Where to Stay

ENGLISH LAKELAND CUMBRIA

The Where to Stay in England series of accommodation guides, published by the English Tourist Board in conjunction with England's regional tourist boards, contains details of establishments which have registered with the English Tourist Board under the official voluntary registration scheme approved and supported by the Government. This scheme provides information needed for the planning and development of tourist facilities in the future. It also gives hoteliers and other providers of tourist and holiday accommodation the chance to tell you, the customer, about the accommodation which they are offering during 1982.

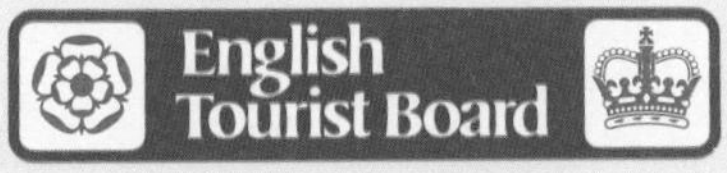

A FAIR DEAL

All establishments registered with the English Tourist Board and appearing in this guide have agreed to adhere to the English Tourist Board's Code of Conduct.

The code helps to ensure a fair deal and to assist in developing the bond of confidence and goodwill between the providers of tourist and holiday accommodation and their customers.

THE CODE OF CONDUCT

In addition to fulfilling its statutory obligations, including having applied for a certificate under the Fire Precautions Act 1971 (if applicable), the management undertakes to observe the following Code of Conduct:

1. To ensure high standards of courtesy and cleanliness; catering and service appropriate to the type of establishment.

2. To describe fairly to all visitors and prospective visitors the amenities, facilities and services provided by the establishment, whether by advertisement, brochure, word of mouth or any other means. To allow visitors to see accommodation, if requested, before booking.

3. To make clear to visitors exactly what is included in all prices quoted for accommodation, meals and refreshments, including service charge, taxes and other surcharges. Details of charges for additional services or facilities available should also be made clear. If applicable the establishment should comply with the provisions of the Hotel Industry's voluntary Code of Booking Practice.

4. To adhere to, and not to exceed, prices current at time of occupation for accommodation or other services.

5. To advise visitors at the time of booking, and subsequently of any change, if the accommodation offered is in an unconnected annexe, or similar, or by boarding out, and to indicate the location of such accommodation and any difference in comfort and amenities from accommodation in the main establishment.

6. To give each visitor, on request, details of payments due and a receipt, if required.

7. To deal promptly and courteously with all enquiries, requests, reservations, correspondence, and complaints from visitors.

Note: Paragraph 4 is intended as a protection against 'gazumping' that is to say the sudden raising of prices of accommodation above the normal tariff ('current prices') on days when, due to heavy demand, accommodation in the locality is in short supply. The 'current prices' may be higher than those indicated in this guide due to changes after the guide went to press.

CONTENTS

All establishments in this guide have registered with the English Tourist Board for 1982. This means that the proprietor has agreed to abide by the Tourist Board Code of Conduct (see fold-out section at the front of the book). As you travel around England watch out for the sign which indicates a registered establishment.

HAVE A HAPPY HOLIDAY

HOW TO USE THIS GUIDE

In this accommodation guide we have endeavoured to provide you with as much information as possible in the space available. The information is presented in a straightforward manner and although it is easy to interpret some explanations may be helpful. To get maximum benefit from this guide we recommend that you read the following notes and in particular those on **Prices** and **Making a Booking.**

The accommodation listed in this guide is divided into the following types:

SERVICED ACCOMMODATION

The various types of serviced accommodation are identified by a code letter in the left margin of the page immediately before the name and address of the establishment.

Type A - Hotels
Establishments which provide accommodation and breakfast and at least one other main meal and service to residents and non-residents without special contract.

Type B - Other hotels and guest houses
Establishments, including hotels not falling within type A, which provide accommodation and breakfast and at least one other main meal and service for residents only.

Type C - Motels and motor hotels
Establishments also falling within the definition of type A but catering especially for the motorist with parking for each bedroom/accommodation unit.

Type D - Inns
Establishments other than hotels and motels, licensed for the sale of alcoholic liquor, having a bar open to members of the public and providing accommodation and breakfast and often other meals and/or bar food.

Type E - Bed and breakfast accommodation
Establishments (except farmhouses – type F) which provide accommodation, some service and breakfast but no other meals.

Type F - Farmhouses
Establishments which provide accommodation with breakfast, some service and often other meals on a working farm. (The size and kind of farm appear in this guide after the name and address, for example Mixed 240 acres.)

The 'Categories of Facilities' numbers explained in the fold-out section of this guide provide a convenient short cut to selecting accommodation most likely to meet your individual requirements. The method is very simple. Just remember – the bigger the number the greater the range of facilities.

ACCOMMODATION FOR GROUPS AND YOUNG PEOPLE

Establishments which cater primarily for groups or which specialise in accommodation for young people.

SELF-CATERING ACCOMMODATION

Establishments which provide accommodation but usually no meals or service and where guests normally make their own arrangements for cooking, day to day cleaning, bed making and so on. Various units are included such as houses, cottages, chalets, flats and houseboats.

The Tourist Board Standards for self-catering are listed at the beginning of the self-catering section of this guide. Establishments which conform to these standards are indicated by a ●. Establishments which conform to all but the minimum room sizes are marked C meaning compact.

CAMPING AND CARAVAN SITES

This covers sites where you can hire a chalet or static caravan and sites with pitches for your own tent, touring caravan or motor caravan.

Establishments which conform to the Tourist Board Standards are indicated by a ●.

PLEASE MENTION 'WHERE TO STAY '82' WHEN MAKING A BOOKING

HOW TO USE THIS GUIDE

ORDER OF LISTING AND ADDRESSES

Establishments are listed under the name of the place where they are situated; or, in the case of isolated spots in the countryside, under the nearest village or town. Town and village names are listed alphabetically and for smaller places an indication of their location is also given. For example '5m N. Anytown' means 5 miles North of Anytown.

If you are looking for accommodation in the vicinity of a town the map section at the back of this guide will enable you to identify places nearby.

Place and county names are not normally repeated in the entries for each establishment but you should ensure that you use the full postal address and post-code when writing.

For example: Letters to the Charlton Hotel, 18 Tilney Street, Homer Cross, Nr. Wikeley, RR0 1TB listed under **Homer Cross (Newshire)** should be addressed:

Charlton Hotel
18 Tilney Street
Homer Cross
Nr. Wikeley
Newshire RR0 1TB

TELEPHONE NUMBERS

The telephone number, exchange name (where this differs from the name of the town under which the establishment is listed) and STD code (in brackets) are given immediately below the address. The STD code applies to calls made anywhere in the UK except for local calls. Codes may be obtained from the operator by dialling 100.

MAP AND INDEX

At the back of this book you will find a map showing the name and location of places which have accommodation listed in this guide. There is also an index which indicates the types of establishment in each location. If you wish to stay for example in or around Anytown, by looking at the map you will be able to identify nearby towns and villages and the index will then tell you whether they have suitable types of accommodation. A number of entries were included just before this guide went to press and therefore may not appear on the map or in the index.

BATHROOMS

The section covering hotels and other serviced accommodation shows the number of public bathrooms available, the number of bedrooms with a private shower but no WC and the number of bedrooms with a private bathroom. A private bathroom consists of a bath and/or shower plus a WC en suite with the bedroom.

Public bathrooms are normally equipped with a bath and sometimes also a shower attachment. A few hotels however have showers only in their public bathrooms and no bath available so this should be checked at the time of booking if it is an important factor.

EVENING MEALS

In the section of this guide covering hotels and other serviced accommodation the twenty-four hour clock has been used to show the starting time for the serving of evening meals and the time when last orders are taken. At smaller hotels and guest houses you may be asked at breakfast time or midday whether you will require a meal that evening. So the time of last order could read, say, *09 30* (9.30am) or *12 00* (noon). The abbreviation 24hr. means that a meal of some kind is always available.

WHEN IS THE ESTABLISHMENT OPEN?

Many hotels and other establishments are open throughout the year; others may close during the winter. We have indicated the opening period numerically, calling January **'1'** and December **'12'**, thus an establishment which is open from March until September will be shown as **3-9.**

YOU WANT A PLACE WITH A , AND A ?

Page iii of the fold-out section at the front of this guide gives the meanings of all the symbols which describe the facilities available at each establishment. If you want a hotel with say a tennis court or conference facilities or you want to be sure that the place you choose will welcome children then fold out the key to symbols and the meanings are then readily to hand whichever page of the guide you are using.

HOW TO USE THIS GUIDE

WILL WE BE ABLE TO GET A DRINK?

Alcoholic drinks are available at all types of accommodation listed in this guide (excepting self-catering) unless the symbol UL appears. The licence to serve drinks may however be restricted, for example to diners only, so you may wish to check this when enquiring about accommodation.

CAN WE TAKE THE DOG WITH US?

Many establishments will accept guests with dogs but we strongly advise you to confirm this at the time of booking when you should also enquire about any extra charges. Some establishments will not accept dogs under any circumstances and these are marked with the symbol ✗.

Visitors from overseas should not bring pets of any kind into Britain unless they are prepared for the animals to go into lengthy quarantine. Owing to the continuing threat of rabies, penalties for ignoring the regulations are extremely severe.

CONFERENCES AND GROUPS

Establishments which can cater for conferences of 10 persons or more have been marked with the symbol T. Rates are often negotiable and the price may be affected by a number of factors such as the time of year, number of people and any special requirements stipulated by the organiser.

There is a special section in this guide listing establishments which cater for groups and young people and many hotels and other establishments will also welcome parties.

HOLIDAYS FOR THE PHYSICALLY HANDICAPPED

The symbol ♿ has been used to mark establishments which have indicated that they meet the minimum requirements listed below and are suitable for physically handicapped guests. However, you are advised to check this and discuss any additional requirements at the time of booking.

1. At least one entrance must have no steps or be equipped with a ramp whose gradient does not exceed 1:12.
2. All doors (including those of WC's, private bathroom etc.) must have at least 74 cm (29 ins) clear opening width, with a head-on approach.
3. All essential accommodation, if not on the ground floor, must be served by an adequately sized lift.
4. All lifts must have gate opening of at least 74 cm (29 ins); lifts must be at least 122 cm (48 ins) deep, and 91 cm (36 ins) wide.
5. At least one bedroom and one public WC must be suitable for the disabled.
6. In bedrooms, private or public bathrooms and WC's used by the disabled, the clearance around beds, and to reach washbasins, WC's etc, must be at least 74 cm (29 ins) and there must be turning space of 122 cm (48ins) by 122cm (48 ins).

Note: Make sure when booking that the management is fully aware of any special requirements.

CREDIT CARDS

We have indicated, under the telephone number in the address column, those credit cards which are accepted by the establishment concerned. The abbreviations are:

Access – Access/Eurocard/Master Charge
Visa – Visa/Barclaycard/Trustcard
C.Bl. – Carte Blanche
Diners – Diners
Amex. – American Express

PLEASE MENTION 'WHERE TO STAY '82' WHEN MAKING A BOOKING

PRICES

The prices appearing in this publication will serve as a useful general guide, but we strongly advise you to check them at the time of booking. This information was supplied to us by proprietors in the summer of 1981 and changes may have occurred since the guide went to press. Prices are shown in pounds sterling and include Value Added Tax and the service charge if made. An asterisk against the price means that no service charge is made and is therefore not included in the quoted price (see also the notes under 'tipping' page 9).

There are many different ways of quoting prices for tourist and holiday accommodation and in order to make this as clear as possible and provide a basis for comparison we have adopted a standardised approach.

For example, in the first section, listing hotels and other serviced accommodation, we show:

1. Price for overnight accommodation with breakfast – single room and double room. The double room price is for two people. If a double room is occupied by one person there is normally a reduction in the quoted tariff, but some hotels may charge the full rate.
2. Price for room, breakfast and evening meal per person per day.
3. Price for room, breakfast and evening meal per person per week.

Establishments may also quote other combinations such as full board on a daily or weekly basis. The symbol **FB** is used to indicate that these terms are available.

ROOM AND BREAKFAST

A number of hotels do not quote or offer an inclusive room and breakfast rate in their published tariff. In such cases the minimum charge for breakfast has been added to the room charge to arrive at a combined price. Some hotels provide a continental breakfast only for the room and breakfast tariff and make an extra charge if a full English breakfast is ordered.

REDUCTIONS FOR CHILDREN

A reduced price is normally quoted for children, especially when sharing a room with their parents. Some establishments, however, do charge the full price when a child occupies a room which might otherwise have been let at the full rate to an adult. The upper age limit for reductions for children may vary according to the establishment and should therefore be checked at the time of booking.

SEASONAL VARIATIONS AND BARGAIN PACKAGES

Prices often vary according to the time of year and are usually substantially lower outside the peak holiday weeks.

Many hotels and other establishments offer special 'package' rates (for example, fully inclusive weekend rates) particularly in the autumn, winter and spring. Further details of bargain packages can be obtained from the hotels themselves or from the English Tourist Board and England's regional tourist boards. Your local travel agent will also have information about these packages and can help you make bookings. Establishments which offer a special Christmas/New Year package have been indicated by means of a holly-leaf symbol.

TOURING CARAVANS, MOTOR CARAVANS AND TENTS

There is no uniform method of quoting prices. For example, some sites charge separately for the pitch, for the parking of the car, and for each person in the party; others quote an all-inclusive price; in between there are various combinations. In order to simplify this and provide a basis for comparison we have indicated the minimum charge for:

1. Car, caravan and two people,
2. Motor caravan and two people,
3. Car, tent and two people.

We think this will serve as a useful general guide, but we should point out that if there are more than two people in your party you may be asked to pay extra. Some sites also make an extra charge for the erection of awnings; and there is sometimes a supplementary charge at weekends.

BOOKING YOUR HOLIDAY

MAKING A BOOKING

When enquiring about accommodation, as well as checking prices and other details, you will need to state your requirements clearly and precisely – for example:

1. Arrival and departure dates with acceptable alternatives if appropriate.
2. The accommodation you need. For example: double room with twin beds, private bath and toilet.
3. The terms you want. For example: room and breakfast; room only; bed, breakfast and evening meal; full board.
4. If you have children with you give their ages, state whether you would like them to share your room or have an adjacent room and mention any special requirements such as a cot.
5. Tell the management about any particular requirements such as a ground floor room or special diet.

Misunderstandings can occur very easily over the telephone so we recommend that all bookings should be confirmed in writing if time permits. Also when first enquiring in writing about a reservation you may find it helpful to use the enquiry coupons at the back of this book which can be cut out and mailed to the establishment(s) of your choice. Remember to include your name and address and please enclose a stamped addressed envelope for each reply or an international reply coupon if writing from outside Britain.

ARRIVING LATE IN THE EVENING

If you will be arriving late in the evening it is advisable to say so at the time of booking and, if you are delayed on your way, then a telephone call to inform the management that you will be late might help to avoid problems on arrival.

IF YOU CANCEL A BOOKING

When you accept offered accommodation, on the telephone, or in writing, you may be entering into a legally binding contract with the proprietor of the establishment. This means that if you cancel a reservation, fail to take up the accommodation or leave prematurely (regardless of the reasons) the proprietor may be entitled to compensation if it can not be relet for all or a good part of the booked period. If a deposit has been paid it is likely to be forfeited and an additional payment may be demanded. In the case of serviced accommodation this is usually two-thirds of the contract price, one-third being deducted for food not consumed and services not rendered. **It is therefore in your interest to advise the management immediately if you have to change your travel plans, cancel a booking or leave prematurely.**

Travel and Holiday Insurance protection policies are available quite cheaply and would safeguard you in the event of your having to cancel or curtail your holiday. Your insurance company or travel agent can advise you further on this; also some hotels offer insurance schemes.

DEPOSITS AND ADVANCE PAYMENTS

For reservations made weeks or months ahead a deposit is usually payable and the amount will vary according to the length of booking, time of year, number in party and so on. The deposit is then deducted from the total bill at the end of the stay.

In the case of self-catering accommodation and caravan/chalet sites often the full amount has to be paid in advance. This may be in two instalments – a deposit at the time of booking and the balance by, say, two weeks before the start of the booked period.

More and more hotels, particularly larger hotels in big towns, now require payment for the room on arrival if a prior reservation has not been made – especially when a guest arrives late and/or with little luggage. Regrettably this practice has become necessary because of the number of guests who have left without paying their bills. If you are asked to pay on arrival it may be advisable to see your room first to ensure that it meets your requirements.

PLEASE MENTION 'WHERE TO STAY '82' WHEN MAKING A BOOKING

BOOKING YOUR HOLIDAY

BOOKING SERVICES & CENTRAL RESERVATIONS OFFICES

The English Tourist Board does not make reservations but many hotel chains and hotel groups have a central reservations office and your local travel agent may also be able to help you. Many Tourist Information Centres provide a Tourist Accommodation Service and these are listed in the regional information pages at the back of this book.

A number of hotel groups and consortia have central reservations offices. Hotels owned by some of the larger groups and consortia have been indicated by the name of the organisation in brackets after the hotel name. All of these have central reservations offices as listed below.

(Anchor)
Anchor Hotels and Taverns. Central Reservations Office, c/o Queens Hotel, Lynchford Road, Farnborough, Hampshire GU14 6AZ.
☎ (0252) 517517

(Best Western)
Best Western Hotels, Interchange House, 26 Kew Road, Richmond, Surrey TW9 2NA.
☎ 01-940 9766

(Br. Trans.)
British Transport Hotels Limited. PO Box 179, St. Pancras Chambers, Euston Road, London NW1 2TU.
☎ 01-278 4211

(Comfort)
Comfort Hotels International, 167 Queensway, London W2 4XG.
☎ 01-221 2626

(Consort)
Consort Hotels, Ryedale Buildings, Piccadilly, York Y01 1PN.
☎ (0904) 20137

(Crest)
Crest Hotels – Europe, Dorland House, 388 The High Road, Wembley, Middlesex HA9 6UG.
☎ 01-903 6422

(De Vere)
De Vere Hotels, The Connaught Rooms, 61-65 Great Queen Street, London WC2B 5DA.
☎ 01-404 0991

(Embassy)
Embassy Hotels, 34 Queen's Gate, London SW7 5JA.
☎ 01-584 8222

(Grand Met.)
Grand Metropolitan Hotels, Grand Metropolitan House, 6-9 Stratford Place, London W1A 4YU.
☎ 01-629 6611 (individuals and small parties) or 01-629 6618 (groups – 9 or more persons).

(Greenall)
Greenall Whitley Hotels, PO Box 27, Loushers Lane, Warrington, Cheshire WA4 6RQ.
☎ (0925) 35471

(Inter)
Inter Hotels, 35 Hogarth Road, London SW5 0QQ.
☎ 01-373 3241

(Ladbroke)
Ladbroke Hotels and Holidays, PO Box 137, Millbuck House, 37 Clarendon Road, Watford, Hertfordshire WD1 1DN.
☎ (92) 46464

(Minotels)
11 Palmeira Mansions, Church Road, Hove, East Sussex BN3 2GA.
☎ (0273) 731908

(Mt. Charlotte)
Mount Charlotte Investments, 2 The Calls, Leeds, West Yorkshire LS2 7JU.
☎ (0532) 444866

(Norfolk)
Norfolk Capital Hotels Ltd, 8 Cromwell Place, London SW7 2JN.
☎ 01-589 7000

(North)
M F North Hotels, 58 Cromwell Road, South Kensington, London SW7 5BZ.
☎ 01-589 1212

(Rank)
Rank Hotels Central Reservation Office, 51 Holland Street, London W8 7JB.
☎ 01-937 8022

(S & N/Thistle)
Thistle Reservations Centre, c/o Kensington Palace Hotel, De Vere Gardens, London W8 5AF.
☎ 01-937 8033

(Swallow)
Swallow Hotels Limited, PO Box 35, Sunderland, Tyne & Wear SR1 3AN.
☎ (0783) 77424

(THF)
Trusthouses Forte, Paramount House, 71-75 Uxbridge Road, London W5 5SL.
☎ 01-567 3444

USEFUL INFORMATION

Hotels and other establishments have a number of legal and statutory responsibilities towards their customers in areas such as the provision of information on prices, the provision of adequate fire precautions and the safeguarding of valuables. Like other businesses, hotels must meet the requirements of the Trade Descriptions Act 1968 when describing and offering accommodation and facilities. The Act aims to protect consumers against misleading statements. When registering with the English Tourist Board establishments agree to abide by a Code of Conduct (see page vi of fold-out section) and in so doing declare that they fulfil all applicable statutory obligations.

PRICE DISPLAY

There is a statutory requirement for establishments which have at least four bedrooms, or eight beds, to display overnight accommodation charges in the reception area or at the entrance. This is to ensure that prospective guests can obtain adequate information about prices before taking up accommodation. When you arrive at a hotel it is in your own interests to check prices and what they include.

TIPPING

Many establishments now levy a service charge automatically and if so this fact must be stated clearly in the offer of accommodation at the time of booking. If the offer is then accepted by the customer the service charge becomes part of the contract. At establishments where a service charge of this kind is made there is no need for guests to give tips to the staff unless some particular or exceptional service has been rendered.

In this guide we have placed an asterisk against the price if a service charge is **not** made and has therefore **not** been included in the price. It is then a matter for the guest to decide for himself which staff to tip and how much. In the case of meals the usual amount is 10% of the total bill.

CHARGES FOR TELEPHONE CALLS

The provision of a telephone for the use of guests can mean considerable overhead expenses for the management, as there is a substantial rental or capital charge on the hotel switchboard and telephone extensions; also there are the wages of the telephone operator.

There are two ways of covering these costs. The first is by including an amount to defray telephone costs in the quoted tariff for all bedrooms. The second method is to levy a small extra service charge on telephone calls made by guests. Many hoteliers think it is unfair to charge all guests whether or not they use the telephone and therefore they make a surcharge on calls put through the hotel's telephone system. Before making long trunk calls within Britain or calls to places outside Britain we advise you to check the charges made.

VALUABLES

Property of value may be deposited for safe-keeping with the proprietor or manager of the hotel who should give you a receipt and who will then generally be liable for the value of the property in the case of loss. For your peace of mind we advise you to adopt this procedure. In establishments which do not accept articles for safe custody, you are advised to keep valuables under your personal supervision.

You may find that proprietors of some hotels and other establishments disclaim, by notice, liability for property brought onto their premises by a guest; however, if a guest engages overnight accommodation in a hotel the proprietor is only permitted to restrict his liability to the minimum imposed upon him under the Hotel Proprietors Act, 1956. Under this Act, a proprietor of a hotel is liable for the value of the loss or damage to any property (other than a motor-car or its contents) of a guest who has engaged overnight accommodation, but if the proprietor has a notice in the form prescribed by that act, his liability is limited to the sum of £50 in respect of one article and a total of £100 in the case of any one guest. These limits do not apply, however, if the guest had deposited the property with him for safe-keeping or if the property is lost through the default neglect or wilful act of the proprietor or his staff.

To be effective any notice intended to disclaim or restrict liability must be prominently displayed in the reception area of, or in the main entrance to, the hotel or other establishment.

WE WELCOME YOUR COMMENTS

In preparing this series of accommodation guides we have tried to anticipate your needs and to set out the information in a straightforward and easy to use style. It may well be, however, that improvements can be made and we welcome your comments and suggestions. The proprietor of every establishment in this guide has agreed to abide by the English Tourist Board's seven point **Code of Conduct.** This is designed to help ensure a fair deal and assist generally in developing the bond of goodwill and confidence between the providers of accommodation and their customers. The Code is printed in full on page vi of the fold-out section at the front of this guide.

PLEASE MENTION 'WHERE TO STAY'82' WHEN MAKING A BOOKING

We naturally hope that you will not have any cause for complaint but problems do inevitably occur from time to time.
If you are dissatisfied, make your complaint to the management immediately at the time of the incident. This gives an opportunity for action to be taken at once to investigate and to put things right without delay. It is extremely difficult to deal effectively with a complaint that is made at a later date.

Information for this publication was collected from proprietors by means of questionnaires and every proprietor has signed a declaration that the information conforms with the requirements of the Trade Descriptions Act, and that he will abide by the English Tourist Board Code of Conduct. The English Tourist Board cannot accept responsibility for any inaccuracy in the information or for any consequences arising from reliance thereon and prices and other details should always be carefully checked at the time of booking. Some, but not all, of the establishments in this guide have been visited by the English Tourist Board. If you have any comments about the places you stay at then please write to us.

We do find it very helpful to receive comments from the public about establishments in **Where to Stay,** and suggestions on how to improve the guides. We would like to hear from you.

HOTELS, MOTELS, INNS, GUESTHOUSES, BED & BREAKFAST AND FARMHOUSES

HOTELS, MOTELS, GUEST HOUSES & OTHER SERVICED ACCOMMODATION

Name and Address: Accommodation Type (See page 3); Town (County); Establishment, Address, Telephone number, Telex, Credit cards accepted	Map Ref.	Category (Key: see front fold-out): Bedrooms	Services	Meals	Prices: Bed and breakfast: Single room overnight	Double room overnight	B & B and evening meal: Per person daily	Per person weekly	Rooms: No. of bedrooms: Single	Double	Family	Bathrooms	Showers	Facilities: Parking–P Garage–G	Evening meals (24 hr. clock)	Months open (1–12)	Symbols
					£ Min. *£ Max.*	£ Min. *£ Max.*	£ Min. *£ Max.*	£ Min. *£ Max.*				Private *Public*		No.of cars	From *Order by*		Key: see fold-out
ALLONBY (Cumbria)	**B2**																
A† East House Guest House, Allonby, Maryport, CA15 6QF. Tel. (090 084) 264 & 276.		1	1	3	*5.00 **5.00*	*10.00 **10.00*	*7.25 **7.25*	*50.00 **50.00*	2	2	3	– *1*	–	P20 –	18 00 *18 00*	1–12	FB
A Ship Hotel, Allonby, Maryport, CA15 6QF. Tel. (090 084) 276.		1	1	3	*5.00 **5.00*	*10.00 **10.00*	*7.25 **7.25*	*50.00 **50.00*	2	4	5	– *2*	–	P20 –	18 00 *18 00*	1–12	FB
ALSTON (Cumbria)	**C2**																
A† Cumberland Hotel, Town Foot, CA9 3HX. Tel. (049 83) 245.		3	3	5	*8.50 **17.00*	*17.00 **20.00*	*13.00 **21.50*	*85.00 **145.00*	1	3	4	2 *1*	–	P3 –	19 00 *21 30*	1–12	FB
A† The George & Dragon Hotel, Garrigill, Nr. Alston, CA9 3DS. Tel. (049 83) 293 & 412.		3	3	4	*8.65 **9.80*	*17.25 **18.55*	*13.25 **16.10*	– –	1	5	–	1 *1*	1	P12 G2	19 00 *20 00*	4–10	FB
A† Hillcrest Hotel, Townfoot, CA9 3RN. Tel. (049 83) 251.		3	4	4	*12.00 –	*20.00 –	*18.00 –	– –	5	4	2	– *3*	1	P15 G3	19 00 *20 00*	1–12	FB
A Lovelady Shield Country House Hotel, Nenthead Rd., CA9 3LF. Tel. (049 83) 203. Credit- Visa, Diners, Amex.		4	4	4	– **12.25*	– **24.50*	– **20.00*	– **127.00*	2	8	2	12 –	–	P20 –	19 15 *20 15*	3–12	
B Cragside House, CA9 3JE. Tel. (049 83) 420.		3	2	2	*6.00 **6.00*	*12.00 **12.00*	*8.75 **8.75*	*57.00 **57.00*	–	2	3	– *2*	–	P6 –	18 00 –	4–10	FB
F Mrs. P. M. Dent, Middle Bayles, CA9 3BS. Tel. (049 83) 383. (Hill 150 acres)		1	1	2	– –	*10.00 **12.00*	*8.00 **9.00*	*49.00 **56.00*	–	1	1	– *1*	–	P2 –	18 00 *16 00*	4–10	
F Mrs. E. Jopling, Loatburn Farm, CA9 3LQ. Tel. (049 83) 544. (Mixed 62 acres)		1	2	2	*4.50 **5.00*	*9.00 **10.00*	*7.00 **7.00*	*42.00 **45.00*	–	1	1	– *1*	–	P4 –	18 00 –	4–12	
AMBLESIDE (Cumbria)	**B2**																
A† Elder Grove Hotel, Lake Rd. LA22 0DB. Tel. (096 63) 2504. Credit- Access, Visa.		4	4	2	*11.00 **12.00*	*22.00 **24.00*	*17.00 **18.00*	*108.00 **115.00*	1	6	2	9 –	–	P9 –	19 30 –	3–11	
A† Fisherbeck Hotel, Lake Rd., LA22 0DH. Tel. (096 63) 3215. Credit- Access.		3	3	4	*11.00 **12.00*	*18.00 **20.00*	*15.50 **16.50*	*100.00 **107.00*	–	12	4	8 *4*	–	P20 –	19 00 *19 00*	2–12	
A† Ghyll Head Hotel, Waterhead, LA22 0HD. Tel. (096 63) 2360.		4	3	4	13.00 *15.00*	26.00 *30.00*	16.00 *18.00*	112.00 *120.00*	1	6	4	11 –	–	P16 –	18 45 *19 45*	1–12	6
A† Kirkstone Foot Country House Hotel, Kirkstone Pass Rd., LA22 9EH. Tel. (096 63) 2232. Credit- Access, Visa, C.Bl., Diners, Amex.		4	3	4	12.50 *14.00*	25.00 *28.00*	21.00 *22.50*	136.50 *147.00*	1	9	2	12 –	–	P30 –	19 30 *20 00*	3–11	
A† Laurel Villa Hotel, Lake Rd., LA22 0DB. Tel. (096 63) 3240.		3	3	2	*10.80 **11.50*	*21.60 **23.00*	*16.50 **17.20*	*105.00 **109.90*	1	7	5	3 *3*	–	P12 –	19 15 *19 15*	3–10	
A† Nanny Brow Country House Hotel, Clappersgate, LA22 9NF. Tel. (096 63) 2036. Credit- Access, Visa.		4	4	4	*13.75 **15.00*	*27.50 **30.00*	*18.50 **20.50*	*125.00 **135.00*	2	10	2	5 *3*	–	P15 –	19 00 *19 30*	1–12	
A† Queens Hotel, Market Pl, LA22 9BU. Tel. (096 63) 2206. Credit- Access, Visa, Amex.		3	3	4	*7.50 **11.50*	*15.00 **23.00*	*10.00 **14.50*	*70.00 **95.00*	4	24	3	15 *5*	–	P2 G4	18 00 *21 00*	1–12	

 You are advised to read the introductory notes and to check prices and other details when booking accommodation

HOTELS, MOTELS, GUEST HOUSES & OTHER SERVICED ACCOMMODATION

Name and Address Accommodation Type (See page 3) **Town (County)** Establishment Address Telephone number, Telex Credit cards accepted	Map Ref.	Category (Key: see front fold-out) Bedrooms	Services	Meals	Bed and breakfast: Single room overnight £ Min. *£ Max.*	Bed and breakfast: Double room overnight £ Min. *£ Max.*	B & B and evening meal: Per person daily £ Min. *£ Max.*	B & B and evening meal: Per person weekly £ Min. *£ Max.*	No. of bedrooms: Single	Double	Family	Bathrooms Private *Public*	Showers	Parking–P Garage–G No. of cars	Evening meals (24 hr. clock) From *Order by*	Months open (1–12)	Symbols Key: see fold-out
AMBLESIDE continued																	
A† Regent Hotel, Waterhead, LA22 0ES. Tel. (096 63) 2254. Credit- Access, Visa, Amex.		3	4	4	*11.00 **14.00*	*22.00 **24.00*	*16.00 **18.50*	*110.00 **125.00*	2	9	1	6 *2*	2	P30 –	19 00 *19 45*	1–12	FB
A† Riverside Hotel, Gilbert Scar Under Loughrigg, Ambleside, LA22 9LJ. Tel. (096 63) 2395.		3	4	4	– –	– –	*15.50 **19.00*	*108.50 **125.00*	2	8	1	2 *3*	–	P12 –	19 00 –	1–12	8
A† Romney Hotel, Waterhead, LA22 0HD. Tel. (096 63) 2219.		3	3	3	– *10.75*	– **20.24*	*15.18 **16.45*	*88.55 **92.40*	5	8	6	– *4*	–	P20 G2	19 00 –	4–10	
A† Rothay Garth Hotel, Rothay Rd., LA22 0EE. Tel. (096 63) 2217. Credit- Visa, Amex.		4	4	3	*13.22 –	*26.44 –	*16.67 –	*106.95 –	2	11	2	5 *3*	2	P13 –	19 00 *18 00*	1–12	
A† Rothay Manor Hotel, Rothay Bridge, LA22 0EH. Tel. (096 63) 3605. Telex 65294. Credit- Diners, Amex.		6	4	4	*34.00 **36.00*	*50.00 **54.00*	*37.00 **40.00*	– –	2	6	4	12 –	–	P30 –	19 30 *21 00*	3–12	
A Royal Yachtsman formerly Salutation Hotel, Lake Rd., LA22 9BX. Tel. (096 63) 2244. Credit- Access, Visa, Amex.		3	5	6	*14.00 –	*23.00 –	– –	– –	6	21	2	1 *5*	–	P70 –	19 00 *22 30*	1–12	FB T
A The Rysdale Hotel, Kelsick Rd., LA22 0EE. Tel. (096 63) 2140. Credit- Access, Visa.		3	4	3	*7.50 –	*15.00 –	*12.00 –	*75.00 –	1	4	3	– *3*	–	– –	19 00 *17 30*	1–12	5
A† Skelwith Bridge Hotel, LA22 9NJ. Tel. (096 63) 2115. Credit- Access, Visa.		4	4	4	14.50 *16.50*	29.00 *33.00*	22.00 *24.00*	135.00 *149.00*	5	17	2	11 *4*	–	P20 –	19 00 *20 45*	2–12	T
A† Vale View Hotel, (Minotels) Lake Rd., LA22 0BH. Tel. (096 63) 3192. Credit- Access, Visa.		4	4	4	10.00 *10.75*	19.00 *20.50*	14.50 *15.50*	91.00 *97.00*	4	14	2	11 *3*	–	P9 –	19 00 *20 00*	3–10	T
A† Walmar Private Hotel, Lake Rd., LA22 0DB. Tel. (096 63) 2454.		3	3	3	*8.50 **9.75*	*17.00 **19.50*	*12.50 **14.50*	*82.50 **94.50*	1	4	3	– *2*	–	– –	19 00 *19 30*	1–11	5 FB
A† Wateredge Hotel, LA22 0EP. Tel. (096 63) 2332. Credit- Access.		4	4	4	*15.50 **16.50*	*31.00 **33.00*	*25.50 **27.00*	*171.50 **182.00*	3	14	1	14 *5*	–	P50 –	19 00 *20 00*	3–12	FB
A† Waterhead Hotel. (Best Western) LA22 0ER. Tel. (096 63) 2566. Credit- Access, Visa, Diners, Amex.		6	4	5	*15.45 **20.70*	*30.90 **41.40*	*23.70 **29.00*	*142.00 **178.00*	2	22	6	30 –	–	P50 –	19 00 *22 00*	1–12	FB T
A† White Lion Hotel, Market Pl., LA22 9DB. Tel. (096 63) 3140.		3	3	3	*12.50 –	*25.00 –	*18.25 –	– –	2	10	2	– *3*	–	P20 G8	19 00 *19 45*	1–11	4 T
B† Balla Wray Country Guest House, High Wray, Ambleside, LA22 0JQ. Tel. (096 63) 3308. Credit- Visa.		3	2	2	*12.50 **14.00*	*25.30 **26.00*	*17.25 **18.00*	*100.00 **120.00*	–	5	3	– *2*	–	P7 –	18 30 –	1–12	5 FB
B† Broad Ings Country House, Skelghyll La., LA22 0HF. Tel. (096 63) 2562.		4	4	4	*10.00 **13.00*	*20.00 **25.00*	*17.00 **20.00*	*107.00 **126.00*	2	4	1	5 *2*	–	P15 G2	19 00 *19 00*	1–12	FB
B† Chapel House Hotel, Kirkstone Rd., LA22 9DZ. Tel. (096 63) 3143.		1	1	2	– –	– –	*9.00 –	– –	2	5	3	– *2*	–	P6 –	19 00 *19 30*	4–11	
B† Compston House Hotel, Compston Rd., LA22 9DJ. Tel. (096 63) 2305.		3	4	3	*8.00 –	*16.00 –	*10.50 –	*72.00 –	1	7	2	– *2*	–	– –	19 00 *18 00*	1–12	

HOTELS, MOTELS, GUEST HOUSES & OTHER SERVICED ACCOMMODATION

Accommodation Type (See page 3)	Name and Address: Town (County) / Establishment / Address / Telephone number, Telex / Credit cards accepted	Map Ref.	Category (Key: see front fold-out): Bedrooms	Services	Meals	Prices: Bed and breakfast: Single room overnight (£ Min. / *£ Max.*)	Double room overnight (£ Min. / *£ Max.*)	B & B and evening meal: Per person daily (£ Min. / *£ Max.*)	Per person weekly (£ Min. / *£ Max.*)	Rooms: No. of bedrooms: Single	Double	Family	Bathrooms (Private / *Public*)	Showers	Facilities: Parking–P Garage–G (No. of cars)	Evening meals (24 hr. clock) (From / *Order by*)	Months open (1–12)	Symbols (Key: see fold-out)
	AMBLESIDE continued																	
Bt	The Gables Hotel, Compston Rd., LA22 9DJ. Tel. (096 63) 3272.		3	4	2	*8.05 **8.05*	*16.10 **16.10*	*11.90 **11.90*	*80.50 **80.50*	4	6	5	2 *3*	1	P8 –	19 00 *17 50*	3–10	3
Bt	Haven Cottage Guest House, Rydal Rd., LA22 9AY. Tel. (096 63) 3270.		3	3	2	– –	– –	*10.75 **12.00*	*69.00 **73.00*	–	5	–	– *1*	–	P6 –	19 00 *18 00*	3–10	10
B	Hillsdale Hotel, Church St., LA22 0BT. Tel. (096 63) 3174.		3	3	2	*6.90 **6.90*	*13.80 **13.80*	*10.75 **10.75*	*72.00 **72.00*	1	3	4	– *1*	1	– –	19 00 *16 00*	1–12	V SP
B	Invergowrie Guest House, Lake Rd., LA22 0DB. Tel. (096 63) 3479.		3	1	2	*8.50 –	*16.00 –	*12.50 –	*85.00 –	1	2	4	– *2*	–	P7 –	18 30 *18 30*	4–10	5 V
Bt	John O Gaunt, Rothay Rd., LA22 0EH. Tel. (096 63) 3310.		3	3	2	*7.50 –	*15.00 –	*11.00 –	– –	–	8	5	– *2*	–	P10 –	18 30 *15 30*	4–10	V FB OAP
B	Kelsick Villa Guest House, Rothay Rd., LA22 0EE. Tel. (096 63) 2385.		2	3	2	*6.50 –	*13.00 –	*10.50 –	– –	1	5	2	– *2*	1	P2 –	19 00 –	2–12	
Bt	Kent House, Lake Rd., LA22 0AD. Tel. (096 63) 3279.		2	1	2	– –	*12.00 **14.00*	*9.00 –	– –	–	4	1	– *1*	–	P2 –	18 00 *16 00*	4–10	OAP
B	Linda's Bed & Breakfast, Shirland, Compston Rd., LA22 9DJ. Tel. (096 63) 2809.		3	3	2	*5.00 **8.00*	*10.00 **16.00*	*8.00 **11.00*	*50.00 **70.00*	1	2	2	– *1*	–	– –	18 00 *21 00*	1–12	V OAP SP T
B	1 Mandall Villas, Rydal Rd., LA22 9AR. Tel. (096 63) 2319.		3	1	2	*5.50 **6.00*	*10.50 **11.00*	*9.00 **9.50*	*58.00 **63.00*	1	–	1	– *1*	–	– –	18 00 –	1–12	
Bt	Norwood House, Church St., LA22 0BT. Tel. (096 63) 3349.		3	1	2	*6.00 **7.50*	*12.00 **15.00*	*9.50 **11.00*	*65.00 **75.00*	2	4	2	– *1*	–	– –	18 30 *14 00*	1–12	
Bt	Oaklands Country House Hotel, Millans Park, LA22 9AG. Tel. (096 63) 2525.		3	4	2	*7.00 **10.00*	*14.00 **20.00*	*12.50 **16.00*	*80.00 **105.00*	1	3	2	1 *1*	3	P8 –	19 00 *16 00*	2–11	V OAP SP
B	Park House, 3 Compston Villas, Compston Rd., LA22 9DJ. Tel. (096 63) 3542.		3	1	2	*5.00 **6.00*	*10.00 **12.00*	*8.00 **9.50*	*53.00 **56.00*	2	4	–	– *1*	–	– –	18 30 *19 00*	2–11	
B	Seven Gates, Rothay Bridge, LA22 0EH. Tel. (096 63) 3179.		4	3	2	*12.00 **15.00*	*20.00 **26.00*	*15.00 **18.00*	*96.00 **117.00*	–	6	1	4 *1*	–	P10 –	19 30 *17 00*	4–10	12 SP
Bt	Smallwood Hotel, Compston Rd., LA22 9DJ. Tel. (096 63) 2330.		3	4	2	*8.00 –	*16.00 –	*12.00 –	*82.00 –	3	6	5	2 *2*	–	P10 –	19 00 *18 00*	1–12	1 SP
B	Thorneyfield, Compston Rd., LA22 9DJ. Tel. (096 63) 2464.		1	1	2	*6.50 **7.50*	*13.00 **15.00*	*10.50 **12.00*	– –	1	3	2	– *1*	–	– –	19 00 *13 00*	1–12	1 M V OAP SP
Bt	Waterwheel Guest House, LA22 9DU. Tel. (096 63) 3286.		1	3	2	– –	*13.00 –	– –	*63.00 –	–	2	2	– *1*	–	– –	19 00 *09 00*	1–12	3
E	Eversly, Low Gale, LA22 0BB. Tel. (096 63) 3311.		1	1	1	*6.50 **6.50*	*12.00 **13.00*	– –	– –	1	3	2	– *1*	–	P3 –	– –	1–12	OAP SP
E	Fisherbeck Farmhouse, Old Lake Rd., LA22 0DH. Tel. (096 63) 2523.		3	1	1	*6.50 **7.50*	*13.00 **15.00*	– –	– –	1	3	1	– *1*	–	P3 –	– –	4–11	
E	Gale Crescent Guest House, Lower Gale, LA22 0BD. Tel. (096 63) 2284.		3	3	1	*6.50 **7.00*	*13.00 **14.00*	– –	– –	2	3	2	– *2*	–	P6 –	– –	4–10	V
Et	Horseshoe Guest House, Rothay Rd., LA22 0EE. Tel. (096 63) 2000.		4	3	1	*8.75 –	*16.00 –	– –	– –	1	5	6	5 *2*	–	P11 –	– –	3–12	V SP
E	Lindenlea, 7 Loughrigg Meadow, LA22 0DZ. Tel. (096 63) 2714.		1	2	1	*5.50 **10.50*	*10.00 **10.50*	– –	– –	–	2	–	– *1*	–	P1 –	– –	1–12	

 You are advised to read the introductory notes and to check prices and other details when booking accommodation

HOTELS, MOTELS, GUEST HOUSES & OTHER SERVICED ACCOMMODATION

Name and Address Accommodation Type (See page 3) Town (County) Establishment Address Telephone number, Telex Credit cards accepted	Map Ref.	Category (Key: see front fold-out) Bedrooms	Services	Meals	Prices: Bed and breakfast Single room overnight £ Min. *£ Max.*	Double room overnight £ Min. *£ Max.*	B & B and evening meal Per person daily £ Min. *£ Max.*	Per person weekly £ Min. *£ Max.*	Rooms: No. of bedrooms Single	Double	Family	Bathrooms Private *Public*	Showers	Facilities: Parking–P Garage–G No. of cars	Evening meals (24 hr. clock) From *Order by*	Months open (1–12)	Symbols Key: see fold-out
AMBLESIDE continued																	
E Meadowbank, Rydal Rd., LA22 9BA. Tel. (096 63) 2710.		3	3	1	*7.00 –	*14.00 –	– –	– –	2	3	2	– *2*	–	P10 –	– –	4–10	
E Riverside, Skelwith Bridge, Ambleside, LA22 9NJ. Tel. (096 63) 3501.		2	2	1	– –	*12.00 **13.00*	– –	– –	–	1	2	– *1*	–	P3 –	– –	3–11	
E Rothay House, Rothay Rd., LA22 0EE. Tel. (096 63) 2434.		3	3	1	– –	*16.00 –	– –	– –	–	3	1	1 *1*	–	P5 –	– –	1–12	
APPLEBY-IN-WESTMORLAND (Cumbria)	**C2**																
A† Appleby Manor Hotel, Roman Rd., CA16 6JD. Tel. Appleby (0930) 51571 & 51207. Telex 64100. Credit- Visa, Amex.		4	5	5	*15.00 **18.50*	*20.00 **28.00*	– –	*135.00 **160.00*	4	14	5	14 *3*	–	P40 G7	19 30 *22 00*	2–12	SP T
A† Courtfield Hotel, Bongate, Appleby-in-Westmorland, CA16 6UP. Tel. Appleby (0930) 51394. Credit- Visa, Diners.		2	4	3	*9.50 –	*19.00 –	*16.50 –	*120.00 –	3	11	1	– *3*	–	P30 G2	19 00 *19 45*	1–12	
A Hoff Lodge, Hoff, Appleby-in-Westmoreland, CA16 6TD. Tel. Appleby (0930) 51875.		3	2	4	*7.00 –	*14.00 –	*10.00 –	*70.00 –	–	2	1	– *1*	–	P20 –	18 30 *21 00*	1–12	FB SP
A† The Tufton Arms Hotel, Market Sq., CA16 6XB. Tel. Appleby (0930) 51593.		4	4	5	10.50 *12.00*	21.00 *23.50*	15.50 *17.00*	96.25 *105.00*	8	19	1	16 *5*	–	P26 G4	19 00 *21 30*	1–12	FB T
A† White Hart Hotel, Boroughgate, Appleby-in-Westmorland, CA16 6XG. Tel. Appleby (0930) 51598.		3	4	4	*9.50 **9.50*	*19.00 **19.00*	– –	– –	1	5	2	– *2*	–	P4 –	18 00 *20 00*	4–12	
B† Bongate House, CA16 6UE. Tel. Appleby (0930) 51245.		3	3	2	*7.50 **7.50*	*15.00 **15.00*	*10.00 **10.00*	*60.00 **60.00*	1	4	2	2 *2*	–	P6 G2	19 00 *18 30*	1–12	SP
B Howgill House, CA16 6UW. Tel. Appleby (0930) 51574.		2	1	2	*6.50 –	*11.00 –	– –	– –	–	2	3	– *1*	–	P6 –	– –	4–10	
D The New Inn, Brampton, Appleby-in-Westmorland, CA16 6JS. Tel. Appleby (0930) 51231.		3	3	5	*7.50 **8.50*	*15.00 **17.00*	*12.00 **13.50*	*90.00 **105.00*	1	3	–	– *2*	–	P22 G1	19 00 *21 30*	1–12	SP
D Royal Oak Inn, Bongate, Appleby-in-Westmorland, CA16 6UN. Tel. Appleby (0930) 51463.		3	3	4	– **8.00*	– **15.00*	– –	– –	2	4	2	– *2*	–	P9 –	18 00 *20 45*	1–12	
F Mrs. M. Wood, Gale House Farm, CA16 6JB. Tel. Appleby (0930) 51380. (Dairy 167 acres)		1	1	2	– **5.50*	– **11.00*	– **8.00*	– **56.00*	–	1	1	– *1*	–	P3 –	19 00 *16 00*	4–9	5
ARNSIDE (Cumbria)	**C3**																
A† Grosvenor Private Hotel, The Promenade, LA5 0AA. Tel. (0524) 761666.		3	3	2	*8.00 **10.00*	*16.00 **20.00*	*12.00 **14.00*	*80.00 **80.00*	3	4	6	– *4*	–	P10 –	18 00 *17 00*	4–10	SP
B† Greystones Guest House, 2 Hazel Gro., Ashleigh Rd., Arnside, Carnforth, Lancs., LA5 0HE. Tel. (0524) 761619.		1	3	2	*6.00 –	*12.00 –	*8.50 –	*59.50 –	1	2	2	– *1*	–	P4 –	18 30 *09 00*	1–12	SP
B† Willowfield Private Hotel, The Promenade, Arnside, Carnforth, Lancs., LA5 0AD. Tel. (0524) 761354.		2	3	2	*6.50 –	*13.00 –	*10.25 –	*71.75 –	2	3	4	– *2*	–	P7 –	18 15 *14 00*	1–12	7

You are advised to read the introductory notes and to check prices and other details when booking accommodation

HOTELS, MOTELS, GUEST HOUSES & OTHER SERVICED ACCOMMODATION

Name and Address Accommodation Type (See page 3) Town (County) Establishment Address Telephone number, Telex Credit cards accepted	Map Ref.	Category (Key: see front fold-out) Bedrooms	Services	Meals	Prices: Bed and breakfast Single room overnight £ Min. / £ Max.	Double room overnight £ Min. / £ Max.	B & B and evening meal Per person daily £ Min. / £ Max.	Per person weekly £ Min. / £ Max.	Rooms: No. of bedrooms Single	Double	Family	Bathrooms Private / Public	Showers	Facilities: Parking–P / Garage–G No. of cars	Evening meals (24 hr. clock) From / Order by	Months open (1–12)	Symbols Key: see fold-out
ASKHAM (Cumbria) (4m S. Penrith)	C2																
D† Queen's Head Inn, Askham, Nr. Penrith, CA10 2PF. Tel. Hackthorpe (093 12) 225.		3	4	4	15.30 / *15.62*	29.37 / *31.25*	27.17 / *28.12*	– / –	–	5	3	1 / *2*	–	P30 / –	20 00 / *19 30*	1–12	10
BAMPTON GRANGE (Cumbria) (3m NW. Shap)	C2																
D Crown & Mitre Hotel, Bampton Grange, Penrith, CA10 2QR. Tel. Bampton (093 13) 225.		2	2	2	*8.00 / –	*16.00 / –	*11.50 / –	*76.45 / –	1	3	2	– / *2*	–	P10 / –	18 30 / *19 30*	1–12	OAP SP
BARBON (Cumbria) (3m NNE. Kirkby Lonsdale)	C3																
A Barbon Inn, Barbon, Via Carnforth, Lancs, LA6 2LJ. Tel. (046 836) 233. Credit- Visa, Diners, Amex.		3	3	5	12.14 / *12.14*	24.28 / *24.28*	23.28 / *23.28*	162.93 / *162.93*	3	7	–	– / *4*	–	P17 / G8	19 30 / *21 30*	1–12	FB SP
BARROW-IN-FURNESS (Cumbria)	B3																
A Duke of Edinburgh Hotel, Abbey Rd., LA14 5QR. Tel. (0229) 21039. Credit- Access, Visa, Amex.		3	4	5	– / **11.50*	– / **17.50*	– / **16.50*	– / –	7	18	1	2 / *4*	–	P10 / G4	18 00 / *21 30*	1–12	FB T
A Roman House Hotel, Abbey Rd., LA13 9JN. Tel. (0229) 25294.		3	2	2	*8.50 / –	*17.00 / –	*12.00 / –	– / –	4	4	1	– / *2*	–	P10 / –	18 00 / *19 00*	1–12	
A† Victoria Park Hotel, Victoria Rd., LA14 5JY. Tel. (0229) 21159. Credit- Access, Visa.		4	5	5	17.00 / *20.00*	24.00 / *28.00*	– / –	– / –	25	10	–	14 / *5*	1	P50 / –	19 00 / *21 30*	1–12	SP
A White House Hotel, Abbey Rd., LA13 9AE. Tel. (0229) 27303. Credit- Access, Visa, Diners, Amex.		3	5	5	*15.00 / **17.00*	*24.00 / **26.00*	*20.50 / **22.50*	*122.50 / **130.50*	21	8	–	2 / *6*	–	P80 / G10	18 30 / *21 30*	1–12	FB OAP SP
B East Mount Private Hotel, Abbey Rd., LA13 9AD. Tel. (0229) 25242.		3	3	2	*8.62 / **8.62*	*14.95 / **14.95*	*12.64 / **12.64*	– / –	4	7	1	– / *2*	–	P12 / –	18 00 / *13 00*	1–12	
BASSENTHWAITE (Cumbria)	B2																
A† Armathwaite Hall, Bassenthwaite, Keswick, CA12 4RE. Tel. Bassenthwaite Lake (059 681) 551. Credit- Access, Visa, Diners, Amex.		5	6	5	*19.00 / **24.00*	*30.00 / **50.00*	*27.50 / **32.50*	– / –	5	28	3	36 / *2*	–	P100 / G6	19 30 / *21 30*	1–12	SP T
A† Bassenfell Manor Hotel, Bassenthwaite, Nr. Keswick, CA12 4RL. Tel. Bassenthwaite Lake (059 681) 366. Credit- Access, Visa, C.Bl., Diners.		4	4	4	*9.50 / –	*17.00 / –	*15.50 / –	*97.65 / –	3	12	4	6 / *4*	–	P20 / –	19 00 / *21 00*	3–11	OAP SP T
A Link House, Bassenthwaite Lake, Dubwath, Cockermouth, CA13 9YD. Tel. Bassenthwaite Lake (059 681) 291.		4	4	4	*8.00 / –	*19.00 / **19.00*	*13.50 / –	*94.50 / **99.00*	2	4	–	5 / *1*	–	P16 / –	19 00 / *20 00*	5–12	OAP SP
A† Ouse Bridge Hotel, Dubwath, Bassenthwaite Lake, CA13 9YD. Tel. Bassenthwaite Lake (059 681) 322.		3	3	2	*10.50 / **11.00*	*21.00 / **22.00*	*12.75 / **13.50*	*85.00 / **90.00*	2	4	4	– / *3*	–	P16 / –	19 00 / –	1–12	2
A† Overwater Hall Hotel, Ireby, Carlisle, CA15 1HH. Tel. Bassenthwaite Lake (059 681) 566. Credit- Access, Visa.		5	4	4	*18.00 / **20.00*	*22.00 / **26.00*	*18.00 / **27.50*	*110.00 / **178.00*	–	10	3	9 / *2*	–	P25 / G1	19 00 / *20 45*	2–12	OAP SP T
A Ravenstone Hotel, Bassenthwaite, Nr. Keswick, CA12 4QG. Tel. Bassenthwaite Lake (059 681) 240.		3	3	2	*12.50 / **12.50*	*25.00 / **25.00*	*15.50 / **15.50*	*92.00 / **92.00*	1	2	9	– / *4*	–	P14 / –	19 00 / *19 00*	4–10	

You are advised to read the introductory notes and to check prices and other details when booking accommodation

HOTELS, MOTELS, GUEST HOUSES & OTHER SERVICED ACCOMMODATION

Name and Address Accommodation Type (See page 3) Town (County) Establishment Address Telephone number, Telex Credit cards accepted	Map Ref.	Category (Key: see front fold-out) Bedrooms	Services	Meals	Prices: Bed and breakfast Single room overnight £ Min. £ Max.	Double room overnight £ Min. £ Max.	B & B and evening meal Per person daily £ Min. £ Max.	Per person weekly £ Min. £ Max.	Rooms: No. of bedrooms Single	Double	Family	Bathrooms Private Public	Showers	Facilities: Parking–P Garage–G No. of cars	Evening meals (24 hr. clock) From Order by	Months open (1–12)	Symbols Key: see fold-out
BASSENTHWAITE continued																	
Bt Kiln Hill Bassenthwaite, Keswick, CA12 4RG. Tel. Bassenthwaite Lake (059 681) 454.		3	3	3	*6.00 –	*12.00 –	*8.50 –	*55.00 –	1	1	4	– *2*	–	P20 –	18 00 *19 00*	1–12	FB SP
Bt Melbecks Farm, Bassenthwaite, Nr. Keswick, CA12 4QX. Tel. Bassenthwaite Lake (059 681) 588.		1	2	2	*6.50 **7.00*	*13.00 **14.00*	*11.00 **11.50*	*63.00 **66.00*	–	3	–	– *1*	–	P5 –	19 30 *20 30*	1–12	
Dt Castle Inn Hotel, Bassenthwaite, Keswick, CA12 4RG. Tel. Bassenthwaite Lake (059 681) 401. Telex 64103. Credit- Access, Visa, Amex.		4	4	4	23.50 –	35.00 –	– –	– –	1	19	1	21 –	–	P100 –	19 30 *20 30*	1–10 12	7 SP T
Dt Pheasant Inn, Bassenthwaite Lake, Wythop, Nr. Cockermouth, CA13 9YE. Tel. Bassenthwaite Lake (059 681) 234.		4	3	4	15.00 *15.00*	30.00 *30.00*	23.00 *23.00*	161.00 *161.00*	5	15	–	12 *4*	–	P80 –	19 00 *20 30*	1–12	SP
Et Lakeside, Dubwath, Bassenthwaite Lake, Nr. Cockermouth, CA13 9YD. Tel. Bassenthwaite Lake (059 681) 358.		3	3	1	*5.50 **6.50*	*11.00 **13.00*	– –	– –	1	2	1	– *1*	–	P6 G1	– –	1–12	5 SP
F Mrs. M. Gilmore, Hill Farm, Bassenthwaite, Keswick, CA12 4RJ. Tel. Bassenthwaite Lake (059 681) 498. (Mixed 14 acres)		1	1	2	*5.50 –	*11.00 –	*8.50 –	–	1	–	2	1 *1*	–	P4 G2	19 00 *21 00*	1–12	6
F Mrs. D. Mattinson, Bassenthwaite Hall Farm, Bassenthwaite, Keswick, CA12 4QP. Tel. Bassenthwaite Lake (059 681) 279. (Mixed 135 acres)		1	1	2	*5.50 **5.50*	*10.50 **11.00*	*9.00 **9.50*	*63.00 **63.00*	–	2	1	– *1*	–	P6 –	19 00 –	5–11	
BECKERMET (Cumbria)	B2																
Dt Royal Oak Hotel, CA21 2XB. Tel. (094 684) 551.		6	3	4	*16.00 **16.00*	*24.00 **24.00*	– –	– –	2	6	–	8 –	–	P20 –	19 00 *22 00*	1–12	SP
BEETHAM (Cumbria) (2m SE. Milnthorpe)	C3																
At Wheatsheaf Hotel, Beetham, Nr. Milnthorpe, LA7 7AL. Tel. Milnthorpe (044 82) 2123. Credit- Access.		3	5	4	– *9.50*	– *16.50*	15.00 –	105.00 –	–	3	1	2 *3*	–	P60 G8	19 00 *20 50*	1–12	
BERRIER (Cumbria) (8m W. Penrith)	B2																
Bt Low Murrah, Berrier, Nr. Penrith, CA11 OXD. Tel. Skelton (085 34) 230.		3	3	2	*7.00 –	*14.00 –	*11.00 –	*75.00 –	–	2	1	– *1*	–	P5 –	19 00 –	2–11	
BLAWITH (Cumbria) (6m S. Coniston)	B3																
A Highfield, Blawith, Ulverston, LA12 8EG. Tel. Lowick Bridge (022 985) 238.		3	3	3	*8.00 **9.00*	*16.00 **18.00*	*13.50 **14.50*	*85.00 **95.00*	1	5	2	5 *3*	1	P20 G2	19 00 *20 30*	1–12	FB SP
Ft R. D. Carlsen, Apple Tree Holme Farm, Blawith, via Ulverston, LA12 8EL. Tel. Lowick Bridge (022 985) 618. (Mixed 5 acres)		4	4	2	– –	– –	*15.00 **17.00*	*99.75 **113.15*	–	1	2	3 –	–	P6 –	19 30 *21 30*	1–12	

HOTELS, MOTELS, GUEST HOUSES & OTHER SERVICED ACCOMMODATION

Accommodation Type (See page 3)	Name and Address: Town (County) / Establishment / Address / Telephone number, Telex / Credit cards accepted	Map Ref.	Category (Key: see front fold-out): Bedrooms	Services	Meals	Prices: Bed and breakfast: Single room overnight (£ Min. / £ Max.)	Double room overnight (£ Min. / £ Max.)	B & B and evening meal: Per person daily (£ Min. / £ Max.)	Per person weekly (£ Min. / £ Max.)	Rooms: No. of bedrooms: Single	Double	Family	Bathrooms (Private / Public)	Showers	Facilities: Parking–P / Garage–G (No. of cars)	Evening meals (24 hr. clock) (From / Order by)	Months open (1–12)	Symbols (Key: see fold-out)
	BOOTLE (Cumbria)	B3																
F	Mrs. D. Cole, Flatts Cottage, Bootle Station, LA19 5XT. Tel. (065 78) 732. (Mixed 6 acres)		1	2	2	– / –	– / –	– / –	*35.00 / *35.00	–	2	–	– / 1	–	P3 / –	18 00 / –	1–12	
Ft	Mrs. M. Hogg, Foldgate Farm, Corney, Bootle, Millom, LA19 5TN. Tel. (065 78) 660. (Mixed 90 acres)		1	2	2	*6.50 / –	*12.00 / –	*10.00 / –	*65.00 / –	–	2	1	– / 1	–	P8 / –	18 00 / –	1–12	
F	Mrs. A. Woodend, Borrowdale Ground, Corney, Bootle, Nr. Millom, LA19 5TX. Tel. (065 78) 659. (Dairy 50 acres)		1	3	2	– / –	– / –	*8.00 / –	*56.00 / –	1	2	2	– / 1	–	P6 / –	19 00 / –	3–9	
	BORROWDALE (Cumbria)	B2																
At	Borrowdale Gates Hotel, Grange in Borrowdale, Keswick, CA12 5UQ. Tel. (059 684) 204.		4	4	4	*13.50 / *15.50	*27.00 / *31.00	*19.50 / *21.50	*130.00 / *145.00	2	12	1	6 / 3	3	P40 / –	19 00 / 21 30	1–12	FB
At	Borrowdale Hotel, Borrowdale, Keswick, CA12 5UY. Tel. (059 684) 224.		4	4	4	– / –	– / –	21.90 / –	– / –	10	26	1	35 / 1	2	P100 / –	19 00 / 20 15	2–12	
A	Knotts View Guest House, Stonethwaite, Borrowdale, Keswick. CA12 5XG. Tel. (059 684) 604.		x	1	2	– / *7.00	– / *14.00	– / *9.75	– / –	–	3	1	– / 1	–	P4 / –	19 00 / –	1–12	
At	Langstrath Hotel, Borrowdale, Keswick, CA12 5XG. Tel. (059 684) 239.		3	3	3	*10.00 / *11.00	*20.00 / *22.00	*14.50 / *15.50	*94.00 / *94.00	1	10	3	– / 3	–	P20 / –	19 00 / 15 00	3–10 / 12	FB
At	Scafell Hotel, Rosthwaite Borrowdale, Nr. Keswick, CA12 5XB. Tel. (059 684) 208.		4	4	4	*11.25 / *14.00	*22.50 / *28.00	*20.00 / *22.50	*126.00 / *143.50	10	11	1	9 / 4	–	P50 / –	19 00 / 20 00	3–11	
B	The Grange, Grange-in-Borrowdale, Keswick, CA12 5UQ. Tel. (059 684) 251.		3	2	2	– / *7.50	– / *15.00	– / *12.50	– / *84.00	1	5	1	1 / 2	–	P7 / –	19 00 / –	4–10	
Bt	Greenbank Country Guest House, Borrowdale, Keswick, CA12 5UY. Tel. (059 684) 215.		3	3	2	*7.50 / –	*15.00 / –	*12.50 / –	*82.50 / –	1	5	4	– / 2	–	P10 / –	19 00 / 17 00	1–12	
B	Hazel Bank Hotel, Rosthwaite, Borrowdale, Nr. Keswick, CA12 5XB. Tel. (059 684) 248.		3	4	3	– / –	– / –	*13.80 / –	*89.00 / –	2	6	1	4 / 2	–	P12 / –	19 00 / –	3–10	
Bt	Royal Oak Hotel, Rosthwaite, Borrowdale, Nr. Keswick, CA12 5XB. Tel. (059 684) 214. Credit- Access.		3	3	2	*11.25 / *11.25	*18.00 / *24.00	*13.50 / *16.50	*87.50 / *108.50	2	6	4	3 / 4	–	P12 / –	19 00 / 19 00	1–11	
Bt	Seatoller House, Seatoller, Borrowdale, Keswick, CA12 5XN. Tel. (059 684) 218.		3	3	2	– / –	– / –	*14.50 / –	*87.00 / –	–	2	6	– / 3	–	P15 / –	19 00 / –	3–11	5
Et	Leathes Head Hotel, Borrowdale, Keswick, CA12 5UY. Tel. (059 684) 247.		3	2	1	*10.50 / –	*21.00 / –	– / –	– / –	1	9	–	3 / 2	–	P25 / –	– / –	4–11	
E	Yew Craggs Guest House, Rosthwaite, Borrowdale, Keswick, CA12 5XB. Tel. (059 684) 260.		x	3	1	– / –	*14.00 / *16.00	– / –	– / –	–	3	2	– / 1	–	P6 / –	– / –	2–10	6
F	Mrs. D. M. Jenkinson, Seatoller Farm, Borrowdale, Keswick, CA12 5XN. Tel. (059 684) 232. (Mixed 100 acres)		1	2	2	*6.50 / *7.50	*12.00 / *14.00	*11.00 / *13.00	*60.00 / *65.00	1	5	–	– / 1	–	P8 / –	18 45 / –	3–10	

 You are advised to read the introductory notes and to check prices and other details when booking accommodation

HOTELS, MOTELS, GUEST HOUSES & OTHER SERVICED ACCOMMODATION

Name and Address Accommodation Type (See page 3) Town (County) Establishment Address Telephone number, Telex Credit cards accepted	Map Ref.	Category (Key: see front fold-out) Bedrooms	Services	Meals	Prices: Bed and breakfast Single room overnight £ Min. £ Max.	Double room overnight £ Min. £ Max.	B & B and evening meal Per person daily £ Min. £ Max.	Per person weekly £ Min. £ Max.	Rooms: No. of bedrooms Single	Double	Family	Bathrooms Private Public	Showers	Facilities: Parking–P Garage–G No.of cars	Evening meals (24 hr. clock) From Order by	Months open (1–12)	Symbols Key: see fold-out
BRAITHWAITE (Cumbria)	**B2**																
A† Coledale Inn, Braithwaite, Keswick, CA12 5TN. Tel. (059 682) 272.		3	3	4	*9.35 *10.50*	*18.70 *21.00*	*14.00 *15.20*	*95.00 *102.00*	–	5	3	– *2*	4	P15 –	19 00 *19 15*	3–11	
A Edith House, Whinlatter Pass, Braithwaite, Nr. Keswick, CA12 5TW. Tel. (059 682) 409. Credit- Access, Visa.		1	3	3	– *10.75*	– *17.50*	– *15.80*	– *88.55*	2	5	2	– *2*	–	P16 –	19 00 *21 00*	1–12	F B
A† Ivy House Hotel, Braithwaite, Keswick, CA12 5SY. Tel. (059 682) 338. Credit- Access, Visa, C.Bl., Diners, Amex.		4	4	4	*18.00 *21.00*	*36.00 *42.00*	*26.00 *29.00*	*175.00 *200.00*	–	8	1	9 –	–	P9 –	19 00 *20 30*	3–12	
A† Middle Ruddings Hotel, Braithwaite, Keswick, CA12 5RY. Tel. (059 682) 436.		4	4	4	10.50 –	20.00 –	16.50 –	110.00 –	3	11	2	8 *3*	–	P20 G1	19 00 *20 30*	2–12	
B† The Homestead, Braithwaite, Keswick, CA12 5RY. Tel. (059 682) 229.		1	2	2	*5.50 *6.00*	*11.00 *12.00*	*8.00 *9.00*	*55.00 *61.00*	2	3	4	– *1*	–	P16 G1	19 00 *19 00*	1–12	
C† Braithwaite Motor Inn, (Consort) Braithwaite, Keswick, CA12 5TD. Tel. (059 682) 444. Credit- Access, Visa, Diners, Amex.		5	4	5	*18.00 *22.00*	*30.00 *37.00*	*22.00 *25.00*	*120.00 *140.00*	–	35	–	35 –	–	P40 –	19 00 *21 30*	2–12	
BRAMPTON (Cumbria)	**C1**																
A† Farlam Hall, CA8 2NG. Tel. Hallbankgate (069 76) 234. Credit- Access.		4	4	4	*17.00 *19.00*	*32.00 *36.00*	*25.50 –	– –	2	9	–	6 *3*	–	P35 –	20 00 *20 00*	1 3–12	
B Garth House, Greenfield La., CA8 1AY. Tel. (069 77) 2193 & 3364.		4	3	2	*9.00 *10.00*	*18.00 *20.00*	*13.00 *15.00*	– –	1	1	2	3 *1*	–	P4 G2	18 00 *20 00*	4–10	8
B Woodside, Hallbankgate, CA8 1JY. Tel. Hallbankgate (069 76) 301.		1	1	2	– –	*10.00 *12.00*	*7.00 *9.00*	*40.00 *45.00*	–	1	1	– *2*	–	P3 –	18 00 –	1–11	3
D† Blacksmiths Arms, Talkin Village, Brampton. CA8 1LE. Tel. (069 77) 3452.		3	3	4	*8.00 *9.00*	*14.00 *18.00*	– –	– –	–	3	–	1 *1*	–	P10 –	19 00 *20 00*	4–10	
D† Hare & Hounds Inn, Talkin Village, Brampton, CA8 1LE. Tel. (069 77) 3456.		4	4	4	*8.00 *9.00*	*14.50 *16.50*	– –	– –	1	2	–	2 *1*	–	P12 –	19 00 *21 00*	1–12	12
D† Ye Olde Scotch Arms, CA8 1SB. Tel. (069 77) 2397.		1	1	1	*6.00 –	*12.00 –	– –	– –	1	2	1	– *2*	–	P20 –	– –	1–12	
E Kirby Moor, Longtown Rd., CA8 2AB. Tel. (069 77) 2021.		3	2	1	*7.00 *8.00*	*14.00 *16.00*	– –	– –	–	1	2	– *1*	–	P8 –	– –	4–10	
F Mrs. A. Forster, High Nook Farm, Low Row, Brampton, CA8 2LU. Tel. Hallbank Gate (069 76) 273. (Stock Rearing 100 acres)		1	2	2	*5.00 *5.00*	*10.00 *10.00*	*6.50 *6.50*	*42.00 *42.00*	–	1	1	– *1*	–	P3 –	18 00 *18 00*	5–10	3
BROUGHTON-IN-FURNESS (Cumbria)	**B3**																
A† Eccle Riggs Hotel, (Minotels) Foxfield Rd., LA20 6BN. Tel. (065 76) 398 & 240. Credit- Access, Visa.		4	4	4	*12.00 *13.50*	*22.00 *25.00*	*18.50 *20.00*	*115.00 *125.00*	3	5	5	4 *3*	–	P100 –	19 00 *20 50*	1–12	
B Cobblers Cottage, Griffin St., LA20 6HH. Tel. (065 76) 413.		3	2	2	*5.75 –	*11.50 –	*9.25 –	*60.00 –	–	2	1	– *1*	–	– –	19 00 *17 00*	3–10	2

HOTELS, MOTELS, GUEST HOUSES & OTHER SERVICED ACCOMMODATION

Accommodation Type (See page 3)	Name and Address: Town (County) / Establishment / Address / Telephone number, Telex / Credit cards accepted	Map Ref.	Category: Bedrooms	Services	Meals	Bed and breakfast: Single room overnight £ Min. / *£ Max.*	Double room overnight £ Min. / *£ Max.*	B & B and evening meal: Per person daily £ Min. / *£ Max.*	Per person weekly £ Min. / *£ Max.*	No. of bedrooms: Single	Double	Family	Bathrooms Private / *Public*	Showers	Parking–P / Garage–G: No. of cars	Evening meals (24 hr. clock): From / *Order by*	Months open (1–12)	Symbols (Key: see fold-out)
	BROUGHTON-IN-FURNESS continued																	
B	Fair View, LA20 6ES. Tel. (065 76) 368.		3	3	2	– –	– –	*8.00 –	– –	1	3	1	– *1*	–	P5 –	18 30 –	3–11	
B†	High Duddon Guest House, Duddon Bridge, Broughton-in-Furness, LA20 6ET. Tel. (065 76) 279.		3	4	2	*8.50 –	*16.00 –	*12.00 –	*75.00 –	2	3	6	– *4*	–	P14 –	18 30 *18 30*	1–12	
E	Broomhill, New St., LA20 6JD. Tel. (065 76) 358.		2	1	1	*6.50 **8.00*	*13.00 **16.00*	– –	– –	–	6	–	– *2*	–	P6 G2	– –	1–12	
F	Mrs. P. Hibbert, High Kiln Bank Farm, Seathwaite, Broughton-in-Furness, LA20 6EB. Tel. (065 76) 395. (Mixed 130 acres)		3	3	3	– –	– –	*8.50 –	*59.50 –	1	6	–	– *2*	–	P8 –	18 30 *18 30*	4–10	FB
	BURTON-IN-KENDAL (Cumbria) (11m S. Kendal)	**C3**																
A†	Clawthorpe Hall Hotel, LA6 1NU. Tel. Burton (0524) 781166. Credit- Access, Visa, Diners, Amex.		5	4	5	*15.50 –	*25.00 –	*20.00 –	*120.00 –	7	22	6	32 *4*	3	P100 –	19 30 *21 45*	1–12	FB
	BUTTERMERE (Cumbria)	**B2**																
A	Bridge Hotel, Buttermere, Nr. Cockermouth, CA13 9UZ. Tel. (059 685) 252.		4	4	4	*14.00 **15.50*	*26.00 **30.00*	*22.00 **24.00*	*125.00 **140.00*	3	17	–	14 *4*	–	P30 G2	19 30 *20 30*	4–10	FB
B†	Dalegarth Guest House, Buttermere, Cockermouth, CA13 9XA. Tel. (059 685) 233.		x	2	2	*10.00 –	*15.50 –	*11.75 –	*66.00 –	2	7	2	– *2*	–	P12 –	19 00 *19 00*	4–10	
B†	Lanthwaite Gate Guest House, Buttermere, Nr. Cockermouth, CA13 9UY. Tel. Lorton (090 085) 270.		2	1	2	– –	– –	*12.00 –	– –	1	3	1	– *1*	–	P5 G3	19 00 *17 30*	2–11	4
D†	The Fish Hotel, Buttermere, Cockermouth, CA13 9XA. Tel. (059 685) 253.		3	3	2	*11.00 –	*22.00 –	*16.00 –	*88.00 –	2	6	3	1 *4*	–	P35 –	19 00 –	3–11	
	CALDBECK (Cumbria)	**B2**																
B†	The Gables, Caldbeck, Wigton, CA7 8EL. Tel. (069 98) 373.		1	1	2	*5.00 –	*10.00 –	*8.00 –	*50.00 –	–	2	–	– *1*	–	P2 –	17 30 *19 30*	1–12	
B†	High Greenrigg House, Caldbeck, Wigton, CA7 8HD. Tel. (069 98) 430.		3	3	3	*8.00 **10.00*	*16.00 **20.00*	*13.00 **15.00*	*91.00 **105.00*	4	4	–	– *3*	–	P12 –	19 00 –	1–12	FB
	CALDERBRIDGE (Cumbria)	**B2**																
B	Fair Hill, Calderbridge, Seascale, CA20 1DY. Tel. Beckermet (094 684) 296.		1	1	2	– –	*11.00 **11.00*	– –	– –	–	1	1	– *1*	–	P3 –	18 00 *19 00*	1–12	
D†	Stanley Arms Hotel, (S & N) Calderbridge, Seascale, CA20 1DN. Tel. Beckermet (094 684) 235 & 599. Credit- Access, Visa.		3	3	4	*12.00 –	*24.00 –	*18.00 **20.00*	*126.00 **140.00*	1	8	–	– *3*	–	P30 –	18 30 *22 00*	1–12	
	CARLISLE (Cumbria)	**B1**																
A†	Central Hotel, Victoria Viaduct, CA3 8AL. Tel. (0228) 20256. Credit- Access, Visa, C.Bl., Amex.		3	6	4	*13.50 **17.00*	*22.00 **27.00*	*17.00 **22.50*	– –	22	57	4	22 *12*	–	G25 –	19 00 *21 00*	1–12	

 You are advised to read the introductory notes and to check prices and other details when booking accommodation

HOTELS, MOTELS, GUEST HOUSES & OTHER SERVICED ACCOMMODATION

CARLISLE continued

Name and Address (Accommodation Type (See page 3); Town (County); Establishment, Address, Telephone number, Telex, Credit cards accepted)	Category: Bedrooms	Category: Services	Category: Meals	Prices: Bed and breakfast – Single room overnight (£ Min. / *£ Max.*)	Prices: Bed and breakfast – Double room overnight (£ Min. / *£ Max.*)	Prices: B & B and evening meal – Per person daily (£ Min. / *£ Max.*)	Prices: B & B and evening meal – Per person weekly (£ Min. / *£ Max.*)	Rooms: No. of bedrooms – Single	Rooms: Double	Rooms: Family	Rooms: Bathrooms (Private / *Public*)	Rooms: Showers	Facilities: Parking–P Garage–G (No. of cars)	Facilities: Evening meals (24 hr. clock) (From / *Order by*)	Facilities: Months open (1–12)	Facilities: Symbols (Key: see fold-out)
A† Crown Hotel, Wetheral, Carlisle, CA4 8ES. Tel. (0228) 60208. Credit- Access, Visa, Diners, Amex.	6	5	5	*24.95 –	*38.95 –	– –	– –	3	43	4	50 –	–	P80 –	19 00 *21 30*	1–12	
A† Crown and Mitre Hotel, (Comfort) English St., CA3 8HZ. Tel. (0228) 25491. Telex 64183. Credit- Access, Visa, Diners, Amex.	5	5	5	*19.50 **24.00*	*34.00 –	*21.50 **25.50*	– –	22	66	6	94 –	–	P25 G25	19 00 *22 00*	1–12	
A Cumbria Park Hotel, 32 Scotland Rd., CA3 9DG. Tel. (0228) 22887.	4	4	4	*12.50 **15.00*	*18.50 **22.00*	*17.50 **20.00*	*122.50 **140.00*	14	12	3	11 *8*	–	P30 –	18 30 *19 30*	1–12	
A† Cumbrian Hotel, (Thistle) Court Sq., CA1 1QX. Tel. (0228) 31951. Telex 64287. Credit- Access, Visa, C.Bl., Diners, Amex.	5	5	5	*28.75 –	*39.50 –	– –	– –	23	44	3	70 *2*	–	P100 –	19 00 *21 30*	1–12	
A† Hilltop Hotel, (Swallow) London Rd., CA1 2PQ. Tel. (0228) 29255. Telex 64292. Credit- Access, Visa, Diners, Amex.	5	5	5	16.00 *27.00*	25.25 *36.50*	– –	– –	23	92	8	101 *5*	–	P350 G1	18 30 *21 45*	1–12	FB
A† Killoran Country House Hotel, The Green, Wetheral, Carlisle, CA4 8ET. Tel. Wetheral (0228) 60200. Credit- Access, Visa.	3	4	4	– **12.50*	– **24.00*	– **20.00*	– **125.00*	2	4	3	– *3*	–	P40 G3	19 00 *21 15*	1–12	FB
A Park House Hotel, Kingstown, Carlisle, CA6 4BY. Tel. (0228) 26028.	1	1	3	*6.90 **8.00*	*11.50 **14.00*	– –	– –	1	6	1	1 *2*	–	P50 –	17 30 *22 00*	1–12	FB
A† Royal Hotel, 9 Lowther St., CA3 8ES. Tel. (0228) 22103.	3	3	3	8.00 *8.00*	15.00 *15.00*	10.50 *12.00*	– –	3	18	4	– *5*	–	– –	17 30 *19 00*	1–12	
B Crossroads House, Brisco, Exit 42, M6, CA4 0QZ. Tel. (0228) 28994.	2	2	2	– **6.50*	– **13.00*	– **9.50*	– **66.50*	2	3	1	– *1*	–	P30 –	18 00 *20 00*	1–12	
B Redruth House, 46 Victoria Place, CA1 1EX. Tel. (0228) 21631.	3	2	2	*6.50 **6.50*	*12.00 **12.00*	*9.75 –	*65.00 –	1	3	1	– *1*	–	– –	19 00 *11 00*	1–12	
C Carlisle Truck Inn Motel, Exit 44–M6 Kingstown, Carlisle, CA3 0JR. Tel. (0228) 34192. Credit- Visa, Amex.	2	2	5	*8.00 –	*16.00 –	 –	– –	24	38	–	62 *3*	–	P200 –	17 00 *24 00*	1–12	
C† Crest Hotel, (Crest) Kingstown, CA4 0HR. Tel. (0228) 31201. Telex 64201. Credit- Access, Visa, C.Bl., Diners, Amex.	5	4	5	*30.00 **34.60*	*38.00 **42.00*	*38.00 **40.00*	– –	–	100	8	108 –	–	P200 –	18 30 *22 00*	1–12	
D† Metal Bridge Inn, (S & N) Floriston, Nr. Carlisle, CA6 4HG. Tel. (0228) 74206. Credit- Access, Visa.	1	2	4	*9.00 –	*18.00 –	– –	– –	2	1	2	– *1*	–	P20 –	18 00 *22 00*	1–12	
D† String of Horses Inn & Restaurant, Faugh, Heads Nook, Carlisle, CA4 9EG. Tel. Hayton (022 870) 297. Credit- Access, Visa, C.Bl., Diners, Amex.	6	5	6	*21.00 **23.00*	*28.50 **39.50*	– –	– –	–	13	–	13 –	–	P50 –	18 00 *22 50*	1–12	
E† East View Guest House, 110 Warwick Rd., CA1 1JU. Tel. (0228) 22112.	1	3	1	*5.50 **6.00*	*11.00 **12.00*	– –	– –	2	4	2	– *3*	–	– –	– –	1–12	3
E Kenilworth, 34 Lazenby Ter., London Rd., CA1 2PZ. Tel. (0228) 26179.	1	2	1	*6.00 **10.00*	*10.00 **12.00*	– –	– –	–	4	2	– *1*	–	P5 –	– –	1–12	

HOTELS, MOTELS, GUEST HOUSES & OTHER SERVICED ACCOMMODATION

Name and Address Accommodation Type (See page 3) **Town (County)** Establishment Address Telephone number, Telex Credit cards accepted	Map Ref.	Category (Key: see front fold-out) Bedrooms	Services	Meals	Prices: Bed and breakfast Single room overnight £ Min. *£ Max.*	Double room overnight £ Min. *£ Max.*	B & B and evening meal Per person daily £ Min. *£ Max.*	Per person weekly £ Min. *£ Max.*	Rooms: No. of bedrooms Single	Double	Family	Bathrooms Private *Public*	Showers	Facilities: Parking–P Garage–G No. of cars	Evening meals (24 hr. clock) From *Order by*	Months open (1–12)	Symbols Key: see fold-out
CARLISLE continued																	
E Roburn Guest House, 38 London Rd., CA1 2EL. Tel. (0228) 24668.		2	2	1	*6.50 **7.50*	*11.00 **13.00*	– –	– –	1	1	2	– *1*	–	P2 G2	– –	1–12	
E White Lea House, 191 Warwick Rd., CA1 1LP. Tel. (0228) 33139.		3	2	1	*6.00 **6.00*	*11.00 **12.00*	– –	– –	1	1	1	– *1*	–	P2 G2	– –	1–12	
F Mrs. D. Nicholson, Willow Grove, Kirklinton, Carlisle, CA6 6DD. Tel. Kirklinton (022 875) 326. (Beef 24 acres)		1	2	2	*6.00 –	*12.00 –	*9.00 –	– –	–	2	1	– *1*	–	P4 –	17 00 *19 00*	3–12	FB
F Mrs. J. L. Rawstron, Beech Holme, Cardewlees, Carlisle, CA5 6LF. Tel. Dalston (0228) 710646. (Dairy 68 acres)		1	3	2	*5.50 **6.00*	*11.00 **12.00*	*7.50 **8.50*	*50.00 **55.00*	1	1	1	– *1*	–	P3 –	18 00 –	4–10	
CARTMEL (Cumbria)	**B3**																
A† Aynsome Manor Hotel, Cartmel, Grange-over-Sands, LA11 6HH. Tel. (044 854) 276. Credit- Access.		4	3	4	– –	– –	*22.00 **26.40*	*124.00 **184.80*	2	11	3	13 *3*	–	P20 –	19 00 *20 30*	1–12	
A† The Grammar Hotel, Cartmel, Grange-over-Sands. LA11 7SG. Tel. (044 854) 367.		4	4	4	*11.00 **12.00*	*21.00 **24.00*	*16.50 **18.00*	– –	2	8	2	12 –	–	P30 –	18 30 *21 30*	1–12	FB
A† Priory Hotel, Cartmel, Grange-over-Sands, LA11 6QB. Tel. (044 854) 267.		3	3	4	*10.00 **12.00*	*20.00 **24.00*	*14.50 **17.50*	*95.00 **115.00*	2	8	–	5 *2*	–	P8 –	19 00 *20 00*	3–11	
B St. Mary's Lodge, Cartmel, Grange-over-Sands, LA11 6PN. Tel. (044 854) 379.		3	3	2	*8.25 **9.35*	*16.50 **18.70*	*14.85 **15.95*	*102.00 **110.00*	1	4	1	– *2*	–	P7 –	19 00 –	4–10	
CARTMEL FELL (Cumbria)	**B3**																
F† Mrs. D. Newton, Lightwood Farm, Cartmel Fell, Grange-over-Sands, LA11 6NP. Tel. Newby Bridge (044 83) 31454. (Beef 100 acres)		1	3	1	*6.00 –	*12.00 –	– –	– –	–	2	–	– *1*	–	P6 –	– –	1–12	
CASTERTON (Cumbria) (1m N. Kirkby Lonsdale)	**C3**																
D† Pheasant Inn, Casterton, Kirkby Lonsdale. LA6 2RX. Tel. Kirkby Lonsdale (0468) 71230.		4	4	5	– –	– –	18.00 *22.00*	– –	1	5	–	3 *2*	–	P50 –	19 00 *22 00*	1–12	
CASTLE CARROCK (Cumbria) (4m S. Brampton)	**C1**																
D Weary Sportsman Inn, Castle Carrock, Carlisle, CA4 9LU. Tel. Hayton (022 870) 230.		1	3	3	*6.00 **6.50*	*12.00 **13.00*	*7.00 **11.00*	*55.77 **58.65*	–	2	2	– *1*	–	P12 –	19 00 *22 00*	1–12	FB
COCKERMOUTH (Cumbria)	**B2**																
A Allerdale Court Hotel, Market Pl., CA13 9NR. Tel. (0900) 823654. Credit- Access, Visa, Amex.		4	4	5	*11.00 **16.00*	*16.00 **22.00*	*17.00 **22.50*	– –	8	18	1	18 *5*	–	– –	18 30 *21 30*	1–12	FB
A† Globe Hotel, Main St., CA13 9LE. Tel. (0900) 822126. Credit- Access, Visa.		3	4	4	*14.00 **14.00*	*20.00 **25.00*	*17.50 –	*122.50 –	16	15	1	7 *7*	1	G20 –	18 30 *21 30*	1–12	

 You are advised to read the introductory notes and to check prices and other details when booking accommodation

HOTELS, MOTELS, GUEST HOUSES & OTHER SERVICED ACCOMMODATION

Type	Name and Address (Town (County), Establishment, Address, Telephone number, Telex, Credit cards accepted)	Map Ref.	Category: Bedrooms	Services	Meals	Prices: Bed and breakfast – Single room overnight (£ Min. / £ Max.)	Double room overnight (£ Min. / £ Max.)	B & B and evening meal – Per person daily (£ Min. / £ Max.)	Per person weekly (£ Min. / £ Max.)	Rooms: No. of bedrooms – Single	Double	Family	Bathrooms (Private / Public)	Showers	Parking–P Garage–G (No. of cars)	Evening meals (24 hr. clock) (From / Order by)	Months open (1–12)	Facilities: Symbols (Key: see fold-out)
	COCKERMOUTH continued																	
A†	Hundith Hill Hotel, CA13 9TH. Tel. (0900) 822092. Credit- Amex.		4	4	2	*9.50 / *11.50	*19.00 / *23.00	*15.00 / *17.00	*98.00 / *112.00	3	13	4	8 / 3	–	P30 / –	19 00 / 19 00	3–11	
A†	Trout Hotel, Crown St., CA13 0EJ. Tel. (0900) 823591.		5	3	5	*18.00 / *19.00	*30.00 / –	*26.00 / *27.00	– / –	4	12	–	15 / 1	–	P100 / –	19 00 / 21 30	1–12	FB SP
A†	Wordsworth Hotel, Main St., CA13 9JS. Tel. (0900) 822757.		3	3	5	*14.00 / *16.00	*22.50 / *25.00	*21.50 / *23.50	*125.00 / *135.00	3	13	2	4 / 2	9	P20 / G6	18 30 / 21 30	1–12	FB SP
B	Croft House, 6–8 Challoner St., CA13 9QS. Tel. (0900) 822532.		3	1	2	– / *6.50	– / *13.00	– / *9.00	– / *63.00	2	6	1	– / 2	–	P4 / –	18 00 / –	4–10	GAP
E	Bouch House, Deanscales, Cockermouth, CA13 0SL. Tel. (0900) 822753.		1	2	1	*6.00 / *6.00	*12.00 / *12.00	– / –	– / –	1	2	–	– / 1	–	P5 / –	– / –	1–12	
E	The Rook, 9 Castlegate, CA13 9EU. Tel. (0900) 822441.		3	2	1	*6.50 / *7.00	*13.00 / *14.00	– / –	– / –	2	2	1	– / 2	–	– / –	– / –	1–12	
F	Mrs. R. Clark, Mosser Gate Farm, High Mosser, Cockermouth, CA13 0SR. Tel. (0900) 822387. (Mixed 600 acres)		1	1	2	*5.50 / *6.00	– / –	*8.50 / *9.00	– / –	2	2	2	– / 3	–	P6 / –	18 30 / –	4–10	
F	Mrs. D. E. Richardson, Pardshaw Hall, CA13 0SP. Tel. (0900) 822607. (Mixed 5 acres)		1	2	2	*5.50 / –	*11.00 / –	*7.50 / –	*52.00 / –	2	1	1	– / 1	–	P4 / G1	18 00 / 18 30	1–12	GAP SP
F	Mr. & Mrs. C. B. Williams, Wood Farm, Mosser, Cockermouth, CA13 0RB. Tel. (0900) 823403. (Stock Rearing 60 acres)		1	3	3	– / –	– / –	*8.50 / *9.00	– / –	–	3	1	– / 2	–	P6 / –	– / –	1–12	FB SP
	CONISTON (Cumbria)	**B3**																
A†	Low Bank Ground Country House Hotel, LA21 8AA. Tel. (096 64) 525.		4	3	2	13.50 / 14.75	27.00 / 29.50	22.00 / 25.00	154.00 / 175.00	–	2	2	4 / 4	–	P10 / –	19 30 / 19 30	2–12	SP
A†	Yewdale Hotel, Yewdale Rd., LA21 8DU. Tel. (096 64) 280.		3	3	4	– / –	*16.00 / *18.00	– / –	– / –	–	6	–	– / 2	–	P6 / –	19 00 / 21 00	1–12	GAP SP
B†	Shepherds Villa, LA21 8EE. Tel. (096 64) 337.		2	3	2	*6.50 / *6.50	*13.00 / *13.00	*10.50 / *10.50	*67.00 / *67.00	1	4	3	– / 2	–	P9 / –	19 00 / 15 00	3–10	
B	Townson Ground, East of Lake Rd., LA21 8AA. Tel. (096 64) 272.		1	1	2	*6.00 / *6.50	*12.00 / *13.00	*9.50 / *10.50	*66.50 / *73.50	1	1	2	– / 1	–	P10 / –	18 30 / –	1–12	3
B†	Wheelgate, Little Arrow, Coniston, LA21 8AU. Tel. (096 64) 418.		3	2	2	– / –	– / –	*12.50 / *12.50	*78.00 / *78.00	–	6	–	– / 1	–	P6 / G1	19 00 / –	4–10	5
D†	Crown Hotel LA21 8EA. Tel. (096 64) 243.		3	3	3	*8.50 / –	*17.00 / –	*14.00 / –	– / –	1	2	3	– / 2	–	P30 / –	19 00 / 20 00	1–12	FB
E	How Head Cottage, East of Lake Coniston, LA21 8AA. Tel. (096 64) 594.		3	2	1	– / –	*12.00 / *15.00	– / –	– / –	–	3	–	– / 1	–	P3 / –	– / –	1–12	
F	Mrs. Batty, Bank Ground Farm, LA21 8AA. Tel. (096 64) 264. (Mixed 26 acres)		3	2	2	*5.50 / –	*11.00 / –	*9.00 / –	*62.00 / –	–	3	5	– / 2	–	P10 / –	18 00 / –	1–12	

Accommodation Type (See page 3). Category Key: see front fold-out.

HOTELS, MOTELS, GUEST HOUSES & OTHER SERVICED ACCOMMODATION

Type	Name and Address (Town (County); Establishment, Address, Telephone number, Telex, Credit cards accepted)	Map Ref.	Bedrooms	Services	Meals	Single room overnight £ Min. £ Max.	Double room overnight £ Min. £ Max.	B & B and evening meal: Per person daily £ Min. £ Max.	Per person weekly £ Min. £ Max.	Single	Double	Family	Bathrooms Private Public	Showers	Parking–P Garage–G (No. of cars)	Evening meals (24 hr. clock) From Order by	Months open (1–12)	Symbols (Key: see fold-out)
	CONISTON continued																	
F†	Mrs. E. Youdell, Spoon Hall, LA21 8AW. Tel. (096 64) 391. (Hill 100 acres)		1	2	2	*6.00 –	*12.00 –	*9.00 –	– –	–	3	1	– 1	–	P6 –	18 30 –	4–10	
	CROGLIN (Cumbria) (4m NE. Kirkoswald)	C2																
D	Robin Hood Inn, Croglin, Carlisle, CA4 9RZ. Tel. (076 886) 227.		3	2	3	*10.00 –	*16.00 –	*12.50 –	– –	–	2	1	– 1	–	P30 –	18 00 22 00	1–12	SP
	CROOKLANDS (Cumbria) (6m SE. Kendal)	C3																
A†	Crooklands Hotel, (Best Western) Crooklands, Nr. Milnthorpe, LA7 7NW. Tel. (044 87) 432. Telex 61686. Credit- Access, Visa, Amex.		5	4	5	*25.00 –	*35.00 *38.00	– –	– –	–	18	1	15 2	–	P120 –	19 00 21 30	1–12	V TV SP T
	CROSBY RAVENSWORTH (Cumbria) (6m SW. Appleby-in-Westmorland)	C2																
F	D.M. Willison, Croft House Farm, Crosby Ravensworth, Penrith, CA10 3JP. Tel. Ravensworth (093 15) 286. (Mixed 100 acres)		1	3	2	*6.00 –	*12.00 –	*9.00 –	*63.00 –	1	4	2	– 2	–	P6 –	19 30 21 30	1–12	10 V TV OAP
	CROSBY-ON-EDEN (Cumbria)	C1																
A†	Crosby Lodge Hotel, Crosby-on-Eden, Carlisle, CA6 4QZ. Tel. (022 873) 618. Credit- Diners, Amex.		4	4	4	*20.00 *25.00	*35.00 *40.00	*30.00 *40.00	– –	1	9	1	9 1	–	P40 –	19 30 21 00	2–12	TV
A	Newby Grange Restaurant & Hotel, Crosby-on-Eden, Nr. Carlisle, CA6 4RA. Tel. (022 873) 645. Credit- Access.		4	4	5	*10.00 *15.00	*20.00 –	*15.00 –	– –	1	9	4	4 4	–	P200 –	18 00 22 30	1–12	V TV FB OAP SP
	DALSTON (Cumbria)	B1																
A†	Dalston Hall, (Best Western) Dalston, Carlisle, CA5 7JX. Tel. Carlisle (0228) 710271. Credit- Access, Visa, C.Bl., Diners, Amex.		5	4	5	*16.00 *22.00	*27.00 *34.00	– –	– –	9	9	–	13 2	–	P100 –	19 30 21 30	1–12	V TV SP T
	DENT (Cumbria)	C3																
A†	George & Dragon Hotel, Main St., LA10 5QL. Tel. (058 75) 256. Credit- Access.		3	3	4	– *10.50	– *19.00	– –	– –	–	7	2	– 2	–	P14 –	19 00 22 00	1–12	TV SP
D	Sportsman Inn, Cowgill, Dent, Sedbergh, LA10 5RG. Tel. (058 75) 282.		1	1	3	– –	*15.00 *17.00	– –	– –	–	3	–	– 1	–	P30 –	19 00 22 00	1–12	14 V SP
F†	Mrs. A. Handley, Helmside Farm, Dent, Sedbergh, LA10 5SY. Tel. (058 75) 230. (Mixed 140 acres)		1	1	2	– –	*12.00 *15.00	*8.00 *10.00	– *65.00	–	2	1	– 1	–	P4 –	19 00 –	1–12	TV
	EGREMONT (Cumbria)	B2																
A†	Blackbeck Inn, (Best Western) Blackbeck, Nr. Egremont, CA22 2NY. Tel. Beckermet (094 684) 661. Credit- Access, Visa, Amex.		6	4	5	21.79 –	31.74 –	– –	– –	7	14	1	22 –	–	P100 –	18 30 21 30	1–12	V TV SP T

Accommodation Type (See page 3). Category key: see front fold-out.

 You are advised to read the introductory notes and to check prices and other details when booking accommodation

HOTELS, MOTELS, GUEST HOUSES & OTHER SERVICED ACCOMMODATION

Type	Town (County) / Establishment, Address, Telephone number, Telex, Credit cards accepted	Map Ref.	Bedrooms	Services	Meals	Bed and breakfast: Single room overnight (£ Min. / £ Max.)	Bed and breakfast: Double room overnight (£ Min. / £ Max.)	B & B and evening meal: Per person daily (£ Min. / £ Max.)	B & B and evening meal: Per person weekly (£ Min. / £ Max.)	No. of bedrooms: Single	No. of bedrooms: Double	No. of bedrooms: Family	Bathrooms (Private / Public)	Showers	Parking–P Garage–G (No. of cars)	Evening meals (24 hr. clock) (From / Order by)	Months open (1–12)	Symbols (Key: see fold-out)
	EGREMONT continued																	
E	Old Vicarage Guest House, Nr. Thornhill, Egremont, CA22 2NX. Tel. Beckermet (094 684) 577.		3	1	1	– *5.50*	– *11.00*	– –	– –	–	2	3	– *2*	–	P8 –	– –	1–12	
	ELTERWATER (Cumbria)	B2																
B	Fellside, Lane Ends, Elterwater, Nr. Ambleside, LA22 9HN. Tel. Langdale (096 67) 678.		1	2	2	*6.50 –	*13.00 –	*10.50 –	*73.50 –	2	2	–	– *2*	–	P4 –	19 00 –	1–12	8
D†	Britannia Inn, Elterwater, Ambleside, LA22 9HP. Tel. Langdale (096 67) 210.		3	3	4	*11.75 **12.35*	*23.50 **24.70*	*18.95 **20.00*	*124.95 **132.65*	2	7	1	– *2*	–	P10 –	19 00 *19 00*	1 3–10 12	FB
	ENNERDALE (Cumbria)	B2																
A†	Shepherd's Arms Hotel, Ennerdale Bridge, CA23 3AR. Tel. Lamplugh (094 686) 249.		4	3	4	*9.00 **10.50*	*18.00 **21.00*	*15.50 **17.00*	– –	1	5	–	2 *2*	–	P12 –	19 00 *20 30*	2–12	SP
F	Mrs. K. Rawling, Hollins, Ennerdale, Cleator, CA23 3AL. Tel. Lamplugh (094 686) 391. (Livestock Rearing 800 acres)		1	1	2	*5.00 **6.00*	*10.00 **12.00*	*7.00 **8.00*	*49.00 **56.00*	–	2	1	– *1*	–	P4 –	18 30 –	4–10	
	ESKDALE (Cumbria)	B3																
A	Brook House, Boot, Eskdale, CA19 1TG. Tel. (094 03) 288.		2	3	3	*8.50 –	*17.00 –	*12.50 –	*80.00 –	–	4	2	– *2*	–	P8 –	19 00 *20 30*	1–12	
D†	Bower House Inn, Eskdale, Holmrook, CA19 1TD. Tel. (094 03) 244.		4	3	4	*15.00 **17.00*	*20.00 **22.00*	*17.00 **19.00*	– –	2	7	5	7 *2*	–	P60 G4	19 00 *21 00*	1–12	SP
D†	Woolpack Inn, Boot, Eskdale, CA19 1TH. Tel. (094 03) 230.		3	3	2	*10.00 **10.50*	*20.00 **21.00*	*16.50 **17.00*	*115.50 **119.00*	–	7	–	– *1*	4	P15 –	19 00 *19 00*	3–10	
F	Mrs. G. M. Temple, Gill Bank Farm, Boot, Holmrook, CA19 1TG. Tel. (094 03) 292. (Hill 67 acres)		1	2	3	*5.00 **6.00*	*10.00 **12.00*	*8.00 **10.00*	*56.00 **70.00*	1	2	–	– *1*	–	P6 –	18 00 *20 30*	1–12	FB
	GILSLAND (Cumbria)	C1																
F	Mrs. J. Lawson, Clarkes Hill Farm, Gilsland, Carlisle, CA6 7DF. Tel. (069 72) 208. (Mixed 165 acres)		1	2	3	– –	– –	*8.00 –	*56.00 –	1	2	3	– *1*	–	P8 –	18 00 –	3–10 12	FB
	GOSFORTH (Cumbria)	B2																
A†	Gosforth Hall Hotel, Gosforth, Seascale, CA20 1AZ. Tel. (094 05) 322.		3	3	4	*13.50 **15.00*	*24.00 **25.50*	*20.50 **22.00*	– –	4	8	–	2 *4*	–	P40 –	19 30 *20 45*	1–12	5
A	The Hob Thross Restaurant, The Square, CA20 1AL. Tel. (094 05) 440 & 572.		1	2	4	12.50 *12.50*	22.50 *22.50*	22.00 –	110.00 *115.00*	1	2	–	– *2*	–	– –	18 30 *20 30*	1–12	SP
F	Mrs. S. Martin, Bank House Farm, Gosforth, Nr. Seascale, CA20 1ED. Tel. Gosforth (094 05) 496. (Mixed 95 acres)		1	1	2	*6.00 –	– –	– –	– –	1	3	1	– *1*	–	P10 –	18 00 *18 00*	1–12	

HOTELS, MOTELS, GUEST HOUSES & OTHER SERVICED ACCOMMODATION

Name and Address Accommodation Type (See page 3) **Town (County)** Map Ref. Establishment Address Telephone number, Telex Credit cards accepted	Category (Key: see front fold-out) Bedrooms	Services	Meals	Prices: Bed and breakfast Single room overnight £ Min. *£ Max.*	Double room overnight £ Min. *£ Max.*	B & B and evening meal Per person daily £ Min. *£ Max.*	Per person weekly £ Min. *£ Max.*	Rooms: No. of bedrooms Single	Double	Family	Bathrooms Private *Public*	Showers	Facilities Parking–P Garage–G No. of cars	Evening meals (24 hr. clock) From *Order by*	Months open (1–12)	Symbols Key: see fold-out
GRANGE-OVER-SANDS (Cumbria) B3																
A† Hotel Commodore, Main St., LA11 6DY. Tel. (044 84) 2055 & 2381. Credit- Visa.	3	3	4	10.25 *11.00*	20.50 *21.50*	15.25 *15.75*	106.75 *110.25*	4	7	1	– *2*	–	P9 G2	18 30 *20 00*	1-12	FB
A† The Cumbria Grand Hotel, Lindale Rd., LA11 6EN. Tel. (044 84) 2331. Credit- Access, Visa, C.Bl., Diners, Amex.	4	5	5	*18.50 **20.50*	*33.00 **35.00*	*25.50 **26.50*	*159.00 **165.00*	1	88	4	59 *12*	–	P200 G10	19 00 *22 00*	1-12	
A† Grange Hotel, (Best Western) Lindale Rd., LA11 6EJ. Tel. (044 84) 3666. Telex 65294. Credit- Access, Visa, Diners, Amex.	4	4	6	*14.85 **22.00*	*29.70 **39.60*	*23.10 **30.80*	*145.55 **194.05*	6	22	4	22 *3*	–	P30 –	19 00 *22 30*	1-12	
A† Grayrigge Hotel, Kents Bank Rd., LA11 7HD. Tel. (044 84) 2345.	3	3	3	*7.50 **8.50*	*15.00 **17.00*	*13.00 **14.00*	*70.00 **75.25*	10	15	14	3 *9*	–	P40 G6	18 00 *19 30*	1-12	FB
A Graythwaite Manor Hotel, Fernhill Rd., LA11 7JE. Tel. (044 84) 2001.	4	4	4	– –	– –	16.60 *26.75*	110.50 *180.00*	9	19	–	12 *8*	–	P20 G15	19 00 *19 30*	1-12	
A† Hampsfell Hotel, Hampsfell Rd., LA11 6BG. Tel. (044 84) 2567.	3	3	4	*8.00 **10.00*	*16.00 **20.00*	*10.00 **14.00*	*65.00 **80.00*	1	4	3	2 *3*	–	P8 –	18 30 *16 30*	1-12	5 FB
A Hardcragg Hall, Grange Fell Rd., LA11 6BJ. Tel. (044 84) 3353.	4	4	5	*10.20 **11.20*	*20.40 **23.85*	– –	– –	2	5	1	3 *2*	–	P20 G2	18 00 *21 30*	1-12	
A† Kents Bank Hotel, (Guestaccom) Kentsford Rd., Kents Bank, LA11 7BB. Tel. (044 84) 2054. Credit- Access, Visa.	4	4	4	*8.25 **9.35*	*16.50 **18.70*	*12.75 **13.75*	*83.00 **92.50*	–	3	–	5 *2*	–	P20 –	19 00 *20 00*	1-12	
A† Methven Hotel, Kents Bank Rd., LA11 7DU. Tel. (044 84) 2031.	3	4	4	*6.90 **7.90*	*13.80 **16.00*	*10.00 **12.00*	*70.00 **84.00*	2	9	3	3 *4*	–	P14 –	19 00 *19 00*	4-10	3 FB
A† Netherwood Hotel, LA11 6ET. Tel. (044 84) 2552.	4	5	4	12.50 *15.50*	25.00 *31.00*	17.50 *20.00*	122.50 *140.00*	5	14	4	17 *4*	–	P60 G4	19 00 *20 30*	1-12	FB
A† Prospect House, Hotel & Restaurant, LA11 7DJ. Tel. (044 84) 2116.	3	3	2	*7.00 –	*14.00 –	*9.75 –	*59.50 –	2	4	2	– *2*	–	P2 G2	18 00 –	3-10	
B† Avondale, Kentsford Rd., Kents Bank, LA11 7BB. Tel. (044 84) 2804.	2	3	2	*5.50 **6.00*	*11.00 **12.00*	*7.50 **8.00*	*52.00 **55.00*	3	4	2	– *2*	–	P3 –	18 00 *16 30*	2-11	
B Berners Close Hotel, (Mt. Charlotte) Kents Bank Rd., LA11 7DL. Tel. (044 84) 2059.	1	2	3	*8.00 –	*14.50 –	– –	– –	22	25	4	– *7*	–	P30 –	18 45 –	1-12	FB
B Clare House, Park Rd., LA11 7HQ. Tel. (044 84) 3026.	4	3	3	– –	– –	*13.80 **17.25*	*80.50 **103.50*	1	10	4	5 *2*	–	P16 –	18 45 –	4-10	
B Craiglands Hotel, Methven Ter., Kents Bank Rd., LA11 7DP. Tel. (044 84) 2348.	3	4	2	*7.00 **7.65*	*13.20 **14.50*	*9.45 **10.40*	*63.90 **70.80*	3	10	5	1 *2*	–	P6 G1	18 30 *18 00*	3-10	
B Holme Lea Guest House, Kentsford Rd., Kents Bank, LA11 7BB. Tel. (044 84) 2545.	1	3	2	*6.00 **6.50*	*12.00 **13.00*	*8.00 **8.50*	*56.00 **59.50*	2	3	2	– *2*	–	P4 G1	18 30 –	2-10	
B† Lymehurst Hotel, Kents Bank Rd., LA11 7EY. Tel. (044 84) 3076.	3	4	3	– **8.10*	– **15.20*	– **10.50*	– **70.00*	2	5	3	1 *1*	–	P10 –	18 30 –	1-12	FB

HOTELS, MOTELS, GUEST HOUSES & OTHER SERVICED ACCOMMODATION

Accommodation Type (See page 3)	Name and Address: Town (County), Establishment, Address, Telephone number, Telex, Credit cards accepted	Map Ref.	Category (Key: see front fold-out): Bedrooms	Services	Meals	Prices: Bed and breakfast: Single room overnight (£ Min. / £ Max.)	Double room overnight (£ Min. / £ Max.)	B & B and evening meal: Per person daily (£ Min. / £ Max.)	Per person weekly (£ Min. / £ Max.)	Rooms: No. of bedrooms: Single	Double	Family	Bathrooms (Private / Public)	Showers	Facilities: Parking–P Garage–G (No. of cars)	Evening meals (24 hr. clock) (From / Order by)	Months open (1–12)	Symbols (Key: see fold-out)
	GRANGE-OVER-SANDS continued																	
B†	Lyndene Guest House, Kentsford Rd., Kents Bank, LA11 7BB. Tel. (044 84) 3189.		1	2	3	*4.75 *5.50	*9.50 *11.00	*6.50 *7.25	*42.50 *46.00	1	1	2	– 2	–	P1 G1	18 00 17 30	1–11	FB
B	Milton House, Fell Rd., LA11 6DH. Tel. (044 84) 3398.		3	2	2	*6.00 *6.50	*12.00 *13.00	*8.00 *8.50	*53.00 *56.00	–	1	2	– 1	–	P3 –	18 30 –	3–10	5
B	Thornfield House, Kents Bank Rd., LA11 7DT. Tel. (044 84) 2512.		3	3	2	– –	*13.00 –	*10.00 –	*70.00 –	–	4	2	– 1	–	P6 –	19 00 14 00	4–10	6
B†	Thornleigh, Esplanade, LA11 7HH. Tel. (044 84) 2733.		3	3	3	9.00 *11.00*	18.00 *22.00*	10.50 *13.25*	73.50 *92.75*	6	13	7	– 7	–	P10 –	18 45 –	1–12	FB
	GRASMERE (Cumbria)	**B2**																
A†	Beck Steps Guest House, Parrock Green, LA22 9SY. Tel. (096 65) 348.		3	3	2	*8.00 *10.00	*16.00 *20.00	*13.00 *15.00	*89.00 *92.00	1	7	1	3 4	–	P8 –	19 00 –	3–11	4
A†	Bridge House Hotel, Stock La., LA22 9SN. Tel. (096 65) 425.		3	3	2	*12.50 *13.50	*25.00 *28.00	*18.50 *20.00	*120.00 *130.00	2	9	1	4 3	–	P20 –	19 00 –	3–11	
A†	Gold Rill Hotel, LA22 9PU. Tel. (096 65) 486.		4	4	4	– –	– –	*25.50 *26.50	*170.00 *177.00	6	15	2	14 2	–	P30 –	19 30 20 30	3–11	5
A†	Grasmere Red Lion Hotel, LA22 9SS. Tel. (096 65) 456. Credit- Access, Visa, Diners, Amex.		5	4	4	19.20 –	33.44 –	– –	– –	7	24	6	28 5	–	P40 –	19 00 21 00	3–11	
A†	Michaels Nook Country House Hotel, LA22 9RP. Tel. (096 65) 496.		6	4	4	– –	– –	*33.00 *48.00	*210.00 *330.00	–	10	–	10 –	–	P10 G2	19 30 20 30	1–12	12
A†	Moss Grove Hotel, Grasmere, Nr. Ambleside, LA22 9SW. Tel. (096 65) 251.		3	3	2	10.00 *10.50*	20.00 *25.00*	16.25 *16.75*	103.25 *106.75*	4	9	2	3 3	–	P10 G1	19 00 19 30	4–10	
A†	Oak Bank Hotel, Broadgate, Grasmere, LA22 9TA. Tel. (096 65) 217. Credit- Access, Visa, Diners, Amex.		3	3	4	*10.50 *14.00	*20.00 *28.00	*16.50 *21.50	*104.00 *127.00	2	11	–	7 2	–	P12 –	19 00 19 30	3–11	5
A†	Prince of Wales Hotel, (Mt. Charlotte) LA22 9PR. Tel. (096 65) 666. Credit- Access, Visa, Diners, Amex.		5	5	4	*22.50 –	*36.50 –	– –	– –	15	58	7	80 –	–	P90 –	19 00 21 00	1–12	
A†	Ravenswood Hotel, LA22 9TA. Tel. (096 65) 277.		3	4	4	*11.50 *13.50	*23.00 *27.00	*18.50 *20.50	*125.00 *139.00	1	10	–	6 3	–	P14 –	19 00 19 30	3–12	
A†	Swan Hotel, (THF) LA22 9RF. Tel. (096 65) 551. Credit- Access, Visa, C.Bl., Diners, Amex.		4	5	4	21.00 *26.00*	32.50 *36.50*	– –	– –	5	36	–	25 5	–	P40 –	19 00 20 45	1–12	
A	Titteringdales, Pye La., LA22 9RQ. Tel. (096 65) 439.		3	3	2	*8.50 *9.50	*17.00 *19.00	*13.50 *14.50	*93.00 *100.00	1	2	2	– 1	–	P8 –	19 00 16 00	3–11	
A†	Wordsworth Hotel, LA22 9SW. Tel. (096 65) 592. Telex 65329. Credit- Access, Visa, Diners, Amex.		6	5	5	*21.00 –	*45.00 –	*33.00 –	– –	2	32	2	36 –	–	P54 G2	19 00 21 30	1–12	FB
B†	Banerigg Guest House, LA22 9PW. Tel. (096 65) 204.		3	3	2	*8.25 –	*16.00 –	*12.25 –	*80.00 –	1	2	2	– 2	–	P9 –	19 00 15 00	3–11	
B†	Dunmail Guest House, Keswick Rd., LA22 9RE. Tel. (096 65) 256.		3	2	2	*7.00 *8.00	*14.00 *16.00	*11.00 *12.00	*75.00 *80.00	1	3	1	– 1	–	P6 –	18 30 –	1–12	2

HOTELS, MOTELS, GUEST HOUSES & OTHER SERVICED ACCOMMODATION

Type	Name and Address (Town (County); Establishment, Address, Telephone number, Telex, Credit cards accepted)	Map Ref.	Bedrooms	Services	Meals	Single room overnight £ Min. £ Max.	Double room overnight £ Min. £ Max.	B & B and evening meal: Per person daily £ Min. £ Max.	B & B and evening meal: Per person weekly £ Min. £ Max.	Single	Double	Family	Bathrooms Private Public	Showers	Parking–P Garage–G (No. of cars)	Evening meals (24 hr. clock) From Order by	Months open (1–12)	Symbols (Key: see fold-out)
	GRASMERE continued																	
B†	Harwood Hotel, Red Lion Sq., LA22 9SP. Tel. (096 65) 248.		3	3	2	*9.00 *10.50	*18.00 *21.00	*13.50 *15.00	*82.50 *87.00	3	7	1	– 3	–	P6 –	19 00 –	3–11	5 SP
B†	Lake View Guest House, Lake View Dr., LA22 9TD. Tel. (096 65) 384.		3	3	2	*9.00 *9.00	*18.00 *18.00	*14.00 *14.00	*93.00 *93.00	2	4	–	– 1	–	P10 –	18 30 –	3–10	
B	Meadow Brow, LA22 9RR. Tel. (096 65) 275.		3	3	2	– –	*18.00 *18.00	*16.00 *16.00	*100.00 *100.00	–	5	–	– 1	–	P10 –	19 00 –	3–11	
B	Rothay Lodge Guest House, LA22 9RH. Tel. (096 65) 341.		3	3	2	*7.59 *7.59	*15.18 *15.18	*11.64 *11.64	*79.69 *79.69	1	3	2	– 2	–	P6 –	19 00 –	1–12	
E	Chestnut Villa, Keswick Rd., LA22 9RE. Tel. (096 65) 218.		2	3	1	*7.00 *7.50	*14.00 *15.00	– –	– –	2	2	2	– 1	–	P10 –	– –	1–12	
	GREAT SALKELD (Cumbria) (4m NE. Penrith)	C2																
F†	Mrs. R. Walker, Wetheral House Holiday Farm, Great Salkeld, Penrith CA11 9NA. Tel. Lazonby (076 883) 314. (Mixed 50 acres)		3	3	2	*5.50 –	*11.00 –	*7.50 –	*50.00 –	–	2	4	1 3	–	P18 –	18 30 –	3–12	OAP SP
	GRETNA (Cumbria)	B1																
A†	The Gretna Chase Hotel, Gretna, Carlisle, CA6 5JB. Tel. (046 13) 517.		3	4	5	*14.00 *16.00	*24.00 *28.00	*16.00 *23.00	*99.00 *158.00	2	7	1	3 2	1	P50 –	19 00 21 30	1–12	SP
	HAVERIGG (Cumbria)	B3																
A†	Foxcroft Hotel, Haverigg, Millom, LA18 4NF. Tel. Millom (0657) 2417.		1	3	2	*6.50 *8.00	*13.00 *14.00	*9.00 *10.00	*63.00 *70.00	1	2	1	– 2	–	P12 –	18 00 20 00	1–12	FB
	HAWESWATER (Cumbria)	C2																
A†	Haweswater Hotel, Bampton, Nr. Penrith, CA10 2RP. Tel. Bampton (093 13) 235. Credit- Access, Visa, Diners.		3	4	4	*12.50 –	*25.00 –	*16.75 –	*105.00 –	4	12	–	– 4	3	P20 G10	19 00 20 00	1–12	SP
	HAWKSHEAD (Cumbria)	B3																
A	Field Head House, Outgate, Nr. Hawkshead, LA22 0PY. Tel. (096 66) 240. Credit- Visa, Diners, Amex.		4	5	2	*12.00 *15.00	*24.00 *30.00	*21.00 *24.00	*132.00 *151.00	2	7	–	4 2	–	P12 G3	19 30 21 00	1–12	SP T
A†	Ormandy Hotel, Grizedale, Hawkshead, Nr. Ambleside, LA22 0QH. Tel. (096 66) 532.		4	3	4	16.87 –	23.75 –	– –	– –	–	4	1	5 –	–	P25 –	19 00 20 30	2–12	
A†	Tarn Hows Hotel, Hawkshead, Nr. Ambleside, LA22 0PR. Tel. (096 66) 330. Credit- Access, Visa, Amex.		5	4	4	*11.50 *19.00	*23.00 *38.00	*22.50 *28.00	*150.00 *196.00	7	21	2	21 3	–	P40 –	19 30 20 30	1 3–12	T
B†	Greenbank, Hawkshead, Ambleside, LA22 0NS. Tel. (096 66) 497.		2	3	2	*7.00 *14.00	– –	*10.00 –	*65.00 –	1	5	2	– 2	–	P8 –	18 45 –	1–12	3 OAP SP
B†	Highfield House Hotel, Hawkshead Hill, Ambleside, LA22 0PN. Tel. (096 66) 344.		3	3	2	11.00 12.75	22.00 25.50	15.75 17.50	105.00 115.00	2	6	4	2 3	–	P12 –	19 00 19 00	1–11	2 SP
B†	Ivy House Hotel, Main St., LA22 0NS. Tel. (096 66) 204.		3	3	2	*8.50 *10.00	*17.00 *20.00	*12.50 *14.00	*72.00 *88.00	1	7	3	1 4	–	P12 –	19 00 17 00	3–11	

You are advised to read the introductory notes and to check prices and other details when booking accommodation

HOTELS, MOTELS, GUEST HOUSES & OTHER SERVICED ACCOMMODATION

Type	Name and Address (Town (County); Establishment, Address, Telephone number, Telex, Credit cards accepted)	Map Ref.	Category: Bedrooms	Services	Meals	Bed and breakfast: Single room overnight £ Min. / £ Max.	Double room overnight £ Min. / £ Max.	B & B and evening meal: Per person daily £ Min. / £ Max.	Per person weekly £ Min. / £ Max.	No. of bedrooms: Single	Double	Family	Bathrooms Private / Public	Showers	Parking–P Garage–G (No. of cars)	Evening meals (24 hr. clock) From / Order by	Months open (1–12)	Symbols (Key: see fold-out)
	HAWKSHEAD continued																	
Bt	Rough Close Country House, Hawkshead, Ambleside, LA22 0QF. Tel. (096 66) 370.		3	3	2	*9.00 *9.00*	*18.00 *18.00*	*15.00 *15.00*	*95.00 *95.00*	–	5	1	– 1	–	P12 –	– –	4–10	5 TV
Dt	Kings Arms Hotel, Hawkshead, Nr. Ambleside, LA22 0NZ. Tel. (096 66) 372 & 363.		3	3	5	– *9.50*	– *19.00*	– –	– –	–	4	2	– 1	–	– –	18 00 22 00	1–12	TV SP
F	Mrs. F. E. Batty, Low Loanthwaite, Outgate, Hawkshead, LA22 0NL. Tel. (096 66) 535. (Small holding 3 acres)		1	1	2	*6.00 –	*12.00 –	*8.50 –	– –	1	1	1	– 1	–	P3 –	18 00 –	1–12	
F	Mrs. R. Geldard, High Wray Farm, Wray, Hawkshead, Nr. Ambleside, LA22 0JE. Tel. Ambleside (096 63) 2280. (Mixed 220 acres)		1	1	1	– *6.00*	– *13.00*	– –	– –	1	1	1	– 1	–	P6 –	– –	1–12	TV OAP SP
	HESKET NEWMARKET (Cumbria) (8m SE. Wigton)	B2																
F	Mrs. D. Studholme, Newlands Grange, Hesket Newmarket, Caldbeck, Wigton, CA7 8HP. Tel. Caldbeck (069 98) 676. (Mixed 70 acres)		1	2	2	*4.50 –	*9.00 –	*7.50 –	– –	1	1	1	– 1	–	P4 –	18 30 –	4–10	TV
	HEVERSHAM (Cumbria) (6m SW. Kendal)	C3																
At	The Bluebell At Heversham, Princes Way, Milnthorpe, LA7 7EE. Tel. Milnthorpe (044 82) 3159. Credit- Access, Visa.		4	4	4	14.00 *18.00*	22.00 *26.00*	18.50 *27.00*	– –	11	17	–	12 4	–	P100 –	19 00 21 15	1–12	V TV FB SP T
E	Leasgill Cottage, Heversham, Milnthorpe, LA7 7EX. Tel. Milnthorpe (044 82) 3542.		1	2	1	*5.50 *6.50*	*11.00 *13.00*	– –	– –	1	3	–	– 1	–	P4 –	– –	4–10	3 TV
	HIGH HESKET (Cumbria) (8m SE. Carlisle)	C2																
Bt	Tauranga Guest House, High Hesket, Carlisle, CA4 0HS. Tel. Southwaite (069 93) 334.		2	2	3	*6.00 –	*12.00 –	*10.00 –	– –	–	2	2	– 1	–	P20 –	18 00 –	1–12	TV
	HOLMROOK (Cumbria)	B3																
B	Carleton Green, CA19 1YX. Tel. (094 04) 608.		3	3	2	– *9.00*	– *18.00*	– *14.50*	– *86.00*	1	5	–	1 2	–	P6 –	19 00 –	4–10	8 V TV
Bt	Lutwidge Arms Hotel, CA19 1UH. Tel. (094 04) 230.		3	3	2	*9.50 –	*16.00 –	*13.50 –	*80.86 –	4	4	3	– 2	–	P20 G11	19 00 19 00	4–10	2 TV
D	Bridge Inn, Santon Bridge, Holmrook, Seascale. CA19 1UX. Tel. Wasdale (094 06) 221.		3	3	3	*8.50 *10.00*	*17.00 *19.00*	*13.75 *15.25*	*86.75 *94.75*	1	14	3	5 4	–	P75 –	19 00 22 00	1–12	TV FB OAP SP
F	Mrs. J. Leak, Hill Farm, CA19 1UG. Tel. (094 04) 217. (Dairy 140 acres)		1	2	2	*5.00 –	*10.00 –	*7.00 –	*49.00 –	1	1	2	– 1	–	P4 –	18 00 –	4–11	TV
	IREBY (Cumbria) (5m NE. Bassenthwaite Lake)	B2																
B	Ladyswood, Ireby, CA5 1EX. Tel. Low Ireby (096 57) 482.		4	4	2	*9.00 *14.00*	*18.00 *24.00*	*13.00 *17.50*	*78.00 *105.00*	–	3	2	5 1	–	P9 –	19 00 –	4–10	V TV OAP SP

HOTELS, MOTELS, GUEST HOUSES & OTHER SERVICED ACCOMMODATION

Name and Address — Accommodation Type (See page 3) — Town (County), Establishment, Address, Telephone number, Telex, Credit cards accepted	Map Ref.	Category (Key: see front fold-out) Bedrooms	Services	Meals	Prices: Bed and breakfast — Single room overnight (£ Min. / £ Max.)	Double room overnight (£ Min. / £ Max.)	B & B and evening meal — Per person daily (£ Min. / £ Max.)	Per person weekly (£ Min. / £ Max.)	Rooms: No. of bedrooms — Single	Double	Family	Bathrooms (Private / Public)	Showers	Facilities: Parking–P Garage–G (No. of cars)	Evening meals (24 hr. clock) (From / Order by)	Months open (1–12)	Symbols (Key: see fold-out)
KENDAL (Cumbria)	C3																
A† Castlesteads Restaurant, Oxenholme, Nr. Kendal, LA9 7PR. Tel. (0539) 27000. Credit- Access, Diners, Amex.		3	3	5	*8.00 / *8.00*	*16.00 / *16.00*	*15.00 / *15.00*	*100.00 / *100.00*	–	3	–	– / *1*	–	P12 / G1	19 00 / *21 30*	1–12	TV FB OAP SP
A† County Hotel, (Thistle) Station Rd., LA9 6BT. Tel. (0539) 22461. Credit- Access, Visa, C.Bl., Diners, Amex.		5	5	5	*23.00 / –	*34.00 / –	– / –	– / –	3	26	2	24 / *2*	–	P40 / –	19 00 / *21 30*	1–12	V TV SP T
A† Heaves Hotel, Nr. Kendal, LA8 8EF. Tel. Sedgwick (0448) 60269 & 60396. Credit- Access, Visa, Amex.		3	4	4	*12.50 / *14.00*	*25.00 / *28.00*	*18.00 / *19.50*	– / –	4	9	3	5 / *3*	–	P24 / –	19 00 / *19 30*	1–12	TV FB OAP SP T
A High Laverock House Hotel, Mealbank, Kendal, LA8 9DJ. Tel. (0539) 23082. Credit- Diners.		4	3	4	*14.00 / –	*21.00 / –	– / –	– / –	–	6	2	8	–	P60 / –	19 00 / *21 00*	1–12	TV OAP SP
A† Romney Private Hotel, 72 Milnthorpe Rd., LA9 5HG. Tel. (0539) 20956 & 22495. Credit- Visa.		3	3	2	*8.15 / –	*15.10 / –	– / –	– / –	–	4	3	– / *2*	–	P50 / –	19 00 / –	1–12	TV
A† Shenstone Country Hotel, LA8 8AA. Tel. (0539) 21023.		3	3	4	13.00 / *13.00*	25.00 / *26.00*	17.50 / *18.00*	121.00 / *124.50*	3	8	2	2 / *3*	–	P20 / –	19 00 / *20 00*	1–12	TV
A† Woolpack Hotel, (Swallow) Stricklandgate, LA9 4ND. Tel. (0539) 23852. Telex 53168. Credit- Access, Visa, Diners, Amex.		6	5	4	16.35 / *21.00*	24.80 / *29.00*	– / –	– / –	12	41	5	58 / *2*	–	P150 / –	19 00 / *21 00*	1–12	V TV FB SP T
B† Beck House, Bridge End, Old Hutton, Kendal, LA8 0NH. Tel. (0539) 20754.		3	3	2	*6.00 / *6.00*	*12.00 / *12.00*	*10.00 / *10.00*	*65.00 / *65.00*	–	2	1	– / *2*	–	P4 / –	19 00 / *20 00*	1–12	TV
B Brandside Guest House, 42 Milnthorpe Rd., LA9 5AU. Tel. (0539) 22158.		3	2	2	*6.00 / *6.50*	*10.00 / *11.00*	*8.00 / *8.50*	*45.00 / *55.00*	1	4	2	– / *2*	–	P7 / –	18 00 / *19 00*	1–12	V TV OAP
B Brantholme, 7 Sedbergh Rd., LA9 6AD. Tel. (0539) 22340.		4	3	3	*11.00 / *12.00*	*13.00 / *16.00*	*11.00 / *13.00*	*77.00 / *84.00*	–	2	1	3 / –	–	P6 / –	18 30 / *17 30*	2–11	TV FB OAP SP
B† Ewebank High Barn, Old Hutton, Kendal, LA8 0NS. Tel. (0539) 25449.		1	2	2	– / –	– / –	*9.00 / *11.00*	*63.00 / *77.00*	–	1	1	– / *1*	–	P2 / –	18 00 / *10 00*	1–12	V TV OAP SP T
B The Glen, Oxenholme, Nr. Kendal, LA9 7RF. Tel. (0539) 26386.		1	1	2	– / –	*12.00 / –	*10.00 / –	*70.00 / –	–	1	1	2 / –	–	P8 / –	18 00 / –	5–9	6 TV
B† Headlands Private Hotel, 53 Milnthorpe Rd., LA9 5QG. Tel. (0539) 20424.		3	3	2	*7.50 / *7.50*	*15.00 / *15.00*	*11.45 / *11.45*	*75.00 / *75.00*	1	2	4	– / *1*	–	P10 / –	18 30 / *17 30*	1–12	V TV
B Highgate Hotel, 128 Highgate, LA9 4HE. Tel. (0539) 24229.		2	3	2	*8.63 / *9.20*	*17.25 / *18.40*	*13.23 / *13.80*	– / –	4	7	1	– / *2*	–	P16 / –	18 30 / *20 00*	1–12	TV
B Hillside Guest House, 4 Beast Banks, LA9 4JW. Tel. (0539) 22836.		3	2	2	*6.25 / *6.50*	*12.50 / –	*8.50 / –	*59.50 / –	–	5	1	– / *2*	–	– / –	18 00 / *13 00*	1–12	TV
B Lyndhurst, 8 South Rd., LA9 5QH. Tel. (0539) 21860.		3	3	2	*7.00 / *10.00*	*11.00 / *12.00*	*9.50 / *10.50*	*63.00 / *70.00*	–	3	2	– / *2*	–	P4 / –	18 00 / –	1–12	TV
B† Rocklands Country House Hotel, Plumgarths, Crook Rd., LA8 8LX. Tel. (0539) 20605.		3	3	4	*9.00 / *11.00*	*16.00 / *18.00*	*14.00 / *15.00*	– / –	1	6	2	– / *3*	–	P16 / –	18 30 / *19 00*	4–10	V TV FB SP
B Rose Cottage Guest House, 46 Milnthorpe Rd., LA9 5AU. Tel. (0539) 24219.		3	1	2	*5.95 / *5.95*	*11.00 / *11.00*	*7.95 / *7.95*	*52.50 / *52.50*	1	3	4	– / *1*	–	P8 / –	18 00 / *19 00*	1–12	V TV

 You are advised to read the introductory notes and to check prices and other details when booking accommodation

HOTELS, MOTELS, GUEST HOUSES & OTHER SERVICED ACCOMMODATION

Type	Name and Address — Accommodation Type (See page 3); Town (County); Establishment; Address; Telephone number, Telex; Credit cards accepted	Map Ref.	Category (Key: see front fold-out) — Bedrooms	Services	Meals	Prices — Bed and breakfast: Single room overnight (£ Min. / £ Max.)	Double room overnight (£ Min. / £ Max.)	B & B and evening meal: Per person daily (£ Min. / £ Max.)	Per person weekly (£ Min. / £ Max.)	Rooms — No. of bedrooms: Single	Double	Family	Bathrooms (Private / Public)	Showers (Private / Public)	Facilities — Parking–P Garage–G (No. of cars)	Evening meals (24 hr. clock) (From / Order by)	Months open (1–12)	Symbols (Key: see fold-out)
	KENDAL continued																	
E	Mrs. F. M. Grimshaw, Meadow Bank, Shap Rd., LA9 6NY. Tel. (0539) 21926.		3	2	1	*6.00 / *6.50	*12.00 / *13.00	– / –	– / –	1	3	2	– / 2	–	P6 / –	– / –	1–12	
E	Woodside Guest House, 119 Windermere Rd., LA9 5EP. Tel. (0539) 20355.		1	1	1	*5.00 / *6.00	*10.00 / *12.00	– / –	– / –	1	2	–	– / 1	–	P4 / –	– / –	3–10	
F	Mrs. S. Beaty, Garnett House Farm, Burneside, Kendal, LA9 5SF. Tel. (0539) 24542. (Mixed 270 acres)		2	3	2	–	*12.00 / –	*8.00 / –	– / –	–	2	2	– / 1	–	P6 / –	19 00 / 16 00	1–12	
F	Mrs. A. E. Bell, Hill Fold Farm, Burneside, Kendal, LA8 9AU. Tel. (0539) 22574. (Mixed 210 acres)		3	2	2	–	*10.00 / –	*8.00 / –	*52.00 / –	–	1	2	– / 1	–	P6 / –	19 00 / 16 00	1–12	
F	Mrs. E. Gardner, Natland Mill Beck Farm, Kendal, LA9 7LH. Tel. (0539) 21122. (Mixed 100 acres)		1	2	1	*6.50 / –	*11.00 / –	– / –	– / –	–	2	1	– / 1	–	P4 / –	– / –	3–10	
F	Mrs. A. M. Harper, Hutton Park, New Hutton, Kendal, LA8 0AY. Tel. (0539) 20565. (Mixed 375 acres)		1	1	2	*5.50 / –	*10.00 / –	*7.00 / –	*49.00 / –	1	3	–	– / 1	–	P6 / –	18 30 / –	3–11	8
F	Mrs. M. Hoggarth, Low Hundhowe Farm, Bowston, Burneside, Kendal, LA8 9AB. Tel. (0539) 22060. (Mixed 225 acres)		2	3	3	– / –	*12.00 / –	*8.50 / –	*58.00 / –	–	3	1	– / 2	–	P4 / –	18 30 / –	4–10	
F	Mrs. D. M. Knowles, The Hollins, New Hutton, Kendal, LA8 0AG. Tel. (0539) 24341. (Mixed 14 acres)		1	2	2	*5.00 / –	*10.00 / –	*7.00 / –	– / –	–	1	1	– / 1	–	P3 / –	18 30 / –	3–11	
F	Mrs. Olive M. Knowles, Cragg Farm, New Hutton, Nr. Kendal, LA8 0BA. Tel. (0539) 21760. (Mixed 175 acres)		1	1	2	*5.00 / *6.00	*10.00 / *12.00	*8.00 / *9.00	– / –	–	1	1	– / 1	–	P3 / –	18 30 / 19 00	4–10	
F	Mrs. I. D. Scales, Greenbank Farm, Crook, Nr. Kendal, LA8 9HR. Tel. Staveley (0539) 821216. (Mushroom 15 acres)		3	3	2	*6.50 / *6.50	*13.00 / *13.00	*11.00 / *11.00	*77.00 / *77.00	–	3	2	– / 1	–	P6 / –	19 00 / 19 00	3–11	10
F	Mrs. T. A. White, Bridge House, Garnett Bridge, LA8 9AZ. Tel. Selside (053 983) 288 & Kendal (0539) 24460. (Small Holding 3 acres)		1	1	2	–	*14.00 / –	*11.00 / –	– / –	–	2	1	– / 2	–	P6 / G2	19 00 / 19 45	1–12	
	KENTMERE (Cumbria) (9m NW. Kendal)	C2																
F	Mrs. J. E. Salkeld, High Fold, Kentmere, Staveley, Kendal, LA8 9JP. Tel. Staveley (0539) 821531. (Mixed 500 acres)		1	1	2	–	*10.00 / –	*6.50 / –	*45.50 / –	–	–	2	– / 1	–	P2 / –	18 00 / 18 00	3–10	
	KESWICK (Cumbria)	B2																
A†	The Bay Tree, 1 Wordsworth St., CA12 4HU. Tel. (0596) 73313.		3	3	4	– / *7.95	– / *15.90	*9.50 / *10.95	*65.00 / *73.50	–	4	3	– / 1	–	– / –	19 00 / 19 00	1–12	
A†	Chaucer House Hotel, Ambleside Rd., CA12 4DR. Tel. (0596) 72318. Credit- Access.		3	3	4	*9.50 / *11.00	*18.50 / *21.00	*13.50 / *17.00	*85.00 / *95.00	10	19	6	– / 9	9	P25 / –	18 30 / 19 30	3–10	
A†	County Hotel, Penrith Rd., CA12 4HF. Tel. (0596) 72341.		3	4	4	*8.20 / *10.25	*16.40 / *20.50	*12.60 / *15.75	*83.00 / *105.00	7	15	4	– / 5	–	P20 / –	19 00 / 20 00	1–12	

HOTELS, MOTELS, GUEST HOUSES & OTHER SERVICED ACCOMMODATION

Name and Address Accommodation Type (See page 3) Town (County) — Map Ref. Establishment Address Telephone number, Telex Credit cards accepted	Category Key: see front fold-out Bedrooms	Services	Meals	Prices Bed and breakfast Single room overnight	Double room overnight	B & B and evening meal Per person daily	Per person weekly	Rooms No. of bedrooms Single	Double	Family	Bathrooms	Showers	Facilities Parking–P Garage–G	Evening meals (24 hr. clock)	Months open (1–12)	Symbols
				£ Min. *£ Max.*	£ Min. *£ Max.*	£ Min. *£ Max.*	£ Min. *£ Max.*				Private *Public*		No.of cars	From *Order by*		Key: see fold-out
KESWICK continued																
A† Crow Park Hotel, The Heads, CA12 5ER. Tel. (0596) 72208. Credit- Access, Visa.	4	3	2	*8.50 **8.50*	*17.00 **17.00*	*11.50 **13.50*	*80.00 **85.00*	5	17	4	20 *4*	–	P15 –	18 45 *19 00*	3–11	SP
A† Derwentwater Hotel, (Inter) Portinscale, Keswick, CA12 5RE. Tel. (0596) 72538. Telex 64418. Credit- Access, Visa, Diners, Amex.	4	5	4	*16.50 **19.50*	*27.00 **31.00*	*18.50 **20.50*	– –	6	29	7	33 *5*	–	P60 –	19 00 *20 30*	1–12	SP T
A† George Hotel, (Mt. Charlotte) St. John St., CA12 5AZ. Tel. (0596) 72076. Credit- Access, Visa, Amex.	3	3	2	*14.00 –	*25.50 –	– –	– –	5	10	2	– *5*	–	P5 –	19 00 *20 15*	1–12	V FB GAP SP T
A† Grange Hotel, Manor Brow. CA12 4BA. Tel. (0596) 72500.	3	3	4	*9.80 **9.80*	*19.60 **21.90*	*15.80 **16.95*	*103.10 **118.65*	2	3	2	1 *2*	4	P40 –	19 00 *21 00*	1–12	V FB GAP SP T
A† Keswick Hotel, (THF) Station Rd., CA12 4NQ. Tel. (0596) 72020. Telex 64200. Credit- Access, Visa, C.Bl., Diners, Amex.	5	5	5	– *23.15*	– *36.30*	– –	– –	14	50	–	64 –	–	P50 G50	19 00 *21 30*	1–12	SP T
A† King's Arms Hotel, Main St., CA12 5BL. Tel. (0596) 72083. Credit- Access, Visa, Diners, Amex.	3	3	4	*12.00 **13.50*	*22.00 **27.00*	– –	– –	6	14	–	1 *4*	–	P4 –	19 00 *20 30*	3–12	SP
A Lairbeck Hotel, Vicarage Hill, CA12 5QB. Tel. (0596) 73373.	4	4	4	*10.20 **11.50*	*20.40 **22.50*	*16.70 **18.30*	*116.00 **128.00*	2	5	6	5 *3*	–	P25 –	18 30 *19 30*	1–12	
A† The Lake Hotel, Lake Rd., CA12 5BZ. Tel. (0596) 72069.	3	3	4	10.50 *11.50*	21.00 *23.00*	16.00 *18.00*	105.00 *119.00*	2	17	1	4 *6*	–	P18 G12	15 00 *16 00*	4–10	V SP
A† Lodore Swiss Hotel, CA12 5UX. Tel. Borrowdale (059 684) 285. Telex 64305.	6	6	4	*25.00 –	*50.00 –	*33.00 –	– –	12	60	–	72 *1*	–	P80 G24	19 00 *21 00*	3–11	V FB
A† Lyzzick Hall Hotel, Nr. Keswick, CA12 4PY. Tel. (0596) 72277.	3	4	3	*10.90 **12.00*	*21.80 **24.00*	*13.85 **15.25*	*88.00 **95.00*	2	6	10	1 *4*	6	P25 –	19 00 –	3–11	GAP SP
A† Mary Mount Hotel, CA12 5UU. Tel. Borrowdale (059 684) 223. Telex 64305.	5	4	4	*23.00 –	*36.00 –	*25.00 –	– –	1	14	–	15 –	–	P40 –	19 00 *20 30*	1–12	SP
A† Millfield Hotel, Penrith Rd., CA12 4HB. Tel. (0596) 72099.	3	4	4	*14.80 **14.80*	*28.40 **32.00*	*19.30 **19.30*	*116.00 **116.00*	6	13	6	6 *5*	–	P20 –	19 00 *20 30*	3–11	V
A Priorholm Hotel, Borrowdale Rd., CA12 5DD. Tel. (0596) 72745.	3	4	3	*9.00 –	*18.00 –	*12.25 –	*81.00 –	1	5	2	– *2*	–	P7 –	19 30 –	1–12	FB GAP SP
A† Queens Hotel, Main St., CA12 5JF. Tel. (0596) 73333. Credit- Access, Visa, Diners, Amex.	4	4	4	*10.00 **12.20*	*20.50 **24.80*	– –	*99.75 **114.75*	10	16	6	12 *6*	–	G25 –	19 00 *20 00*	3–11	V FB SP T
A† Red House Hotel, CA12 4QA. Tel. (0596) 72211. Credit- Amex.	3	4	4	*11.00 **14.30*	*23.00 **32.00*	*17.00 **21.00*	*98.00 **120.00*	3	16	4	12 *3*	–	P25 G5	19 00 *20 00*	3–11	V FB
A† Royal Oak Hotel, (THF) Station St., CA12 5HH. Tel. (0596) 72965. Credit- Access, Visa, C.Bl., Diners, Amex.	4	4	5	15.65 *22.65*	25.30 *32.30*	– –	– –	19	39	8	30 *19*	–	P42 –	19 00 *21 30*	1–12	V SP T
A† Skiddaw Grove Hotel, Vicarage Hill, CA12 5QB. Tel. (0596) 73324.	4	4	4	*10.00 **11.00*	*20.00 **22.00*	*15.00 **16.00*	*100.00 **107.00*	2	9	1	5 *2*	1	P12 –	18 30 *19 30*	3–11	7 V FB SP

 You are advised to read the introductory notes and to check prices and other details when booking accommodation

HOTELS, MOTELS, GUEST HOUSES & OTHER SERVICED ACCOMMODATION

Name and Address Accommodation Type (See page 3) **Town (County)** Establishment Address Telephone number, Telex Credit cards accepted	Map Ref.	Category (Key: see front fold-out) Bedrooms	Services	Meals	Prices: Bed and breakfast Single room overnight £ Min. *£ Max.*	Double room overnight £ Min. *£ Max.*	B & B and evening meal Per person daily £ Min. *£ Max.*	Per person weekly £ Min. *£ Max.*	Rooms: No. of bedrooms Single	Double	Family	Bathrooms Private *Public*	Showers	Facilities Parking–P Garage–G No.of cars	Evening meals (24 hr. clock) From *Order by*	Months open (1–12)	Symbols Key: see fold-out
KESWICK continued																	
A† Skiddaw Hotel, 29–31 Main St., CA12 5BN. Tel. (0596) 72071. Credit- Access, Visa, Diners, Amex.		4	4	4	14.00 –	25.00 –	20.50 –	– –	19	28	5	23 *6*	–	P16 –	19 00 *21 00*	1–12	SP
A† Tower Hotel, Portinscale, Keswick, CA12 5RD. Tel. (0596) 73099.		3	3	4	*10.00 **11.00*	*20.00 **22.00*	*14.50 **15.50*	*96.00 **103.00*	4	17	6	7 *3*	–	P50 –	19 00 *19 30*	1–12	FB OAP SP T
A Underscar, CA12 4PH. Tel. (0596) 72469. Credit- Access, Visa.		3	4	3	*11.00 –	*20.50 –	– –	– –	5	20	6	5 *8*	–	P18 –	19 00 *19 30*	4–10	OAP SP T
A† Walpole Hotel, Station Rd., CA12 4NA. Tel. (0596) 72072.		4	4	4	*10.25 **11.80*	*20.25 **23.30*	*15.75 **18.10*	*105.00 **120.00*	3	8	6	10 *2*	–	P9 –	19 00 *20 30*	1–12	
B† Acorn House Private Hotel, Ambleside Rd., CA12 4DL. Tel. (0596) 72553.		3	3	2	– –	*15.00 **16.00*	*11.70 **12.70*	*78.00 **85.00*	–	6	3	– *3*	–	P8 –	18 30 *14 30*	4–10	
B† Allerdale House, 1 Eskin St., CA12 4DH. Tel. (0596) 73891.		3	3	2	*6.00 **6.50*	*12.00 **13.00*	*8.75 **9.25*	*61.25 **64.75*	1	3	2	– *3*	3	P3 –	18 00 *18 30*	1–11	
B An Darach, 49 Wordsworth St., CA12 4BZ. Tel. (0596) 73912.		1	3	2	– **6.00*	– **12.00*	– **8.50*	– **59.00*	1	1	–	– *1*	–	P2 –	17 30 –	1–11	10 M FB OAP SP T
B Avondale Guest House, 20 Southey St., CA12 4EF. Tel. (0596) 72735.		3	3	2	*6.00 **6.50*	*12.00 **13.00*	*9.00 **9.50*	*60.00 **63.00*	–	3	2	– *1*	–	– –	18 00 *17 00*	1–12	FB OAP
B† Beckside, 5 Wordsworth St., CA12 4HU. Tel. (0596) 73093.		2	2	2	– –	*11.20 **11.20*	*8.50 **8.50*	*59.50 **59.50*	–	3	–	– *1*	–	– –	18 30 –	1–12	M
B Beckstones, 51 Eskin St., CA12 4DG. Tel. (0596) 72709. Credit- Amex.		2	1	2	*5.50 **6.00*	*11.00 **12.00*	*8.00 **8.50*	*56.00 **59.50*	3	3	–	– *1*	–	– –	17 30 –	4–10	10
B† Braemar Guest House, 21 Eskin St., CA12 4DQ. Tel. (0596) 73743.		3	2	2	*6.00 –	*12.00 –	*8.00 –	– –	2	2	1	– *1*	–	– –	18 30 *18 30*	4–10	SP
B† Burleigh Mead & Hazeldene Hotels, The Heads, CA12 5ER. Tel. (0596) 72750 & 72106.		3	3	3	*7.50 **9.50*	*15.00 **19.00*	*11.50 **14.00*	*77.00 **95.00*	3	11	15	– *6*	–	P16 –	18 30 *16 00*	3–11	OAP SP
B The Cartwheel, 5 Blencathra St., CA12 4HW. Tel. (0596) 73182.		3	3	2	*6.00 **6.50*	*12.00 **13.00*	*9.50 **10.00*	*42.00 **45.50*	1	3	2	– *1*	–	– –	18 30 *18 30*	1–12	5 SP
B Cathay Guest House, 30 Stanger St., CA12 5JU. Tel. (0596) 72621.		2	3	2	*6.00 –	*11.00 –	*8.50 –	*56.00 –	1	1	4	– *1*	–	– –	18 30 –	1–12	OAP SP
B† Clarence House, 14 Eskin St., CA12 4DQ. Tel. (0596) 73186.		2	2	2	*6.70 **6.70*	*13.40 **13.40*	*10.60 **10.90*	*71.00 **73.00*	3	3	2	– *2*	–	– –	18 30 *18 00*	1–12	M FB SP
B Mrs. J. E. Cox, 15 Helvellyn St., CA12 4EN. Tel. (0596) 73848.		1	2	2	*6.00 **6.00*	*12.00 **12.00*	*9.00 **9.00*	*60.00 **60.00*	1	–	2	– *1*	–	– –	18 30 *18 30*	1–12	
B† Cragside Licensed Guest House, 39 Blencathra St., CA12 4HX. Tel. (0596) 73344.		3	3	2	*6.25 **6.85*	*12.50 **13.70*	*9.50 **10.35*	*65.00 **70.00*	–	5	–	– *1*	–	– –	18 30 *16 00*	4–10	3
B Cranlea Guest House, 13 Stanger St., CA12 5JU. Tel. (0596) 73611.		3	1	2	*5.50 **6.00*	*11.00 **12.00*	*7.25 **8.00*	– –	1	3	1	– *1*	–	– –	19 00 –	1–12	

HOTELS, MOTELS, GUEST HOUSES & OTHER SERVICED ACCOMMODATION

Name and Address Accommodation Type (See page 3) **Town (County)** Establishment Address Telephone number, Telex Credit cards accepted	Map Ref.	Category (Key: see front fold-out) Bedrooms	Services	Meals	Prices: Bed and breakfast Single room overnight £ Min. *£ Max.*	Double room overnight £ Min. *£ Max.*	B & B and evening meal Per person daily £ Min. *£ Max.*	Per person weekly £ Min. *£ Max.*	Rooms: No. of bedrooms Single	Double	Family	Bathrooms Private *Public*	Showers	Facilities: Parking–P Garage–G No. of cars	Evening meals (24 hr. clock) From *Order by*	Months open (1–12)	Symbols Key: see fold-out
KESWICK continued																	
Bt Cumbria Hotel, 1 Derwentwater Pl., Ambleside Rd., CA12 4DR. Tel. (0596) 73171. Credit- Access, Amex.		3	3	2	*8.50 –	*17.00 –	*12.50 –	*81.55 –	3	2	4	– *2*	–	P8 –	19 00 *19 00*	4–10	
Bt Dalkeith House, 1 Leonard St., CA12 4EJ. Tel. (0596) 72696.		2	3	2	*6.75 **7.65*	*13.50 **15.30*	*9.75 **11.00*	*66.00 **75.00*	1	3	2	– *2*	–	– –	18 30 *17 00*	1–12	OAP SP
B Dorchester Guest House, 17 Southey St., CA12 4EG. Tel. (0596) 73256.		1	2	2	*6.00 **7.00*	*12.00 **14.00*	*8.00 **9.00*	*56.00 **63.00*	1	4	3	– *1*	–	– –	19 00 *18 00*	4–10	
Bt Easedale Hotel, Southey St., CA12 4HL. Tel. (0596) 72710.		2	2	2	*7.75 –	*15.00 –	*12.00 –	– –	2	8	–	– *3*	2	– –	18 30 *18 30*	4–10	OAP
Bt Edwardene Guest House, 24–26 Southey St., CA12 4EF. Tel. (0596) 73586.		3	3	2	*7.00 –	*14.00 –	*11.00 –	*77.00 –	2	3	6	– *2*	–	– –	19 00 *17 00*	1–12	
B Foye House, 23 Eskin St., CA12 4DQ. Tel. (0596) 73288.		3	2	2	*6.25 –	*12.50 –	*10.35 –	*70.00 –	3	3	–	– *1*	–	– –	18 30 –	1–12	5
Bt Gale Hotel, Underskiddaw, Keswick, CA12 4PL. Tel. (0596) 72413.		3	3	2	*7.50 **8.50*	*15.00 **17.00*	*12.50 **13.50*	*84.00 **84.00*	2	5	7	– *5*	–	P12 –	19 00 –	3–11	
B Glendale Guest House, 7 Eskin St., CA12 4DH. Tel. (0596) 73562.		2	1	2	*6.00 –	*12.00 –	*8.80 –	*60.00 –	1	4	2	– *1*	–	– –	18 30 *16 30*	1–12	10
B Greystone Guest House, 22 Skiddaw St., CA12 4BY. Tel. (0596) 72184.		2	2	2	*6.00 –	*12.00 –	*8.00 –	*56.00 –	–	2	1	– *1*	–	– –	18 30 *14 00*	4–10	3 SP
Bt Greystones, Ambleside Rd., CA12 4DP. Tel. (0596) 73108.		3	3	3	*7.00 –	*14.00 –	*10.00 –	*70.00 –	2	4	4	1 *1*	3	P5 G1	18 30 *18 30*	1–12	FB OAP SP T
Bt Hall Garth, 37 Blencathra St., CA12 4HX. Tel. (0596) 72627.		3	3	2	*6.00 –	*12.00 –	*8.50 –	*58.00 –	1	3	1	– *1*	–	– –	19 00 –	1–12	SP
B Harvington House, 19 Church St., CA12 4DX. Tel. (0596) 73511.		3	1	2	*5.25 **5.50*	*10.50 **10.50*	*8.00 **8.00*	*56.00 **56.00*	1	2	3	– *1*	–	– –	18 30 *12 00*	4–10	3
Bt The Heights Hotel, Castlerigg, CA12 4TE. Tel. (0596) 72251.		3	3	2	*9.00 **10.00*	*18.00 **20.00*	*13.00 **14.00*	*90.00 **91.00*	2	8	4	– *4*	–	P30 G3	18 30 *18 30*	4–10	FB OAP SP
Bt Highfield Hotel, The Heads, CA12 5ER. Tel. (0596) 72508.		3	4	2	*10.00 –	*16.50 –	*12.95 –	*90.65 –	1	7	2	1 *2*	–	– –	19 00 –	4–10	5
B Hillcrest Guest House, The Heads, CA12 5ER. Tel. (0596) 72714.		1	1	2	*5.75 **5.75*	*11.50 **11.50*	*9.20 **9.20*	*62.40 **62.40*	1	6	2	– *2*	3	– –	19 00 *18 00*	4–10	3
Bt Howe Keld Guest House, 5–7 The Heads, CA12 5ES. Tel. (0596) 72417.		3	4	2	*6.90 **7.75*	*13.30 **14.50*	*10.00 **11.30*	*70.00 **73.50*	3	10	2	– *4*	–	P11 G2	19 00 *18 00*	1–12	OAP SP T
Bt Laurel Bank Guest House, Laurel Bank, Penrith Rd., CA12 4LJ. Tel. (0596) 73006.		3	2	2	*6.00 **7.00*	*11.00 **12.00*	*9.50 **10.00*	*64.00 **68.00*	2	3	1	– *2*	–	P6 G1	18 30 –	3–10	
B Leonardsfield House, 3 Leonards St., CA12 4EJ. Tel. (0596) 74170.		2	3	2	*5.00 **6.50*	*10.00 **13.00*	*8.00 **10.00*	– –	2	3	3	– *2*	–	– –	18 30 *19 00*	1–11	1 OAP SP
B Littlefield, 32 Eskin St., CA12 4DG. Tel. (0596) 72949.		2	1	2	*6.10 –	*12.20 –	*8.85 –	*61.00 –	1	3	2	– *1*	–	– –	18 30 *17 00*	2–11	5

You are advised to read the introductory notes and to check prices and other details when booking accommodation

HOTELS, MOTELS, GUEST HOUSES & OTHER SERVICED ACCOMMODATION

Accommodation Type (See page 3)	Town (County) / Establishment / Address / Telephone number, Telex / Credit cards accepted	Map Ref.	Category: Bedrooms	Category: Services	Category: Meals	Prices: Bed and breakfast – Single room overnight (£ Min. / £ Max.)	Prices: Bed and breakfast – Double room overnight (£ Min. / £ Max.)	Prices: B & B and evening meal – Per person daily (£ Min. / £ Max.)	Prices: B & B and evening meal – Per person weekly (£ Min. / £ Max.)	Rooms: No. of bedrooms – Single	Rooms: Double	Rooms: Family	Rooms: Bathrooms (Private / Public)	Rooms: Showers	Facilities: Parking–P Garage–G (No. of cars)	Facilities: Evening meals (24 hr. clock) (From / Order by)	Facilities: Months open (1–12)	Facilities: Symbols (Key: see fold-out)
	KESWICK continued																	
B	Lyndhurst Guest House, 22 Southey St., CA12 4EF. Tel. (0596) 72303.		3	3	2	*5.00 *6.00*	*10.00 *12.00*	*9.00 *10.00*	*63.00 *70.00*	1	2	2	– 1	–	– –	18 00 *12 00*	1–12	UL TV
B	Lynwood Guest House, 12 Ambleside Rd., CA12 4DL. Tel. (0596) 72081.		3	3	2	– –	*12.00 –	*9.00 –	– –	–	4	4	– 2	–	– –	18 30 –	1–12	3 TV
B	Ravensworth Private Hotel, Station St., CA12 5HH. Tel. (0596) 72476.		3	3	2	*8.50 *9.00*	*15.00 *16.00*	*11.00 *11.50*	*75.00 *78.00*	1	7	1	– 2	–	P4 –	19 00 *16 00*	1–12	UL TV
B	Richmond House, 37–39 Eskin St., CA12 4DG. Tel. (0596) 73965.		3	3	4	*6.00 *7.00*	*12.00 *14.00*	*10.00 *11.00*	*70.00 *77.00*	3	5	3	2 3	–	– –	19 00 *18 00*	1–10 12	V TV FB OAP SP
B†	Rickerby Grange, (Guestaccom) Portinscale, Keswick, CA12 5RH. Tel. (0596) 72344.		3	4	2	*8.00 –	*16.00 –	*11.50 –	*74.80 –	1	6	1	3 2	2	P10 –	18 30 *18 30*	3–11	V TV OAP SP
B†	Ridgeway Guest House, 25 Stanger St., CA12 5JY. Tel. (0596) 72582.		3	2	2	*6.00 *6.50*	*13.00 *14.00*	*9.00 *9.50*	*63.00 –	–	4	1	– 1	–	P5 –	18 30 –	3–10	UL V TV SP
B†	Shemara Guest House, 27 Bank St., CA12 5JZ. Tel. (0596) 73936.		2	3	2	– –	*11.50 *13.00*	*8.75 *9.50*	– –	–	2	3	– 1	–	P5 –	18 30 –	3–11	M UL V TV
B	Silverdale Hotel, Blencathra St., CA12 4HT. Tel. (0596) 72294.		3	4	2	*8.75 *8.75*	*17.50 *17.50*	*11.50 *11.50*	*73.00 *73.00*	2	8	2	– 3	–	P8 –	18 45 *17 00*	1–12	V TV
B†	Stoneycroft Hotel, Newlands Valley, Keswick, CA12 5TS. Tel. Braithwaite (0596 82) 240.		4	4	2	– –	*16.00 *18.50*	*11.50 *13.25*	*75.00 *87.00*	–	4	2	3 1	–	P20 –	18 30 –	4–10	5 TV FB OAP SP
B†	Sunnyside, 25 Southey St., CA12 4EF. Tel. (0596) 72446.		2	3	2	*7.00 *7.00*	*14.00 *14.00*	*10.25 *10.25*	*68.00 *68.00*	1	4	3	– 3	–	P7 –	18 30 *15 30*	4–10	8 M UL TV
B†	Tarn Hows Guest House, 5 Eskin St., CA12 4DH. Tel. (0596) 73217.		3	2	3	– –	*11.90 –	*8.25 –	*57.75 –	–	4	1	– 1	–	P1 –	18 30 *16 00*	1–12	UL TV SP
B†	West View Guest House, The Heads, CA12 5ES. Tel. Keswick (0596) 73638.		2	3	2	*7.50 –	*15.00 –	*11.75 –	*77.00 –	–	6	2	– 2	–	– –	18 30 –	3–11	TV
B	Woodford House Guest House, The Heads, CA12 5ER. Tel. (0596) 72148.		3	3	2	*6.90 *7.48*	*13.80 *14.96*	*10.35 *11.50*	*72.45 *80.50*	8	6	3	– 3	–	P5 –	19 00 –	3–11	UL V OAP SP
B†	Woodlands Guest House, Brundholme Rd., CA12 4NL. Tel. (0596) 72399.		3	3	2	*7.00 *7.50*	*14.00 *15.00*	*10.50 *11.00*	*65.00 *70.00*	1	4	2	– 1	–	P10 –	18 30 *18 30*	3–10	6 UL TV SP
D	Swinside Inn, Newlands Valley, Keswick, CA12 5UE. Tel. Braithwaite (059 682) 253.		2	3	3	*8.00 *8.50*	*16.00 *17.00*	– –	– –	1	4	3	– 2	–	P100 –	18 00 *20 45*	1–12	M V TV
D	Twa Dogs Inn, Penrith Rd., CA12 4JU. Tel. (0596) 72599.		3	2	1	– –	*16.00 *18.00*	– –	– –	–	3	2	– 1	–	P15 –	– –	1–12	5 TV
E†	Brierholme Guest House, 21 Bank St., CA12 5JZ. Tel. (0596) 72938.		2	3	1	*6.00 *7.00*	*12.00 *14.00*	– –	– –	2	3	2	– 1	–	P5 –	– –	1–12	M UL
E	Monkstone, 62 Blencathra St., CA12 4HX. Tel. (0596) 73250.		3	2	1	– –	*10.50 *11.50*	– –	– –	–	3	–	– 1	–	P3 –	– –	4–10	5 UL TV OAP
E†	Parkfield, The Heads, CA12 5ES. Tel. (0596) 72328.		3	3	1	*7.00 –	*14.00 –	– –	– –	1	5	1	– 1	–	P8 –	– –	3–10	2 TV
E	Mrs. J. Thorburn, 19 Stanger St., CA12 5JU. Tel. (0596) 72495.		3	2	1	*6.00 *6.50*	*11.00 *12.00*	– –	– –	2	2	1	– 1	–	P2 –	– –	4–10	5 UL TV
E	The Vale, 17 Stanger St., CA12 5JU. Tel. (0596) 73618.		3	3	1	– –	*11.00 *13.00*	– –	– –	–	2	2	– 1	–	– –	– –	1–12	2 UL TV OAP SP

Category key: see front fold-out.

HOTELS, MOTELS, GUEST HOUSES & OTHER SERVICED ACCOMMODATION

Type	Name and Address Town (County) Establishment Address Telephone number, Telex Credit cards accepted	Map Ref.	Bedrooms	Services	Meals	Single room overnight £ Min. *£ Max.*	Double room overnight £ Min. *£ Max.*	Per person daily £ Min. *£ Max.*	Per person weekly £ Min. *£ Max.*	Single	Double	Family	Bathrooms Private *Public*	Showers	Parking–P Garage–G No. of cars	Evening meals (24 hr. clock) From *Order by*	Months open (1–12)	Symbols Key: see fold-out
	KESWICK continued																	
F	Mrs. J. Ray, Applethwaite Farm, Applethwaite, Keswick, CA12 4PN. Tel. (0596) 72608. (Mixed 120 acres)		1	1	2	– *–*	•11.00 *•12.00*	•10.00 *•11.00*	•68.00 *•73.00*	–	3	–	– *1*	–	P3 –	 *–*	1–12	
F	Mrs. E. M. Stamper, Millbeck Farm, Millbeck, Keswick, CA12 4PS. Tel. (0596) 72358. (Mixed 80 acres)		2	2	2	•5.50 *•5.50*	•11.00 *•11.00*	•9.50 *–*	•66.50 *•66.50*	–	2	2	– *2*	–	P8 –	19 00 *18 00*	4–10	
F	Mrs. M. E. Thompson, Low Grove Farm, Millbeck, Keswick, CA12 4PS. Tel. (0596) 72103. (Mixed 140 acres)		1	3	2	•5.00 *•6.50*	•10.00 *•12.00*	•8.00 *•9.00*	•55.00 *•63.00*	–	2	1	– *1*	–	P4 –	18 30 *19 30*	4–10	
	KINGS MEABURN (Cumbria) (4m NW. Appleby-in-Westmorland)	C2																
D	White Horse Inn, Kings Meaburn, Penrith, CA10 3BU. Tel. Morland (093 14) 256.		2	3	2	•5.50 *•8.00*	•11.00 *•16.00*	•9.00 *•11.00*	•63.00 *•77.00*	–	2	1	– *1*	2	P3 –	19 00 *–*	4–10	
	KIRKBY LONSDALE (Cumbria)	C3																
A	Red Dragon Hotel, Main St., Kirkby Lonsdale, Via Carnforth, Lancs., LA6 2AH. Tel. (0468) 71205.		3	3	4	•9.00 *•10.00*	•16.00 *•18.00*	•14.00 *•15.00*	•90.00 *•105.00*	2	7	1	– *2*	2	P6 G2	18 30 *19 30*	4–10	
A†	Royal Hotel Market Square, Kirkby Lonsdale, Via Carnforth, Lancs. LA6 2AE. Tel. (0468) 71217 & 71519. Credit- Access, Visa, Diners, Amex.		4	4	5	15.00 *20.00*	25.00 *35.00*	– *–*	– *–*	4	18	2	16 *4*	–	P30 G10	19 00 *22 00*	1–12	
E	Brant Howe, Fairbank, Kirkby Lonsdale, via Carnforth, Lancashire, LA6 2DU. Tel. (0468) 71832.		3	2	1	– *–*	•14.00 *–*	– *–*	– *–*	–	1	2	– *1*	–	P6 G1	– *–*	1–12	
F	Mrs. L. M. Lee, Whaitber Farm, Westhouse, Nr. Kirkby Lonsdale, Carnforth, Lancs., LA6 3PQ. Tel. Ingleton (0468) 41476. (Mixed 47 acres)		1	2	2	•6.50 *•7.00*	•12.00 *•14.00*	•9.50 *•11.00*	•54.00 *•60.00*	1	1	1	– *1*	–	P6 –	18 00 *20 00*	1–12	
	KIRKBY STEPHEN (Cumbria)	C2																
A	Jolly Farmers Guest House, 63 High St., CA17 4QT. Tel. (0930) 71063.		3	3	3	•6.50 *•7.00*	•12.00 *•13.00*	•9.50 *•10.00*	– *–*	2	4	1	– *2*	–	P14 G1	18 30 *19 30*	1–12	12
F	Mrs. D. Harper, Wrenside Farm, Kaber, Kirkby Stephen, CA17 4HZ. Tel. Kirkby Stephen (0930) 71614. (Mixed 100 acres)		1	2	2	•5.50 *•7.00*	•11.00 *•14.00*	•6.50 *•8.00*	•42.00 *•50.00*	–	3	1	– *1*	–	P3 –	18 00 *19 30*	4–10	
	KIRKOSWALD (Cumbria)	C2																
A†	Prospect Hill Hotel, (Guestaccom) Kirkoswald, Penrith, CA10 1ER. Tel. Lazonby (076 883) 500. Credit- Visa, Diners, Amex.		3	3	4	•10.45 *•18.70*	•20.90 *•28.00*	•16.50 *•24.75*	•108.35 *•156.88*	2	7	2	2 *3*	1	P24 –	19 15 *20 30*	1 3–12	
	KIRKSANTON (Cumbria) (6m SE. Bootle)	B3																
B†	Croft Cottage, Kirksanton, Millom, LA18 4NW. Tel. Millom (0657) 2582.		1	2	2	•5.00 *–*	•10.00 *–*	•8.50 *–*	•55.00 *–*	–	5	1	– *2*	–	P5 –	18 00 *–*	1–12	

Accommodation Type (See page 3) — Category Key: see front fold-out

You are advised to read the introductory notes and to check prices and other details when booking accommodation

HOTELS, MOTELS, GUEST HOUSES & OTHER SERVICED ACCOMMODATION

Name and Address Accommodation Type (See page 3) Town (County) Establishment Address Telephone number, Telex Credit cards accepted	Map Ref.	Category (Key: see front fold-out) Bedrooms	Services	Meals	Prices: Bed and breakfast Single room overnight £ Min. *£ Max.*	Double room overnight £ Min. *£ Max.*	B & B and evening meal Per person daily £ Min. *£ Max.*	Per person weekly £ Min. *£ Max.*	Rooms: No. of bedrooms Single	Double	Family	Bathrooms Private *Public*	Showers	Facilities: Parking–P Garage–G No. of cars	Evening meals (24 hr. clock) From *Order by*	Months open (1–12)	Symbols Key: see fold-out
LAKESIDE (Cumbria) (10m NE. Ulverston)	**B3**																
B The Knoll Guest House, Lakeside, Ulverston, LA12 8AU. Tel. Newby Bridge (044 83) 1347 or Barrow (0229) 24628.		3	3	2	*7.00 **8.00*	*14.00 **16.00*	*11.00 **12.00*	*68.00 **72.00*	3	4	3	– *2*	–	P8 –	– *18 30*	4–10	SP
LANERCOST (Cumbria)	**C1**																
A New Bridge Hotel, Lanercost, Brampton, Nr. Carlisle, CA8 2HG. Tel. Brampton (069 77) 2224.		3	3	4	– **13.75*	*25.85 **29.15*	*22.00 –	– –	4	8	1	3 *3*	–	P40 –	19 30 *20 30*	1–12	SP
LANGDALE (Cumbria)	**B2**																
A† Langdales Hotel, Great Langdale, Ambleside, LA22 9JF. Tel. (096 67) 253.		4	4	4	*15.00 –	*30.00 –	*22.00 –	*140.00 –	3	14	3	16 *2*	–	P50 –	19 30 *20 15*	1–12	SP
A† New Dungeon Ghyll Hotel, Gt. Langdale, Nr. Ambleside, LA22 9JX. Tel. (096 67) 213.		4	4	4	*10.94 –	*21.88 –	*16.99 –	*111.93 –	6	10	3	9 *3*	–	P40 –	19 00 *19 00*	4–11	
A Old Dungeon Ghyll Hotel, Gt. Langdale, Ambleside, LA22 9JY. Tel. (096 67) 272.		3	3	3	*10.00 –	*20.00 –	*17.50 –	*110.00 –	7	9	1	– *3*	–	P150 –	19 30 *19 30*	2–12	
A† Pillar Hotel, Great Langdale, Nr. Ambleside, LA22 9JB. Tel. (096 67) 656. Credit- Access.		3	4	3	*10.00 **12.00*	*20.00 **24.00*	*12.20 **20.10*	*85.40 **126.30*	10	13	4	3 *4*	–	P30 –	19 00 *20 00*	2–12	SP
D† Three Shires Inn, Little Langdale, Ambleside, LA22 9NZ. Tel. (096 67) 215.		3	3	4	– **12.00*	– **22.00*	– **21.00*	– –	1	6	–	– *2*	–	P12 G2	19 00 *21 00*	1–12	2 FB SP
F Mrs. S. Harryman, Fell Foot Farm, Little Langdale, Ambleside, LA27 9PE. Tel. (096 67) 294. (Mixed 431 acres)		1	1	2	– –	*12.00 **14.00*	*10.00 **12.00*	– –	–	2	1	– *1*	–	P4 –	– *18 30*	4–10	3 FB
F Mrs. J. Toms, Middlefell Farm, Gt. Langdale, Ambleside, LA22 9JU. Tel. (096 67) 684. (Stock Rearing 260 acres)		2	1	2	– –	*14.00 **17.00*	*11.00 **12.50*	*75.00 **85.00*	–	3	1	– *1*	–	P5 –	18 30 *18 30*	4–10	
LITTLE CLIFTON (Cumbria) (5m SW. Cockermouth)	**B2**																
C† Crossbarrow Motel, Little Clifton, Workington, CA14 1XS. Tel. Workington (0900) 61443. Credit- Access, Visa.		3	3	5	*17.00 –	*22.50 –	–	–	–	26	–	26 –	–	P20 –	19 00 *21 30*	1–12	
LONGTOWN (Cumbria)	**B1**																
B Glenesk Guest House, Arthuret Rd., Longtown, Nr. Carlisle, CA6 5SJ. Tel. (0228) 791275.		2	3	2	*6.00 **6.00*	*12.00 **12.00*	*8.50 **10.00*	– **63.00*	3	3	2	– *2*	–	P8 –	19 00 –	1–12	
LORTON (Cumbria) (4m SE. Cockermouth)	**B2**																
D Horseshoe Inn, High Lorton, Cockermouth, CA13 9UQ. Tel. (090 085) 214.		1	1	4	– –	*16.00 –	– –	– –	–	2	1	– *2*	–	P20 –	19 00 *21 00*	1–12	
F Mrs. P. M. Blair, Hope Farm, Lorton, Cockermouth, CA13 9UD. Tel. (090 085) 226. (Mixed 10 acres)		1	1	1	– –	*10.00 –	– –	– –	–	1	1	– *1*	–	P4 –	– –	4–10	

HOTELS, MOTELS, GUEST HOUSES & OTHER SERVICED ACCOMMODATION

Accommodation Type (See page 3); Town (County); Establishment, Address, Telephone number, Telex, Credit cards accepted. Category — Key: see front fold-out. Prices: £ Min. / £ Max. Bathrooms/Showers: Private / *Public*. Parking: No. of cars (P = Parking, G = Garage). Evening meals (24 hr. clock): From / *Order by*. Symbols — Key: see fold-out.

Type	Name and Address	Map Ref.	Bedrooms	Services	Meals	B&B Single room overnight £ Min. / *£ Max.*	B&B Double room overnight £ Min. / *£ Max.*	B&B and evening meal Per person daily £ Min. / *£ Max.*	B&B and evening meal Per person weekly £ Min. / *£ Max.*	No. of bedrooms: Single	Double	Family	Bathrooms Private / *Public*	Showers Private	Parking–P Garage–G	Evening meals From / *Order by*	Months open (1–12)	Symbols
	LORTON continued																	
F	Mrs. M. A. Steel, Crag End Farm, Rogerscale, Lorton, Cockermouth, CA13 0RG. Tel. (090 085) 658. (Mixed 250 acres)		1	1	2	*6.50 / **6.50*	*13.00 / **13.00*	*8.50 / **8.50*	*59.50 / **59.50*	1	2	3	– / *2*	–	P10 / –	18 00 / *18 00*	1–12	
	LOW HESKET (Cumbria) (7m SE. Carlisle)	C2																
A†	The Manor, Barrock Park, Low Hesket, Carlisle, CA4 0JS. Tel. Southwaite (069 93) 681. Credit- Access, Visa, Diners, Amex.		5	4	5	*18.50 / **25.00*	*37.00 / **38.25*	*30.00 / **38.80*	*210.00 / **271.60*	11	26	–	37 / *–*	–	P50 / –	19 00 / *21 30*	1–12	
	LOWESWATER (Cumbria)	B2																
A	Grange Hotel, Loweswater, Cockermouth, CA13 0SU. Tel. Lamplugh (094 686) 211.		2	2	3	*10.50 / **12.00*	*20.00 / **24.00*	*16.50 / **18.00*	*103.00 / **113.00*	4	12	1	3 / *5*	5	P20 / G2	17 00 / *18 00*	1–12	1
A†	Scale Hill Hotel, Loweswater, Nr. Cockermouth, CA13 9UX. Tel. Lorton (090 085) 232.		4	3	4	15.00 / *19.00*	27.00 / *34.00*	22.00 / *27.50*	140.00 / *164.00*	4	8	2	6 / *3*	–	P20 / –	19 30 / *19 45*	3–11	
D†	Kirkstile Inn, Loweswater, Cockermouth, CA13 0RU. Tel. Lorton (090 085) 219.		3	3	4	*15.46 / **22.78*	*20.61 / **28.30*	– / –	– / –	–	7	1	7 / *2*	–	P40 / –	18 00 / *22 00*	1–12	
E†	Lorton Park, High Lorton, Cockermouth, CA13 9UG. Tel. Lorton (090 085) 223.		3	1	1	*8.50 / **10.00*	– / –	– / –	– / –	–	2	–	– / *1*	–	P4 / –	– / –	4–10	
	LOWICK (Cumbria) (5m N. Ulverston)	B3																
A†	Meadows Hotel, (Guestaccom) Lowick Green, Nr. Ulverston, LA12 8DX. Tel. Lowick Bridge (022 985) 276.		3	3	4	*8.00 / **8.50*	*16.00 / **17.00*	*12.75 / **13.50*	*81.00 / **86.00*	–	3	1	– / *1*	–	P15 / –	19 00 / *22 00*	1–12	
D†	Farmers Arms Hotel, (S & N) Lowick Green, Nr. Ulverston, LA12 8DT. Tel. Greenodd (022 986) 277. Credit- Access, Visa.		3	3	4	*10.00 / –	*20.00 / –	– / –	– / –	4	7	1	– / *3*	–	P100 / –	19 00 / *21 30*	1–12	
	LYTH VALLEY (Cumbria) (5m WSW. Kendal)	C3																
A†	Damson Dene Country Hotel & Restaurant, Crosthwaite, Nr. Bowness-on-Windermere, LA8 8JE. Tel. Crosthwaite (044 88) 227. Credit- Access, Visa, Amex.		5	6	6	*16.00 / **17.00*	*32.00 / **34.00*	*20.25 / **21.25*	*133.00 / **140.00*	2	18	4	22 / *1*	–	P100 / –	18 30 / *23 00*	1–12	
A†	Lyth Valley Hotel, Crosthwaite, Kendal, LA8 8DB. Tel. Crosthwaite (044 88) 233.		4	3	4	*9.00 / **10.00*	*17.00 / **21.00*	*17.00 / **18.50*	– / –	2	5	3	3 / *2*	–	P70 / –	19 00 / *20 30*	1–12	
	MARYPORT (Cumbria)	B2																
D	Rivendell Inn, Dearham, Maryport, CA15 7JP. Tel. (090 081) 2769.		3	3	3	*5.75 / **6.90*	*11.50 / **13.80*	*9.20 / **10.35*	*64.40 / **72.45*	–	6	1	4 / *2*	–	P12 / G1	17 00 / *23 00*	1–12	FB
	MILNTHORPE (Cumbria)	C3																
D†	Ship Inn, (S & N) Sandside, LA7 7HW. Tel. (044 82) 3113.		2	3	2	*6.50 / **6.50*	*13.00 / **13.00*	*9.50 / **10.50*	*63.00 / **63.00*	2	3	–	– / *1*	–	P70 / –	18 00 / *19 45*	1–12	FB
E	Monarch Grill & Guest House, 11 The Square, LA7 7QJ. Tel. (044 82) 3677. Credit- Access, Visa, Diners, Amex.		2	1	1	*6.50 / **8.50*	*13.00 / **17.00*	– / –	– / –	4	4	1	– / *2*	–	– / –	– / –	1–12	

You are advised to read the introductory notes and to check prices and other details when booking accommodation

HOTELS, MOTELS, GUEST HOUSES & OTHER SERVICED ACCOMMODATION

Accommodation Type (See page 3). Category key: see front fold-out. Prices in £ Min. / *£ Max.* Bathrooms: Private / *Public*. Parking–P, Garage–G: No. of cars. Evening meals (24 hr. clock): From / *Order by*. Symbols: Key: see fold-out.

Type	Name and Address (Town (County); Establishment, Address, Telephone number, Telex, Credit cards accepted)	Map Ref.	Bedrooms	Services	Meals	Bed and breakfast: Single room overnight £ Min. / *£ Max.*	Bed and breakfast: Double room overnight £ Min. / *£ Max.*	B & B and evening meal: Per person daily £ Min. / *£ Max.*	B & B and evening meal: Per person weekly £ Min. / *£ Max.*	No. of bedrooms: Single	Double	Family	Bathrooms Private / *Public*	Showers	Parking–P Garage–G (No. of cars)	Evening meals (24 hr. clock) From / *Order by*	Months open (1–12)	Symbols
	MUNGRISDALE (Cumbria)	B2																
B†	The Mill, Mungrisdale, Penrith, CA11 0XR. Tel. Threlkeld (059 683) 659.		3	4	2	*9.50 / **10.00*	*19.00 / **20.00*	*13.00 / **14.50*	*90.00 / **102.00*	2	5	2	– / *3*	–	P10 / –	19 00 / –	3–10	
F†	Mrs. J. M. Tiffin, Wham Head Farm, Hutton Roof, Mungrisdale, Penrith, CA11 0XS. Tel. Skelton (085 34) 289. (Mixed 126 acres)		1	1	2	*6.00 / –	*12.00 / –	*8.50 / –	*58.00 / –	–	2	2	– / *1*	–	P6 / –	18 00 / –	4–10	
F†	Mrs. C. Weightman, Near Howe Farm, Mungrisdale, Troutbeck, Penrith, CA11 0SH. Tel. Threlkeld (059 683) 678. (Mixed 350 acres)		2	3	2	– / –	*12.00 / –	*8.50 / –	– / –	–	4	1	– / *2*	–	P10 / G2	19 00 / *19 00*	3–10	
F	Mrs. O. Wilson, High Beckside Farm, Mungrisdale, Penrith, CA11 0XR. Tel. Threlkeld (059 683) 636. (Mixed 150 acres)		1	2	2	– / –	– / **10.00*	– / **8.50*	– / **56.00*	–	1	1	– / *1*	–	P2 / –	18 30 / –	5–10	
	NEWBY BRIDGE (Cumbria)	B3																
A†	Lakeside Hotel, Newby Bridge, Nr. Ulverston, LA12 8AT. Tel. (0448) 31207. Telex 65149. Credit- Access, Amex.		5	6	4	15.00 / *17.90*	26.00 / *35.75*	14.75 / *23.86*	108.84 / *129.60*	10	80	5	95 / –	–	P100 / G6	18 30 / *21 30*	1–12	
A†	Newby Bridge Hotel, Newby Bridge, Nr. Ulverston, LA12 8NA. Tel. (0448) 31222. Credit- Access, Visa, Amex.		3	4	5	*14.00 / –	*23.00 / –	– / –	– / –	7	9	2	2 / *2*	–	P50 / G10	19 00 / *22 30*	1–12	
A†	Swan Hotel, (Inter) Newby Bridge, Ulverston, LA12 8NB. Tel. (0448) 31681. Credit- Access, Visa, Diners, Amex.		5	4	5	*21.00 / **30.00*	*38.00 / **46.50*	*28.00 / **44.00*	– / –	7	16	13	36 / *2*	–	P100 / –	19 00 / *21 30*	1–12	
E	Landing Cottage, Lakeside, Newby Bridge, Nr. Ulverston, LA12 8AS. Tel. (0448) 31719.		4	3	1	*6.75 / **7.50*	– / –	– / –	– / –	–	3	2	2 / *2*	–	P6 / –	– / –	3–10	
	ORTON (Cumbria)	C2																
C†	Tebay Mountain Lodge Motel, Orton, Penrith, CA10 3XG. Tel. (058 74) 351. Credit- Access, Visa, Diners, Amex.		6	2	2	*18.50 / –	*28.00 / –	– / –	– / –	–	22	10	32 / –	–	P40 / –	19 00 / *21 00*	1–12	
D	George Hotel, Orton, Nr. Penrith, CA10 3RJ. Tel. (058 74) 229.		3	2	4	*10.50 / –	*21.00 / –	– / –	– / –	2	4	1	– / *2*	–	G4 / –	18 00 / *22 00*	1–12	
	PENRITH (Cumbria)	C2																
A†	Abbotsford Hotel, Wordsworth St., CA11 7CY. Tel. (0768) 63940 & 62687.		3	3	5	*10.00 / **12.00*	*19.25 / **24.00*	*15.20 / **17.20*	*88.55 / **103.95*	3	3	5	2 / *2*	–	P8 / G4	18 30 / *21 30*	1–12	
A†	Brantwood Country House Hotel, Stainton, Nr. Penrith, CA11 0EP. Tel. (0768) 62748.		4	4	5	– / *14.95*	– / *23.00*	– / –	– / –	–	6	–	6 / *2*	–	P38 / G2	19 00 / *22 00*	1–12	
A	Edenhall Hotel, Edenhall, Penrith CA1 8SX. Tel. Langwathby (076 881) 454. Credit- Access, Visa, Diners, Amex.		5	4	4	*10.50 / –	*21.00 / –	*16.10 / **16.10*	– / **109.00*	6	16	6	28 / –	–	P80 / G10	19 00 / *20 30*	1–12	
A†	George Hotel, CA11 7SH. Tel. (0768) 62696.		5	5	4	*15.00 / **16.00*	*27.00 / **28.00*	*20.00 / **21.00*	– / –	9	21	–	30 / –	–	P30 / –	19 00 / *20 30*	1–12	

HOTELS, MOTELS, GUEST HOUSES & OTHER SERVICED ACCOMMODATION

Accommodation Type (See page 3)	Name and Address: Town (County), Establishment, Address, Telephone number, Telex, Credit cards accepted	Map Ref.	Category: Bedrooms	Services	Meals	Prices: Bed and breakfast — Single room overnight	Double room overnight	B & B and evening meal — Per person daily	Per person weekly	Rooms: No. of bedrooms — Single	Double	Family	Bathrooms	Showers	Facilities: Parking–P Garage–G	Evening meals (24 hr. clock)	Months open (1–12)	Symbols
	Key: see front fold-out					£ Min. £ Max.	£ Min. £ Max.	£ Min. £ Max.	£ Min. £ Max.				Private Public		No. of cars	From Order by		Key: see fold-out
	PENRITH continued																	
A†	Queens Head Hotel, Tirril, Penrith, CA10 2JF. Tel. (0768) 63219.		3	3	5	*10.50 *11.00	*21.00 *22.00	*15.00 *16.00	*100.00 *107.00	2	6	–	– 3	–	P36 –	19 30 21 30	1–12	TV SP
A†	Round Thorn Country Hotel, Beacon Edge, Penrith, CA11 8SJ. Tel. (0768) 63952. Credit- Access, Visa, Diners, Amex.		4	5	5	*13.20 *15.50	*20.70 *23.00	*13.50 *18.00	*84.00 *115.50	2	9	3	7 1	6	P200 G2	19 00 24 00	1–12	V TV FB OAP SP T
A	Station Hotel, Castlegate, CA11 7JB. Tel. (0768) 62072.		2	3	4	*7.00 *8.50	*12.50 *15.50	*9.50 *11.50	*70.00 *85.00	4	14	2	– 5	–	P6 G4	18 30 20 30	1–12	V TV FB OAP T
A	Woodland House Hotel, Wordsworth St., CA11 7QY. Tel. (0768) 64177.		3	3	4	*6.75 *7.00	*13.50 *14.00	*10.70 *10.95	*74.90 *76.65	2	4	2	– 2	–	P12 G1	18 30 19 00	1–12	V TV SP
B	Brandelhow Guest House, 1 Portland Pl., CA11 7QN. Tel. (0768) 64470. Credit- Amex.		3	3	2	*7.00 *9.00	*11.00 *13.00	*7.50 *9.00	*52.00 *56.00	–	2	4	– 2	–	P4 –	17 50 17 50	1–12	UL V TV OAP
B†	Limes Country Hotel, Redhills, Stainton, Penrith, CA11 0DT. Tel. (0768) 63343.		3	3	2	*8.00 –	*13.80 –	*10.35 –	*69.00 –	2	4	2	– 2	–	P12 –	18 30 18 00	1–12	UL TV FB OAP SP
B	Noonhowe, Melkinthorpe, Penrith, CA10 2DR. Tel. Hackthorpe, (093 12) 464.		3	3	2	*6.00 –	*12.00 –	*9.50 –	*64.00 –	2	3	–	– 1	2	P10 –	18 00 19 30	1–12	UL TV
B	Voreda View, 2 Portland Pl., CA11 7QN. Tel. (0768) 63395.		2	2	2	*6.00 *7.50	*12.00 *15.00	*9.50 *12.00	– –	1	2	4	– 2	–	P1 –	18 00 19 00	1–12	M UL TV OAP
B	Whitrigg House, Clifton, Penrith, CA10 2EE. Tel. (0768) 64851.		3	3	3	*11.00 *11.00	*16.00 *16.00	*16.00 *16.00	*112.00 *112.00	–	6	2	1 2	–	P8 G3	19 00 21 00	1–12	5 TV FB SP
D	Royal Hotel, Wilson Row, CA11 7PZ. Tel. (0768) 62670.		3	3	4	*7.00 *7.00	*12.00 *12.00	*8.00 *8.00	*56.00 *56.00	–	2	2	– 1	–	P3 –	18 00 20 00	1–12	V TV
E	Low Street Cottage, Plumpton, Penrith, CA11 0JD. Tel. Plumpton (076 884) 276.		1	2	1	*5.00 *5.00	*10.00 *10.00	– –	– –	–	3	–	– 1	–	P4 –	– –	4–10	UL TV
F†	Mrs. M. Harris, Whitbarrow Farm, Berrier, Penrith, CA11 0XB. Tel. Greystoke (085 33) 366. (Dairy 220 acres)		1	3	2	– –	*11.50 –	*8.00 –	*50.00 –	–	4	2	– 2	–	P3 –	18 00 13 00	3–10	UL TV
F	Mrs. J. Mathews, Roundthorn Farmhouse, Beacon Edge, Penrith, CA11 8SJ. Tel. (0768) 62299. (Smallholding 2 acres)		1	3	2	*6.00 *6.00	*12.00 *12.00	*9.00 *9.00	*63.00 *63.00	–	1	1	– 1	–	P8 –	19 00 20 30	1–12	
F	Mrs. D. M. Shadwick, Woodlands Farm, Stainton, Penrith, CA11 0ES. Tel. (0768) 62265. (Mixed 11 acres)		1	1	1	*5.50 *6.00	*11.00 *12.00	– –	– –	1	2	–	– 1	–	P3 –	– –	3–10	UL TV
F	Mrs. S. M. Smith, Highgate Farm, CA11 0SE. Tel. Greystoke (085 33) 339. (Mixed 400 acres)		2	3	2	*6.00 *7.00	*12.00 *14.00	*9.00 *10.00	*58.00 *65.00	1	3	–	– 1	–	P6 –	18 00 18 00	4–10	UL TV
	PENTON (Cumbria) (7m NE. Longtown)	C1																
F†	Mrs. J. F. Lawson, Craigburn, Penton, Longtown, Carlisle, CA6 5QP. Tel. Nicholforest (022 877) 214. (Mixed 220 acres)		3	2	2	*5.50 *6.00	*11.00 *12.00	*8.50 *9.50	*57.00 *65.00	2	4	4	– 3	–	P10 –	18 00 14 00	1–12	UL V TV SP

 You are advised to read the introductory notes and to check prices and other details when booking accommodation

HOTELS, MOTELS, GUEST HOUSES & OTHER SERVICED ACCOMMODATION

Name and Address: Accommodation Type (See page 3); Town (County); Establishment, Address, Telephone number, Telex, Credit cards accepted	Map Ref.	Category (Key: see front fold-out): Bedrooms	Services	Meals	Prices: Bed and breakfast: Single room overnight (£ Min. / £ Max.)	Double room overnight (£ Min. / £ Max.)	B & B and evening meal: Per person daily (£ Min. / £ Max.)	Per person weekly (£ Min. / £ Max.)	Rooms: No. of bedrooms: Single	Double	Family	Bathrooms (Private / Public)	Showers (Private / Public)	Facilities: Parking–P, Garage–G (No. of cars)	Evening meals (24 hr. clock) (From / Order by)	Months open (1–12)	Symbols (Key: see fold-out)
PENTON continued																	
F† Mrs. M. M. Sisson, Bessiestown Farm, Penton, Nr. Carlisle, CA6 5QP. Tel. Nicholforest (022 877) 219. (Mixed 50 acres)		2	2	2	*6.00 *7.00*	*12.00 *14.00*	*11.00 *12.00*	*65.00 *75.00*	–	5	–	– *1*	–	P6 –	18 30 –	1–12	UL
RAVENGLASS (Cumbria)	B3																
A† Pennington Arms Hotel, Main St., CA18 1SD. Tel. (065 77) 222 & 626.		3	4	5	*8.90 *11.90*	*17.80 *23.80*	*12.90 *17.90*	*90.30 *125.30*	8	21	12	4 *10*	1	P50 G2	18 00 *22 00*	1–12	
B† Holly House Hotel, CA18 1SQ. Tel. (065 77) 230.		3	3	5	*7.50 *8.00*	*14.00 *15.00*	– –	– –	2	5	2	– *2*	–	P12 –	18 00 *21 30*	1–12	SP
RAVENSTONEDALE (Cumbria)	C2																
A† The Fat Lamb, Cross Bank, Fell End, Ravenstonedale, Kirkby Stephen, CA17 4LL. Tel. Newbiggin-on-Lune (058 73) 242.		3	4	5	*10.00 *11.00*	*16.00 *18.00*	*13.00 *14.50*	*91.00 *101.50*	–	4	2	– *2*	–	P60 G3	18 00 *22 00*	1–12	FB SP
RENWICK (Cumbria) (3m NE. Kirkoswald)	C2																
A† Highland Hall, Renwick, Penrith, CA10 1JL. Tel. Lazonby (076 883) 375.		4	3	4	– –	*18.50 –	*16.75 –	– –	–	3	1	1 *1*	–	P4 –	19 30 *19 30*	3–11	FB
RYDAL (Cumbria)	B2																
A† The Glen Rothay, Rydal Nr. Ambleside, LA22 9LR. Tel. Ambleside (099 63) 2524. Credit- Access, Visa, Diners, Amex.		4	4	4	*19.50 –	*33.00 –	*23.95 –	*148.00 –	1	8	2	11 *1*	–	P45 –	19 30 *19 30*	2–12	SP
A† Rydal Lodge Hotel, Rydal, Ambleside, LA22 9LR. Tel. Ambleside (096 63) 3208. Credit- Access.		3	3	2	*10.80 *10.80*	*17.60 *17.60*	*14.80 –	*97.00 *97.00*	–	7	1	– *3*	–	P12 –	19 00 *14 00*	4–10	
A White Moss House, Rydal Water, Grasmere, LA22 9SE. Tel. Grasmere (096 65) 295.		4	3	2	– –	– –	*35.00 *37.00*	*231.00 *245.00*	–	7	–	7 –	–	P10 –	20 00 *19 30*	3–10	
ST. BEES (Cumbria)	B2																
A† Seacote Hotel, Beach Rd., CA27 0ES. Tel. (094 685) 777. Credit- Access, Visa.		6	5	5	*16.00 *16.00*	*25.00 *28.00*	*21.00 *22.00*	*147.00 –	5	16	1	22 –	–	P80 –	19 00 *21 45*	1–12	SP
B Fern Bank, High House Rd., CA27 0BZ. Tel. (094 685) 468.		1	2	2	*5.50 *6.00*	*11.00 *12.00*	*8.00 *8.50*	*50.00 *55.00*	1	3	–	– *2*	–	P5 –	18 00 *20 00*	1–12	UL
B Sea View House, Sea Mill La., CA27 0BD. Tel. (094 685) 352.		3	3	3	*5.50 *6.00*	*11.00 *11.00*	*8.50 *8.50*	– –	–	2	1	– *1*	–	P6 G1	18 20 –	1–12	UL FB SP
SATTERTHWAITE (Cumbria) (4m SSW. Hawkshead)	B3																
F† Mrs. J. Crabtree, Force Mill Farm, Satterthwaite, Ulverston, LA12 8LQ. Tel. (022 984) 205. (Stock Rearing 54 acres)		3	3	4	– –	– –	10.50 –	66.00 –	–	4	–	– *2*	–	P8 –	19 00 *20 30*	1–12	FB SP
SAWREY (Cumbria)	B3																
A† Sawrey Hotel, Far Sawrey, Nr. Ambleside, LA22 0LQ. Tel. Windermere (096 62) 3425 & 4651.		3	4	4	*10.50 *11.50*	*21.00 *23.00*	*14.50 *15.50*	*95.00 *102.00*	3	12	3	3 *4*	–	P30 –	19 00 *20 45*	1–12	SP

HOTELS, MOTELS, GUEST HOUSES & OTHER SERVICED ACCOMMODATION

Type	Name and Address (Town (County), Establishment, Address, Telephone number, Telex, Credit cards accepted)	Map Ref.	Category: Bedrooms	Category: Services	Category: Meals	Prices: Bed and breakfast – Single room overnight	Prices: Bed and breakfast – Double room overnight	Prices: B & B and evening meal – Per person daily	Prices: B & B and evening meal – Per person weekly	Rooms: No. of bedrooms – Single	Rooms: Double	Rooms: Family	Rooms: Bathrooms	Rooms: Showers	Facilities: Parking–P Garage–G	Facilities: Evening meals (24 hr. clock)	Facilities: Months open (1–12)	Facilities: Symbols
Accommodation Type (See page 3)			Key: see front fold-out			£ Min. *£ Max.*	£ Min. *£ Max.*	£ Min. *£ Max.*	£ Min. *£ Max.*				Private *Public*		No.of cars	From *Order by*		Key: see fold-out
	SAWREY continued																	
A	Sawrey House Private Hotel, Sawrey, Nr. Ambleside, LA22 0LF. Tel. Hawkshead (096 66) 387.		3	3	3	*8.00 **9.50*	*16.00 **19.00*	*13.00 **15.00*	*90.00 **105.00*	2	6	4	2 *3*	2	P20 –	19 00 –	1–12	TV OAP SP
	SEASCALE (Cumbria)	B3																
A†	Scawfell Hotel, CA20 1QU. Tel. (0940) 28400 & 28207. Credit- Access, Visa, Diners.		3	4	5	14.00 *15.50*	27.00 *30.00*	21.00 –	136.50 *145.00*	5	32	5	6 *10*	–	P120 G8	19 00 *21 30*	1–12	V TV FB OAP SP
	SEBERGHAM (Cumbria) (10m SSW. Carlisle)	B2																
F	Mrs. E. M. Johnston, Bustabeck, Sebergham, Carlisle, CA5 7DX. Tel. Raughton Head (069 96) 339. (Mixed 72 acres)		1	2	2	*4.50 –	*9.00 –	*8.00 –	*50.00 –	–	3	–	– *2*	–	P4 –	18 00 –	5–9	UL TV
	SEDBERGH (Cumbria)	C3																
A†	Oakdene Country Hotel, Garsdale Rd., LA10 5JN. Tel. (0587) 20280.		3	3	4	*10.00 **12.00*	*20.00 **24.00*	*15.50 **20.50*	– –	–	5	1	1 *2*	–	P14 –	19 30 *20 00*	1–12	V SP
E	Rose Cottage, Hallbank, Hawes Rd., LA10 5JW. Tel. (0587) 20864.		1	2	1	– –	*11.00 **12.00*	– –	– –	–	1	–	1 –	–	P1 –	– –	1–12	UL TV
	SHAP (Cumbria)	C2																
A	Brookfield, Shap, Penrith, CA10 3PZ. Tel. (093 16) 397.		3	4	4	*7.00 **7.50*	*13.00 **14.00*	*12.00 **13.00*	– –	1	4	2	– *1*	–	P25 G5	19 30 *20 15*	2–12	V TV
A	Greyhound Hotel, Main St., CA10 3PW. Tel. (093 16) 474 & 662. Credit- Access, Visa.		4	4	5	11.55 *12.65*	23.10 *25.30*	16.55 –	115.85 –	3	12	2	7 *4*	–	P60 –	18 00 *22 00*	1–12	V TV FB OAP SP
A†	Shap Wells Hotel, CA10 3QU. Tel. (093 16) 628. Credit- Visa, C.Bl., Diners, Amex.		3	5	5	10.75 –	21.50 –	16.00 –	– –	13	44	6	30 *9*	–	P100 G4	19 00 *21 30*	2–12	V TV FB OAP
D	Kings Arms Hotel, Main St., Shap, Penrith, CA10 3NU. Tel. (093 16) 277.		3	3	2	*8.50 **10.50*	*17.00 **25.00*	*11.00 **13.00*	*60.00 **80.00*	–	4	2	– *2*	–	P20 –	19 00 *22 00*	1–12	V TV OAP SP
F	Mrs. S. Hodgson, Green Farm, Shap, Penrith, CA10 3PW. Tel. (093 16) 619. (Mixed 167 acres)		1	1	1	– –	*11.00 –	– –	– –	–	2	1	– *1*	–	P4 –	– –	4–9	UL TV
F†	Mrs. S. J. Thompson, Southfield Farm, Shap, Penrith, CA10 2NX. Tel. (093 16) 282. (Mixed 100 acres)		1	3	1	– –	*10.00 **13.00*	– –	– –	–	1	1	– *1*	–	P3 –	– –	4–10	10 UL TV
	SILECROFT (Cumbria)	B3																
B	Whicham Old Rectory, Silecroft, Millom, LA18 5LS. Tel. Millom (0657) 2954.		3	3	2	*6.50 **7.00*	*13.00 **14.00*	*10.00 **11.00*	*65.00 **70.00*	1	2	2	– *3*	–	P6 –	18 00 *21 00*	1–12	UL V TV
D	Miners Arms, Silecroft Nr. Millom, LA18 5LP. Tel. Millom (0657) 2325 & 2691. Credit- Visa, Diners, Amex.		3	3	4	*6.50 **7.50*	*13.00 **14.00*	*9.00 **10.00*	*56.00 **63.00*	1	1	1	– *2*	–	P40 –	18 00 *20 00*	1–12	TV OAP

 You are advised to read the introductory notes and to check prices and other details when booking accommodation

HOTELS, MOTELS, GUEST HOUSES & OTHER SERVICED ACCOMMODATION

Name and Address Accommodation Type (See page 3) **Town (County)** Establishment Address Telephone number, Telex Credit cards accepted	Map Ref.	Category (Key: see front fold-out) Bedrooms	Services	Meals	Prices: Bed and breakfast Single room overnight £ Min. *£ Max.*	Double room overnight £ Min. *£ Max.*	B & B and evening meal Per person daily £ Min. *£ Max.*	Per person weekly £ Min. *£ Max.*	Rooms: No. of bedrooms Single	Double	Family	Bathrooms Private *Public*	Showers	Parking–P Garage–G No. of cars	Evening meals (24 hr. clock) From *Order by*	Months open (1–12)	Facilities: Symbols Key: see fold-out
SILLOTH (Cumbria)	B1																
A† Golf Hotel, Criffel St., Silloth-on-Solway, Carlisle, CA5 4AB. Tel. (0965) 31438. Credit- Access, Diners, Amex.		4	4	5	•10.50 *•17.00*	•20.00 *•32.00*	– *–*	•100.00 *•150.00*	7	13	3	14 *4*	–	– –	19 00 *21 30*	1–12	SP
A† Queens Hotel, Park Ter., Silloth, Carlisle, CA5 4DQ. Tel. (0965) 31373. Credit- Access.		4	4	5	•12.00 *•15.00*	•26.00 *•30.00*	•18.00 *•21.00*	•110.00 *•130.00*	5	14	3	11 *3*	–	G12 –	19 00 *21 50*	1–12	FB OAP SP
A† Skinburness Hotel, (Minotels) CA5 4QY. Tel. (0965) 31468. Credit- Access, Visa.		4	4	5	•12.50 *•14.50*	•23.00 *•26.00*	– *–*	•70.00 *•81.00*	9	13	1	9 *4*	–	P150 G5	19 00 *21 30*	1–12	OAP SP
B Mitchell's, 11 Esk St., CA5 4BU. Tel. (0965) 31528.		1	1	2	•5.50 *•6.50*	•11.00 *•12.00*	•7.00 *•8.00*	•45.00 *•50.00*	1	1	1	– *1*	–	P3 –	17 30 *13 00*	1–12	
B Nith View, 1 Pine Ter., Skinburness Rd., CA5 4DT. Tel. (0965) 31542.		3	3	4	•6.25 *•6.50*	•12.50 *•13.00*	•9.00 *•9.50*	– *–*	1	1	2	– *1*	–	P6 –	18 00 *16 00*	4–10	
F Mrs. D. M. Greenup, Nook Farm, Beckfoot, Silloth, CA5 4LG. Tel. Allonby (090 084) 279. (Dairy 90 acres)		1	1	2	•5.00 *–*	•10.50 *–*	•7.50 *–*	•49.00 *–*	–	1	1	– *1*	–	P4 –	18 00 *–*	4–10	OAP
SPARK BRIDGE (Cumbria) (3m S. Coniston Water)	B3																
A Bridgefield House, Sparkbridge, Ulverston, LA12 8DA. Tel. Lowick Bridge (022 985) 239.		3	3	3	•10.35 *•10.35*	•20.70 *•20.70*	•17.25 *•17.25*	•144.90 *•144.90*	1	4	1	– *2*	–	P8 –	19 30 *16 00*	1–12	FB SP
F† Mrs. M. Harrison, Bridgefield Farm, Sparkbridge, Ulverston, LA12 8DA. Tel. Lowick Bridge (022 985) 652. (Mixed 210 acres)		1	2	1	– *–*	•10.00 *–*	– *–*	– *–*	–	1	1	– *1*	–	P4 –	– *–*	4–10	
STAVELEY (Cumbria)	C3																
B Millholme, Ings, Staveley, Nr. Kendal, LA8 9PY. Tel. (0539) 821309.		3	3	2	– *•6.00*	•12.00 *•12.00*	•8.50 *–*	– *–*	1	7	–	– *2*	–	P14 –	18 30 *17 30*	3–10	5
TEBAY (Cumbria)	C2																
B Barbara's Cottage, Gaisgill, Tebay, Penrith, CA10 3UA. Tel. Orton (058 74) 340.		1	3	2	•4.50 *•4.50*	•9.00 *•9.00*	•8.50 *•8.50*	•55.50 *•55.50*	–	1	1	– *1*	–	P3 –	19 30 *20 00*	1–12	3
B Carmel House, Tebay, Nr. Penrith, CA10 3TH. Tel. Orton (058 74) 651.		1	2	2	– *•5.00*	– *•10.00*	– *•7.00*	– *•35.00*	1	3	–	– *1*	–	P6 –	19 00 *19 00*	1–12	FB
TEMPLE SOWERBY (Cumbria)	C2																
A† Temple Sowerby House, Temple Sowerby, Nr. Penrith, CA10 1RZ. Tel. Kirkby Thore (093 06) 578. Credit- Access, Visa.		4	4	2	•15.00 *•20.00*	•30.00 *•40.00*	•25.00 *•30.00*	– *–*	2	8	2	10 *1*	–	P12 –	20 00 *20 00*	3–12	5 OAP SP
E Moss View Guest House, Temple Sowerby, Penrith, CA10 1RZ. Tel. Kirkby Thore (093 06) 657.		1	2	1	– *•4.50*	– *•9.00*	– *–*	– *–*	1	1	1	– *1*	–	P3 –	– *–*	1–12	
THIRLMERE (Cumbria)	B2																
F Mrs. J. Hodgson, Stybeck Farm, Thirlmere, Keswick, CA12 4TN. Tel. Keswick (0596) 73232. (Mixed 165 acres)		2	1	2	•7.00 *–*	•13.00 *–*	•10.50 *–*	•73.50 *–*	–	2	1	– *1*	–	P3 –	18 30 *–*	3–11	4

HOTELS, MOTELS, GUEST HOUSES & OTHER SERVICED ACCOMMODATION

Accommodation Type (See page 3)	Name and Address: Town (County) / Establishment / Address / Telephone number, Telex / Credit cards accepted	Map Ref.	Category (Key: see front fold-out): Bedrooms	Services	Meals	Prices: Bed and breakfast: Single room overnight (£ Min. / £ Max.)	Double room overnight (£ Min. / £ Max.)	B & B and evening meal: Per person daily (£ Min. / £ Max.)	Per person weekly (£ Min. / £ Max.)	Rooms: No. of bedrooms: Single	Double	Family	Bathrooms (Private / Public)	Showers (Private / Public)	Facilities: Parking–P Garage–G (No. of cars)	Evening meals (24 hr. clock) (From / Order by)	Months open (1–12)	Symbols (Key: see fold-out)
	THORNTHWAITE (Cumbria) (3m NW. Keswick)	B2																
A†	Ladstock Country House Hotel, Thornthwaite, Keswick, CA12 5RZ. Tel. Braithwaite (059 682) 210.		3	3	3	*10.00 *10.00	*20.00 *22.00	*15.00 *16.00	*90.00 *97.00	1	13	3	1 5	15	P20 –	19 00 15 00	3–10	
A†	Swan Hotel, Thornthwaite, Keswick, CA12 5SQ. Tel. Braithwaite (059 682) 256.		4	4	4	10.80 –	21.60 –	17.50 –	119.00 –	1	14	–	6 2	–	P60 G3	18 45 20 15	3–11	
B†	Thornthwaite Hall Guest House, Thornthwaite, Keswick, CA12 5SA. Tel. Braithwaite (059 682) 424.		3	2	2	– –	– –	*11.00 –	*72.00 –	2	2	1	– 1	–	P5 –	19 00 –	4–10	2
B	Thwaite Howe Hotel, Thornthwaite, Keswick, CA12 5SA. Tel. Braithwaite (059 682) 281.		4	4	4	– –	*26.00 *28.00	*17.90 *19.00	*108.00 *125.00	–	8	–	8 –	–	P20 –	19 00 17 00	3–10	6
C†	Wood End Country House Hotel & Restaurant, Thornthwaite, Keswick, CA12 5SL. Tel. Braithwaite (059 682) 206.		5	4	4	*13.00 *15.00	*25.00 *29.00	*20.00 *21.50	*112.00 *126.00	1	6	1	7 1	–	P30 –	19 00 20 30	1–12	10 FB
	THRELKELD (Cumbria) (4m NE. Keswick)	B2																
B	Cobble Rigg, Kiln How, Threlkeld, Keswick, CA12 4SG. Tel. (059 683) 329.		1	1	2	– –	*11.00 –	*7.50 –	*49.00 –	–	1	1	– 1	–	P2 –	18 00 –	4–10	
F	Mrs. R. Marr, Sycamore House, Threlkeld, Keswick, CA12 4RX. Tel. (059 683) 234. (Mixed 30 acres)		1	1	2	– –	*10.00 –	*7.50 –	– –	–	1	2	– 1	–	P3 –	18 50 14 00	4–10	1
	TROUTBECK, PENRITH (Cumbria)	B2																
B†	Netherdene Guest House, CA11 0SJ. Tel. Greystoke (085 33) 475.		2	3	2	*5.50 *7.00	*11.00 *14.00	*8.00 *10.00	*56.00 *70.00	–	2	2	– 2	–	P6 –	18 30 –	3–11	
D†	Troutbeck Hotel, CA11 0SJ. Tel. Greystoke (085 33) 243.		2	3	2	*5.75 *6.33	*11.50 *12.66	*9.78 *10.35	– –	–	2	3	– 1	5	P50 –	18 00 –	1–12	
F	Mrs. R. Bird, Askew Rigg Farm, CA11 0SZ. Tel. Threlkeld (059 683) 638. (Mixed 200 acres)		1	2	2	*5.50 –	*11.00 –	*8.50 –	– –	1	1	2	– 1	–	P6 –	18 00 –	1–12	
F†	P. Fellows, Lane Head Farm, CA11 0SY. Tel. Threlkeld (059 683) 220. (Mixed 110 acres)		3	3	2	*7.00 –	*14.00 –	*11.00 –	– *75.00	–	2	3	– 1	–	P10 –	19 00 17 30	3–10	
	TROUTBECK, WINDERMERE (Cumbria)	B3																
B	The Toft, Town End LA23 1LB. Tel. Ambleside (096 63) 3320.		1	2	2	– –	– –	*11.00 *12.00	*72.50 *79.00	–	3	–	– 1	–	P4 –	19 00 –	4–10	7
D	Mortal Man Hotel, LA23 1PL. Tel. Ambleside (096 63) 3193.		4	3	4	– –	– –	*25.50 *28.00	*170.00 *187.50	2	13	–	10 2	–	P30 –	19 30 20 00	2–11	5
F	Mrs. Jean Beaty, Long Green Head Farm, LA23 1PR. Tel. Ambleside (096 63) 2012. (Mixed 1000 acres)		1	2	1	– *6.00	*12.00 –	– –	– –	–	1	2	– 1	–	P4 –	– –	3–10	5
	ULLSWATER (Cumbria)	C2																
A†	Brackenrigg Hotel, Watermillock, Ullswater, Nr. Penrith, CA11 0LP. Tel. Pooley Bridge (085 36) 206. Credit- Access, Visa.		2	3	4	*9.50 *11.00	*19.00 *22.00	*16.50 *18.00	*99.00 *115.00	2	5	4	– 2	–	P56 –	19 00 21 00	4–10	FB

You are advised to read the introductory notes and to check prices and other details when booking accommodation

HOTELS, MOTELS, GUEST HOUSES & OTHER SERVICED ACCOMMODATION

Name and Address — Accommodation Type (See page 3) — Town (County), Establishment, Address, Telephone number, Telex, Credit cards accepted	Map Ref.	Category (Key: see front fold-out) Bedrooms	Services	Meals	Prices — Bed and breakfast: Single room overnight	Double room overnight	B & B and evening meal: Per person daily	Per person weekly	Rooms — No. of bedrooms: Single	Double	Family	Bathrooms	Showers	Facilities — Parking–P Garage–G	Evening meals (24 hr. clock)	Months open (1–12)	Symbols
					£ Min. £ Max.	£ Min. £ Max.	£ Min. £ Max.	£ Min. £ Max.				Private Public		No. of cars	From Order by		Key: see fold-out
ULLSWATER continued																	
A Crown Hotel, Pooley Bridge, Penrith, CA10 2NP. Tel. Pooley Bridge (085 36) 217. Credit- Visa.		3	3	4	*13.50 *18.50	*18.50 *21.50	– –	– –	–	5	–	– 1	–	P5 –	19 30 20 30	3–10	
A Fairlight Restaurant & Guest House, Glenridding, Penrith, CA11 0PD. Tel. Glenridding (085 32) 397.		1	1	4	*7.50 *8.50	*15.00 *17.00	– –	– –	–	3	1	– 1	–	P9 –	19 00 21 30	4–10	SP
A† Glenridding Hotel, (Minotels) Glenridding, Ullswater, CA11 0PB. Tel. Glenridding (085 32) 228. Credit- Access, Visa, Diners, Amex.		4	4	4	*12.00 *14.50	*24.00 *29.00	*15.50 *22.00	*108.50 *140.00	10	29	3	29 3	–	P30 –	19 00 20 30	1–12	SP T
A Howtown Hotel, Ullswater, Penrith, CA10 2ND. Tel. Pooley Bridge (085 36) 514.		3	4	4	– –	– –	*15.00 –	*90.00 –	3	11	1	– 5	–	P20 –	19 00 20 30	4–10	FB
A† Leeming House Hotel, (Prestige) Ullswater, Nr. Penrith, CA11 0JJ. Tel. Pooley Bridge (085 36) 444. Credit- Access, Visa, Diners, Amex.		5	4	4	28.00 28.00	56.00 56.00	43.60 67.60	– –	2	22	–	24 3	–	P40 –	19 30 21 00	2–12	8 FB SP T
A† Old Church Hotel, Watermillock, Penrith, CA11 0JN. Tel. Pooley Bridge (085 36) 204.		4	4	4	– –	– –	*22.00 *27.00	*137.00 *145.00	3	9	1	7 1	–	P30 –	19 30 20 30	4–10	FB
A Rampsbeck Hotel, on Ullswater, Watermillock, Nr. Penrith, CA11 0LP. Tel. Pooley Bridge (085 36) 442. Credit- Access.		4	4	4	*13.50 –	*27.00 –	*19.50 –	*117.00 –	5	13	1	8 4	–	P100 –	19 00 21 00	1–12	FB T
A† Sharrow Bay Country House Hotel, Ullswater, Penrith, CA10 2LZ. Tel. Pooley Bridge (085 36) 301 & 483.		5	4	4	– –	– –	*37.00 *55.00	– –	6	23	–	21 4	–	P20 G4	20 00 20 45	3–12	13
A† Ullswater Hotel, Glenridding, Penrith, CA11 0PA. Tel. Glenridding (085 32) 444. Telex 64357. Credit- Access, Visa, C.Bl., Diners, Amex.		4	4	4	*20.00 *22.00	*40.00 *44.00	*29.00 *31.00	– –	6	32	10	48 –	–	P160 –	19 00 20 30	1–12	OAP SP T
E Bridge House, Glenridding, Penrith, CA11 0PA. Tel. Glenridding (085 32) 236. Credit- Access.		1	1	1	– –	*13.00 –	– –	– –	–	3	3	– 2	–	P7 –	– –	3–11	
E Knotts Mill Country Guest House, Watermillock, Penrith, CA11 0JN. Tel. Pooley Bridge (085 36) 472.		3	1	1	– –	*14.00 *15.00	– –	– –	–	2	3	– 1	–	P10 –	– –	4–10	
F† Mrs. J. Cox, Bank House Farm, Matterdale End, Penrith, CA11 0LF. Tel. Glenridding (085 32) 302. (Mixed 12 acres)		3	2	2	*5.50 –	*11.00 –	*10.00 –	*65.00 –	1	1	1	– 1	–	P2 G1	19 00 16 00	1–12	SP
ULVERSTON (Cumbria)	**B3**																
A Hill Foot Hotel & Country Club, Hill Foot, LA12 7SE. Tel. (0229) 52166.		5	3	4	– –	30.00 30.00	– –	– –	–	6	–	6 –	–	P50 –	19 00 21 30	1–12	SP
A† Lonsdale House Hotel, Daltongate, LA12 7BD. Tel. (0229) 52598 & 53960. Credit- C.Bl., Amex.		4	3	4	13.37 17.78	25.30 29.09	18.37 22.78	– –	11	11	–	14 2	–	P40 –	19 00 20 30	1–12	
A† Railway Hotel, Princes St., LA12 7NQ. Tel. (0229) 52208.		3	4	4	*10.00 *11.00	*17.00 *19.00	*15.50 *16.50	*75.00 *85.00	2	4	2	– 2	–	P40 G2	19 00 21 00	1–12	FB SP T

HOTELS, MOTELS, GUEST HOUSES & OTHER SERVICED ACCOMMODATION

Type	Name and Address (Town (County); Establishment, Address, Telephone number, Telex, Credit cards accepted)	Map Ref.	Category: Bedrooms	Category: Services	Category: Meals	Bed and breakfast: Single room overnight (£ Min. / £ Max.)	Bed and breakfast: Double room overnight (£ Min. / £ Max.)	B & B and evening meal: Per person daily (£ Min. / £ Max.)	B & B and evening meal: Per person weekly (£ Min. / £ Max.)	No. of bedrooms: Single	No. of bedrooms: Double	No. of bedrooms: Family	Bathrooms (Private / Public)	Showers	Parking-P / Garage-G (No. of cars)	Evening meals (24 hr. clock) (From / Order by)	Months open (1–12)	Symbols (Key: see fold-out)
	ULVERSTON continued																	
A†	Sefton House Hotel, 34 Queen St., LA12 7AF. Tel. (0229) 52190.		4	4	5	*13.50 *18.40	*25.00 *34.50	*18.50 *23.40	– –	2	7	1	6 2	–	P3 G3	18 00 21 30	1–12	SP
D	Sun Inn, Market St., LA12 7AY. Tel. (0229) 55044. Credit- Amex.		3	3	4	*6.50 *8.50	*13.00 *20.00	*7.75 *11.25	*42.00 *56.00	–	9	2	2 3	–	P10 –	18 00 20 00	1–12	V FB OAP SP T
	UNDERBARROW (Cumbria)	C3																
A†	Greenriggs Country House Hotel, Underbarrow, Nr. Kendal, LA8 8HF. Tel. Crosthwaite (044 88) 387.		4	4	3	*14.00 *15.00	*28.00 *30.00	*19.00 *21.00	*125.00 *139.00	2	9	2	7 2	–	P40 –	20 00 21 00	2–12	SP T
F	Mrs. C. M. Simpson, High Gregg Hall Farm, Underbarrow, Kendal, LA8 8BL. Tel. Crosthwaite (044 88) 318. (Mixed 100 acres)		1	2	2	– –	*10.00 *10.00	*7.00 *7.00	*49.00 *49.00	–	2	–	– 1	–	P3 –	18 30 –	4–10	
	WASDALE (Cumbria)	B2																
A†	Low Wood Hall Hotel, Netherwasdale, Seascale, CA20 1ET. Tel. (094 06) 289.		3	2	2	*9.75 *9.75	*19.50 *19.50	*15.00 *15.00	*100.00 *100.00	1	8	3	– 3	–	P12 –	19 00 19 00	1–12	SP
A†	Wasdale Head Inn, Wasdale Head, Gosforth. CA20 1EX. Tel. Wasdale (094 06) 229. Credit- Access, Visa.		4	3	4	*14.60 *16.00	*29.21 *32.20	*21.50 *24.15	*165.00 *185.50	2	6	2	10 –	–	P50 –	19 15 20 00	1–12	V OAP SP
B†	Greendale Guest House, Greendale, Wasdale, Nr. Seascale, CA20 1EU. Tel. (094 06) 243.		1	2	3	– –	*12.00 *14.00	– –	– –	–	3	–	– 1	–	P30 –	18 00 20 00	4–10	
D	Strands Hotel, Netherwasdale, Seascale, CA20 1ET. Tel. (094 06) 237.		3	3	3	*9.20 *12.00	*18.40 *24.00	*13.80 *18.00	*87.00 *126.00	1	6	–	– 3	–	P20 –	18 00 21 20	1–12	
E†	Old Vicarage, Netherwasdale, via Seascale, CA20 1ET. Tel. Wasdale (094 06) 232.		3	2	1	– –	*17.00 *17.00	– –	– –	–	1	1	– 1	–	P4 –	– –	1–12	
	WELTON (Cumbria) (8m SW. Carlisle)	B2																
B	Fiddlers Close, CA5 7EW. Tel. Raughton Head (069 96) 410.		3	3	4	*6.00 *7.00	*12.00 *14.00	*8.00 *10.00	*50.00 *60.00	2	2	–	– 2	–	P4 –	18 00 20 00	1–12	V FB OAP SP
	WHITEHAVEN (Cumbria)	B2																
A†	Roseneath Country House Hotel, Low Moresby, Whitehaven, CA28 6RX. Tel. (0946) 61572. Credit- Access, Visa, Diners.		5	5	4	12.00 18.00	22.00 27.50	– –	– –	2	7	–	7 1	–	P20 –	19 30 20 45	1–12	12 SP T
B	Glenlea Guest House, Stanford Hill, Whitehaven, CA28 6PS. Tel. (0946) 3873.		3	3	4	*7.50 *8.50	*15.00 *17.00	*10.00 *12.00	*70.00 *84.00	1	2	2	– 1	–	P8 G4	18 00 20 00	1–12	2 V
F	Mrs. M. Bowe, Shaw Farm, Moor Row, Whitehaven, CA24 3LB. Tel. Cleator Moor (0946) 810470. (Beef 100 acres)		1	2	1	*5.50 *6.00	*11.00 *12.00	– –	– –	–	3	–	– 1	–	P3 G1	– –	1–12	V

 You are advised to read the introductory notes and to check prices and other details when booking accommodation

HOTELS, MOTELS, GUEST HOUSES & OTHER SERVICED ACCOMMODATION

Name and Address Accommodation Type (See page 3) Town (County) / Establishment / Address / Telephone number, Telex / Credit cards accepted	Map Ref.	Category (Key: see front fold-out) Bedrooms	Services	Meals	Prices: Bed and breakfast Single room overnight £ Min. £ Max.	Double room overnight £ Min. £ Max.	B & B and evening meal Per person daily £ Min. £ Max.	Per person weekly £ Min. £ Max.	Rooms: No. of bedrooms Single	Double	Family	Bathrooms Private Public	Showers	Facilities: Parking–P Garage–G No. of cars	Evening meals (24 hr. clock) From Order by	Months open (1–12)	Symbols Key: see fold-out
WIGTON (Cumbria)	**B2**																
A Royal Oak Hotel, 5 West St., CA7 9NP. Tel. (096 54) 2393.		3	4	4	*6.50 *6.50	*13.00 *13.00	*9.00 *9.00	*63.00 *63.00	2	6	2	– 2	–	P12 G6	18 00 21 30	1–12	5 V TV FB OAP SP
E Spittal Rigg, CA7 0ES. Tel. (096 54) 3375.		1	1	1	*5.50 *6.00	*11.00 *12.00	– –	– –	1	2	–	– 1	–	P3 –	– –	1–12	UL
F Mrs. S. Todhunter, Drumleaning Farm, CA7 0NU. Tel. (096 54) 2230. (Mixed 90 acres)		1	1	1	*5.00 –	*10.00 –	– –	– –	–	1	1	– 1	–	P2 G2	– –	4–10	UL
WINDERMERE (Cumbria)	**B3**																
A† Applegarth Hotel., College Rd., LA23 1BU. Tel. (096 62) 3206. Credit- Access, Amex.		3	3	4	*7.50 *10.00	*15.00 *20.00	*11.00 *14.50	*72.00 *95.00	1	8	3	1 3	–	P6 G1	19 00 20 00	1–12	V TV FB SP
A† Beech Hill Hotel, Cartmel Fell, LA23 1EX. Tel. (096 62) 2137. Telex 67415. Credit- Access, Visa, C.Bl., Diners, Amex.		5	5	4	*25.00 *30.00	*39.50 *45.00	– –	– –	2	40	3	45 –	–	P52 –	19 30 21 30	1–12	V TV FB OAP SP T
A† Beechwood Private Hotel, South Craig, Beresford Rd., LA23 2JG. Tel. (096 62) 3403.		3	3	3	– *9.20	– *18.40	– *14.50	– *101.00	2	4	2	– 1	–	P8 –	18 45 20 30	2–10	6 UL V TV FB OAP SP
A† Belsfield Hotel, (THF) Kendal Rd., LA23 3EL. Tel. (096 62) 2448. Telex 65238. Credit- Access, Visa, C.Bl., Diners, Amex.		5	5	5	22.65 28.15	35.30 40.80	– –	– –	10	63	–	67 5	–	P80 –	19 00 21 30	1–12	V TV SP T
A† Bordriggs Country House Hotel, Longtail Hill, LA23 3JA. Tel. (096 62) 3567.		4	4	4	*11.65 –	*23.30 –	*17.50 –	*115.50 –	1	7	2	10 –	–	P14 –	18 30 19 30	1–12	V TV OAP SP
A† Burnside Hotel, (THF) Kendal Rd., LA23 3EP. Tel. (096 62) 2211. Credit- Access, Visa, C.Bl., Diners, Amex.		5	4	4	20.65 23.65	30.80 36.30	– –	– –	7	17	6	24 –	–	P70 –	19 00 21 30	1–12	V TV SP T
A† Cranleigh Hotel, Kendal Rd., LA23 3EW. Tel. (096 62) 3293.		3	4	4	*10.00 *12.00	*28.00 *32.00	*15.00 *17.00	*90.00 *110.00	3	6	2	3 2	4	P8 –	19 00 20 00	3–11	TV SP
A† Earlston Hotel, Thornbarrow Rd., LA23 2DF. Tel. (096 62) 3636.		4	4	3	*10.00 –	*20.00 –	*17.80 –	*113.25 –	4	7	6	8 2	–	P17 –	19 00 18 00	1–12	TV OAP SP T
A† Eastbourne Hotel, Biskey Howe Rd., LA23 2JR. Tel. (096 62) 3525. Credit- Access, Visa.		3	3	2	*9.25 *10.35	*17.50 *19.70	*15.00 *16.10	– –	–	6	3	– 2	–	P3 –	19 00 20 00	1–12	TV FB
A† Ellerthwaite Lodge, New Rd., LA23 2LA. Tel. (096 62) 5115.		6	4	5	10.00 15.00	20.00 30.00	15.00 20.00	90.00 120.00	1	10	1	12 –	–	P20 –	19 00 22 00	2–12	V TV SP T
A† Fairfield Hotel, Brantfell Rd., LA23 3AE. Tel. (096 62) 3772. Credit- Access, Visa, Diners, Amex.		1	3	2	*10.50 *12.50	*21.00 *25.00	*16.50 *19.50	*108.00 *128.00	1	3	4	5 1	–	P10 –	19 00 17 00	3–11	5 TV SP
A† Fir Garth Hotel, Ambleside Rd., LA23 1EU. Tel. (096 62) 3562.		3	3	4	*11.22 –	*22.44 –	*18.12 –	– –	1	5	15	21 –	–	P26 –	18 30 20 30	1–12	V TV OAP SP
A† Grey Walls Hotel, Elleray Rd., LA23 1AG. Tel. (096 62) 3741. Credit- Access, Diners, Amex.		4	4	4	*12.50 *13.50	*25.00 *27.00	*19.40 *20.40	*114.80 *121.80	4	10	3	14 3	2	P19 G4	19 00 20 00	3–11	V TV FB T

HOTELS, MOTELS, GUEST HOUSES & OTHER SERVICED ACCOMMODATION

Name and Address Accommodation Type (See page 3) Town (County) Establishment Address Telephone number, Telex Credit cards accepted	Map Ref.	Category (Key: see front fold-out) Bedrooms	Services	Meals	Prices: Bed and breakfast Single room overnight £ Min. *£ Max.*	Double room overnight £ Min. *£ Max.*	B & B and evening meal Per person daily £ Min. *£ Max.*	Per person weekly £ Min. *£ Max.*	Rooms: No. of bedrooms Single	Double	Family	Bathrooms Private *Public*	Showers	Facilities: Parking–P Garage–G No. of cars	Evening meals (24 hr. clock) From *Order by*	Months open (1–12)	Symbols Key: see fold-out
WINDERMERE continued																	
A† Hideaway Hotel, Phoenix Way, LA23 1DB. Tel. (096 62) 3070.		4	4	4	*8.00 **10.00*	*16.00 **20.00*	*14.00 **19.00*	*115.00 **130.00*	1	10	4	12 *1*	–	P20 –	19 00 *20 00*	2–12	FB OAP SP
A† Hilton House Hotel, New Rd., LA23 2EE. Tel. (096 62) 3934.		4	3	4	*8.25 **9.50*	*16.50 **19.00*	*13.50 **15.95*	*87.50 **104.50*	1	4	2	3 *1*	–	P12 –	18 45 *20 30*	1–12	OAP SP
A† Holbeck Ghyll Hotel, Holbeck La., LA23 1LU. Tel. Ambleside (096 63) 2375.		4	4	2	12.50 *17.00*	25.00 *34.00*	19.00 *25.00*	116.00 *150.00*	2	8	2	8 *2*	–	P12 –	19 15 *20 00*	3–10	
A† Knoll Hotel, Lake Rd., LA23 2JF. Tel. (096 62) 3756.		3	3	2	10.50 –	21.00 –	14.00 –	98.00 –	4	4	4	3 *4*	–	P15 –	19 00 *19 00*	3–10	3 FB
A† Langdale Chase Hotel, LA23 1LW. Tel. Ambleside (096 63) 2201. Credit- Access, Visa, Diners, Amex.		5	5	4	19.00 –	36.00 –	– –	– –	7	23	6	30 *5*	–	P50 –	19 00 *20 45*	1–12	FB SP
A† Lindeth Fell Country House Hotel, LA23 3JP. Tel. (096 62) 3286. Credit- Access, Visa.		4	3	4	*16.50 –	*33.00 –	*24.50 –	– –	2	8	3	13 –	–	P20 –	19 00 –	3–10	5
A† Lindeth Howe Country House, Longtail Hill, Storrs Pk., LA23 3JF. Tel. (096 62) 5759.		3	4	4	*18.00 **20.00*	*23.00 **26.00*	*16.50 **19.00*	*110.00 **130.00*	–	4	3	– *3*	–	P8 –	19 00 *16 30*	3–10	SP
A† Linthwaite Hotel, LA23 3JA. Tel. (096 62) 3688.		4	4	2	*15.20 **20.00*	*30.00 **40.00*	*23.00 **28.00*	*146.00 **175.00*	2	11	–	11 *1*	–	P20 –	19 30 *19 00*	4–10	8
A† Low Wood Hotel, LA23 1LP. Tel. Ambleside (096 63) 3338. Telex 65273. Credit- Access, Visa, Diners, Amex.		4	5	6	*13.90 **16.80*	*27.80 **33.60*	*21.60 **24.50*	*126.00 **147.00*	29	61	6	66 *21*	–	P200 –	18 30 *22 30*	3–11	FB SP T
A† Mountain Ash Hotel, Ambleside Rd., LA23 1AT. Tel. (096 62) 3715. Credit- Access, Visa, Diners, Amex.		3	3	4	*12.00 **15.00*	*22.00 **35.00*	*19.50 **22.50*	*130.00 **150.00*	9	16	4	7 *6*	–	P27 –	18 30 *19 30*	2–12	FB OAP SP T
A† Oakfold Private Hotel, Beresford Rd., LA23 2JG. Tel. (096 62) 3239.		3	3	5	– –	– –	*14.00 –	*96.00 –	1	5	1	– *1*	–	P10 –	19 00 *21 30*	2–12	5 SP
A† Old England Hotel, (THF) LA23 3DF. Tel. (096 62) 2444. Telex 65194. Credit- Access, Visa, C.Bl., Diners, Amex.		5	5	5	– *33.00*	– *48.00*	– –	– –	18	62	4	84 –	–	P60 –	19 30 *21 30*	1–12	SP T
A† Priory Hotel, Rayrigg Rd., LA23 1EX. Tel. (096 62) 4377. Credit- Access, Visa, C.Bl., Diners, Amex.		5	4	5	*25.00 **28.00*	*38.00 **43.00*	– –	– –	2	11	2	15 –	–	P30 –	19 30 *21 30*	1–12	SP T
A† Ravensworth Hotel, Ambleside Rd., LA23 1BA. Tel. (096 62) 3747. Credit- Access, Visa.		4	4	2	*10.60 **15.00*	*15.20 **30.00*	*11.35 **19.85*	*63.00 **113.00*	4	6	3	13 –	–	P13 –	19 00 *19 00*	3–11	SP
A† Rosemount Private Hotel, Lake Rd., LA23 2EQ. Tel. (096 62) 3739. Credit- Access, Visa.		3	5	4	*7.50 **8.50*	*15.00 **17.00*	*12.50 **14.50*	*85.00 **98.00*	2	4	2	2 *2*	1	P6 G2	18 00 *18 00*	1–12	FB OAP SP T
A† Royal Hotel, (Best Western) LA23 3DB. Tel. (096 62) 3045 & 5267. Credit- Access, Visa, C.Bl., Diners, Amex.		4	4	5	*13.65 **20.00*	*27.30 **40.00*	*22.25 **27.00*	*142.00 **175.00*	7	17	5	29 *5*	–	P15 G5	18 30 *22 30*	1–12	FB SP T

You are advised to read the introductory notes and to check prices and other details when booking accommodation

HOTELS, MOTELS, GUEST HOUSES & OTHER SERVICED ACCOMMODATION

Accommodation Type (See page 3)	Name and Address: Town (County) / Establishment / Address / Telephone number, Telex / Credit cards accepted	Category – Bedrooms	Category – Services	Category – Meals	Bed and breakfast: Single room overnight £ Min. / £ Max.	Bed and breakfast: Double room overnight £ Min. / £ Max.	B & B and evening meal: Per person daily £ Min. / £ Max.	B & B and evening meal: Per person weekly £ Min. / £ Max.	No. of bedrooms: Single	No. of bedrooms: Double	No. of bedrooms: Family	Bathrooms Private / Public	Showers	Parking–P Garage–G No. of cars	Evening meals (24 hr. clock) From / Order by	Months open (1–12)	Symbols (Key: see fold-out)
	WINDERMERE continued																
A†	St. Martins Hotel, Lake Rd., LA23 3DE. Tel. (096 62) 3731. Credit- Access.	3	4	4	11.50 –	22.00 –	18.00 –	104.00 –	5	10	2	4 *3*	–	P12 –	19 00 *20 00*	3–10	TV FB
A†	St Mary's Cottage Hotel, Ambleside Rd., LA23 1AX. Tel. (096 62) 3192.	4	4	4	– –	*28.00 **36.00*	*18.00 **22.00*	– –	–	6	–	6 –	–	P9 –	19 30 *21 30*	3–11	TV OAP SP
A†	Sun Hotel, Troutbeck Bridge, Windermere LA23 1HH. Tel. (096 62) 3274. Credit- Access, Visa, Diners.	3	3	5	*9.00 **10.00*	*15.60 **16.50*	*14.00 **15.00*	*90.00 **105.00*	–	6	3	1 *2*	–	P12 –	18 00 *22 30*	1–12	V TV OAP SP
A†	Westbourne Hotel, Biskey Howe Rd., LA23 2SR. Tel. (096 62) 3625. Credit- Access, Visa.	3	4	2	*9.25 **10.25*	*18.50 **20.50*	*14.50 **15.50*	*98.00 **105.00*	3	4	3	– *3*	2	P14 –	18 30 *19 00*	1–12	V TV SP
A	White Lodge Hotel, Lake Rd., LA23 2JS. Tel. (096 62) 3624.	3	4	4	*11.00 **13.00*	*20.00 **24.00*	*15.00 **17.00*	– –	2	6	2	3 *2*	–	P16 –	19 00 *20 00*	3–11	V TV FB OAP SP T
A†	Wild Boar Hotel, Crook, Nr. Windermere, LA23 3NF. Tel. (096 62) 5225. Credit- Access, Visa, Diners, Amex.	6	4	4	*18.40 **21.50*	*36.80 **43.00*	*28.50 **31.70*	*185.00 **207.00*	–	35	3	38 –	–	P60 G4	19 00 *21 00*	1–12	V TV FB SP T
A†	Windermere Hotel, LA23 1AL. Tel. (096 62) 2251. Telex 667986. Credit- Access, Visa, Diners, Amex.	5	4	4	*15.50 **17.25*	*29.90 **33.35*	*20.45 **22.20*	*143.15 **155.40*	17	56	7	58 *4*	–	P80 –	19 00 *20 45*	2–12	V TV OAP SP T
A†	Windermere Hydro Hotel, (Mt. Charlotte) Helm Rd., LA23 3BA. Tel. (096 62) 4455. Telex 65196. Credit- Access, Visa, Diners, Amex.	6	5	4	*22.50 –	*38.00 –	– –	– –	14	72	10	96 –	–	P100 –	18 45 *20 30*	1–12	V TV SP T
A†	Yorkshire House Hotel, 1 Upper Oak St., LA23 2LB. Tel. (096 62) 6124 & 4689. Credit- Visa.	3	4	5	*7.50 **7.50*	*15.00 **15.00*	*10.50 **10.50*	*73.50 **73.50*	1	2	3	– *1*	6	P5 –	17 30 *24 00*	1–12	V TV FB OAP SP T
B	Acton House, 41 Craig Walk, LA23 2HB. Tel. (096 62) 5340.	3	3	2	– –	*9.50 **10.50*	*7.25 **8.00*	*48.00 **53.00*	–	3	–	– *1*	–	P2 –	18 45 *09 30*	2–11	TV OAP
B	Adam Place, 1 Park Ave., LA23 2AR. Tel. (096 62) 4600.	3	2	2	*6.00 **6.50*	*12.00 **13.00*	*9.00 **9.50*	*58.50 **63.00*	1	2	1	– *1*	–	P4 –	18 30 *16 00*	3–10	V TV
B	The Archway, 13 College Rd., LA23 1BY. Tel. (096 62) 5613.	3	3	2	*6.50 **7.00*	*13.00 **14.00*	*10.20 **10.70*	*68.00 **71.50*	1	2	3	– *1*	–	P3 –	18 30 *16 00*	1–12	TV
B†	Boston House, The Terrace, LA23 1AJ. Tel. (096 62) 3654.	3	3	2	*5.50 **7.00*	*11.00 **14.00*	*9.00 **11.00*	*57.00 **69.00*	1	2	3	– *2*	2	P5 –	18 45 –	3–11	V TV OAP
B	Bowfell Cottage, Middle Entrance Dr., LA23 3JY. Tel. (096 62) 4835.	1	1	2	*6.00 **6.50*	*12.00 **13.00*	*8.00 **10.00*	*55.00 **65.00*	–	2	1	– *1*	–	P4 –	18 00 *22 00*	1–12	TV OAP SP
B†	Braemount House, Sunny Bank Rd., LA23 2EN. Tel. (096 62) 5967. Credit- Access, Visa.	5	4	3	– –	– *22.00*	*14.00 **16.50*	– **100.00*	–	3	1	4 –	–	P4 –	19 00 –	1–12	V TV FB OAP SP
B†	Brendon Chase, College Rd., LA23 1BU. Tel. (096 62) 5638.	3	3	2	*6.50 **7.00*	*12.50 **13.00*	*10.00 **10.50*	*65.00 **68.50*	2	3	4	1 *3*	–	P6 –	18 00 *19 00*	1–12	V TV OAP SP

HOTELS, MOTELS, GUEST HOUSES & OTHER SERVICED ACCOMMODATION

Name and Address Accommodation Type (See page 3) Town (County) / Establishment / Address / Telephone number, Telex / Credit cards accepted	Map Ref.	Category (Key: see front fold-out) Bedrooms	Services	Meals	Prices: Bed and breakfast — Single room overnight	Bed and breakfast — Double room overnight	B & B and evening meal — Per person daily	B & B and evening meal — Per person weekly	Rooms: No. of bedrooms — Single	Double	Family	Bathrooms	Showers	Facilities: Parking–P Garage–G	Evening meals (24 hr. clock)	Months open (1–12)	Symbols
					£ Min. £ Max.	£ Min. £ Max.	£ Min. £ Max.	£ Min. £ Max.				Private Public		No. of cars	From Order by		Key: see fold-out
WINDERMERE continued																	
B† Broadview Guest House, 7 Woodland Rd., LA23 2AE. Tel. (096 62) 2367.		3	3	2	*7.00 *7.50	*12.00 *14.00	*9.50 *10.50	*63.50 *70.50	–	2	3	– 2	–	– –	18 00 14 00	1-12	SP
B† Brooklands, Ferry View, LA23 3JB. Tel. (096 62) 2344.		3	3	2	– –	– –	*12.50 *14.37	*87.50 *97.75	1	3	2	2 1	1	P6 –	19 00 –	1-12	SP
B† Castle View Guest House, 131 Craig Walk, LA23 3AX. Tel. (096 62) 2954.		3	3	2	*6.00 *6.50	*12.00 –	*8.50 *9.00	*56.00 *60.00	1	5	1	– 2	–	P7 –	18 30 –	2-11	FB
B Clifton House, Ellerthwaite Rd., LA23 2AH. Tel. (096 62) 4968.		3	3	2	*6.00 *7.00	*12.00 *14.00	*10.00 *11.00	*63.00 *75.00	1	4	1	1 1	1	P5 G1	19 00 17 00	1-12	5 FB
B† The Cottage, Elleray Rd., LA23 1AG. Tel. (096 62) 3128.		3	3	3	– –	*11.50 –	*10.00 –	*66.00 –	–	4	2	– 2	–	P6 –	19 00 19 00	1-12	SP
B† Crag Brow Cottage, Helm Rd., LA23 3BU. Tel. (096 62) 4080.		4	3	4	*11.50 –	*23.00 –	– –	– –	–	4	–	4 –	–	P6 –	19 15 –	1-12	SP
B Dalegarth Private Hotel, Lake Rd., LA23 2EQ. Tel. (096 62) 5052.		3	2	2	– –	*16.00 *19.00	*16.10 *18.40	*105.00 *122.00	–	7	1	1 2	1	P6 –	18 30 –	1-12	SP
B† Denehurst, Queens Dr., LA23 3EL. Tel. (096 62) 4710.		3	3	3	*6.00 *6.00	*12.00 *12.00	*10.00 *10.00	*65.00 *65.00	1	3	3	– 1	–	– –	19 00 –	1-12	FB OAP
B† Elim Bank Hotel, Lake Rd., LA23 2JJ. Tel. (096 62) 4810.		3	3	2	– *13.23	– *19.55	– *15.52	– *108.64	1	5	1	– 2	–	P6 –	19 30 17 30	1-11	
B† Elim Lodge Guest House, Biskey Howe Rd., LA23 2JP. Tel. (096 62) 4271.		3	2	2	– –	*12.00 *13.00	*9.50 *10.00	*65.00 *68.00	–	2	3	– 1	–	P10 –	18 30 15 00	1-12	
B Garth Cottage, 1 Woodlands Rd., LA23 2AE. Tel. (096 62) 4273.		2	3	2	*6.00 –	*10.00 –	*7.50 –	*52.50 –	–	3	–	– 2	–	P2 –	18 00 –	1-12	OAP
B† Glenville, Lake Rd., LA23 2EQ. Tel. (096 62) 3371.		3	3	4	*8.00 *10.50	*14.00 *19.00	*14.00 *17.00	*90.00 *115.00	1	7	1	1 2	–	P12 –	19 00 09 00	1-12	OAP SP
B Greenriggs Guest House, 8 Upper Oak St., LA23 2LB. Tel. (096 62) 2265.		3	2	2	*5.50 *5.50	*11.00 *11.00	*9.00 *9.00	*60.00 *60.00	1	3	2	– 2	–	P3 –	19 00 17 30	3-10	
B Greenwood House, 2 North Ter., Lake Rd., LA23 3AU. Tel. (096 62) 2123.		2	3	2	– *6.00	– *10.00	*8.50 –	– *59.50	–	2	2	– 1	–	– –	18 00 –	1-12	M OAP
B Haisthorpe, Holly Rd., LA23 2AF. Tel. (096 62) 3445.		3	3	2	– *6.50	– *13.00	– *10.50	– *70.00	2	5	–	– 1	–	– –	18 30 16 00	3-10	8
B† Hawksmoor, Lake Rd., LA23 2EQ. Tel. (096 62) 2110.		2	3	2	*6.50 *8.00	*13.00 *16.00	*10.75 *12.25	*73.00 *82.00	–	4	2	– 1	–	P10 –	18 30 18 00	2-11	M
B 2 Holly Cottages, Rayrigg Rd., LA23 3BZ. Tel. (096 62) 4250.		3	2	2	*6.25 *7.25	*12.50 *14.50	*10.50 *12.00	*69.00 *79.50	1	4	2	– 2	–	P4 –	19 00 15 00	2-11	OAP SP
B† Holly Lodge, 6 College Rd., LA23 1BX. Tel. (096 62) 3873.		3	3	2	*9.00 *10.00	*11.00 *13.00	*9.00 *12.00	*53.00 *65.00	–	6	4	– 3	–	P6 –	18 30 16 00	1-12	
B Kenilworth Guest House, Holly Rd., LA23 2AF. Tel. (096 62) 4004.		3	3	2	*6.25 –	*12.50 –	*10.00 –	*66.00 –	1	5	1	– 1	–	– –	18 30 12 00	3-10	OAP
B Kirkwood Guest House, Prince's Rd., LA23 2DD. Tel. (096 62) 3907.		1	3	2	*5.75 *6.25	*11.50 *12.50	*10.25 *11.75	*64.00 *64.00	2	2	3	– 2	–	– –	19 00 –	1-12	

You are advised to read the introductory notes and to check prices and other details when booking accommodation

HOTELS, MOTELS, GUEST HOUSES & OTHER SERVICED ACCOMMODATION

Type	Name and Address (Town (County), Establishment, Address, Telephone number, Telex, Credit cards accepted)	Category: Bedrooms	Services	Meals	B&B Single room overnight £ Min. / *£ Max.*	B&B Double room overnight £ Min. / *£ Max.*	B&B and evening meal Per person daily £ Min. / *£ Max.*	B&B and evening meal Per person weekly £ Min. / *£ Max.*	Single	Double	Family	Bathrooms Private / *Public*	Showers Private / *Public*	Parking–P Garage–G (No. of cars)	Evening meals (24 hr. clock) From / *Order by*	Months open (1–12)	Symbols
	WINDERMERE continued																
B†	Laurel Cottage, St. Martin's Sq., LA23 2EE. Tel. (096 62) 5594.	3	2	2	*6.00 / **7.50*	*12.00 / **15.00*	*10.00 / **12.00*	*70.00 / **84.00*	1	6	1	– / *1*	2	P3 / –	19 00 / *17 30*	1–12	UL TV SP Ad
B	Little Longtail, Ferry View, LA23 3JB. Tel. (096 62) 3884.	3	2	2	*7.00 / **7.00*	*13.00 / **13.00*	*10.00 / **10.00*	*67.50 / **67.50*	1	1	3	– / *2*	–	P4 / –	18 30 / –	4–10	UL V TV FB
B†	Lonsdale Hotel, Lake Rd., LA23 2JJ. Tel. (096 62) 3348. Credit- Access.	4	3	4	*9.00 / **10.25*	*18.00 / **20.50*	*14.75 / **16.00*	*96.25 / **105.87*	2	5	4	7 / *1*	–	P10 / –	18 30 / *16 00*	2–11	3 V TV OAP SP T Ad
B†	Mylne Bridge, Brookside, Lake Rd., LA23 2BX. Tel. (096 62) 3314.	3	4	3	*8.00 / –	*16.00 / –	*13.25 / –	*88.00 / –	1	10	2	4 / *2*	–	P15 / –	18 30 / *17 00*	2–12	7 TV OAP SP Ad
B	Oakfield, 46 Oak St., LA23 1EN. Tel. (096 62) 5692.	3	3	2	*6.50 / **7.00*	*12.00 / **13.00*	*9.00 / **10.00*	*60.00 / **65.00*	1	1	3	– / *1*	–	– / –	18 00 / *18 30*	1–12	UL TV SP
B†	Oakthorpe Hotel, High St., LA23 1AF. Tel. (096 62) 3547.	3	2	2	*8.50 / **8.50*	*17.00 / **19.00*	*13.50 / **14.50*	– / –	7	10	4	– / *5*	7	P18 / –	19 00 / –	3–11	TV OAP SP
B	Oldfield House, Oldfield Rd., LA23 2BY. Tel. (096 62) 3250.	3	1	2	*6.00 / –	*12.00 / –	*10.00 / **12.00*	– / –	–	1	2	– / *1*	–	P4 / –	19 00 / *16 00*	1–12	UL TV
B†	Orrest Close, 3 The Terrace, LA23 1AJ. Tel. (096 62) 3325.	3	3	2	*5.70 / **7.00*	*11.40 / **14.00*	– / –	– / –	2	3	2	– / *3*	–	P8 / –	– / –	1–12	UL TV OAP SP Ad
B†	Orrest Head House, Kendal Rd., LA23 1JG. Tel. (096 62) 4315.	2	2	2	*6.75 / **7.75*	*13.50 / **15.50*	*11.50 / **13.50*	*80.00 / **87.50*	1	5	1	– / *1*	–	P10 / –	18 30 / –	4–10	10 V TV
B†	Prospect House Guest House, High St., LA23 1AF. Tel. (096 62) 4205.	3	2	2	*6.50 / **7.50*	*12.00 / **14.00*	*10.50 / **11.50*	*70.00 / **75.00*	1	4	3	– / *2*	–	– / –	18 30 / *17 00*	1–12	UL V TV SP
B†	St. John's Lodge, Lake Rd., LA23 2EQ. Tel. (096 62) 3078.	3	4	4	*6.50 / **8.00*	*13.00 / **16.00*	*10.50 / **12.00*	*70.00 / **78.00*	1	4	2	– / *1*	4	P7 / –	19 00 / *16 00*	1–12	2 V TV FB OAP SP
B†	South View, Cross St., LA23 1AE. Tel. (096 62) 2951.	3	3	2	*6.00 / **7.00*	*12.00 / **14.00*	*9.50 / **10.50*	*62.00 / **70.00*	–	3	1	– / *2*	–	P5 / –	18 30 / *18 30*	1–12	UL TV SP Ad
B†	Thornbank, 4 Thornbarrow Rd., LA23 2EW. Tel. (096 62) 3724. Credit- Visa, Amex.	4	5	4	*7.00 / **9.50*	*14.00 / **21.00*	*12.00 / **17.00*	*81.00 / **114.00*	2	7	3	5 / *3*	1	P12 / –	19 00 / *18 00*	1–12	UL V TV FB OAP SP T Ad
B	Tudor House Restaurant & Guest House, Ellerthwaite Sq., LA23 1DP. Tel. (096 62) 2421.	2	3	2	*6.50 / **8.00*	*13.00 / **16.00*	*9.50 / **11.00*	*65.00 / **70.00*	–	5	–	– / *1*	–	P4 / –	– / –	4–10	V TV SP
B†	Waverley Hotel, College Rd., LA23 1BX. Tel. (096 62) 3546 & 5026.	3	3	2	*8.63 / **9.78*	*16.10 / **17.82*	*12.65 / **14.95*	*88.55 / **104.65*	3	4	4	– / *2*	–	P8 / –	19 00 / *20 00*	1–12	V TV OAP SP Ad
B	West View, Cross St., LA23 1AE. Tel. (096 62) 5140.	1	3	2	*6.00 / **7.00*	*11.00 / **12.00*	*7.75 / **9.00*	*50.00 / **60.00*	–	3	1	– / *2*	–	P3 / –	18 30 / *14 00*	1–12	UL V TV OAP
B†	Westlake Guest House, Lake Rd., LA23 2EQ. Tel. (096 62) 3020.	3	4	4	– / –	*14.00 / **18.00*	*12.00 / **14.00*	*80.00 / **95.00*	–	3	3	– / *1*	4	P7 / –	18 30 / *19 00*	1–12	V TV OAP SP
B	White Rose Guest House, Broad St., LA23 2AB. Tel. (096 62) 5180.	3	3	4	*6.00 / **7.00*	*12.00 / **14.00*	*9.00 / **11.00*	*63.00 / **77.00*	–	2	3	– / *1*	–	P5 / –	18 30 / *19 00*	2–11	UL V TV FB OAP SP
B†	Willowsmere Hotel, Ambleside Rd., LA23 1ES. Tel. (096 62) 3575. Credit- Access, Visa, Diners, Amex.	3	3	2	*8.50 / **10.00*	*17.00 / **20.00*	*14.00 / **16.00*	*80.00 / **87.00*	3	12	1	8 / *2*	–	P20 / G2	19 00 / *18 00*	3–11	5 V TV SP T Ad

Accommodation Type (See page 3). Category key: see front fold-out. Symbols key: see fold-out.

HOTELS, MOTELS, GUEST HOUSES & OTHER SERVICED ACCOMMODATION

Name and Address Accommodation Type (See page 3) Town (County) / Establishment / Address / Telephone number, Telex / Credit cards accepted	Map Ref.	Category (Key: see front fold-out) Bedrooms	Services	Meals	Prices: Bed and breakfast Single room overnight £ Min. *£ Max.*	Double room overnight £ Min. *£ Max.*	B & B and evening meal Per person daily £ Min. *£ Max.*	Per person weekly £ Min. *£ Max.*	Rooms: No. of bedrooms Single	Double	Family	Bathrooms Private *Public*	Showers	Facilities: Parking–P Garage–G No. of cars	Evening meals (24 hr. clock) From *Order by*	Months open (1–12)	Symbols Key: see fold-out
WINDERMERE continued																	
C† Burn How Motel, Back Belsfield Rd., LA23 3HH. Tel. (096 62) 4486. Credit- Amex.		6	4	5	*16.00 **18.00*	*32.00 **35.00*	*24.00 –	– –	–	10	8	18 –	–	P18 –	19 00 *21 30*	3–12	[V] [TV] [SP]
D Albert Hotel, Queen's Square, LA23 3BY. Tel. (096 62) 3241 & 4059.		3	3	1	– –	*15.00 **22.00*	– –	– –	–	5	1	– *2*	–	P7 –	– –	1–12	[V] [TV] [T]
E† Beckmead, 5 Park Ave., LA23 2AR. Tel. (096 62) 2757.		3	2	1	*6.25 –	*12.50 –	– –	– –	1	2	1	– *1*	–	– –	– –	2–11	[TV]
E Belsfield Guest House, 4 Belsfield Ter., Kendal Rd., LA23 3EQ. Tel. (096 62) 5823.		3	3	1	– –	*13.00 –	– –	– –	–	3	4	– *2*	–	– –	– –	3–11	[TV]
E† Briscoe Lodge, Ellerthwaite Rd., LA23 2AH. Tel. (096 62) 2928.		2	1	1	– –	*10.00 **10.00*	– –	– –	–	2	1	– *1*	–	– –	– –	4–10	9 [TV]
E† Elim House, Biskey Howe Rd., LA23 2JP. Tel. (096 62) 2021.		3	2	1	*7.00 **7.00*	*12.00 **13.00*	– –	– –	–	5	2	– *1*	–	P6 –	– –	3–10	3 [TV]
E† Field House, Kendal Rd., LA23 3EQ. Tel. (096 62) 2476.		3	3	1	– –	*15.00 **17.00*	– –	– –	–	4	4	– *2*	–	– –	– –	4–10	[TV] [OAP]
E Fir Trees Guest House, Lake Rd., LA23 2EQ. Tel. (096 62) 2272.		4	2	1	– –	*13.00 **16.00*	– –	– –	–	4	2	2 *1*	–	P8 G2	– –	1–12	3 [TV] [OAP] [SP]
E† Glenburn, New Rd., LA23 2EE. Tel. (096 62) 2649.		3	2	1	*7.00 **9.00*	*12.00 **19.00*	– –	– –	2	2	5	1 *2*	–	P11 –	– –	1–12	[M] [TV]
E† Hazeldene, Lake Rd., LA23 2JJ. Tel. (096 62) 2523.		2	2	1	*6.00 –	*12.00 –	– –	– –	1	2	3	– *1*	–	– –	– –	1–12	3 [M] [TV]
E† The Old Bakery, High St. Ter., High St., LA23 1AF. Tel. (096 62) 2512.		2	2	1	*5.00 **6.00*	*10.00 **12.00*	– –	– –	1	2	–	– *1*	–	– –	– –	1–12	[TV]
E Old Court House, Lake Rd., LA23 3BJ. Tel. (096 62) 3718.		3	2	1	*6.00 **7.00*	*12.00 **13.00*	– –	– –	1	4	1	– *2*	–	P4 G1	– –	3–10	[TV]
E† Rockside, Church St., LA23 1AQ. Tel. (096 62) 5343.		3	3	1	*6.50 **7.50*	*13.00 **15.00*	– –	– –	3	5	5	– *4*	1	P12 –	– –	1–12	[V] [TV] [SP]
E Stonecroft, Beresford Rd., LA23 2JG. Tel. (096 62) 2901.		3	3	1	– –	*11.00 **15.00*	– –	– –	–	2	2	– *1*	–	P5 –	– –	1–12	[TV] [SP]
E† Villa Lodge, Cross St., LA23 1AE. Tel. (096 62) 3318.		3	4	1	– –	*12.00 **14.00*	– –	– –	–	4	3	– *2*	–	P8 –	– –	1–11	[TV]
E Virginia Cottage, 1 Crown Villas, Kendal Rd., LA23 3EJ. Tel. (096 62) 4891.		3	1	1	*7.00 **7.50*	*14.00 **15.00*	– –	– –	1	2	1	– *1*	–	– –	– –	1–12	9 [V] [OAP] [SP]
E Winbrook, 30 Ellerthwaite Rd., LA23 2AH. Tel. (096 62) 3213.		3	2	1	*5.50 **6.00*	*11.00 **12.00*	– –	– –	–	4	1	1 *1*	–	P6 –	– –	1–12	[TV]
F Mrs. E. M. Tuer, The Common Farm, LA23 1JQ. Tel. (096 62) 3433. (Dairy 160 acres)		1	2	1	– –	*12.00 –	– –	– –	–	3	–	– *1*	–	P3 –	– –	4–10	[TV]
WITHERSLACK (Cumbria)	**B3**																
A The Old Vicarage, Witherslack, Grange-over-Sands, LA11 6RS. Tel. (044 852) 381.		4	3	2	*15.00 **15.00*	*24.00 **24.00*	*19.50 **22.50*	*132.50 **152.50*	–	1	2	3 –	–	P10 –	18 30 *20 30*	1–12	[V] [TV] [SP]

 You are advised to read the introductory notes and to check prices and other details when booking accommodation

HOTELS, MOTELS, GUEST HOUSES & OTHER SERVICED ACCOMMODATION

Name and Address Accommodation Type (See page 3) **Town (County)** Establishment Address Telephone number, Telex Credit cards accepted	**Map Ref.**	**Category** (Key: see front fold-out) Bedrooms	Services	Meals	**Prices** Bed and breakfast Single room overnight	Double room overnight	B & B and evening meal Per person daily	Per person weekly	**Rooms** No. of bedrooms Single	Double	Family	Bathrooms	Showers	**Facilities** Parking–P Garage–G	Evening meals (24 hr. clock)	Months open (1–12)	Symbols
					£ Min. *£ Max.*	£ Min. *£ Max.*	£ Min. *£ Max.*	£ Min. *£ Max.*				Private *Public*		No.of cars	From *Order by*		Key: see fold-out
WORKINGTON (Cumbria)	**B2**																
A Beckstone Hotel, Harrington, Workington, CA14 5PP. Tel. Harrington (0946) 831666.		**5**	**4**	**5**	– **17.50*	– **24.50*	*20.10 **24.50*	– –	–	6	1	6 *1*	–	P50 –	17 00 *21 30*	1–12	V TV FB SP
A Westland Hotel, Branthwaite Rd., CA14 4SS. Tel. (0900) 4544.		**5**	**5**	**5**	18.00 *21.00*	24.00 *28.00*	– –	– –	10	34	4	43 *3*	–	P200 –	19 00 *21 30*	1–12	V TV FB SP T
B Dower House, 22 Portland Sq., CA14 5DL. Tel. (0900) 5906.		**1**	**2**	**2**	*6.50 **7.25*	*11.50 **10.50*	*8.00 **8.00*	*50.00 **50.00*	–	3	4	– *2*	2	P1 –	18 30 *15 30*	1–12	UL V TV FB OAP SP
B† Morven Guest House, Main Rd., Siddick, Workington, CA14 1LE. Tel. (0900) 2118.		**3**	**3**	**2**	*6.50 **8.00*	*13.00 **15.00*	*9.00 **10.50*	*56.00 **60.00*	1	5	2	– *3*	–	P18 –	18 00 *16 00*	1–12	TV

ACCOMMODATION FOR GROUPS AND YOUNG PEOPLE

ACCOMMODATION FOR GROUPS & YOUNG PEOPLE

Name and Address Town (County) / Establishment / Address / Telephone number, Telex	Map Ref.	Accommodates: Men	Women	Individuals	Groups	Ages accepted (Min. / Max.)	Bedrooms & Beds: Number of bedrooms: Single	Double and twin	To sleep 3 or more persons	Beds: Total number	Baths: Number of private bathrooms	Number of public baths/showers	Prices: Per person: Overnight bed only (£ Min. / £ Max.)	Overnight bed and breakfast (£ Min. / £ Max.)	Weekly full board (£ Min. / £ Max.)	Months open (1–12)	Symbols (Key: see fold-out)
ALSTON (Cumbria)	C2																
High Plains Lodge Outdoor Centre, CA9 3DD. Tel. (049 83) 886. Contact Chris Jones, Y.M.C.A. Office, Herrington Burn, Houghton-le-Spring, Tyne & Wear, Tel. Fencehouses (0385) 852822 & 853085. Price includes food, instruction & equipment		✓	✓	✓	✓	8 –	–	–	10	56	–	5	*7.50 –	– –	*52.50 –	1–12	UL V TV T
AMBLESIDE (Cumbria)	B2																
Carlisle Diocesan Conference House, Rydal Hall, LA22 9LX. Tel. (096 63) 2050. Contact The Warden,		✓	✓	✓	✓	– –	4	19	5	58	1	8	*6.32 –	*7.86 –	*86.10 *86.10*	1–12	V TV
† YWCA Iveing Cottage, Old Lake Rd., LA22 0DJ. Tel. (096 63) 2340. Contact F. M. Bliss,		✓	✓	✓	✓	7 –	1	3	8	50	–	5	– –	– *5.05*	*29.15 *40.65*	2–10	UL V
BASSENTHWAITE (Cumbria)	B2																
† Kiln Hill Barn, Bassenthwaite, Keswick, CA12 4RG. Tel. Bassenthwaite Lake (059 681) 454. Contact Mr. B. Smith,		✓	✓	✓	✓	– –	2	7	6	45	–	6	– –	*4.00 *4.25*	*45.00 *48.00*	1–12	UL V TV
DENT (Cumbria)	C3																
Whernside Cave & Fell Centre, Dent, Sedbergh, LA10 5RE. Tel. (058 75) 213. Contact M. K. Lyon, The Warden,		✓	✓	✓	✓	7 70	–	2	6	36	–	12	*2.00 *3.50*	*5.00 *5.00*	*50.00 *100.00*	1–12	UL V
GREYSTOKE (Cumbria)	C2																
Lattendales Guest House, Greystoke, Penrith, CA11 0UE. Tel. (085 33) 229. Contact The Wardens,		✓	✓	✓	✓	– –	5	3	1	14	–	3	– –	– –	*80.00 *85.00*	1–12	UL V
KESWICK (Cumbria)	B2																
Castlerigg Manor Residential Youth Centre, Manor Brow, Keswick, CA12 4AR. Tel. (0596) 72711. Contact Booking Secretary,		✓	✓	✓	✓	– –	9	11	10	70	–	16	– *4.00*	– *5.50*	– *77.00*	1–12	V TV
THRELKELD (Cumbria)	B2																
† Blencathra Centre, Threlkeld, Keswick, CA12 4SG. Tel. (059 683) 601. Contact The Manager.		✓	✓	–	✓	– –	–	26	16	107	–	7	*2.60 *3.20*	– –	– –	1–12	UL
ULVERSTON (Cumbria)	B3																
Manjushri Institute, College for Buddhist Studies, Conishead Priory, LA12 9QQ. Tel. (0229) 54019. Contact Ms. Emily Streng, or Roy Tyson,		✓	✓	✓	✓	16 –	2	4	5	65	–	6	*2.80 *7.20*	*3.50 *7.90*	*39.60 *70.60*	1–12	UL V

You are advised to read the introductory notes and to check prices and other details when booking accommodation

A Guide to English Food & Drink

DID YOU KNOW that there are vineyards producing English WINE in more than 20 different counties in England? CHEESE-rolling festivals are still held in some English villages? Over 1,000 different BEERS are brewed in England? YORKSHIRE PUDDING Day is celebrated in Harrogate, Yorkshire on the 24th May? There's a GINGERBREAD Shop in Ashbourne, a MUSTARD Shop in Norwich and even a BAKEWELL PUDDING Shop in Bakewell?

...And where to enjoy it

These are just a hint of the fascinating details you'll find in this colourful new 148 page Guide to English Food and Drink.

Published by the English Tourist Board as part of the TASTE OF ENGLAND promotion, the 1982 Guide also lists hundreds of hotels, restaurants, pubs and teaplaces where you can find good traditional English fare. All are clearly marked on regional location maps, and details are also given of food fairs, drinks festivals and country gatherings where you can join in the local celebrations – and taste the produce.

You can even try out some of England's traditional dishes at home, by following the many tempting recipes given in the Guide.

Whether you are holidaying in England, travelling through the country on business or just enjoying a day out, keep this Guide with you – and your eyes open for the distinctive Taste of England symbol. Then you'll have a chance to enjoy the true flavour of England.

A GUIDE TO ENGLISH FOOD AND DRINK is available, price 95p, from bookshops, newsagents and most Tourist Information Centres or by post (plus 25p postage and packing) from the English Tourist Board, 4 Grosvenor Gardens, London SW1W 0DU.

Picture Guide to places to stay

Cumbria, English Lakeland, the most beautiful corner of England is one of the best known and best loved holiday areas in Britian. The National park has, for many years, been carefully protected to maintain its strikingly, unspoiled beauty.

Early spring daffodils, colourful masses of rhododendrons and azaleas throughout early summer, and the soft browns and greens of autumn contrasting with the changing light and colour of the lakes contribute to the romantic spectacle.
Less well known, but equally attractive, are the scenic Pennine foothills of the pastoral Eden Valley on the eastern side of Cumbria.

There are splendid beaches and magnificent views along the county's southern and western coastline with popular family resorts like Silloth on the shores of the Solway and Arnside (Vikings lair) which has retained its beauty by resisting massed tourist invasion for many years.

The Cathedral city of Carlisle is the gateway to Roman history along Hadrian's Wall, and in this north-eastern part of the county you will find many picturesque villages and country inns.

The county is full of excellent accommodation and all parts of the region are accessible easily during a long weekend or longer holiday. Wherever you go I think you will agree with me that Cumbria is "the most beautiful corner of England".

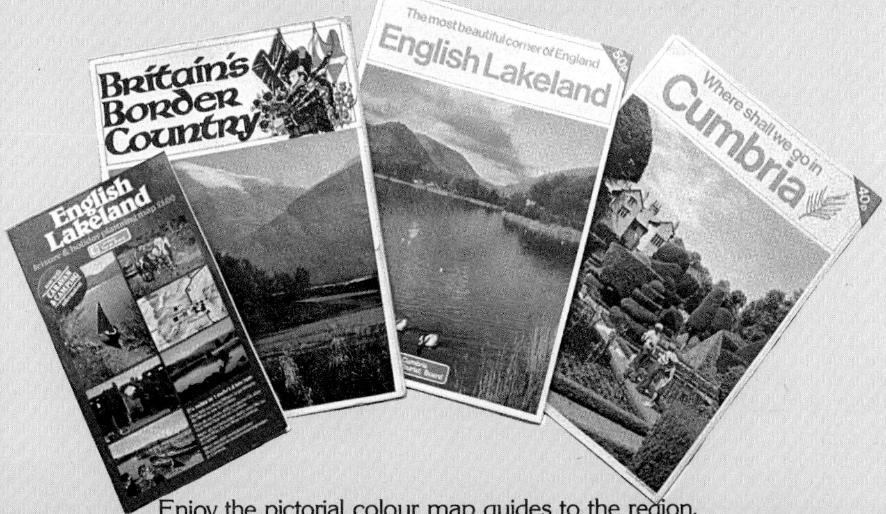

Enjoy the pictorial colour map guides to the region.
Order your copies on the publications order form at the back of this guide

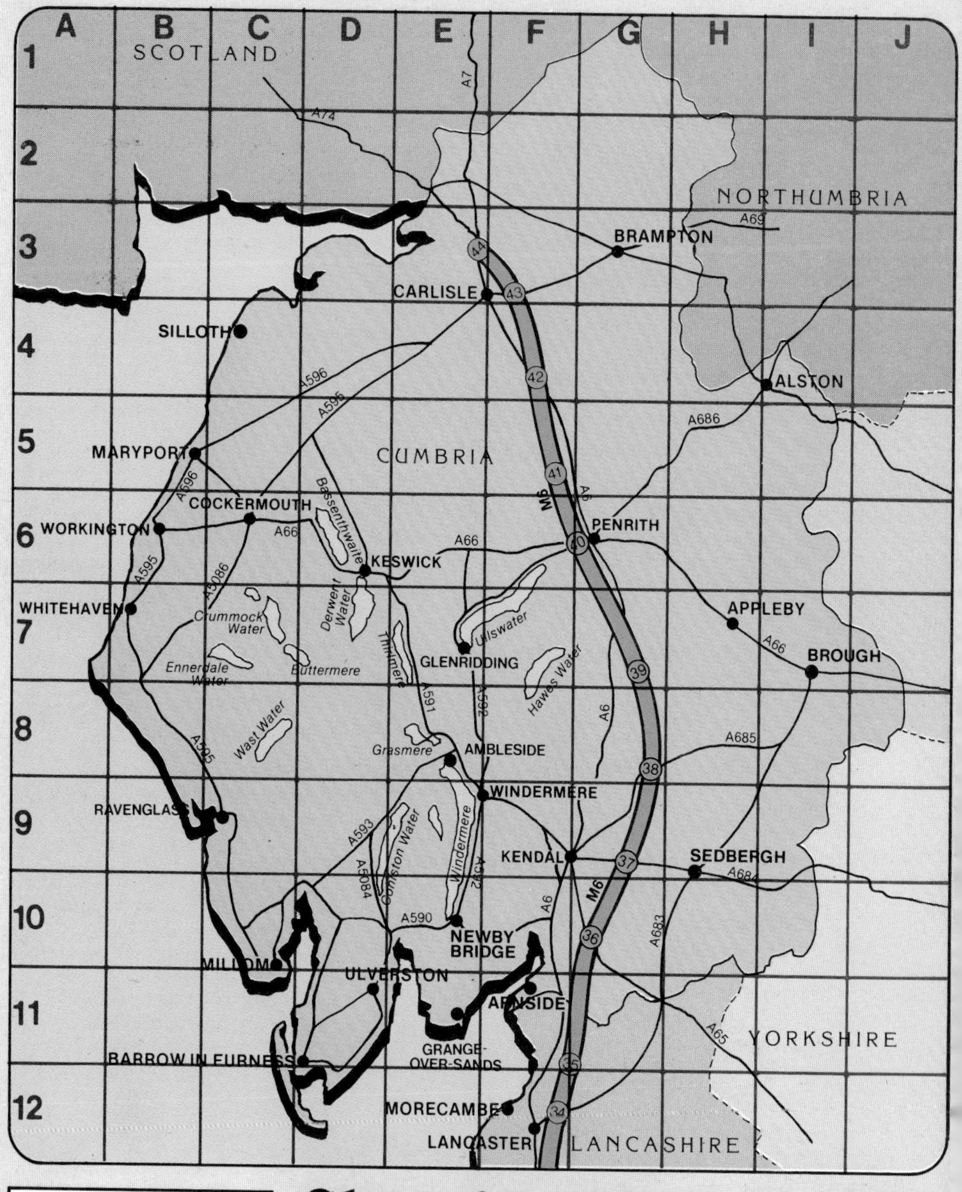

Choosing where to stay

On the next two pages there is an index listing every establishment in this section. You can choose from either self-catering holidays or hotels and guest-houses.

Against each entry you will find a map reference which, when you look at the grid on the map, will tell you where your hotel is. To the right of the index, there is a page number which will lead you directly to a full description of the accommodation of your choice.

All hotels, guest-houses and self-catering accommodation in this section would welcome your telephone call or letter requesting either further information or your holiday booking.

Self-catering holidays
(non-serviced accommodation)

Map Ref	Establishment	Page
F.9.	Applethwaite Luxury Apartments, WINDERMERE	46
F.5.	Arcos, HUTTON JOHN, Nr. Penrith	47
E.11.	Aynsome Manor Park, CARTMEL	51
G.5.	Banktop Courtyard, LAZONBY	49
E.9.	The Barn, Old Heathwaite, WINDERMERE	84
E.9.	Beaumont Luxury Flats, WINDERMERE	46
E.9.	Biskey Howe Flats, WINDERMERE	55
C.10.	Brockwood Park, BROUGHTON IN FURNESS	51
F.8.	Browfoot Farm, KENTMERE	96
	Border Holiday Homes	92 & 94
E.9.	Canterbury Flats, BOWNESS	44 & 45
	Cottage Life, SOUTH LAKELAND	90
	Country Holidays, CUMBRIA	56
D.11.	Crayrock, BARROW IN FURNESS	92
C.6.	Croft Cottages, COCKERMOUTH	53
E.8.	Dove Nest, WINDERMERE	55
G.5.	Eden Grove Holiday Cottages, LAZONBY, Nr. Penrith	53
D.11.	The Falls, MANSRIGGS, Nr Ulverston	56
D.7.	Fieldside Grange, KESWICK	90
C.8.	Greendale Flats, WASDALE	52
D.6.	Greta Side Court, KESWICK	87
F.9.	Heathwaite Howe, WINDERMERE	85
F.6.	High House, THACKTHWAITE	85
E.4.	Holiday cottage, Nr Carlisle, WELTON, Nr. Dalston	94
E.9.	Howe Foot Holiday Flats, WINDERMERE	95
G.3.	Long Byres, TALKIN HEAD, Nr. Brampton	49
E.11.	Longlands, CARTMEL	86
G.2.	Lynebank Holiday Cottages, ROADHEAD, Nr. Carlisle	91
	Mackays Agency, CUMBRIA	85
F.5.	The Manor, LOW HESKET, Nr. Carlisle	54
C.6.	Midtown Cottages & Brigham Farm, HIGH LORTON, Nr. Cockermouth & KESWICK	43
C.6.	Old Corn Mill PAPCASTLE Nr. Cockermouth	95
E.9.	Ottersholme, BOWNESS	51
F.9.	Plumgarths Holiday Flats CROOK, Nr. Kendal	49
	Self-Caterers Association, CUMBRIA	88 & 89
E.6.	Setmabanning Farm, THRELKELD, Nr. Penrith	90
E.9.	Spinnery Cottage, BOWNESS	47
	Stock Park Estate, CUMBRIA	50
E.4.	Welton Plaines, WELTON Nr Dalston	86
F.9.	Woodlea, WINSTER, Nr Bowness	55
E.9.	Wordsworth Court, BOWNESS-ON-WINDERMERE	56

Caravan & Camp Sites

Map Ref	Establishment	Page
F.9.	Ashes Lane Caravan Park, STAVELEY	84
F.6.	Beckses Caravan Park, PENRUDDOCK	93
B.7.	Inglenook Caravan Park, LAMPLUGH	94
E.11.	Lakeland Caravan Park FLOOKBURGH	92
D.6.	Low Briery Holiday Village, KESWICK	48
E.6.	Morte Point Caravans, THRELKELD & MUNGRISEDALE	91
	Rentacamp, CONISTON & STAVELEY	54
C.4.	Stanwix Park, SILLOTH	95
F.6.	Ullswater Caravan & Camp Site, ULLSWATER	47

Hotels & Guest Houses
(serviced accommodation)

Map Ref	Establishment	Page
D.6.	Acorn House Hotel, KESWICK	65
C.6.	Allerdale Court Hotel, COCKERMOUTH	42
D.6.	Allerdale House, KESWICK	57
E.9.	Applegarth Hotel, WINDERMERE	65
E.8.	Balla Wray Guest House, HIGH WRAY, Nr. Ambleside	30
D.6.	Bay Tree Guest House, KESWICK	76
E.8.	Becksteps Guest House, GRASMERE	81
E.9.	Beechwood Hotel, WINDERMERE	77
F.2.	Bessiestown Farm, PENTON, Nr Carlisle	72
F.10.	Blue Bell Hotel, HEVERSHAM, Nr. Milnthorpe	26
E.9.	Bordriggs Country House Hotel, WINDERMERE	12
D.7.	Borrowdale Gates Hotel, GRANGE IN BORROWDALE	76
E.9.	Boston House, WINDERMERE	58
E.9.	Braemount House, WINDERMERE	82
E.8	Broad Ings Country House, AMBLESIDE	37
E.9.	Brooklands Hotel, WINDERMERE	59
D.6.	Burleigh Mead & Hazeldene Hotels, KESWICK	33
E.9.	Burn How Motel, BOWNESS ON WINDERMERE	80
D.6.	Chaucer House Hotel, KESWICK	24
D.6.	Clarence House, KESWICK	60
D.6.	Coledale Inn, BRAITHWAITE, Nr Keswick	57
E.8.	Compston House, AMBLESIDE	33
E.9.	Crag Brow Cottage, BOWNESS ON WINDERMERE	66
D.6.	Cragside Guest House. KESWICK	63
E.9	Cranleigh Hotel, BOWNESS ON WINDERMERE	67
G.10.	Crooklands Hotel, CROOKLANDS	14
B.6.	Crossbarrow Motel, LITTLE CLIFTON	68
D.6.	Crow Park Hotel, KESWICK	41
I.4.	Cumberland Hotel, ALSTON	62
D.6.	Cumbria Hotel, KESWICK	63
E.4.	Dalston Hall Hotel, DALSTON	70
F.9.	Damson Dene Hotel, CROSTHWAITE, Nr Kendal	9
E.9.	Earlston Hotel, BOWNESS ON WINDERMERE	29
D.6.	Easdale Hotel, KESWICK	63
E.9.	Ellerthwaite Lodge Hotel, WINDERMERE	19
	English Lakes Hotels, AMBLESIDE BOWNESS · CROOK	31
	Farmhouse Accommodation Bookings CUMBRIA	82
E.9.	Fairfield Hotel, BOWNESS ON WINDERMERE	79
E.8.	The Gables Hotel, AMBLESIDE	13
E.8.	Ghyll Head Hotel, WATERHEAD, Ambleside	15
E.7.	Glenridding Hotel, GLENRIDDING, Ullswater	14
E.8.	Glen Rothay Hotel, RYDAL, Nr Ambleside	6
E.11.	Grammar Hotel, CARTMEL	71
E.11.	Grange Hotel, GRANGE OVER SANDS	40

Hotels & Guest Houses

(serviced accommodation)

Hotels & Guest Houses

(serviced accommodation)

NANNY BROW
COUNTRY HOUSE HOTEL

Ambleside, Cumbria. Tel. Ambleside (09663) 2036

Nanny Brow is peacefully set in 5 acres of gardens and woodland offering panoramic views down the Brathay Valley towards the Langdales yet only 1½ miles from the centre of Ambleside. Built in 1907 the hotel is a haven of gracious country house charm with up to date facilities including tea/coffee making in all bedrooms, full central heating and adjacent private car park. We also offer lawn tennis, croquet and private river fishing. The quality of our home cooked 6 course dinners is well known and personal service is our trademark. Residential licence

Commended by the British Tourist Authority.

Write or phone Geoff or Cheryl Kershaw for brochure and tariff. AA* RAC**

SCAFELL HOTEL

ROSTHWAITE, BORROWDALE, CUMBRIA CA12 5XB
Telephone: Borrowdale (059-684) 208

Situated in the heart of the Borrowdale Valley, just off the main road which goes on to Honister Pass and Buttermere, the Scafell Hotel was formerly a Coaching Inn frequented by travellers making the journey over Honister Pass from Keswick to Cockermouth.

Tastefully Modernised it still retains its old charm and character.
23 Bedrooms — Private Bathrooms Available — Our Dining Room/Restaurant (Open to Non Residents) is renowned for its Fine Food and Wines. Five Course Table D' Hote, A La Carte of Grill Menus available. Fully Licensed with Cocktail and Public (Riverside) Bar Selling Real Ale, both well noted for Bar Lunches.

EGON RONAY — ASHLEY COURTENAY — SIGNPOST RECOMMENDED

A British Tourist Authority commended Country Guest House

AA Listed RAC

THE MILL

Mungrisdale, Penrith
Cumbria CA11 0XR
Telephone Threlkeld (059683) 659

Delightfully situated at the foot of the mountains in grounds bounded by a trout stream, this former Mill Cottage (dated 1651) provides nine comfortable bedrooms, and all facilities for a relaxing holiday.

Pam and David Wood are the owners who ensure that only the best of freshly prepared appetising food is served, and a good selection of wines are available for their guests.

"We find they return for more — may we send you a brochure?"

The Glen Rothay

AA ** RAC

Rydal Nr. Ambleside

Facing peaceful Rydalwater, our 17th century Country House Hotel is the perfect location for touring the whole of Lakeland, or just relaxing with the hotel boats, bicycles, or a gentle stroll around the Lake. Golf facilities at Threlkeld are available free to guests.

Tasteful rooms of character, all with private facilities and superb traditional English cooking, using only the freshest of produce, ensure a pleasant and relaxing break or holiday.

For Honeymoons or that special occasion, we have two rooms with four-poster beds: the Rydal Suite with balcony overlooking the lake, and the Rothay Room. The house adjoins Dora's Field, immortalised by Wordsworth and has strong links with the Lake Poets.

BADGER BAR & GARDEN PATIO – REAL ALE – BARGAIN BREAKS

Feb. – June Nov. – Dec.

Please write or ring for brochure and tariff Ambleside (09663) 2524.

Iain and Sandra Garside — Resident proprietors.

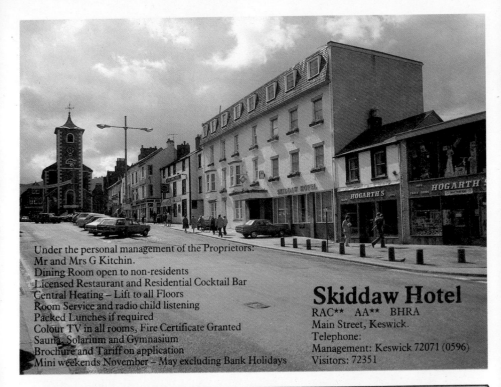

Under the personal management of the Proprietors:
Mr and Mrs G Kitchin.
Dining Room open to non-residents
Licensed Restaurant and Residential Cocktail Bar
Central Heating – Lift to all Floors
Room Service and radio child listening
Packed Lunches if required
Colour TV in all rooms, Fire Certificate Granted
Sauna, Solarium and Gymnasium
Brochure and Tariff on application
Mini weekends November – May excluding Bank Holidays

Skiddaw Hotel

RAC** AA** BHRA
Main Street, Keswick.
Telephone:
Management: Keswick 72071 (0596)
Visitors: 72351

Lindeth Fell Country House Hotel

Bowness-on-Windermere, Cumbria
Tel: Windermere (096 62) 3286 Visitors 4287
AA★★RAC★★ Ashley Courtenay and Signpost recommended

Lindeth Fell is a charming Country Mansion set in 6½ acres of landscaped gardens and ideally situated in the heart of English Lakeland.
Lindeth Fell offers its guests a unique relaxing and total atmosphere — with excellent varied cuisine and wine cellar.
Tea making facilities are provided, central heating throughout, ample car parking, lawn tennis, croquet, putting, fishing from our own tarn.
Open Feb. to Nov. Licensed. Colour brochure on request s.a.e. please.

DO YOU LIKE A Family run Hotel, with a truly caring personal service.
Quiet, fully modernised rooms with this view.
Being known by your name, not your room number.
Good fresh food, cooked with care.
Home made Bread, Cheese, and Jam.
If so, you will like:

HIGHFIELD HOTEL

AA **THE HEADS, KESWICK.** BTA RAC
Telephone: (0596) 72508.
Please ask Mr. & Mrs. C. M. Jordan for a Colour brochure.

The Hideaway Hotel

PHOENIX WAY, WINDERMERE
WINDERMERE (09662) 3070

This 2 star hotel is personally run by the owners, Tim and Jackie Harper. They have received a special award from the British Tourist Authority for their cuisine every year since 1978. Hearty meals and a fine selection of personally chosen wines are served by friendly staff in the elegant restaurant.

Log fires welcome you in the cosy bar and comfortable lounge and central heating is fitted throughout the hotel. All 11 bedrooms have private facilities.

Ideally hidden away down a quiet lane and away from the hustle and bustle, it is most centrally situated for all the amenities of this beautiful region.

Recommended by Ashley Courtenay Signpost, Les Routiers, and others, with special commendation from the British Tourist Authority.

Very reasonable rates for Reservations and brochures:

Windermere (09662) 3070

IVY HOUSE HOTEL

Hawkshead, Nr. Ambleside, Cumbria LA22 0NS
Telephone: Hawkshead 204

Resident Proprietors: Mr. & Mrs. C. J. Williams
Restaurant Licence AA Listed

A georgian residence of great character Ivy House is centrally situated in the quaint and attractive village of Hawkshead.
We are a family run Hotel with a friendly and informal atmosphere and good home cooking.
Motel type units with private facilities available for 4-6 people.

May we send you a brochure with full details. **Chris and Betty Williams.**

Riverside Hotel

Gilbert Scar, Under Loughrigg,
Ambleside, Cumbria LA22 9LJ.
Tel: Ambleside 2395 (Code 096-63)

A small Country Hotel, tastefully modernised throughout and beautifully situated in a lovely and peaceful riverside setting. Secluded on a quiet lane and yet only a few minutes walk from the centre of Ambleside. Personally supervised by the proprietors who provide delicious meals and every comfort in an atmosphere as friendly and relaxing as it is professional.

AA LICENSED RAC
Ashley Courtenay Recommended

Please 'phone or send stamp for Colour Brochure — Resident Proprietors Gillian and Alan Rhone

LANGSTRATH HOTEL

Stonethwaite, Borrowdale, Keswick, Cumbria
Tel: (059 684) 239

A small family-run hotel offering unique personal service.
Quietly situated with magnificent views. Ideal walking base.
Excellent home cooking and well-stocked bar.
Additional Self-catering facilities available.

Lyzzick Hall Hotel

Nr. Keswick. Tel: (0596) 72277

Residential Licence (Cellar Bar)

Large Car Park Swimming Pool

A charming Country House Hotel with excellent views of the Lakeland mountains and countryside.

Bedrooms (twins, doubles and family rooms, many with showers) are comfortable and well appointed.

A pleasant relaxing dining room where freshly cooked meals are served.

Comfortable, spacious lounges with pleasant outlooks, one with colour TV.

The heated swimming pool is situated in a sheltered part of the two acres of lawns and gardens.

The Hotel with its pleasant surroundings is ideal for restful and family holidays at reasonable terms.

We offer a pleasant & friendly welcome. Brochure and tariff on request. **SAE please to Mr. & Mrs. I. Atkinson.**

THE GABLES PRIVATE HOTEL

Compston Road
Ambleside, Cumbria LA22 9DJ

Situated in open position, overlooking the Park and Tennis Courts etc. and Loughrigg Fell. Within three minutes of the Bus Station and Bus Tour Centre for Drives throughout the Lake District. Convenient to the head of Lake Windermere for Boating, Launch or Steamer Trips

Two comfortable Lounges one with TV
Hot and cold water in all bedrooms.
Our aim is to give you satisfaction and comfort.
Home cooking and personal attention. Free Car Park.
Fire Certificate. Residential Licence.
Central Heating.

Telephone: Ambleside (09663) 3272

Resident Proprietors: Mr. and Mrs. K. Robinson
AA & RAC Listed

SEATOLLER HOUSE

Borrowdale, Keswick, Cumbria
Tel: Borrowdale (059 684) 218

Set in a sheltered position at the head of the unspoiled Borrowdale valley, Seatoller House is over 300 years old and has been a guest house for over a century. It is known for its homely, informal atmosphere and for its good food (residential licence). Modern facilities have not changed its traditional character. It is ideal for walkers who want easy access to the high hills, and as a centre from which to explore the Lakes.

Recommended in **The Good Hotel Guide.**

St Martin's Hotel

****AA Bowness-on-Windermere RAC ****
Telephone (09662) 3731

Situated in level surroundings in the village centre — close to the lake, boats and shops.

St Martin's is a family run, licensed hotel with a friendly atmosphere. There is central heating throughout and some rooms have private bathrooms. Fresh home cooked food is served and a wide choice of dishes are offered for each meal.

We are happy to cater for special diets and for the need of children.

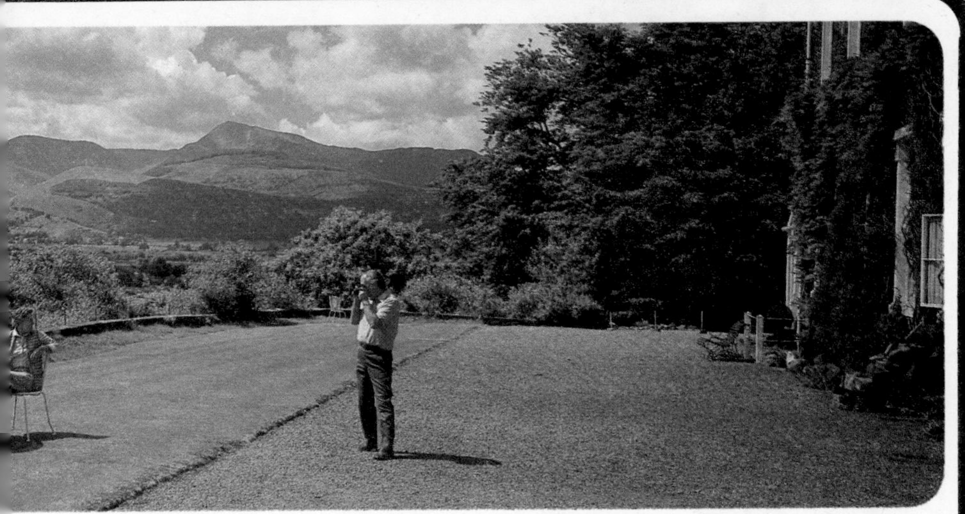

The Hotel can promise a carefree holiday in the most beautiful of surroundings with ample facilities on our premises including spacious lounges, one with television, and a cosy downstairs bar adjoining billiards and table tennis rooms. Outside in the extensive informal gardens and woods there is a putting green which is very popular after dinner on warm evenings, a swimming pool and even an adventure tree for exploring children.

Although the Lake District is so compact that it can be enjoyed without excessive driving, we are able to help guests plan a variety of alternative excursions using public transport on land and water while short outings can be arranged with our mini-bus. Weekday golf on the recently opened nine holes of the Keswick Golf Club and use of our little sailboat on Derwentwater are both available free of charge while for those wishing to walk we are able to assist with advice and suggestions.

Please write or telephone (0596-72211) for our Brochure and Tariff for the coming year which we will be pleased to send by return together with other information on facilities available for our guests.

Children and dogs are especially welcome

Leeming Country House Hotel

Ullswater,
Watermillock
Cumbria

24 Bedrooms
All baths en suite

Tel: Pooley Bridge
(Code 08536) 444

Non Residents
Welcome

A warm welcome awaits all guests arriving at Leeming, a truly magnificent Georgian House on the shores of Lake Ullswater. Arguably the most beautiful setting for a Hotel, unsurpassed in England, and yet situated just 6 miles from the M6 Motorway Junction 40. Leeming House is run by the resident owners Mike and Ginny Fitzpatrick, with enormous help from the young and friendly staff. The Hotel is luxuriously furnished throughout and the English Cuisine and Continental Wines superb. The grounds amounting to 20 acres of formal gardens and natural woodland extend to the Lake shore where sailing, water ski-ing, wind surfing and Trout fishing are immediately at hand, while Penrith Golf Club (par 69) is within easy reach.

Hillsdale Hotel

Church Street, Ambleside

Tel: Ambleside (09663) 3174
Resident Proprietors: Allan and Margaret Crombie

This is a small family run hotel centrally situated in Ambleside. The clean, well equipped rooms and friendly, attentive service ensure a relaxing holiday.

We have an excellent reputation for home cooked meals with interesting menus making this one of the best hotels in the Lake District. Please send S.A.E. for Brochure and Tariff.

AA and RAC Listed
Central Heating in all rooms.

Rothay Manor

Hotel & Restaurant
Ambleside, Cumbria, LA22 0EH
Tel: Ambleside (096-63) 3605

Egon Ronay, Signpost, Ashley Courtenay
*AA***RAC*
B.T.A. Commended Country House Hotel

Bronwen Nixon and her two sons invite you to their well-known Hotel and Restaurant in the heart of the English Lakes. This elegant Regency House has 12 comfortable bedrooms, all with private bathroom, colour TV, GPO telephone and central heating. The relaxed atmosphere of the Hotel and its renowned Restaurant make it ideal for the discerning guest. Non-residents are most welcome. Open March to December inclusive, with reduced rates in the winter.
Every day we serve Morning Coffee, Buffet Lunch 12.30-2.00, Afternoon Tea and Dinner 7.30-9.00 p.m.

★ Ample parking.
★ Central heating.
★ Close to bowling, putting, tennis, etc.
★ Laundry and drying facilities
★ Close to all amenities.
★ Open all year.
★ Fire certificate.

AA & RAC Listed

Rothay Garth Hotel

Licensed

Ambleside
ENGLISH LAKELAND
Telephone: Ambleside 2217 (STD 09663)

Resident Proprietors: David and Margaret Parott, David and Jill Smith.
A warm welcome awaits you in this charming family run hotel in its own grounds, with delightful views over fells. We aim to make everyone's stay a pleasant and happy one, with friendly service and good home cooking.

SAWREY HOUSE

Private Hotel: Residential Licence
Telephone: Hawkshead 387

Set in the heart of beautiful Lakeland this delightful house stands in its own grounds in a prominent position overlooking Esthwaite Water and Coniston Fell.

Very peaceful and quiet, the hotel offers friendly service and good food. There are twelve bedrooms with hot and cold water.

Colour Brochure on request to the proprietors:
Mr. and Mrs. W. D. Lambert
Sawrey House, SAWREY, Nr. Ambleside, Cumbria.
RAC and AA Listed

AA RAC

★ *Colour television*
★ *Restaurant*
★ *Residential licence*
★ *Comfortable bar lounge*
★ *Children welcome*
★ *Private parking*
★ *Fire certificate*

Waterhead, Ambleside,
Cumbria LA22 0HD

Telephone: Ambleside (09663) 2219

A small family hotel set in spacious gardens with magnificent views over Windermere Lake from all rooms.

A warm and friendly atmosphere with good English cooking.

Resident Proprietors: Joyce E. Boow and Doris E. Nevinson.

SCALE HILL HOTEL

Loweswater, Nr. Cockermouth, Cumbria CA13 9UX

Telephone: Lorton (090085) 232 **Cockermouth 6 miles** **Keswick 12 miles**

Resident Proprietors: M. E. & S. Thompson

A 17th century Coaching Inn with all modern comforts situated in the quiet and beautiful Loweswater Valley where no coaches and caravans are allowed. Quality English food and hospitality in a peaceful area containing 3 lakes and some magnificent scenery. 13 bedrooms (6 with private bath) Fully licensed.

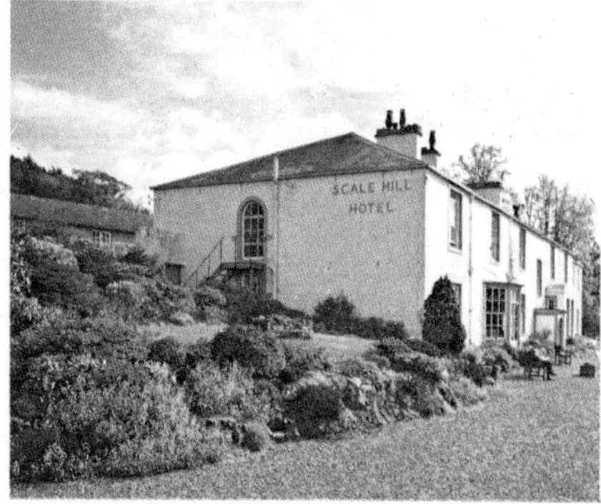

HOTEL

AA Listed

The Smallwood Private Hotel

Compston Road,
Ambleside LA22 9DJ
Telephone: Ambleside
(09663) 2330

Resident proprietors:
Mr. & Mrs. T. E. Armitstead

A small family run hotel, occupying a central position in this pleasant village in the heart of the Lake District.

- ★ ***Only two minutes walk from bus station***
- ★ ***Coach tours leave nearby***
- ★ ***Near to parks and cinema***
- ★ ***Two lounges — one with colour TV***
- ★ ***Separate dining tables***
- ★ ***Central Heating***
- ★ ***Free car parking space***

Friendly service and excellent food with quality and presentation given priority. These are just some of the things which make the Smallwood so highly recommended with a high percentage of returning guests. Further details on request.

Rydal Lodge

As a small family Hotel, we offer:

Friendly personal service
Good English cooking
Comfortable lounges and bedrooms

Pleasant riverside gardens and a central situation

also
Table licence, car park, colour television.

Relax in a country house atmosphere in the heart of Lakeland

Please send for our free brochure:

Mr. & Mrs. E. Warren and family, Rydal, Ambleside, Cumbria LA22 9LR
Telephone: Ambleside (09663) 3208

AA LISTED RAC*

You see the best of Lakeland from Mount Charlotte.

Here are three of the most attractive and distinctive hotels in the whole Lake District. They're in three of the very best spots for enjoying this beautiful region. Each has its own very special style and character. And each gives you the friendly, attentive service that's the hallmark of all Mount Charlotte Hotels.

The George Hotel
AA ** RAC

St John Street, Keswick-on-Derwentwater, Cumbria. Tel: (0596) 72076

The George is a charming 16th century coaching inn, in the centre of Keswick: a perfect base for exploring the beautiful northern lakes and mountains.

The hotel has just 17 comfortable rooms. Its excellent meals, and the real ale served in the bar, have repeatedly earned The George a place in the "Good Pub Guide".

The Prince of Wales Hotel
AA *** RAC

Grasmere, Cumbria.
Tel: (09665) 666

This elegant "country house" style hotel stands in nine acres of its own grounds on the shore of Grasmere itself.

The Prince of Wales is renowned for its excellent cuisine. Each of its 81 bedrooms has a private bathroom, radio, telephone and colour TV.

The Windermere Hydro Hotel
AA *** RAC

Helm Road, Bowness-on-Windermere, Cumbria. Tel: (09662) 4455

A palatial Edwardian hotel, fully yet tastefully modernised, the Hydro stands above the lakeside village of Bowness, commanding a breathtaking view of the lake and mountains beyond.

Each of its 96 luxurious bedrooms has a private bathroom, radio, telephone and colour TV.

Elsewhere in the North of England, and throughout the best parts of Britain, there are 25 other, equally distinctive Mount Charlotte hotels. For details, write to us at 2 The Calls, Leeds LS2 7JU, or phone (0532) 444866.

MYLNE BRIDGE

AA RAC Licensed

Spacious Lounge
Private Facilities
Central Heating
Car Park

Our charming well appointed Hotel is situated in a quiet central position. We offer you a pleasant comfortable holiday with personal service in a warm friendly atmosphere, which combined with our enjoyable home cooking is well recommended by our many regular guests.

For Tariff and Colour Brochure Contact:

JOHN & MARGARET MATTINSON,
LAKE ROAD, WINDERMERE CUMBRIA.
Telephone: (096 62) 3314

Balla Wray Country Guest House

High Wray, Nr. Ambleside, Telephone Ambleside (09663) 3308

Set within 2 acres of beautiful gardens overlooking Lake Windermere. Fishing off own private jetty. Very peaceful and quiet. Balla Wray is surrounded by National Trust land providing ideal walking area. A good centre for the motorist to tour the Lakes.
Hawkshead 2½ miles, Ambleside 4 miles
All bedrooms have own key, H & C, razor points, bedside lights and heating.
Spacious lounge, colour TV, central heating and log fires when necessary. Children welcome, although no facilities for children under 5. Bed, breakfast and evening meal. Self-catering cottage also available.

Please send stamp for brochure to: Mr. & Mrs. B Counsell. AA Listed.

Wild Boar Hotel

Crook, Nr. Windermere

Telephone Windermere (09662) 5225

Dating back to the 18th century the hotel has been tastefully modernised and yet retains its old world charm. Standing in its own grounds amidst the fells one can enjoy a complete air of tranquility and yet be only 3 miles from Bowness with all its sporting activities and 1 mile from Windermere Golf Club. 38 bedrooms, all with private bath/shower & colour TV. The hotel has an established reputation for the finest food coupled with an excellent cellar. A British Tourist Authority Commended Country Hotel and recommended by Egon Ronay and Ashley Courtenay AA***RAC

Waterhead Hotel

Ambleside Cumbria

Telephone Ambleside (09663) 2566

Delightfully situated on the shore of Lake Windermere at Waterhead Bay with superb mountain and lake views. 30 well appointed bedrooms. All with private bath/shower, colour TV. Radio, GPO telephones and intercom to reception office in all bedrooms. Elegant lounges, fully licensed, Stringers Bar, Cocktail Bar. Ample car parking. Hotel recently modernised AA***RAC

Low Wood Hotel

Windermere Cumbria

Telephone Ambleside (09663) 3338 Telex 65273

Low Wood is situated in a setting of unsurpassed natural beauty, standing on the banks of the northern end of Windermere and possessing an unrivalled view of England's highest mountains. There are spacious lawns and gardens running down to the edge of the lake for the private use of hotel guests.

The hotel possesses half a mile of lake frontage with boat launching and mooring facilities and car parking for 200 cars. There are 96 bedrooms, 66 with private bath. The hotel, apart from the usual facilities, has a separate a la carte Restaurant where last orders are taken up to 10.00 p.m. AA***RAC

There are also 8 self-catering flats.

Royal Hotel

Bowness-on-Windermere Cumbria

Telephone Windermere (09662) 3045 or 5267

The ideal hotel for the centre of Lake District activities situated in the heart of Bowness. 100 yards from the lake. The hotel with its own small private gardens has 29 bedrooms, all with private bath/shower, radio and colour TV. The hotel has a separate intimate grill room serving a la carte meals with last orders taken up to 10.30 p.m. A friendly reception and comfortable accommodation awaits you at the Royal Hotel which has been elegantly modernised within. AA**RAC

English Lakes Hotels

Linthwaite Country House Hotel

A Lakeland Hotel with an established reputation for providing the highest standards of cuisine, service, comfort and cleanliness. Set in eight acres of beautiful gardens with magnificent views of Lake Windermere and surrounding mountains.

Bowness-on-Windermere, Cumbria LA23 3JA
Tel: Windermere (096 62), Reception 3688, Residents 2321

Langdales Hotel

Great Langdale, Ambleside English Lakes

A comfortable Country Hotel, with home cooked fresh food and friendly service.

Non residents most welcome

One of the original BTA commended Country House Hotels.

Resident Proprietors: Mr. and Mrs. K. L. Farrar
Tel: Langdale (096-67) 253
AA★★★RAC

Burleigh Mead & Hazeldene Hotels

The Heads, Keswick, Cumbria, CA12 5ER

Beautifully and centrally situated with fine open views over Derwentwater and the Borrowdale and Newlands Valleys. Close to the town centre yet only a few minutes walk from the Lakeside and Friars Crag. Ideal centre for walking and touring. Write or telephone Keswick (0596) 72106 for colour brochure and tariff.

COMPSTON HOUSE HOTEL

Compston Road, Ambleside, English Lakes

(RES. LICENCE)

Compston House is a cheerful and homely hotel overlooking the Mini-Golf and Tennis Courts with fine views of Loughrigg. Close to the bus station, shops and within walking distance of the Lake. There are 10 bedrooms, all well appointed and heated. We will make you very welcome and endeavour to make your holiday a comfortable and happy one. Children sharing parents room, half price.

Generous reductions for a week's stay and a special low season tariff and winter programme. Packed lunches, Morning coffee, Fire certificate, look at these plus features.

A tray of tea on arrival : Early-morning tea making facilities : All rooms heated : Access to your rooms all day : Full English breakfast : A three course dinner plus coffee : ALL INCLUDED IN THE PRICE

Send for our Colour Brochure and Tariff — and be pleasantly surprised.

Telephone: Ambleside (09663) 2305 Reception 3663 Visitors

Be our guests: Christine and Alan Walker.

Lindeth Howe

COUNTRY HOUSE HOTEL

Lindeth Howe licensed luxury country house hotel is set in a beautiful peaceful part of Bowness. Personal service is guaranteed, candlelit dinners, log fires, excellent traditional English meals. Superb Lake views, tea and coffee in all bedrooms, and a beautiful large garden just 5 minutes walk from the Lake.

For brochures and tariff please contact the resident proprietors:

CLIVE and EILEEN BAXTER

Lindeth Howe Country House Hotel, Storrs Park, Bowness-on-Windermere, Cumbria LA23 3JF
Telephone: Windermere (09662) 5759

The Skelwith Bridge Hotel

Skelwith Bridge, Nr. Ambleside, Cumbria
LA22 9JN English Lakes.
Tel: Ambleside 2115 (STD 09663)

A 17th Century Lakeland Inn **AA RAC**

Originally a 17th Century Inn, this friendly Hotel is fully licensed with oak beamed lounges, open log fires and serving wholesome food with a varied wine list. Standing at the gateway to the lovely Langdale Valley this makes it an ideal centre from which to explore our beautiful Lakeland.

Non-Residents are welcome for morning coffee, Bar meals are available lunchtime and evening and Dinners.

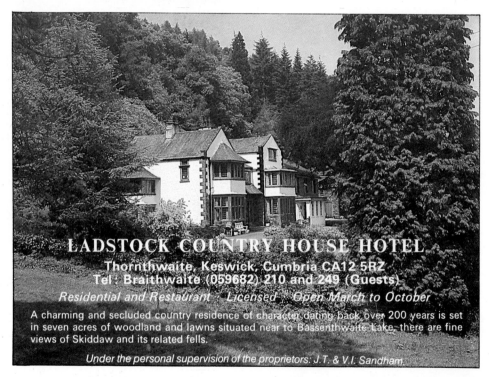

LADSTOCK COUNTRY HOUSE HOTEL

Thornthwaite, Keswick, Cumbria CA12 5RZ
Tel: Braithwaite (059682) 210 and 249 (Guests)

Residential and Restaurant · Licensed · Open March to October

A charming and secluded country residence of character dating back over 200 years is set in seven acres of woodland and lawns situated near to Bassenthwaite Lake, there are fine views of Skiddaw and its related fells.

Under the personal supervision of the proprietors: J.T. & V.I. Sandham.

New Dungeon Ghyll Hotel

G. Langdale, nr. Ambleside

The hotel is situated in one of the most beautiful corners of English Lakeland at the very foot of the famous Langdale Pikes and Dungeon Ghyll Waterfalls.

Open March to Nov. Good food & wines
19 bedrooms Bar Snacks — Teas

Children and Pets welcome.

Brochure on request S.A.E. please

Personally run by owners Pauline & John Booth

Langdale 213

**AA

Millfield Hotel

RAC**

Penrith Road, Keswick, Cumbria CA12 4HB. Telephone: Keswick (0596) 72099.
Manager: Mr. K. G. Fairbairn

The Millfield Hotel has a long established reputation for good food and efficient service, both of which will be appreciated by visitors to Keswick in the very heart of the Lake District.
The Hotel is well situated overlooking the river and Fitz Park but only a few minutes stroll from the town centre with the shores of Derwentwater just beyond. Visitors touring the Lakes by car will find Keswick the ideal centre but within a few miles from town in all directions, the beauty and splendour of the lakes, rivers and mountains provide the perfect setting for a relaxing holiday.
The Millfield Hotel has twenty-five bedrooms (six with private bathroom), a lift to all floors, ample car parking, spacious lounges, bar and elegant dining room all under the personal supervision of the Manager to ensure guests of a warm welcome, thoughtful hospitality and excellent food.

PRIVATE HOTEL

IN THE HEART OF THE LAKES

Tel: WINDERMERE 3239

WE *are quietly situated in spacious grounds, some 10 mins. walk from the lake shore, Bowness village and main tourist & recreation facilities.*
EXCELLENT CUISINE *is offered from a great variety of home cooked dishes, all prepared from fresh local produce and herbs grown in the garden – A hearty English breakfast starts the day. Every comfort and warm hospitality awaits you in our well furnished Country House Hotel.*
NEW PATRONS *are invited to send for colour brochure and sample menus.*

R. E. & G. E. SURTEES, OAKFOLD PRIVATE HOTEL,
BERESFORD ROAD, BOWNESS-ON-WINDERMERE, CUMBRIA LA23 2JG

HAZEL BANK HOTEL

ROSTHWAITE, BORROWDALE, CUMBRIA CA12 5XB

Proprietors: Mr. & Mrs. Doherty & Family.
Residential Licence. **Borrowdale (059684) 248**

This charming old country house stands in 3½ acres of garden and woodland, 200 yards from the main road and at the foot of the Watendlath path. This was the site chosen by Sir Hugh Walpole as the setting for his noval 'Rogue Herries' as well as the birth place of Judith Paris.
We are situated in one of England's loveliest and most peaceful valleys – overlooking the picturesque village of Rosthwaite – with uninterupted views of the mountains which form the very heart of the Lake District.
Whether you decide to visit us in Spring, Summer or Autumn, Hazel Bank Hotel provides a comfortable home for our guests – either walking or touring by car. Four of our bedrooms are provided with private W.C. and showers and the Hotel is under the personal supervision of the resident proprietors.

---

overlooking the peaceful unspoilt

Eden Valley

Prospect Hill Hotel

KIRKOSWALD BY PENRITH

Telephone: Lazonby (076883) **500**

20 minutes off the M6

A farm building complex meticulously converted by the owners between 1974 and 1980.
Red sandstone walls, oak timbers and antiques, combined with taste, quality, service and 'uniqueness'.
. . . . . . but no words from us will get you here . . . . . .
we simply state . . . . .
1979 AA Award Winner · Ashley Courtenay '80-'81-'82 · BTA Restaurant commended '81-'82 ·
Member of Guestaccom '80-'81-'82 (the family of small quality hotels)

Knoll Hotel

LAKE ROAD
Bowness-on-Windermere, Cumbria LA23 2JF
B.H.R.C.A. *AA *RAC
Magnificent views overlooking Lake Windermere

Comfort & Warmth	Peace & Quiet
Good Home Cooking	Cosy Cocktail Bar
Secluded Parking Space	(in own grounds)
Full Fire Certificate	Central Heating

Brochure upon application
Telephone Windermere 3756
Personally supervised by the Resident Owners
Mrs. R. Pinchbeck & Mr. & Mrs. D. Berry

Lane Head Farm

Troutbeck Penrith Cumbria Threlkeld 220

Proprietors Christine and Peter Fellows

A 17th century typical Lakeland farmhouse situated 250 yards from main A66 midway between Penrith and Keswick. Outstanding panoramic views of Lakeland countryside with an attractive garden. The farmhouse has maintained its old character. The bedrooms have been tastefully decorated, with hot and cold water and shaver points (one double and three family). A guest lounge with colour TV and a large diningroom. A feature and one of the attractions of Lane Head is the high standard of food. A large breakfast and a five-course evening meal for healthy appetites on returning from the day's activities.

We will be happy to supply further details.

Allerdale Court Hotel

Market Square, Cockermouth, Cumbria

Telephone: (STD Code 0900) 823654

Dating back to the 17th Century the Allerdale Court Hotel with its genuine oak panelling, beamed ceiling and antique furnishings is a natural setting to enjoy both our wide selection of Traditional Beers and Gourmet French Cooking of our "Pickwick Restaurant".

We have two comfortable lounge bars, a beer garden, TV lounge, and 27 Bedrooms, 17 with Private bath "en suite", all with central heating, radio and tea making facilities.

Centrally situated in the old market square it makes an ideal base to cover the Lake District, the Border Country and the West Cumbria coast. Open all year round, reduced rates close season.

Write or phone for brochure and quotation to Allerdale Court Hotel

PRIVATE RESIDENTIAL HOTEL RAC ★★ FULLY LICENSED FREE HOUSE

Oak Bank Hotel

A well appointed 12 bedroomed hotel, 9 with private facilities, situated in the famous Village of Grasmere, ***(heart of the Lakes).***

The hotel is personally run by the proprietors, Cordon Bleu cooking complemented by a personally chosen wine list.

The accent is on friendly hospitality, open March – November, with reduced rates out of season.

A colour brochure, tariff will gladly be sent on application to:

Attilio & Sharon Savasi,
Oak Bank Hotel, Grasmere,
Cumbria LA22 9TA. Tel: (09665) 217.

MIDTOWN COTTAGES HIGH LORTON, BUTTERMERE VALLEY

EGON RONAY RECOMMENDED

High Lorton is on the Western side of Whinlatter Pass and whilst near several lakes and the high mountains, has remained unspoilt. It is a proper village with a community life, and a pub and village shop in both High & Low Lorton. Between Cockermouth & Keswick, Lorton is only 40 minutes from the motorway but is another world. We provide linen towels, colour TV and we hope everything you need. Recently converted, each cottage has two twin bedded rooms, a bathroom with entrance lobby on the ground floor, and upstairs, a large living room, with dining area and separate kitchen.

Midtown Cottages

BRIGHAM FARM, KESWICK

Newly completed, sleeping 2/4, there are six comfortable flats, well equipped and furnished, and although only ½ mile from the town centre are pleasantly secluded. Keswick is the natural centre of the Lake District, is the hub of the public transport system and allows you to reach any part of the Lake District quickly, with or without your car. Again we provide linen, towels, colour TV and we hope everything you need.

Cottage Living Room

Bargain breaks in Winter.
Personal supervision.
Completely self contained.
Linen & towels provided.
Open all year.
Inspected and approved by the Cumbria & Lakeland Self Caterers Association and "A.A."
For further details and prices, see our line entry in this publication.

OLGA & NEIL HUNTER
12, DERWENT STREET, KESWICK,
CUMBRIA CA12 5AN
Tel: (0596) 74392
(7 Day answering)

Brigham Farm

Canterbury Flats

Quarry Rigg Bowness-on-Windermere Cumbria

AA Listed Member of Cumbria and Lakeland Self-Caterers' Association

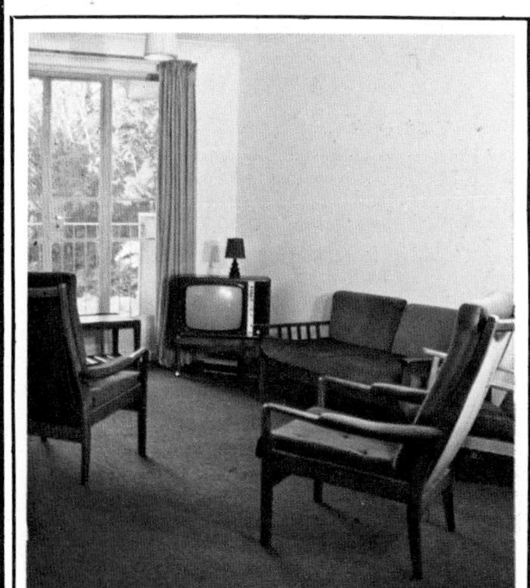

Part of a new development, providing a choice of 22 self-contained flats for holiday lettings, built in the grounds of an old house in the centre of the lakeside village of Bowness.

Lake Windermere, with its rowing boats, steamer pier and glorious views, is less than 5 minutes walk away.

Well furnished, fully equipped
Colour Television in each lounge
All-electric kitchens and hot water
Twin or double beds, plus extra folding Z-beds. Night storage and supplementary heaters. Bathroom with W.C. and shaver point. Cot/high chair can be hired.
Private entrances. Garage or Parking space. Dogs accepted in some flats.
Pay-phone for Canterbury Flat tenants.
Rents include off-peak heating.

Weekly lettings all-year-round.
Short stays of two nights or longer Nov. — March, weekends or mid-week.

Bed linen at no extra cost provided on weekly lettings, or can be hired for short breaks.

Most of the flats in Quarry Rigg will sleep from 2-4 persons (1-bedroomed flats) or from 4-6 persons (2-bedroomed flats). The somewhat larger 2-bedroomed flats in Qurry Rigg Centre sleep up to 6 or 7 persons, look out towards the lake on one side and over the new shopping precinct (reached from Lake Road) on the other. The largest Canterbury Flats are in Quarry Rigg, contain 3 bedrooms and 2 bathrooms, and sleep from 6-9 persons.
Colour brochure (S.A.E. please) from H. E. & S. A. Betham, Flat 41A Quarry Rigg, Windermere, Cumbria. Tel: Windermere (09662) 5216 or Canterbury (0227) 69803.

BEAUMONT LUXURY HOLIDAY FLATS

THORNBARROW ROAD, WINDERMERE LA23 2DG

Tel: Windermere (09662) 5144

Beaumont stands in its own grounds with extensive views of the central fells.

It is a Lakeland stone house divided into self-contained flats for 2-5 people.

All our units are fully equipped to a high standard.

Quiet surroundings
Parking in grounds
Convenient for public transport
Gas central heating
Colour television
Linen provided
Short stays of two nights or more in winter.

ALSO – NEW FOR 1982 –

Three luxury one-bedroom bungalows specially designed for the disabled, suitable for 2-3 people.

Member of Cumbria and Lakeland Self-Caterers' Association.

AA Listed

Illustrated brochure (S.A.E. please) from the Proprietors

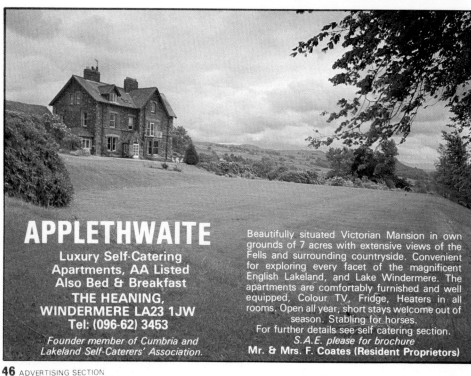

APPLETHWAITE

Luxury Self-Catering Apartments, AA Listed
Also Bed & Breakfast

THE HEANING, WINDERMERE LA23 1JW

Tel: (096-62) 3453

Founder member of Cumbria and Lakeland Self-Caterers' Association.

Beautifully situated Victorian Mansion in own grounds of 7 acres with extensive views of the Fells and surrounding countryside. Convenient for exploring every facet of the magnificent English Lakeland, and Lake Windermere. The apartments are comfortably furnished and well equipped, Colour TV, Fridge, Heaters in all rooms. Open all year, short stays welcome out of season. Stabling for horses.

For further details see self catering section.

S.A.E. please for brochure

Mr. & Mrs. F. Coates (Resident Proprietors)

ULLSWATER AREA

'Arcos', Hutton John,
Penrith, Cumbria.

Reservations: Raymond Cowperthwaite.
Tel: Greystoke (08533) 300.

2 cottages and 2 bungalows. Sleep from 4 to 6 people. Open all year Price range from £75-£160.
Poplar House and Ivy Cottage are situated in the small, peaceful hamlet of Hutton John beside river and woodlands. Furnished and fitted to a high standard with central heating and radiators in all rooms. Continental quilts provided. Rates include electricity and heating
D.G.P.TV.Y.

In the Lake District National park, and under the personal supervision of Proprietors: Mr. & Mrs. D. Dobinson & Sons.

Tents and Touring Pitches.
Separate enclosure for Caravans.
Toilets, Showers, Washer,
Drier, Shop & Licensed Bar.

Self Contained Holiday Houses & Caravans with mains services.

The Ullswater

Caravan Camping & Marine Park.
Watermillock
Penrith
Cumbria

New Childrens Playground

For further particulars & Colour Brochure
Tel: 08536-666
9 am-10 pm

Members of N.F.S.O., A.A., C.T.B., C.C. of Gt. Britain, A.C.S.I.

Lakeside Picnic Area
Boat launching and Motor & Rowing boats for hire.

SELF-CATERING

BOWNESS-ON-WINDERMERE

200 years old Spinnery converted into delightful holiday flats.
Near village and lake yet quiet and secluded.
Bargain Winter Breaks

Bob and Joan Allman-Smith
Spinnery Cottage, Fairfield,
Brantfell Road, Bowness-on-Windermere

Tel: 09662 4884.

"Founder member of Cumbria and Lakeland Self-Caterers' Association."

Low Briery

HOLIDAY VILLAGE

(1½ MILES FROM THE CENTRE OF KESWICK)

EXCELLENTLY APPOINTED

CARAVAN 'HOLIDAY HOMES'

FLATS AND COTTAGES

Set in a peaceful and secluded situation in wooded country with the River Greta flowing alongside and the Lakeland fells towering above.

MAINS WATER, SEWERAGE & ELECTRICITY

Brochures (large S.A.E. please)

GREY ABBEY PROPERTIES LTD (ELLB)
PO BOX 23, COACH RD, WHITEHAVEN, CUMBRIA

Tel: WHITEHAVEN (0946) 3773 – 24 hr. answering service

CLOSE TO HADRIAN'S WALL

LONG BYRES

Talkin Head, Brampton.

Self-Catering Houses (sleep 2-6) on North Pennine Hill Farm. Special facilities include: Farm Shop with Home Cooked Foods, Riding Ponies. Golf and Boating within 3 miles. Excellent for touring Border Country and Lake District.

Winner of British Tourist Authority Award of Merit

Apply: Susan Dean, Kirkhouse, Brampton, Cumbria.
Tel: Hallbankgate (06976) 262.

BANKTOP COURT YARD

A traditional Cumbrian Bank Barn recently converted to four self contained luxury holiday houses, retaining the character of the original Barn and Cobbled Courtyard.

Accommodating from 4-6 persons these houses offer all the amenities expected from a first class establishment including Colour Television. Set in its own grounds, in the village of Lazonby in the beautiful Eden Valley. The Lakes, Dales, North Pennines and Scottish Border Country are all within easy reach. Fishing is available in the River Eden.

Founder Member of Cumbria Self-Caterers' Association

For Brochure and Tariff:
Mrs. Mary Carlyle, Banktop House, Lazonby, Penrith CA10 1AQ.
Telephone: Lazonby (076 883) 268

Between Kendal and Windermere
Open All Year
5 Spacious Flats — Garden Chalet
Sleep 2-6
Central Heating, TV.,
3 acres secluded grounds.

Mr. and Mrs. Jonathan Somervell,
Crook, Kendal, Cumbria LA8 8LE
Tel: Staveley (0539) 821325
evenings

For full details see:
Self-Catering Section — Kendal.
Founder Member Cumbria and Lakeland
Self-Caterers' Association.

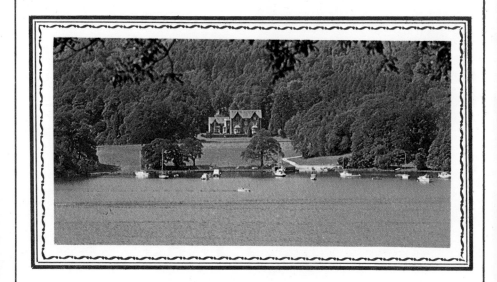

Aynsome Manor Park

Cartmel, Cumbria LA11 6HH
Telephone 044 854 433

Luxury self contained holiday flats, all electric, TV, fridge, bathroom etc. Extensive secluded gardens and grounds with historic Monks Fish Pond.

OTTERSHOLME

Storrs Park, Bowness-on-Windermere

Beautiful luxurious cottage, secluded and **with own private lake frontage**, offers self catering at highest standard.

(Rates from £150 per week)

Also available at Storrs Park — Granton Lodge.

(Rates from £84 per week)

SAE for full details from:

Mrs. L. C. Sinfield, Storrsthwaite, Storrs Park, Bowness-on-Windermere, Cumbria LA23 3LF, or telephone 0448 60394

Brockwood Park Norwegian Lodges

The most luxurious and imaginative self-catering development in the country.

Especially attractive rates for Winter weekends and midweek breaks.

Central Heating : Triple Glazing

Colour Television : Video : Elegant furnishings

Lounge Bar : Meals Service : Games Room

Wide range of facilities for families, children groups :

Activities programme and Brochure:- **The Manager, Brockwood Park, Whicham Valley Nr. Millom, Cumbria. Tel: 0657 2329**

Wasdale

BISKEY HOWE HOLIDAY FLATS

**BISKEY HOWE ROAD
WINDERMERE LA23 3AP**

Tel: Wind'ere (09662) 2323

We offer Luxury Flats fully equipped to a high standard. Linen provided, colour TV, member of Cumbria & Lakeland Self-caterers association. Residential proprietors George and Marjorie Mullen.

DOVE NEST ESTATE & FARM

**Dove Nest Estate and farm offers a unique holiday haven in the heart of magnificent English Lakeland; this perfect combination of away-from-it-all peace and relaxation together with the comfort and convenience of luxury self-catering accommodation in the estate cottages, chalets or apartments.
Estate amenities include Squash Court, Sauna, lake and river fishing.**

Lucas-Egon Ronay and AA recommended.

**Mrs. Elsie Stables,
Dove Nest, Windermere.
Telephone: Ambleside (09663) 2286.**

WOODLEA WINSTER

3 miles from Bowness and Lake Windermere. Comfortable house sleeps 7/8 in quiet Winster Valley. Stream through the garden, all mod cons., plus log fire.

**MRS. C. E. BROCKBANK,
Common Head, Staveley,
Kendal, Cumbria.
Tel: Staveley (0539) 821237**

For more details see self-catering section under "Winster".
Founder member Cumbria & Lakeland Self Caterers Association.

Wordsworth Court

Holiday Cottages, Brantfell Road,
Bowness-on-Windermere
Telephone: (09662) 3302

The cottages are situated in an elevated position within 100 yards of Bowness Bay. Most of them enjoy views of Lake Windermere. Activities include hiring of sailing, rowing or power boats. Easter to September lake steamers sail regularly to Ambleside etc. evening dinner dances and discos. The stone built cottages have recently been converted to provide luxury accommodation. There is a large private car park, all beds are supplied with sheets and attractive covers, colour TV.
Brochure on request (S.A.E. please).

350 Cottages, Farmhouses & Flats

You can take the entire family and the dog for a week's holiday in the wing of a beautiful old country house, with breathtaking Lake District scenery on the doorstep, FOR LESS THAN £60.

More exotic is a 17th century almshouse, complete with minstrel's gallery and a grand piano.

Or what about a 16th century cottage with three feet thick walls designed to sleep four or six Cistercian monks?

If you want to know more about our 350 character cottages, farmhouses, flats and apartments (not to mention the occasional Georgian mansion, converted chapel or former reptile house) then **please write or phone** for our fully illustrated **free** brochure.

Country Holidays

28 High Street, Gargrave, Skipton, BD23 3RW. Telephone (075678) 251 or 776
Telex 517534

RAC Listed *Fire Certificate*

BOSTON HOUSE

The Terrace, Windermere, Cumbria
Tel: (09662) 3654
Resident Proprietors: Sheila and Trevor Holmes

A spacious and comfortable Guest House in an elevated position overlooking Windermere with easy access to bus and train. Sheila and Trevor Holmes and family offer a personal service with good home cooking. Weekly terms Dinner Bed and Breakfast from £57.00.

May we send you our colour brochure?

Thwaite Howe Hotel

Thornthwaite, near Keswick. Telephone (059 682) 281
**** AA**

Try this small select private Country House Hotel for your Lakeland holiday, honeymoon, or short break. Hidden behind Thornthwaite village in 4 acres of lawns and woodland in an elevated position on the edge of Thornthwaite Forest, with superb views looking down Derwent Valley and on to Skiddaw mountain, only a short distance from Bassenthwaite Lake and Derwentwater. We have eight spacious bedrooms all with Private Bath. TV Lounge and quiet lounge with open fires, we maintain a top class table concentrating on good English food with good choice.

Contact resident proprietors: Mr. and Mrs. D. G. Tindall for brochure.

WELL WORTH LOOKING FOR

Lonsdale Hotel

Lake Road, Bowness-on-Windermere, Cumbria
Telephone: (09662) 3348

Small family run hotel only 5 minutes from lake
Centrally situated for shops

★ Honeymoon suite with Four Poster Bed ★ Fire precaution certificate
★ Cocktail bar ★ Lounge with colour TV ★ Views of lake and mountains
★ Some bedrooms with private facilities ★ Good Food and service
★ Car park ★ Golf, fishing, bowls, tennis and riding all nearby.

colour brochure from resident proprietors Rose & Allan Holliday

Highland Hall Renwick Penrith Cumbria

Highland Hall is a small Georgian Country House Hotel. It nestles into the Fells high above the Eden Valley. Here are moorlands, rich in bird life and wild flowers, which give views into Scotland beyond the Solway Firth, far into the Lake District Mountains and south into the Yorkshire Dales.

The small scale of Highland Hall's operation makes it possible to provide cuisine and service of very high quality. Every menu is carefully devised according to the availability of seasonal and local foods; bread and rolls are baked daily using local stoneground flour.

Highland Hall combines the traditional comfort of a small hotel with the cuisine of a good restaurant.

Bookings, Reservations and Brochure: Nigel Long, Lazonby (076 883) 375.

TWA DOGS INN

Penrith Road
Keswick-on-Derwentwater
Cumbria (0596) 72599

ACCOMMODATION OPEN ALL YEAR
Except Christmas and New Year Period

Situated at the heart of Northern Lakeland this is a local inn with a tremendously warm and friendly atmosphere under the personal supervision of the proprietors, Lois and Gordon Hallatt. The modern bedrooms are all equipped with H & C and electric blankets. Centrally Heated.

Bar meals, for which the Inn is noted, are served each day from 12-2 and 6.00-8.30 and from 12-1.30 and 7.00-8.30 on Sundays.

The ideal centre for walking or touring at any time of the year.

The traditional REAL ALE comes from wooden casks.

CLARENCE HOUSE

14 ESKIN STREET
KESWICK
CA12 4DQ

Tel. Keswick (0596) 73186

Bed & Breakfast Dinner, Bed & Breakfast
A.A. Listed Fire Certificate

OPEN ALL SEASONS

A select and friendly guest house, pleasantly situated within easy reach of the lake, parks and town centre.

All bedrooms have hot and cold water, shaving facilities and heating. Lounge with colour TV and coal fire.

Special weekly rates.
Generous reductions for children
Brochure on request — S.A.E. please

Under the personal supervision of the resident owner:
Mrs. Lexie Hartley

The Royal Oak
Rosthwaite

Keswick, Cumbria CA12 5XB

Six miles from Keswick

Ideal for Walkers

Central Heating Residential Licence

Family Run

Closed 1-26 December

Telephone: Borrowdale (059684) 214

Rosemount

A family-run private hotel ideally situated between Windermere and Bowness. Excellent cuisine, cosy lounge, small bar, immaculate bedrooms, full central heating, Fire Certificate, and ample parking space. Above all else, friendly and personal attention. AA and RAC listed.

Lake Road Windermere
Cumbria LA23 2EQ
Telephone Windermere (09662) 3739.

The Hideaway Hotel

PHOENIX WAY, WINDERMERE
WINDERMERE (09662) 3070

This 2 star hotel is personally run by the owners, Tim and Jackie Harper. They have received a special award from the British Tourist Authority for their cuisine every year since 1978. Hearty meals and a fine selection of personally chosen wines are served by friendly staff in the elegant restaurant.

Log fires welcome you in the cosy bar and comfortable lounge and central heating is fitted throughout the hotel. All 11 bedrooms have private facilities.

Ideally hidden away down a quiet lane and away from the hustle and bustle, it is most centrally situated for all the amenities of this beautiful region.

Recommended by Ashley Courtnay Signpost, Les Routiers, and others, with special commendation from the British Tourist Authority.

Very reasonable rates
for Reservations and brochures:

Windermere (09662) 3070

The Cranleigh Hotel

Kendal Road Bowness ~ on ~ Windermere
Telephone: Windermere 3293

The Cranleigh is a quiet Country House Hotel situated in the middle of this lovely Lakeland village, just two minutes walk from Lake Windermere and Bowness Bay. It is small and cosy and well known for its good food and friendly service.

There are nine double or twin bedrooms and three single rooms. Some have private bathroom attached, some have showers and all have the added luxury of complimentary tea and coffee making facilities.

We are proud of our home cooked food. Our speciality is home baking, fresh vegetables and good English meat. We are pleased to provide special diet or vegetarian dishes.

Our Traditional English Breakfast, we are told, is enough to last you till Dinner time, but for those who want something to eat whilst out sightseeing, our picnic lunches are available every day.

There is a comfortable television lounge with a log fire and also a bar lounge in which to relax after dinner or during the day.

We look forward to welcoming you to 'Cranleigh'

Crossbarrow Motel

and Self-Catering Studio Apartments

Little Clifton

Workington 3½ miles · Whitehaven 8 miles · Cockermouth 5 miles

Conveniently situated near Chapel Brow, close to the junction of the Whitehaven (A595) and Workington (A66) roads to Cockermouth. **Between the Lake District National Park and the sea,** with superb views to Skiddaw and the Lakeland Fells.

Crossbarrow Motel, converted from an old stone-built farmhouse and barn.

STUDIO APARTMENTS

Similar to some newer continental establishments

Fully Self-Catering (on weekly basis)
or
Overnight accommodation (with or without meals)

Each apartment is fully self-contained with its own bath/shower room, kitchenette and TV.
Restaurant and bar in the former farmhouse

For forward bookings apply (with large SAE please) to:

Border Eng., Contrs. Ltd. (EL), PO Box 23, Coach Road, Whitehaven, Cumbria
Telephone: Whitehaven (0946) 3773 — 24 hours answering service
or:
Telephone: Crossbarrow Motel — Workington (0900) 61443.

King's Arms Hotel

Keswick-on-Derwentwater Cumbria

Accommodation Historic Interest
Meals Snacks

Telephones:
Reception 72083 *Residents 72466*

The King's Arms is a historic coaching house dating back some two hundred years to the time of George III. The old-world charm and character has been carefully retained whilst providing also the modern amenities which the present-day guest is entitled to expect. The hotel is situated in the town centre. There are 20 bedrooms, each with H & C, electric fires and shaver points, a comfortable residents' lounge with colour television, and a lounge bar. In the dining room you will find an extensive choice on a good English bill of fare. All public rooms, corridors, stairways and some bedrooms are centrally heated. Every facility is offered for an enjoyable holiday at reasonable cost, a brochure and tariff will be sent on request. Credit cards accepted — Access, American Express, Barclaycard, Diners Club.

OPEN MOST OF THE YEAR

Greenbank Guest House

Hawkshead, Cumbria

Telephone: Hawkshead 497 & 289
Table Licence

A well appointed guest house tastefully modernised yet still retaining its old world charm and character. Situated on the perimeter of the picturesque village of Hawkshead. Centrally positioned for exploring the Lake District, within walking distance of the well known beauty spot 'Tarn Hows'.
Ideal for pony trekking, fishing, sailing, fell climbing and all outdoor pursuits.

Warm friendly atmosphere under the personal supervision of the resident proprietors
Mr. & Mrs. A. Hart.
Please send S.A.E. for details.

DALSTON HALL

A magnificent XVIth century Baronial Mansion set in seven acres of landscaped gardens surrounded by a further 200 acres of unspoilt countryside.
Our accommodation is furnished to the highest standard — rooms have bathrooms, telephones and colour televisions. For that special occasion we have four poster honeymoon suites one of which is situated at the top of the Pele Tower and contains a double sunken bath.
The restaurant offers a full a la carte menu, a daily table d'hote and a comprehensive wine list all within quiet, intimate surroundings.
Dalston Hall is ideally situated 4 miles from the centre of Carlisle and 30 minutes from the Lakes; why not break your journey and visit us. Special breaks and honeymoon weekends available.

Contact: Michael Bertano, Freepost, Dalston Hall, Dalston, Carlisle, CA5 7JX (Tel: 0228 710271).

The Grammar Hotel

Cartmel, Grange-over-Sands, Cumbria.
Tel: Cartmel 367

The Grammar Hotel is delightfully situated on the edge of the village of Cartmel with unspoilt views across the park and race course. The Hotel is surrounded by beautiful countryside and woodlands and the nearby 12th Century Priory is a notable feature of the landscape in this cathedral city in miniature. The Hotel was originally the old Cartmel Grammar School and the appearance and character of this fine Georgian building has been retained but the resident owners Alan and Lillian Hewitson convey an atmosphere of a warm and friendly Country Hotel. There are 11 bedrooms all with private bathrooms and showers, also two charming lounges, one as a TV room, large separate dining room and cocktail bar, all fully centrally heated. There is a delightful garden which is a natural sun trap for you to enjoy the peace and quiet. The Hotel is the ideal centre for all Lakeland pursuits, also the seaside and many local amenities.

Table and Residential Licence.

Please send for our free brochure. SAE please,
Alan and Lillian Hewitson.

SOUTH VIEW

Central position but quietly situated. Noted for Good Food and friendly service. Lounge with Colour Television, Tea making facilities in every bedroom, some bedrooms with private bathroom.

B & B from £6.50 per day, £42 per week. S.A.E. for brochure to South Cross Street, Windermere LA23 1AE.

NEWBY BRIDGE HOTEL

At the foot of beautiful Lake Windermere

A friendly Inn with the atmosphere of a pleasant country house, the Newby Bridge takes pride in extending a sense of well-being to its guests.

Our public rooms are warm and comfortable, some with cheery open fires. Bedrooms are particularly bright and well appointed.

Bar Meals are a speciality in the attractive Old English lounge with its massive beams and unusual stone fireplace. Excellent a la carte meals are served in the Tudor Dining Room overlooking the gardens.

Prices are very reasonable and families are made particulrly welcome.

On the A590, Newby Bridge, near Ulverston
Telephone Newby Bridge 31222 (STD 0448)

Bessiestown Farm

Penton, Carlisle, Cumbria
Tel: Nicholforest (022877) 219 RAC/AA listed
Proprietors: Jackie & Margaret Sisson

Indoor Heated Swimming Pool · Riding, Games Room · Childrens Play area

Bessiestown Farm is a Beef & Sheep rearing farm situated in a quiet rural area approximately 17 miles north of Carlisle, ideally suited for breaking your journey to and from Scotland, or as a base for touring the Lake District, South Scotland, The Solway Coast and the Roman Wall. Other facilities within a 10 mile radius include Fishing, Golf, Shooting & beautiful country walks.

Bed, breakfast & evening meals are available in the delightful and spacious farmhouse. The house is central heated, has guests' dining room and lounge with colour TV. There are five modern comfortable letting bedrooms — each with wash hand basins.

Excellent accommodation, friendly atmosphere and good food.

Keswick-on-Derwentwater

The centre for Northern Lakeland with spectacular scenery, ideal for climbers, ramblers and walkers; popular for sailing, wind-surfing and hang-gliding. Less than a tankful carries you to see Rural Crafts, Historic Homes and Gardens, Ancient Castles, Priories and Stone Circles, Watermills, Steam and Miniature Railways. There are launches, cycle and pony hire, mini-bus tours — something for everyone.

Keswick-on-Derwentwater Publicity Association, Keswick

Send this coupon with P.O/Cheque for 50p to WTS 2 Keswick, Cumbria for your Pictorial Guide and Accommodation Register.

Name:..

Address:..

....

....

..............................*Post Code*........

Killoran Country House Hotel, The Green, Wetheral, Carlisle

(Tel: Wetheral 60200 STD 0228)

Licensed; 10 bedrooms; Children welcome; Car park; Brampton 5 miles; Carlisle 3.

Overlooking the village green, ancient church and the lovely River Eden, famous for its trout and salmon, Killoran is a beautiful red sandstone building which was built in 1870. The hotel is surrounded by 2½ acres of secluded grounds and here guests are able to relax in comfort in a peaceful setting and enjoy superb cuisine. Being located just two miles from the M6 motorway (junction 42) this is an ideal touring centre for the Lake District, Hadrian's Wall, Border Country and the Northumbria National Park. It is also a convenient overnight stopping place for tourists travelling to and from Scotland. Carlisle golf course is nearby.

Hampsfell Hotel

Hampsfell Road, Grange-over-Sands Cumbria LA11 6BG

Telephone (04484) 2567

A small country house hotel in own grounds. Some private bathrooms. Quiet and peaceful.

Centrally heated. Private parking. Residential licence. Open all year. Low season Bargain Breaks.

Please send stamp for brochure and details to the resident proprietors, Mr. & Mrs. W. J. Whiteside.

Ravenstone

Standing on the slopes of Skiddaw in two acres of grounds and woodland, five miles from Keswick on A.591 Carlisle road.

If you are looking for a warm welcome, a relaxed, comfortable country house atmosphere with a certain style, traditional English home cooking, an elegant and charming house, quiet and secluded but conveniently placed, a large and comfortable lounge, a separate television room, a games room, a full-sized snooker table, a well stocked bar with an interesting and reasonably priced wine list, family run, central heating, up to fifty per cent reductions for children and all at a figure much lower than you might expect . . .

We shall be delighted to send you a brochure.

Sidney and Ena Tuck

Ravenstone Hotel, near Keswick

Cumbria, CA12 4OG

AA

Telephone Bassenthwaite Lake (059681) 240

RAC

GRANGE-IN-BORROWDALE, KESWICK, CUMBRIA

Resident Proprietors: Mr & Mrs E. Fraser.
Telephone: Borrowdale (059684) 204

Ashley Courtenay
AA & RAC**

Michelin Guide & Signpost recommended Beautifully situated away from traffic noise, and with excellent views of the Borrowdale valley, this old world hotel, with all modern conveniences, will provide you with all the peace and comfort, good food and friendly service, to make your holiday a success. We are tucked away, turn right over Grange Bridge, but only 4 miles from Keswick.

The Bay Tree Guest House, Keswick.

The Bay Tree is a Good Food Guest House, currently listed in many 'Good Food Guides'. Residents lounge and separate colour television lounge. Tastefully furnished bedrooms with tea and coffee making facilities, electric blankets shaver points, full central heating. Residential licence. Situated beside the River Greta and Fitz Park.

1 Wordsworth Street,
Keswick,
Cumbria CA12 4HU

Proprietors:
Pat & John Garner.

WHEN IN KESWICK BE SURE TO VISIT.
THE ACQUISITIVE VIRUS
13 Lake Road, Keswick. Tel: 73874
A shop for people with the Collecting Bug.

Hardcragg Hall

16th Century Manor House

AA* **Hotel and Restaurant** **RAC**
Grange-over-Sands

Hardcragg Hall is a small manor house set in the middle of Grange-over-Sands within easy reach of shops and the promenade. Its history goes back over 400 years and the house reflects these centuries of hospitality in its original floor boards and warm oak panelling. Ideally hidden away from the hustle and bustle. Situated for all the amenities of this beautiful region, with Sea and Coarse Fishing, 3 Golf Courses, Riding, Boating. All within easy reach, Lake Windermere approx., 6 miles. Over the years, many famous people have stayed at Hardcragg, but none was made more welcome than today's visitor who will particularly appreciate the crackling log fires, the comfortable bedrooms and excellent cuisine. Good Bar Lunches. Booking is advisable for dinners.

NOW OPEN FOR MINI WEEKENDS AND FOUR DAY BREAKS (any 4 days) AT VERY REASONABLE RATES.

For a room or a meal, Telephone the new owners Jack and Carol at Grange (04484) 3353 who look forward to sharing their delightful country house with you.

Four ways to enjoy Windermere

They're called Swan, Swift, Teal and Tern. They cruise the lake throughout the holiday season, in traditional style. And what better way to see it?

Windermere is almost too beautiful to be true. Unspoilt, picturesque, enchanting; it's all of these, and more. The variety is astonishing—that's why so many people come back year after year to renew their acquaintance.

Sealink is the only company which operates a regular sailing schedule between Bowness, Ambleside and Lakeside. You can reach Windermere by train via Oxenholme, on the main London-Crewe-Glasgow main line. Sealink's Bowness pier is only 1½ miles away from Windermere by frequent bus service—or you can drive to Lakeside and park there.

Details of sailing times and fares (there are special party rates, too) can be obtained from British Rail stations and appointed travel agents; or direct from The Manager, Sealink Windermere Services, Lakeside, Ulverston, Cumbria LA12 8AS. Telephone Newby Bridge (0448) 31539.

Sealink
Windermere

Woodlands

Brundholme Road, Keswick CA12 4NL.
Telephone Keswick (0596) 72399
AA Listed RAC **Fire Certificate**

A small, select Guest House, quietly situated in its own grounds near the lovely Fitz Park, offering every comfort and traditional English fare. It is a friendly, well-appointed house with two lounges, one with colour TV, and good car parking facilities. Weekly terms are available.

Brochure on request — SAE please
Resident Proprietress - Mrs. Evelyn Staton.

Orrest Close

THE TERRACE, WINDERMERE.

Is a listed building overlooking the Lake. We are close to 'Buses, Trains and Restaurants, and have private parking and a comfortable lounge.

S.A.E. Please to:
Betty & Brian Bradley,
For brochure and tariff or Telephone:
(09662) 3325

Beck Steps Guest House

Grasmere, Cumbria LA22 9SY
Telephone: Grasmere
(096 65) 348

A quiet, friendly guest house which overlooks the village green in the centre of Grasmere.

The house specialises in delicious English fare and each satisfying meal is personally prepared and cooked by the owners, Jim and Emily Fowler, from top quality produce. For those who wish, drinks are served before dinner and a small selection of wine is available.

Central heating is fitted throughout the house and our comfortable lounge has a large log fire which has proved a great favourite with our guests.

Each of the ten bedrooms has washing facilities and some have private bath/shower and toilet.

Private parking is provided alongside the house.

A glance at our brochure will convince you that we offer better class hotel type accommodation at guest house prices.

Why not choose one of our personally inspected, delightful old farmhouses, where you can be sure of a warm welcome from your Cumbrian hosts, good home-cooking and comfortable accommodation in peaceful rural surroundings. Our farms all offer exceptional value and are ideal bases from which to explore Cumbria, either on foot or by car.

FARMHOUSE ACCOMMODATION BOOKINGS

4 HOLLY CLOSE, HEVERSHAM
NR. MILNTHORPE, CUMBRIA
TELEPHONE (04482) 3902

For illustrated details of over fifty farms throughout Cumbria, write to Sue Butcher, enclosing 30p.

Braemount House

SUNNY BANK ROAD, WINDERMERE LA23 2EN
TEL: (09662) - 5967

COME AND BE SPOILED

Braemount House is in a quiet, pleasant but convenient situation between Windermere and Bowness.

We provide a standard of comfort and service which we hope will guarantee you a real holiday.

We offer fresh food, well cooked and cater for all appetites, with a wide choice at breakfast ranging from home-made croissants and fresh fruit juice to enormous English breakfasts. Delicious and satisfying evening meals, Residential Licence and comfortable lounge with open fire make evenings "at home" a pleasure.

Our warm and attractive bedrooms all have their own bathrooms, colour TVs and hot drinks facilities.

Here you will find comfort, relaxation, individual attention and excellent value. It will be our pleasure to spoil you thoroughly.

LAKELAND HOLIDAYS

We offer a personalised Booking service for any visitors requiring accommodation in the North Lakes. Individuals, Conferences, Groups and Package Holidays arranged.

For further information please contact or ring Hazel Wilkinson.
LAKELAND HOLIDAYS, 9 ST. JOHN'S TERRACE, KESWICK, CUMBRIA CA12 4DP.
Tel: KESWICK 0596 72470.

Package Holidays

Historical Houses

Historical Houses & Gardens

Fishing/Angling

Multi-Activity Water Sports

Tastes & Crafts of Cumbria.

Living with your House Plants

Xmas House parties

Link House

Bassenthwaite Lake,
Cockermouth, Cumbria,
CA13 9YD
Bassenthwaite Lake (059681) 291

For warmth, comfort and good food try our Victorian house at the head of Bassenthwaite Lake.

May & Brian Smith

KILN HILL BARN

Accommodation for groups and families.

Ring: May Smith on
Bassenthwaite Lake 454 (059681)

KILN HILL BARN,
BASSENTHWAITE, KESWICK.
CUMBRIA CA12 4RG.

Greystones

ST. JOHN'S TERRACE
AMBLESIDE ROAD, KESWICK

Homely 10 bedrooms Guesthouse
run by the owners and th
Good food
atmosphere
indivi

Proprietors:
FRED & HAZEL
WILKINSON

ASHES LANE CARAVAN & CAMPING PARK

Staveley Nr. Kendal. Tel: (0539) 821119.

22 acres of open undulating countryside with lovely views. All essential amenities. Caravans, M'vans and Tents. S.A.E. for details.

From M6 J36, follow A591 "Windermere" 1¼ dual carriageway — pass "Crook" road sign and follow international camping symbols on left.

From Windermere only 5m on A591 to Kendal. Through Staveley to dual carriageway — make a U-turn at "Crook" road sign. Follow international camping symbols on left.

ROYAL YACHTSMAN

(Salutation Hotel) under new ownership

Lake Road, Ambleside, Cumbria
Telephone: (09663) 2244

Situated in the centre of Ambleside, this comfortable fully licensed hotel offers an ideal base to tour and explore the Lake District.

- ★ ***Bar Lunches and Evening Snacks.***
- ★ ***Packed Lunches.***
- ★ ***Telephone and Tea/Coffee making facilities in each bedroom.***
- ★ ***Car Park & Fire Certificate.***

Set price and A La Carte menu for Dinner, most credit cards welcome.

100 year old Barn converted into

LUXURY HOLIDAY FLAT

Excellent Views, Sleeps 4 persons.

Mrs. J. E. Law,
OLD HEATHWAITE,
WINDERMERE, CUMBRIA LA23 2DH
Tel: (09662) 2410.

WELTON PLAINS HOLIDAY COTTAGES

Six luxury homes in the picturesque hamlet of Welton, 4½ miles from Caldbeck.

Lovely old barns, set in the peaceful and unspoilt Caldew Valley, converted to provide luxury holiday accommodation with all amenities, including central heating, colour televisions and fridge/freezers. Absolutely NO extras — electricity and linen provided free. Large play area and landscaped grounds. Ample parking.

The Solway coast, Lakes, Roman Wall and Pennines are all within easy reach, while pony-trekking, fishing and fell-walking are available locally. Cottages sleep from 4-8. Brochure and tariff on request (S.A.E. please) to Capt. H. V. Hubbard, Welton Plains, Welton, Cumbria, CA5 7ET. Tel: 069 96 459.

Longlands

Cartmel, Cumbria LA11 6HG
Telephone: Cartmel (044854) 475

Set in the beautiful Cartmel Valley within the National Park. Four acres of peaceful secluded woodland five miles from Lake Windermere.
Spacious accommodation of quality in three courtyard cottages, one maisonette, one flat. Colour Television. Fully equipped laundry. Resident proprietors.

Founder Member Cumbria and Lakeland Self-Caterers' Association.

CUMBRIA & LAKELAND SELF-CATERERS' ASSOCIATION

This Association is a voluntary organisation established in 1980, with the support of the Cumbria Tourist Board, to promote a high standard in self-catering throughout the County.

Our members provide quality self-catering houses, cottages, flats or chalets ranging from the simple to the luxurious as may be judged from individual brochures. Members' establishments are inspected to ensure that the properties are clean, properly equipped, comfortable, adequately heated, the decorations and furnishings contribute to a pleasant atmosphere and that the brochure is accurate in all respects.

In choosing to stay with one of our members, we in the Association are confident that you will find everything to your satisfaction. We welcome your comments, recognising that there is always room for improvement, as our aim is to make your holiday in Cumbria a lasting pleasure.

Further details of members' properties may be found in the line entries, listed under each place name, in the self-catering section of this publication. Many may also be found in the Advertisements Section.

For further details about the Association, including our special Winter Breaks leaflet, contact the C.L.S.C.A. Secretary, OLD HEATHWAITE, WINDERMERE LA23 2DH. (S.A.E. please).

ALSTON
Shield Hill Cottages,
Garrigill, Alston.
Alston (049 83) 238

AMBLESIDE
How Head Cottage,
c/o 21 Loughrigg Avenue,
Ambleside (09663) 2461

AMBLESIDE
Luxury Flats. Kirkstone
Foot Country House Hotel,
Ambleside (09663) 2232

AMBLESIDE
Stephen How Cottage
Skelwith Bridge,
Ambleside (09663) 3135

BAILEY
Bailey Mill, Newcastleton,
Roxburghshire.
Roadhead (069 78) 617

BORROWDALE
Derwent Farmhouse,
Grange, Borrowdale, Keswick.
Borrowdale (059 684) 673

BORROWDALE
Newton Place,
Borrowdale, Keswick.
Borrowdale (059 684) 278

BRAITHWAITE Nr. Keswick
Trustclean, Queens Court,
Bentley, Doncaster.
Doncaster (0302) 783193

CUMBRIA & LAKELAND SELF-CATERERS' ASSOCIATION

BRAMPTON Long Byres, Talkin Head, Brampton. Hallbankgate (069 76) 262	**KENTMERE** Browfoot Farm, Nicholson, & Co., Lake Road, Windermere. Windermere (09662) 2291	**WELTON** Well Cottage, Green View, Welton, Dalston, Carlisle. Raughton Head (06996) 230
BROUGHTON-IN-FURNESS Brockwood Park, Whicham Valley, Millom (0657) 2329	**KESWICK area** Brigham Flats & Midtown Cottages, Cockermouth. 12 Derwent St., Keswick 74392	**WIGTON** The Stables, Rosley House, Rosley, Wigton. Wigton (09654) 2665
BROUGHTON-IN-FURNESS Coach House Flats, High Duddon Guest House, Broughton-in-F (06576)279	**KESWICK area** Grey Abbey Properties Ltd., P.O. Box 23, Coach Road, Whitehaven (0946) 3773	**WINDERMERE** The Barn, Old Heathwaite, Windermere (09662) 2410
CARLISLE area Millstone Cottage, Blackhall Wood, Carlisle. Dalston (0228) 710342	**KESWICK** Latrigg, c/o 2 Holemire Cottages, High Lorton. Lorton (090 085) 648	**WINDERMERE** Beaumont Luxury Holiday Flats, Thornbarrow Rd., Windermere (09662) 5144
CARTMEL Longlands, Cartmel, Grange-over-Sands. Cartmel (044 854) 475	**LANGDALE VALLEY** Cottage, c/o Langdales Hotel, Great Langdale, Ambleside. Langdale (09667) 253	**WINDERMERE** Biskey Howe Flats, 1A Biskey Howe Road, Windermere (09662) 2323
CROOK Holiday Cottages, Low Crag, Crook, Kendal. Crosthwaite (044 88) 268	**LAZONBY** Banktop Courtyard, Lazonby, Penrith. Lazonby (076 883) 268	**WINDERMERE** Bowering Holiday Flats, 6 Park Road, Windermere. Newby Bridge (0448) 31202
ELTERWATER Wheelwrights, Elterwater, Ambleside. Langdale (09667) 635	**LOWESWATER** Flats. Scale Hill Hotel, Loweswater, Cockermouth. Lorton (090 085) 232	**WINDERMERE** Canterbury Flats, 41A Quarry Rigg, Lake Rd., W'mere. Tel: (0227) 69803
GRANGE-OVER-SANDS Newlands Holiday Flats, Crown Hill, Grange-over-S (04484) 2659	**SEBERGHAM Near Caldbeck** Monkhouse Hill Farm, Welton, Carlisle. Kendal (0539) 21897	**WINDERMERE** The Heaning, Heaning Lane, Windermere. Tel: (09662) 3453
GRASMERE Meadow Brow, Grasmere, Ambleside. Grasmere (096 65) 275	**ULLSWATER** Arcos. Holiday Cottages Hutton John, Nr. Penrith. Greystoke (08533) 300	**WINDERMERE** Heathwaite Howe, c/o Old Heathwaite, Windermere (09662) 2410
IVEGILL Bungalows, Low Grange, Southwaite, Carlisle. Southwaite (069 93) 432	**ULLSWATER** Dalemain Estate Office, Dalemain, Nr. Penrith. Pooley Bridge (08536) 450	**WINDERMERE** High Riding, Black Beck Wood, Windermere (09662) 4313
KENDAL Dowsonfold Cottage, Summerhow, Kendal. Kendal (0539) 20763	**ULLSWATER** Rose Bank Cottage, Dacre, Penrith. Pooley Bridge (08536) 258	**WINDERMERE** Spinnery Cottage Flats, Brantfell Road, Windermere (09662) 4884
KENDAL Plumgarths Holiday Flats, Crook, Kendal. Staveley (0539) 821325	**ULLSWATER** Waltons Holiday Homes, Stainton, Nr. Penrith. Penrith (0768) 62714	**WINSTER** Woodlea c/o Common Head, Staveley, Kendal. Staveley (0539) 821237

CARAVANS

Threlkeld, Nr. Keswick, Cumbria.
A small genuine farm site just off the Penrith, Keswick road with milking cattle and hill sheep, overlooking Saddleback with Helvellyn behind. The river Glendermakin runs through the site. Marvellous country for walkers and within easy reach of Derwentwater, Ullswater, Grasmere, Windermere, etc. Sailing, boating and steamer trips can be enjoyed. Wide choice of excellently equipped modern Kingsize caravans with electricity, fridge, mains water, drainage and excellent heating. Parking beside caravans. Flush toilets, hot/cold showers, shaver points, laundry room, shop and pony trekking on site. Excellent nearby village shop.

Hutton Roof, Mungrisdale Nr. Keswick, Cumbria.
A new select site with only about 40 static caravans — very quiet and secluded. An obvious choice for those wanting quiet peace. Caravans set in light woodland on a 1,000ft high ridge with magnificent views towards Grt. Calva and High Peak. Excellent toilet block with H/C showers and basins, shaver points, laundry room and shop, riding from site. Some lovely Shetland ponies. Fine woodland walking and within easy reach of Ullswater, Derwentwater, Thirlmere, Grasmere, etc. Wide choice of modern Kingsize caravans with electricity, fridge, very large fires and mains water, equipped to a very high standard. Discount for O.A.P.'s.

Rates £30 — £80 — ask for special 10% discount scheme.
We specialise in early/late cheap holidays and April/Oct. Weekends.

Mount Point Caravans (EL), 17 South Road, Stourbridge, West Midlands.
Telephone Stourbridge 5960.

S.A.E. Essential (Please try to give holiday dates and party details).

THE BEAUTIFUL BORDERS

LYNEBANK HOLIDAY COTTAGES

set on a sheep farm by the forest.

Central Heating — Home from Home — Open all year — Fishing — Riding Walking — Superb Touring Base — Ideal for Children — Pets welcome.

Details from: DOROTHY DOWNER, BANK END FARM, ROADHEAD, CARLISLE CA6 6NU.
Telephone: Roadhead (06978) 644

SELF-CATERING SEASIDE FAMILY HOLIDAYS

Enjoy three holidays rolled into one at this super Holiday Park right on the coast.

Ideal base for touring the Lake District, visiting its many beaches or a whole lot of fun and choice from the many entertainments on site.

There's TV too, in the fully equipped super luxury caravans. Along with other touches of luxury such as hot water, showers and fridge.

The park facilities include heated indoor swimming pool, amusement arcade, playground, children's amusement room, licensed bar, entertainment centre and shop.

Write for free colour brochure (stating holiday dates and telephone number) to: Bourne Holiday Parks, 51-55 Bridge Street, Hemel Hempstead, Herts. Or phone (0442) 48661.

Name ____________________

Address ____________________

____

____________________ P/code ______

BOURNE
HOLIDAY PARKS

GLENRIDDING HOUSE ULLSWATER

Two large flats on the first floor of a period house on the edge of Lake Ullswater with lake frontage. Large pleasant gardens. Beautiful views of the Lake and surrounding fells. Electric heating. Well equipped. Available all year. Sleeps 4-6.

S.A.E. for brochure or phone: Carlisle 0228 34371 office hours; 0228 75344 evenings and weekends.

Border Holiday Homes, Bute House, Rosehill, Carlisle CA1 2SA.

Family Holidays in the English

LAKE DISTRICT

FOR COASTAL AND COUNTRYSIDE SELF-CATERING HOLIDAYS

What could be more relaxing than a week or two in this beautiful area?

CRAYROCK is an established agency that keeps in close touch with it's Holidaymakers thereby specialising in personally organising holidays to suit all requirements.

We have a wide variety of reasonably priced accommodation, including Cottages, Farmhouses, Flats and Caravans in lovely locations ranging from lively Lake District Holiday Centres to remote peaceful Lakeland Valleys, Sea-side Villages with the benefit of Sea and Sand with easy access for touring the Lakes, and the interesting Market Towns of this lovely area!

We'll do our best to make your Holiday your Best Yet!

CRAYROCK LIMITED
39 RAMPSIDE,
BARROW-IN-FURNESS,
CUMBRIA or
Telephone Barrow (0229) 25772

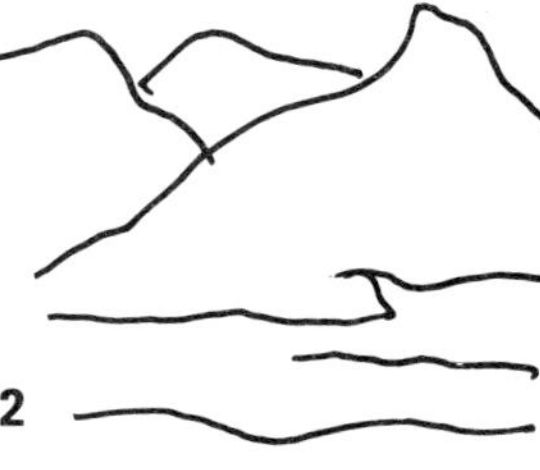

Holiday Cottage Nr. Carlisle

Well Cottage pictured above is situated in the small picturesque rural hamlet of Welton, 8 miles south of Carlisle on the northern fringe of the Lake District. 11 miles from M6 junction 41. Recently renovated throughout. It has a large lounge, well equipped all electric kitchen/dinette, sun lounge, 2nd toilet (on the ground floor). Upstairs there are three good sized bedrooms sleeping 6. Bathroom including shower.

Facilities include — Colour TV, fridge, oil ch., garage and small garden.

Ideal centre for touring Hadrians Wall, Lakes and Border Country.

There is a pub and shop/PO in Welton.

Two day Winter breaks.

Also 6 Berth, 2 Bedroom caravans, fridge, TV, on small quiet sites with mountain views.

S.A.E. for further details and illustrated brochures to: — Mrs. A. E. Ivinson, Green View, Welton, Nr. Dalston, Carlisle CA5 7ES. Tel: Raughton Head (069 96) 230.

Member of the Cumbria & Lakeland Self-Caterers Association.

INGLENOOK CARAVAN PARK

A.A. listed site

Situated 4 miles equally from Lake Ennerdale & Loweswater and 7 miles from Cockermouth. Luxury 2 bedroom caravan with mains services, TV, fridge, fully equipped except linen. Ideally situated just off the A5086 in these beautiful surroundings, an ideal centre to suit all pursuits, only 15 static vans on this A.A. listed site.

Fishing in nearby Cogra Moss; permits from site shop. Laundry room (with spin drier), Shop, telephone.

S.A.E. for illustrated brochure

MRS. A. E. IVINSON, GREEN VIEW, WELTON, NR. DALSTON, CARLISLE, CA5 7ES
Tel: Raughton Head (06996) 230

ALLONBY (Solway Coast)

Beach Croft
Modern detached bungalow
Sleeps up to 7

The Mews
4 self contained houses (Sleeps 4-7)

The properties are near the beach on the outskirts of Allonby Village, designated an area of outstanding natural beauty. Comfortably furnished and well equipped. Gas Central Heating; Gas fires; fitted carpets. TV., Fridge; good centre for touring the Lake District and Scottish Borders. Available all year.

SAE for brochure with colour photos or phone Carlisle (0228) 34371 office hours (022875) 344 evenings and weekends.

Border Holiday Homes, Bute House, Rosehill, Carlisle CA1 2SA

Self catering holidays in luxury apartments and caravans with all mod cons.
Fun for ALL the family at
Stanwix Park
HOLIDAY CENTRE
SILLOTH on SOLWAY
CUMBRIA'S SEASIDE HOLIDAY TOWN
Tourers and Campers Welcome
We recommend advance booking at peak holiday periods
Send for Free Colour Brochure. Dial-A-Brochure Tel. Silloth (0965) 31671

SELF-CATERING ACCOMMODATION

TOURIST BOARD STANDARDS FOR SELF-CATERING

The Tourist Board Standards for self-catering accommodation are given below. Establishments which conform to these standards are indicated by a ●. Establishments which conform to all but the minimum room sizes are marked **C** – meaning compact. We have also printed our recommendations on the kind of information which proprietors should provide to people enquiring about a reservation. This will serve as a useful check list of questions you may want to ask.

ACCOMMODATION - GENERAL

1. Each self-contained unit should have a floor area of not less than 200 sq ft (18.60 sq metres) for a two person unit plus 50 sq ft (4.65 sq metres) for each additional person (this includes living, sleeping, cooking and bathroom areas). Each non self-contained unit should have a floor area of not less than 175 sq ft (16.25 sq metres) for 2 persons plus 50 sq ft (4.65 sq metres) for each additional person.
2. Adequate circulation space must be available during daytime in bedrooms/sleeping areas and living rooms/areas.
3. All bedrooms/sleeping areas must have at least one window which can be opened.
4. All beds (except children's beds) must conform to, or exceed, the following minimum dimensions:
Single beds: 6 ft x 2 ft 6 in (183 x 76 cm)
Double beds: 6 ft x 4 ft (183 x 122 cm)
5. All mattresses must be spring interior, foam or of similar quality and in sound condition. Bedding must be clean.
6. Bedding must be supplied in sufficient quantity as specified in the inventory. For winter, late or early season lettings, the scale of bedding should be increased.
7. Where linen is provided, it must be changed for all new occupants. For lets of two weeks or more, spare linen must be available.

FITTINGS, FURNISHINGS ETC.

1. All units must be provided with: at least one dressing table or equivalent; wardrobe or clothes hanging space; adequate drawer space. Other equipment as specified in the inventory.
2. All fittings, furniture and furnishings in bedrooms/sleeping areas and living rooms/areas must be adequate for the maximum number of occupants.
3. All rooms/areas, passages and staircases must have suitable floor finishes or coverings.
4. All rooms/areas, passages and staircases must have adequate ventilation.
5. All living rooms/areas and kitchens must have windows opening directly into the open air.
6. All windows must be equipped with opaque curtains or blinds.
7. All areas must have adequate heating available, according to season.
8. All bedrooms/sleeping areas, living rooms/areas and kitchens must be adequately lit to the level of at least 100 watts or equivalent per room/area.
9. All passages, corridors and staircases must be adequately lit for the safety of the occupants.

BATHROOMS, WCs

1. All self-contained units must have at least one bathroom equipped with a bath or shower and a washbasin (if there is no washbasin in any bedroom/sleeping area). A mirror must be above, or adjacent to, the washbasin.
2. All self-contained units must have at least one WC, equipped with toilet paper.
3. All non-self-contained units must have at least one bathroom, equipped with a bath or shower, for every 15 guests. Where washbasins are not fitted in each accommodation unit at least one washbasin, having hot and cold running water, must be provided in a bathroom or washroom for every eight guests.
A mirror must be above, or adjacent to, the washbasin.
4. All non-self-contained units must be provided with at least one WC, equipped with toilet paper and disposal bin, for every 10 guests.
Note: The ratios of bathrooms, washbasins and WCs to guests apply within any one building to the maximum number of occupants that can be accommodated within the non-self-contained units within that building.
5. Hot water must be available at all reasonable times.

KITCHENS

1. All units must have a kitchen equipped with either a gas or electric cooker with an oven and a grill and at least two boiling rings. Cookers must be clean and in sound condition and functioning properly.
2. All units must be equipped with a ventilated food storage cupboard or a refrigerator.
3. All sinks must be equipped with a draining board, and hot and drinking water supply.

GENERAL

1. All units must be thoroughly cleaned and checked before every letting.
2. Occupiers must be provided with a key to the entrance door of their unit and, where applicable, a key giving access to the building.
3. If the proprietor is not resident on the premises, his name, address and telephone number, or that of his local agent, who must have a complete set of keys, must be prominently displayed, together with those of emergency services, e.g. doctor, fire, etc.
4. The structure of the unit/building must be in sound condition with no internal dampness.
5. All exterior and interior decorations, furnishings, floor coverings and fittings must be maintained in good condition.
6. All units must be provided with suitable dustbins.

INFORMATION FOR HIRERS

1. The booking form should be accompanied by full details of accommodation, including sleeping arrangements. In addition, the following information should be given:
Car parking arrangements near unit.
Whether or not pets are allowed.
Whether or not arrangements can be made for advance ordering of groceries and other provisions.
Distance of unit from nearest shop(s), post office etc.
Distance of unit from nearest public transport.
Arrangements for refuse collection.
If access to toilet facilities is outside the main building.
2. A map, where necessary, should be provided, showing the location of the unit.

INVENTORY OF EQUIPMENT

The accommodation should contain the following: -

3 blankets or 1 continental quilt and cover per bed.

1 per person
Pillow.
Knife (table & dessert).
Fork (table & dessert).
Spoon (dessert & tea).
Plate (large & small).
Tea cup and saucer.
Cereal/soup plate.
Tumbler.
Egg cup.

2 per person
Coathangers.

1 per unit
Kettle.
Teapot.
Tea caddy.
Saucepan & lid (large, medium and small).
Frying pan.
Colander.
Oven roasting tray.
Casserole dish.
Carving knife and fork.
Bread knife.
Bread/cake container.
Bread and cake plate.
Bread/chopping board.
Fish slice.
Small vegetable knife.
Tin opener.
Corkscrew/bottle opener.
Potato peeler.
Large fruit dish.
Butter dish.
Sugar basin.
Tray.
Milk jug.
Condiment set (2 piece).
Washing-up bowl.
Dustpan and brush.
Broom.
Floor cloth.
Pot scourer/dish mop.
Bucket.
Mirror.
Doormat.
Covered kitchen refuse container.
Fire extinguisher.

2 per unit
Table spoons.
Mixing bowls or basins.
Dusters.
Ash trays.

SELF-CATERING AGENCIES

Listed below are the names and addresses of agencies which have a selection of properties to let at a number of different locations. For further details of the properties and prices all you need do is telephone or write to the agency concerned indicating the time of year when the accommodation is required and also any preferred locations. Prices are based on weekly terms per unit. Low and high season periods may vary from agency to agency but usually the months of June to September make up the high season.

Each of these agencies has registered its properties with the English Tourist Board for 1982 and has agreed to adhere to the Code of Conduct set out below. Agencies marked † are members of the Regional Tourist Board.

AGENCY CODE OF CONDUCT

In addition to fulfilling its statutory obligations, the Agent/Management undertakes to observe the following Code of Conduct.

1. To deal promptly and courteously with all enquiries, reservations and correspondence from clients.

2. To describe fairly to all clients and prospective clients the amenities and facilities at each letting property whether by advertisement, brochure, word of mouth or any other means and where practicable to allow clients to view the accommodation if requested before booking.

3. To inspect every property prior to acceptance and to ensure that the facilities provided there are consistent with the details provided to visitors.

4. To make clear to clients exactly what is included in all prices quoted and what additional charges will be incurred (eg. meter for electricity/gas), and to return promptly any refundable deposit or balance thereof.

5. To give each client details of payments due and a receipt.

6. To ensure that satisfactory arrangements are made for cleaning between each let and that maintenance arrangements, including provisions for dealing with emergencies, have been made for each property; also to ensure that the inventory is checked and items replaced as necessary between lets.

7. To be responsible for taking up any complaint with the proprietor on behalf of the complainant, and where the complaint is found justified to be responsible for making or securing reasonable restitution.

8. To agree on request to allow a representative of the Board the opportunity to look over individual properties at such times as may be convenient to the Agent and the Board.

Blakes Holidays Ltd
Wroxham, Norwich,
Norfolk NR12 8DH.
☎ Wroxham (06053) 2917 (all holiday parks and homes).
Telex: 97114.
1300 properties throughout England individually sited and in holiday parks/villages.
Price range holiday homes: £35.00-£126.00 (low season) £99.00-£330.00 (high season). Months open: 1-12.

Cottage Life
Douglas and Judy Worrall †
1 Elterwater, Ambleside,
Cumbria LA22 9HN.
☎ Langdale (09667) 292.
25 individual properties in Central and Southern Lakeland.
Price range: £65.00-£95.00 (low season) £75.00-£225.00 (high season). Months open: 1-12.

Country Holidays (Skipton) Ltd † Ad
15 High Street, Gargrave, Skipton,
N. Yorks. BD23 3RA.
☎ Gargrave (075678) 251/776.
Telex: 517534.
Houses, bungalows and cottages throughout Cumbria.
Price range: £31.00-£155.00 (low season) £83.00-£299.00 (high season). Months open: 1-12.

English Country Cottages
Claypit Lane, Fakenham,
Norfolk NR21 9AH.
☎ Fakenham (0328) 51155.
Telex: 817252.
Properties throughout Cumbria.
Price range: £75.00-£246.00 (low season) £114.00-£594.00 (high season). Months open: 1-12.

Grey Abbey Properties Ltd †
P.O. Box 23, Coach Road,
Whitehaven, Cumbria CA28 9DF.
☎ Whitehaven (0946) 3773.
70 cottages and flats in Cumbria.
Price range: £37.00-£93.00 (low season) £100.00-£154.00 (high season). Months open: 1-12.

Holidays in Lakeland Ad
Stock Park Estate, Newby Bridge,
Ulverston, Cumbria LA12 8AY.
☎ Newby Bridge (0448) 31549.
300 properties including 20 chalets/caravans in Cumbria.
Price range: £50.00-£120.00 (low season) £65.00-£250.00 (high season). Months open: 3-10.

Lakeland Cottage Holidays †
5 Top Row, Seatoller, Keswick,
Cumbria CA12 5XW.
☎ Braithwaite (059 682) 493.
Properties in Northern Lakeland.
Price range: £50.00-£85.00 (low season) £70.00-£220.00 (high season). Months open: 1-12.

Lowther Estate Management Services †
Estate Office, Lowther, Penrith,
Cumbria CA10 2HG.
☎ Hackthorpe (09312) 392.
10 bungalows and cottages in Northern Lakeland and Eden Valley.
Price range: £30.00-£100.00 (low season). £70.00-£240.00 (high season). Months open: 3-12.

SELF-CATERING AGENCIES

Mackay's Agency Ⓐ
30 Frederick Street,
Edinburgh EH2 2JR, Scotland.
☎ (031) 226 4364.
325 properties throughout Cumbria.
Price range: £35.00-£100.00 (low season) £50.00-£175.00 (high season).
Months open: 3-10.

Nelson and Wycherley
Church Buildings, Grange-over-Sands, Cumbria LA11 6BB.
☎ Grange-over-Sands (044 84) 2301.
24 properties on the Northern shore of Morecambe Bay and in South Lakes area.
Price range: £20.00-£55.00 (low season) £45.00-£95.00 (high season).
Months open: 1-12.

Taylings Holiday Cottages
14 High Street, Godalming,
Surrey GU7 1ED.
☎ Godalming (04868) 28522.
Properties in Cumbria.
Price range: £20.00-£60.00 (low season) £40.00-£380.00 (high season).
Months open: 1-12.

Windermere Holidays †
'Homewood', Storrs Park,
Windermere, Cumbria LA23 3LT.
☎ Windermere (09662) 4175.
14 properties in Southern Lakeland.
Price range: £40.00-£75.00 (low season) £80.00-£180.00 (high season).
Months open: 1-12.

PLEASE MENTION WHERE TO STAY '82' WHEN MAKING A BOOKING

SELF-CATERING ACCOMMODATION

Name and Address: Town (County) / Establishment	Map Ref.	Contact for reservations: Name and address, Telephone number, Telex	Tourist Board Standards	Self-contained: House (or part)	Bungalows	Cottages	Chalets/caravans	Flats/flatlets	Houseboats	Not self-contained: Flats/flatlets	Chalets	Number of persons per unit	Prices per unit per week: Low season £ Min. / £ Max.	High season £ Min. / £ Max.	Months open (1–12)	Symbols (Key: see fold-out)
ALLONBY (Cumbria)	**B2**															
† Beachcroft, Mawbray Rd.		Border Holiday Homes, Bute House, Rosehill, Carlisle, Cumbria, CA1 2SA. Tel. Carlisle (0228) 34371.	●	–	1	–	–	–	–	–	–	7	45.00 / –	– / *150.00*	1–12	GE LHU
† The Mews, School La.		Border Holiday Homes, Bute House, Rosehill, Carlisle, Cumbria, CA1 2SA. Tel. Carlisle (0228) 34371.	●	4	–	–	–	–	–	–	–	4–7	45.00 / –	– / *120.00*	1–12	GE LHU
ALSTON (Cumbria)	**C2**															
† Gilmore Close, The Butts,		Mrs. M. L. Kearton, Market Pl., Alston, Cumbria, CA9 3HS. Tel. (049 83) 210.	●	–	–	5	–	–	–	–	–	2–5	48.30 / *63.25*	74.75 / *103.50*	1–12	GE LF U
Shield Hill Cottages.		Mrs. Wearmouth, Shield Hill House, Garrigill, Alston, Cumbria, CA9 3EX. Tel. (049 83) 238.	●	–	–	2	–	–	–	–	–	8	60.00 / *80.00*	80.00 / *100.00*	1–12	GE LHU
Swans Head Cottage,		Mr. or Mrs. Graves, Swans Head Inn, Townhead, Alston, Cumbria, CA9 3SL. Tel. (049 83) 680.	●	–	–	1	–	–	–	–	–	4	55.00 / *70.00*	85.00 / *105.00*	1–12	GE LFU
AMBLESIDE (Cumbria)	**B2**															
Badgers Rake,		Mrs. P. A. Black, Badgers Rake, Fisherbeck Park., Ambleside, Cumbria LA22 0AJ. Tel. (096 63) 2332.	●	–	–	–	–	4	–	–	–	4–7	30.00 / *45.00*	100.00 / *180.00*	1–12	LN
† Balla Wray Holiday Cottage, Balla Wray Guest House,		Mr. & Mrs. B. Counsell, Balla Wray Guest House, High Wray, Ambleside, Cumbria, LA22 0JQ. Tel. (096 63) 3308.	●	–	–	1	–	–	–	–	–	2–4	92.00 / *95.00*	110.00 / *130.00*	1–12	GE LH U
Borrans Court Holiday Flats, Borrans Rd.		Mr. Bernard Loughran, Ferncliffe, Craiglands Ave., Heysham, Lancashire, Tel. Heysham (0524) 54671.	●	–	–	1	–	9	–	–	–	6	50.00 / –	– / *150.00*	1–12	GE LN
Bungalow, Loughrigg Pk.		Mrs. G. Haigh, 37 Causeway Head, Soyland, Halifax, W. Yorks, HX6 4NH.	●	–	1	–	–	–	–	–	–	6	45.00 / *60.00*	75.00 / *95.00*	1–12	GE LN
5 Busk Cottage.		Mrs. L. M. Williamson, 52 Windermere Pk., Windermere, Cumbria, LA21 1HP. Tel. Windermere (096 62) 3114.	●	–	–	1	–	–	–	–	–	4	30.00 / *50.00*	50.00 / *85.00*	1–12	GE LN
† Byways, Edinboro, Ambleside,		Douglas & Judy Worrall, Cottage Life, Lane Ends Barn, 11 Elterwater, Ambleside, Cumbria, LA22 9HN. Tel. Langdale (096 67) 292.	●	–	–	1	–	–	–	–	–	5	75.00 / –	– / *135.00*	1–12	GE LN
3 Cheapside.		N. D. Bell, 3 Cheapside, Ambleside, Cumbria, LA22 0AB. Tel. (096 63) 3082.	●	–	–	–	–	2	–	–	–	2–6	45.00 / –	– / *75.00*	1–12	GE LN
Cherry Tree Cottage,		Mrs. A. Parker, Cherry Tree Cottage, North Rd., Ambleside, Cumbria, LA22 0DW. Tel. (096 63) 3619.	●	1	–	–	–	–	–	–	–	2–4	50.00 / *65.00*	65.00 / *95.00*	3–11	GE LN

SELF-CATERING ACCOMMODATION

Name and Address: Town (County) / Establishment	Map Ref.	Contact for reservations: Name and address, Telephone number, Telex	Accommodation: Tourist Board Standards	Self-contained: House (or part)	Bungalows	Cottages	Chalets/caravans	Flats/flatlets	Houseboats	Not self-contained: Flats/flatlets	Chalets	Number of persons per unit	Prices per unit per week: Low season (£ Min. / *£ Max.*)	High season (£ Min. / *£ Max.*)	Months open (1–12)	Symbols (Key: see fold-out)
AMBLESIDE continued																
Cop Hill, 4 Gale Howe Park,		Mrs. S. V. Cooke, Woodlands, Evesham Rd., Weethley, Alcester, Warwickshire, B49 5LW. Tel. Alcester (0789) 763615.	●	1	–	–	–	–	–	–	–	7	100.00 *120.00*	150.00 *200.00*	1–12	M LF
The Coppice.		Mrs. E. M. Cervetti, The Coppice, Skelwith Fold, Ambleside, Cumbria, LA22 0HU. Tel. (096 63) 3676.	●	–	–	–	–	1	–	–	–	2–5	50.00 –	– *95.00*	1–12	GE M LN
The Cottage, St. Mary's La.,		Mrs. J. Elleray, 2 Fairview Ter., Ambleside, Cumbria, LA22 9EF. Tel. (096 63) 3379.	●	–	–	–	–	1	–	–	–	4	30.00 –	– *60.00*	1–12	GE M LH
Ellerthwaite Self Catering Properties.		Mr. K. V. Davies, Ellerthwaite, Ellerigg Rd., Ambleside, Cumbria, LA22 9EU. Tel. (096 63) 2020.	●	–	–	–	4	5	–	–	–	3–6	45.00 *50.00*	55.00 *65.00*	3–11	GE M LN
Fell View, Oaks Field, Kirkstone Rd.		Mrs. G. Fowler, Ryde Lodge, Zigzag Rd., Kenley, Surrey. Tel. 01-668 3144.	●	–	1	–	–	–	–	–	–	5	55.00 *70.00*	70.00 *95.00*	1–12	GE M LN
The Garden Flat, 2 Lowfield, Old Lake Rd.,		P. F. Quarmby, 3 Lowfield, Old Lake Rd., Ambleside, Cumbria, LA22 0DH. Tel. (096 63) 2326.	●	–	–	–	–	1	–	–	–	5	30.00 –	60.00 *65.00*	1–12	GE M LF
High Bank Cottage.		Mr. & Mrs. N. C. Murphy, High Bank Cottage, Old Lake Rd., Ambleside, Cumbria, LA22 0AE. Tel. (096 63) 2384.	●	1	–	–	–	–	–	–	–	7	50.00 –	– –	1–12	GE M LF
† 6 High Gale.		M. Garside, 6 High Gale, Ambleside, Cumbria, LA22 0BG. Tel. (09 663) 3420.	●	–	–	–	–	2	–	–	–	4–5	45.00 *45.00*	65.00 *65.00*	1–12	GE M LN
Horseshoe Cottage, 3 Rydal View, Millans Park,		Mrs. M. Wiseman, 34 Edward St., Blackpool, Lancashire, FY1 1BA. Tel. Blackpool (0253) 28936 (day) & 43471 (evening).	●	–	2	1	–	–	–	–	–	4–6	40.00 *70.00*	75.00 *130.00*	1–12	GE M LN T
2 How Head Cottages, Chapel Hill,		Mrs. Lynda Wilson, 21 Loughrigg Ave., Ambleside, Cumbria, LA22 0DG. Tel. (096 63) 2461.	●	–	–	1	–	–	–	–	–	5	50.00 –	100.00 –	1–12	GE M LN
Huyton Hill.		Miss Shuttleworth, Secretary, Huyton Hill, Nr. Ambleside, Cumbria, LA22 0HZ. Tel. (096 63) 3333.	●	–	1	6	–	8	–	–	–	4–6	50.00 *65.00*	85.00 *220.00*	1–12	GE M LH
Kilburn,		Mrs. M. Tebay, Kilburn, Wansfell Rd., Ambleside, Cumbria, LA22 0EG. Tel. (096 63) 2421.	●	–	–	–	–	1	–	–	–	5	40.00 *55.00*	55.00 *70.00*	1–12	GE M LN
Kirkstone Brow Flat.		B. E. Flitters, Kirkstone Brow, Sweden Bridge La., Ambleside, Cumbria, LA22 9EX. Tel. (096 63) 2863.	●	–	–	–	–	1	–	–	–	4	60.00 *60.00*	65.00 *65.00*	1–12	GE M LN

SELF-CATERING ACCOMMODATION

Name and Address: Town (County) / Establishment	Map Ref.	Contact for reservations: Name and address, Telephone number, Telex	Tourist Board Standards	Self-contained: House (or part)	Self-contained: Bungalows	Self-contained: Cottages	Self-contained: Chalets/caravans	Self-contained: Flats/flatlets	Self-contained: Houseboats	Not self-contained: Flats/flatlets	Not self-contained: Chalets	Number of persons per unit	Prices per unit per week: Low season	Prices per unit per week: High season	Months open (1–12)	Symbols
													£ Min. *£ Max.*	£ Min. *£ Max.*		Key: see fold-out
AMBLESIDE continued																
† Kirkstone Foot Country House Hotel.		Mr. & Mrs. S. R. Bateman, Kirkstone Foot Country House Hotel, Kirkstone Pass Rd., Ambleside, Cumbria, LA22 9EH. Tel. (096 63) 2232.	●	–	–	–	–	14	–	–	–	2–7	105.00 *175.00*	136.50 *230.00*	1–12	LF
4 Lake Rd.,		Mrs. G. Howson, Glenburn, New Rd., Windermere, Cumbria, LA23 2EE. Tel. Windermere (096 62) 2649.	●	–	–	–	–	1	–	–	–	5	45.00 *80.00*	90.00 *90.00*	1–12	10 GE LN
Lakeland Holiday Cottages.		J. Dickinson, Old Manor House, Wrea Green, Preston, Lancs., PR4 2WJ. Tel. Kirkham (0772) 682221.	●	–	–	3	–	–	–	–	–	2–7	70.00 –	– *200.00*	4–10	GE LH
13 Loughrigg Ave.,		Mr. & Mrs. A. Faulkner, Market Pl., Ambleside, Cumbria, LA22 9DA. Tel. (096 63) 3263.	●	1	–	–	–	–	–	–	–	6	90.00 *90.00*	90.00 *100.00*	1–12	GE LN
Low Brow Barn, Lake Rd., Waterhead,		Miss J. F. Moore, Moorings, Lake Rd., Waterhead, Ambleside, Cumbria, LA22 0DT. Tel. (096 63) 2250.	●	–	–	1	–	–	–	–	–	4	80.50 *85.50*	– *95.50*	4–10	5 LN
Manor House Cottage, High Wray.		Mrs. Sylvia Harris, High Wray House, High Wray, Ambleside, Cumbria, LA22 0JQ. Tel. (096 63) 2107.	●	–	–	1	–	–	–	–	–	5	70.00 *75.00*	80.00 *85.00*	2–11	GE LN
Oaks Cottage, Oaks Field, Off Kirkstone Rd.		Mr. J. A. Butterworth, White Moss House, Rydal Water, Grasmere, Ambleside, Cumbria, LA22 9SE. Tel. Grasmere (096 65) 295.	●	–	–	1	–	–	–	–	–	2–4	75.00 *95.00*	75.00 *95.00*	1–12	GE LF
† Ramsteads.		Mr. Evans, Ramsteads, Ramsteads Coppice, Outgate, Ambleside, Cumbria, LA22 0NH. Tel. Hawkshead (096 66) 583 & 051–428 2605.	●	–	–	–	8	–	–	–	–	4–6	64.00 *96.00*	98.00 *146.00*	4–10	GE LH
Seven Gates,		Mr. & Mrs. J. Thompson, Seven Gates, Rothay Bridge, Ambleside, Cumbria, LA22 0EH. Tel. (096 63) 3179.	●	–	–	–	2	2	–	–	–	2–4	50.00 –	85.00 –	1–12	LF
Stephen How Cottage,		Mrs. M. A. Dixon, Stephen How, Skelwith Bridge, Ambleside, Cumbria, LA22 9NP. Tel. (096 63) 3135.	●	–	–	1	–	–	–	–	–	2–3	75.00 –	90.00 –	2–11	GE LN
Stock Ghyll Holiday Flats.		M. Horrax, Stock Ghyll Holiday Flats, Kirkstone Rd., Ambleside, Cumbria, LA22 9EW. Tel. (096 63) 3294.	●	2	–	1	2	9	–	15	–	2–8	38.00 *76.00*	46.00 *99.00*	1–12	GE LH
The Studio Flat,		Mrs. J. Tomlinson, Stockghyll Studio, 2 Cheapside, Ambleside, Cumbria, LA22 0AB. Tel. (096 63) 2383 & 3430.	●	–	–	–	–	1	–	–	–	4–5	45.00 *60.00*	70.00 *95.00*	1–12	3 GE LN
Sycamore House, King St.,		Mrs. S. Thomas, Beech House, Victoria Rd., Windermere, Cumbria, LA23 2DL. Tel. Windermere (096 62) 2467.	●	–	–	–	–	1	–	–	–	2–9	25.00 *55.00*	55.00 *90.00*	1–12	GE LH

You are advised to read the introductory notes and to check prices and other details when booking accommodation

SELF-CATERING ACCOMMODATION

Name and Address: Town (County), Map Ref., Establishment	Contact for reservations: Name and address, Telephone number, Telex	Tourist Board Standards	Self-contained: House (or part)	Self-contained: Bungalows	Self-contained: Cottages	Self-contained: Chalets/caravans	Self-contained: Flats/flatlets	Self-contained: Houseboats	Not self-contained: Flats/flatlets	Not self-contained: Chalets	Number of persons per unit	Prices per unit per week: Low season (£ Min. / £ *Max.*)	Prices per unit per week: High season (£ Min. / £ *Max.*)	Months open (1–12)	Symbols (Key: see fold-out)
AMBLESIDE continued															
Wansfell View. 9 Oaksfield, off Kirkstone Rd.,	Mrs. M. W. Lambert, 3 Kingsway, Tynemouth, Tyne & Wear, NE30 2LY. Tel. N. Shields (0632) 575719.	●	1	-	-	-	-	-	-	-	4–6	45.00 *65.00*	70.00 *90.00*	1–12	GE M LN
APPLEBY-IN-WESTMORLAND (Cumbria) C2															
Broad Lea Holiday Homes,	Mrs. A. M. Ewbank, Broad Lea, Broom, Long Marton, Appleby-in-Westmorland, Cumbria, CA16 6JP. Tel. Kirkby Thore (093 06) 236.	●	-	1	1	-	-	-	-	-	7	75.00 *100.00*	100.00 *150.00*	1–12	GE LH
Brow Farm,	Miss W. & D. Swinbank, Brow Farm, Dufton, Appleby-in-Westmorland, Cumbria, CA16 6DF. Tel. Appleby (0930) 51202.	●	-	-	-	1	-	-	-	-	6	- *45.00*	- *60.00*	3–10	GE LN
The Cottage, Murton House.	Mrs. S. E. Guest, Murton House, Murton, Appleby-in-Westmorland, Cumbria, CA16 6NA. Tel. Appleby (0930) 51426.	●	-	-	1	-	-	-	-	-	6	40.00 *40.00*	95.00 *95.00*	1–12	GE M LH
Fell-Foot, Murton, Appleby-in-Westmorland.	Mrs. H. E. Schug, Bongate Moor, Appleby-in-Westmorland, Cumbria, CA16 6LH. Tel. Appleby (0930) 51516.	●	-	-	1	-	-	-	-	-	4	42.00 *42.00*	52.00 *52.00*	3–10	GE LN
Kirkber Farm,	Mrs. Mary M. Bell, Kirkber Farm, Appleby-in-Westmorland, Cumbria, CA16 6JG. Tel. Appleby (0930) 51389.	●	-	-	-	-	-	-	1	-	8	60.00 -	- *125.00*	3–11	GE M LN
Whygill Head.	Mrs. L. M. Watson, Whygill Head, Little Asby, Appleby-in-Westmorland, Cumbria, CA16 6QO. Tel. Kirkby Stephen (0930) 71531.	●	-	-	-	2	-	-	-	-	4–6	- *28.00*	- *30.00*	3–10	GE LN
ARNSIDE (Cumbria) C3															
Briery Bank House.	Mrs. M. K. Oliver, Briery Bank House, Briery Bank, Arnside, Carnforth, Lancs. LA5 0EF. Tel. (0524) 761242.	●	1	-	-	-	-	-	-	-	5	35.00 *40.00*	60.00 *68.00*	1–12	GE M LN
† Hampsfell.	Mr. & Mrs. A. E. & F. W. Anthony, Hampsfell, The Promenade, Arnside, via Carnforth, Lancs., LA5 0AD. Tel. (0524) 761285.	●	-	-	-	-	1	-	-	-	2–5	35.00 *50.00*	60.00 *75.00*	1–12	5 GE M LH
The Homestead.	Mrs. M. E. H. Kelsall, The Homestead, Carr Bank Rd., Milnthorpe, Nr. Arnside, Carnforth, Lancs. LA7 7LE. Tel. (0524) 761213.	●	1	-	-	-	-	-	-	-	5–6	60.00 -	65.00 *85.00*	1–12	GE M LH

You are advised to read the introductory notes and to check prices and other details when booking accommodation

SELF-CATERING ACCOMMODATION

Name and Address: Town (County), Map Ref., Establishment	Contact for reservations: Name and address, Telephone number, Telex	Tourist Board Standards	Self-contained: House (or part)	Self-contained: Bungalows	Self-contained: Cottages	Self-contained: Chalets/caravans	Self-contained: Flats/flatlets	Self-contained: Houseboats	Not self-contained: Flats/flatlets	Not self-contained: Chalets	Number of persons per unit	Prices per unit per week: Low season (£ Min. / *£ Max.*)	Prices per unit per week: High season (£ Min. / *£ Max.*)	Months open (1–12)	Symbols (Key: see fold-out)
ASPATRIA (Cumbria) B2 (8m NE. Maryport)															
41 Arkleby Rd.,	Mr. J. Tinnion, 35 Arkleby Rd., Aspatria, Cumbria, CA5 2BA. Tel. (0965) 20538.	●	-	-	1	-	-	-	-	-	6	60.00 *60.00*	70.00 *70.00*	1–12	GE LN
Chapel House, Blennerhasset, Aspatria, Carlisle,	Miss D. M. Leach, The Old Manse, Blennerhasset, Carlisle, Cumbria, CA5 3RL. Tel. (0965) 20530.	●	1	-	-	-	-	-	-	-	9	- -	60.00 *75.00*	4–10	GE LH
Town Head Farm, Hayton, Aspatria, Carlisle,	Mrs. A. M. Storr, The Red Haven, Hayton, Aspatria, Carlisle, Cumbria, CA5 2NW. Tel. (0965) 20596.	●	1	-	-	-	-	-	-	-	4–6	57.50 -	74.75 -	5–10	GE LN
BACKBARROW (Cumbria) B3															
Bridge House, Backbarrow, Nr. Ulverston,	Mrs. P. M. Bell, Oaklands, 63 Whittingham La., Broughton, Preston, Lancs., PR3 5DB. Tel. Preston (0772) 863065.	●	1	-	-	-	-	-	-	-	8	45.00 *70.00*	80.00 *100.00*	1–12	GE LN
1 The Glen, Backbarrow, Nr. Ulverston.	V. Lord, The Knoll Guest House, Lakeside, Ulverston, Cumbria, LA12 8AU. Tel. Newby Bridge (0448) 31347 or (0229) 24628.	●	-	-	1	-	-	-	-	-	5	50.00 *70.00*	80.00 *90.00*	1–12	GE LH
BAILEY (Cumbria) C1 (5m NE. Longtown)															
Bailey Mill.	Mrs. Pamela Copeland, Bailey Mill, Bailey, Newcastleton, Roxburghshire, TD9 0TR. Tel. Roadhead (069 78) 617.	●	2	-	-	-	-	-	-	-	4–6	48.00 *68.00*	88.00 *108.00*	3–11	GE LF T
BECKFOOT (Cumbria) B2 (3m SW. Silloth)															
Belmont Holiday Home.	Bill James, Belmont House, Beckfoot, Nr. Silloth, Cumbria, CA5 4LF. Tel. Allonby (090 084) 340 (Evenings).	●	1	-	-	-	-	-	-	-	5	40.00 -	- *80.00*	4–10	GE LN T
BEETHAM (Cumbria) C3 (2m SE. Milnthorpe)															
† Keiths Cottage & Whinscar Cottage, 32 & 30 Leighton Beck Rd., Beetham, Via Milnthorpe,	Mrs. Dorothy A. Scott, Overleigh House, East Cliff, Preston, Lancs., PR1 3JE. Tel. Preston (0772) 53545.	●	-	-	2	-	-	-	-	-	5–7	55.00 -	- *130.00*	1–12	GE LN T
BOOTLE (Cumbria) B3															
Beckside Farm Pony Trekking Centre, Bootle, Nr. Millom,	J. D. Southward, Broom Hill, Bootle, Nr. Millom, Cumbria, LA19 5UN. Tel. (065 78) 736.	●	1	-	-	1	-	-	-	-	8	40.00 -	- *143.00*	1–12	GE LN
Briar Grove, Bootle, Millom.	Mrs. H. R. Grice, Hinning House, Bootle, Millom, Cumbria, LA19 5TJ. Tel. (065 78) 205.	●	-	-	1	-	-	-	-	-	6	45.00 *50.00*	65.00 *75.00*	4–10	GE LN

 You are advised to read the introductory notes and to check prices and other details when booking accommodation

SELF-CATERING ACCOMMODATION

Name and Address: Town (County) / Establishment	Map Ref.	Contact for reservations: Name and address, Telephone number, Telex	Tourist Board Standards	Self-contained: House (or part)	Bungalows	Cottages	Chalets/caravans	Flats/flatlets	Houseboats	Not self-contained: Flats/flatlets	Chalets	Number of persons per unit	Prices per unit per week: Low season (£ Min. / £ Max.)	High season (£ Min. / £ Max.)	Months open (1–12)	Symbols (Key: see fold-out)
BORROWDALE (Cumbria)	**B2**															
† Castle How, Rosthwaite, Borrowdale, Keswick,		Mr. & Mrs. J. Grange, Yew Tree Cottage, Ullock, Portinscale, Keswick, Cumbria, CA12 5SP. Tel. Braithwaite (059 682) 493.	●	–	1	1	–	–	–	–	–	5	60.00 / –	– / *145.00*	1–12	GE LF
Derwent Farm, Grange-in-Borrowdale, Keswick,		Mrs. C. R. Blinston, 82 Causeway Side, Linthwaite, Huddersfield, W. Yorkshire, HD7 5NW. Tel. Huddersfield (0484) 842066.	●	–	–	–	–	2	–	–	–	3–5	55.00 / *70.00*	60.00 / *80.00*	1–12	GE LN
High Seat, Manesty, Keswick,		Mrs. Leyland, Youdale Knot, Manesty, Keswick, Cumbria, CA12 5UG. Tel. (059 684) 663.	●	–	1	–	–	–	–	–	–	2–12	60.00 / –	– / *95.00*	1–12	6 GE LN
High Stile Cottage, Top Row, Seatoller, Borrowdale.		Mrs. P. M. Brannan, Lingy Acre, Portinscale, Keswick, Cumbria, CA12 5TX. Tel. Keswick (0596) 72717.	●	–	–	1	–	–	–	–	–	5	80.00 / *100.00*	120.00 / *140.00*	4–10	GE LN
Kiln How & Rose Cottage, Rosthwaite, Borrowdale, Nr. Keswick,		Mr. & Mrs. L. K. Weller, Rose Cottage, Rosthwaite-in-Borrowdale, Cumbria, CA12 5XB. Tel. (059 684) 209.	●	–	–	–	–	5	–	–	–	2–8	45.00 / *55.00*	60.00 / *120.00*	1–12	GE LH
† Newton Place.		Mr. & Mrs. C. A. Locker, Newton Place, Borrowdale, Keswick, Cumbria, CA12 5UY. Tel. (059 684) 278.	●	–	–	1	–	3	–	–	–	5–6	38.00 / *54.00*	103.00 / *120.00*	1–12	GE LF
† Scale Force Cottage & Ghyllside Cottage, Seatoller, Borrowdale, Keswick.		Mr. & Mrs. J. Grange, Yew Tree Cottage, Ullock, Portinscale, Keswick, Cumbria, CA12 5SP. Tel. Braithwaite (059 682) 493.	●	–	–	2	–	–	–	–	–	6	75.00 / –	– / *200.00*	1–12	GE LF
BRAITHWAITE (Cumbria)	**B2**															
† 3 Crown Cottages, Braithwaite, Keswick,		Receptionist, Braithwaite Motor Inn, Braithwaite, Keswick, Cumbria, CA12 5TD. Tel. (059 682) 444.	●	–	–	1	–	–	–	–	–	4	35.00 / *45.00*	100.00 / *140.00*	1–12	LH
Hawthorn Cottage, Braithwaite, Keswick.		Mrs. J. L. Boucher, Dalegarth, Buttermere, Cockermouth, Cumbria, CA13 9XA. Tel. Buttermere (059 685) 233.	●	–	–	1	–	–	–	–	–	4–6	50.00 / –	– / *85.00*	4–10	GE LN
Kinn Cottage, Braithwaite, Keswick.		Mrs. P. M. Brannan, Lingy Acre, Portinscale, Keswick, Cumbria, CA12 5TX. Tel. Keswick (0596) 72717.	●	–	–	1	–	–	–	–	–	5	80.00 / *100.00*	120.00 / *140.00*	3–10	GE LN
I. Melbecks.		R. Pattinson, I. Melbecks, Braithwaite, Keswick, Cumbria, CA12 5TL. Tel. (059 682) 219.	●	1	–	2	–	–	–	–	–	8–9	– / *63.00*	– / *80.00*	1–12	GE LH
† Moss Garth & Moss Gate, Braithwaite, Keswick,		Trustclean Ltd., Queens Ct., Bentley, Doncaster, S. Yorks., DN5 9QH. Tel. Doncaster (0302) 783193.	●	1	–	–	–	–	–	1	–	2–8	60.00 / –	– / *178.00*	1–12	GE LH

SELF-CATERING ACCOMMODATION

Name and Address: Town (County) / Establishment	Map Ref.	Contact for reservations: Name and address, Telephone number, Telex	Tourist Board Standards	Self-contained: House (or part)	Self-contained: Bungalows	Self-contained: Cottages	Self-contained: Chalets/caravans	Self-contained: Flats/flatlets	Self-contained: Houseboats	Not self-contained: Flats/flatlets	Not self-contained: Chalets	Number of persons per unit	Prices per unit per week: Low season (£ Min. / £ Max.)	Prices per unit per week: High season (£ Min. / £ Max.)	Months open (1–12)	Symbols (Key: see fold-out)
BRAITHWAITE continued																
The Old Farmhouse Mews Cottages,		J. D. Broadbent, The Old Farmhouse, Braithwaite, Nr. Keswick, Cumbria, CA12 5SY. Tel. (059 682) 431.	C	-	-	7	-	2	-	-	-	6	44.00 / *80.00*	61.00 / *100.00*	1–10 12	GE LN
† Primrose Cottage, Main St.		Mr. & Mrs. J. Grange, Yew Tree Cottage, Ullock, Portinscale, Keswick, Cumbria, CA12 5SP. Tel. (059 682) 493.	●	-	-	1	-	-	-	-	-	4–5	65.00 / -	- / *125.00*	1–12	GE LF
BRAMPTON (Cumbria)	**C1**															
Cleugh Head Farm Cottage.		Mrs. M. E. Smith, Cleugh Head, Low Row, Brampton, Cumbria, CA8 2JB. Tel. Hallbankgate (069 76) 283.	●	1	-	-	-	-	-	-	-	7	30.00 / *50.00*	65.00 / *75.00*	1–12	LN
† Long Byres, Talkin Head, Brampton,		Mrs. Susan Dean, Kirkhouse, Brampton, Cumbria, CA8 1JR. Tel. Hallbankgate (069 76) 262.	●	-	-	7	-	-	-	-	-	2–6	40.00 / *60.00*	90.00 / *120.00*	1–12	LF
† Old Gables, 9 High Cross St.,		Mrs. E. P. Bell, The Post Office, Lazonby, Penrith, Cumbria, CA10 1BX. Tel. Lazonby (076 883) 242 & 437.	●	-	-	-	-	1	-	-	-	5	50.00 / -	90.00 / *110.00*	1–12	LN
BROUGH (Cumbria)	**C2**															
3 Kings Ter, Upper Market St.,		Mrs. J. C. McIvor, The Cottage, Victoria Rd., Church Brough, Kirkby Stephen, Cumbria, CA17 4EJ. Tel. (093 04) 597.	●	1	-	-	-	-	-	-	-	6	45.00 / *45.00*	60.00 / *70.00*	1–12	GE LH
Todds House, N. Stainmore, Brough.		Mrs. M. D. Willis, 112 Moorside Rd., Urmston, Manchester, Lancs., M31 3RF. Tel. 061-748 3651.	●	-	-	1	-	-	-	-	-	11	70.00 / *70.00*	95.00 / *95.00*	4–10	GE LN
BROUGHTON-IN-FURNESS (Cumbria)	**B3**															
Brockwood Park,		Mr. Joe Cant, Brockwood Park, Whicham Valley, Broughton-in-Furness, Millom, Cumbria, LA18 5JS. Tel. Millom (0657) 2329.	●	-	-	-	30	-	-	-	-	4–8	75.00 / *97.00*	210.00 / *265.00*	1–12	LF
Broomhill.		Mrs. A. I. Shipman, Broomhill New St., Broughton-in-Furness, Cumbria, LA20 6JD. Tel. (065 76) 358.	●	-	-	-	-	-	-	3	-	2–6	59.00 / *89.00*	69.00 / *102.00*	1–12	GE LH
† Coach House.		Mr. & Mrs. D. V. Walker, High Dudden Guest House, Broughton-in-Furness, Cumbria, LA20 6ET. Tel. (065 76) 279.	●	-	-	-	-	2	-	-	-	4–8	45.00 / *65.00*	85.00 / *140.00*	1–12	GE LF
Cockley Beck Cottage.		Mrs. G. Akrigg, Cockley Beck Farm, Seathwaite, Broughton-in-Furness, Cumbria, LA20 6EQ. Tel. (065 76) 480.	●	-	-	1	-	-	-	-	-	4–6	45.00 / -	- / *70.00*	1–12	GE LN

You are advised to read the introductory notes and to check prices and other details when booking accommodation

SELF-CATERING ACCOMMODATION

Name and Address: Town (County) / Establishment	Map Ref.	Contact for reservations: Name and address, Telephone number, Telex	Tourist Board Standards	Accommodation: Self-contained: House (or part)	Bungalows	Cottages	Chalets/caravans	Flats/flatlets	Houseboats	Not self-contained: Flats/flatlets	Chalets	Number of persons per unit	Prices: Per unit per week: Low season (£ Min. / £ Max.)	High season (£ Min. / £ Max.)	Months open (1–12)	Symbols (Key: see fold-out)
BROUGHTON-IN-FURNESS continued																
Furness Bungalow, Station Rd.		Mrs. Linda Pogson, The Haven, 57A Main St., Warton, Carnforth, Lancs., LA5 9NX. Tel. Carnforth (052 473) 2290.	●	-	1	-	-	-	-	-	-	6	45.00 *60.00*	70.00 *90.00*	3–10	GE LN
Hazel Head Cottage.		Mrs. G. Lowery, Hazel Head Farm, Ulpha, Broughton-in-Furness, Cumbria, LA20 6DX. Tel. (065 76) 531.	●	-	-	1	-	-	-	-	-	5	57.50 -	- *86.25*	4–10	5 GE LN
Hole House Farm, Ulpha, Broughton-in-Furness,		W. Melville M. Tyson, Wreaks End House, Broughton-in-Furness, Cumbria, LA20 6BS. Tel. (065 76) 216.	●	1	-	-	-	-	-	-	-	6–7	65.00 -	- *90.00*	3–11	GE LN
Park Stile Cottage, Syke House,		Mrs. A. C. Willis, Lane End Farm, Waberthwaite, Millom, Cumbria, LA19 5YJ. Tel. Ravenglass (065 77) 262.	●	-	-	1	-	-	-	-	-	5	59.00 *77.00*	77.00 *115.00*	1–12	11 GE LN
† Thornthwaite Farm.		Jean Jackson, Thornthwaite Farm, Woodland, Broughton-in-Furness, Cumbria, LA20 6DF. Tel. (065 76) 340.	●	-	-	1	2	-	-	-	-	5–6	40.00 -	- *70.00*	1–12	GE LF
Undercragg, Seathwaite,		Mrs. J. Hartley, Turner Hall, Seathwaite, Broughton-in-Furness, Cumbria, LA20 6EE. Tel. (065 76) 420.	●	-	-	1	-	-	-	-	-	6	- -	90.00 -	1–12	GE LN
† Water Walk Mill, Duddon Bridge, Broughton-in-Furness,		Mrs. H. Parsons, Glebelands, Broughton-in-Furness, Cumbria, Tel. (065 76) 379.	●	1	-	-	-	-	-	-	-	6–8	50.00 *60.00*	70.00 *100.00*	1–12	GE LH
BURGH-BY-SANDS (Cumbria)	**B1**															
Hollygarth Cottage, Monkhill, Burgh-by-Sands, Carlisle,		Mr. & Mrs. L. Higdon, 4 St. Georges Cres., Stanwix, Carlisle, Cumbria, CA3 9NL. Tel. Carlisle (0228) 24978.	●	-	-	1	-	-	-	-	-	5	40.00 *60.00*	75.00 *95.00*	1–12	GE LF
BURTON-IN-KENDAL (Cumbria) (11m S. Kendal)	**C3**															
Lime Field House, Farleton, Nr. Burton-in-Kendal,		Mr. & Mrs. C. J. R. Ratcliff, 4 Ribblesdale Pl., Preston, Lancashire, PR1 3NA. Tel. Preston (0772) 58427.	●	-	-	1	-	-	-	-	-	2–7	70.00 -	- *140.00*	1–12	GE LN
Tyee Cottage, Tanpits La.		J. I. H. & J. M. Coates, Larchwoods, Huby, York, Yorks., YO6 1HS. Tel. Easingwold (0347) 810411.	●	-	-	1	-	-	-	-	-	6	45.00 -	- *70.00*	1–12	GE LN
BUTTERMERE (Cumbria)	**B2**															
† Midtown Cottages, High Lorton, Lorton Vale, Buttermere Valley, Nr. Cockermouth,		Olga Hunter, 12 Derwent St., Keswick, Cumbria, CA12 5AN. Tel. Keswick (0596) 74392.	●	-	-	4	-	-	-	-	-	4	68.00 *120.00*	110.00 *150.00*	1–12	LF

SELF-CATERING ACCOMMODATION

Name and Address: Town (County), Map Ref., Establishment	Contact for reservations: Name and address, Telephone number, Telex	Tourist Board Standards	Self-contained: House (or part)	Bungalows	Cottages	Chalets/caravans	Flats/flatlets	Houseboats	Not self-contained: Flats/flatlets	Chalets	Number of persons per unit	Prices per unit per week: Low season £ Min. / £ Max.	High season £ Min. / £ Max.	Months open (1–12)	Symbols (Key: see fold-out)
BUTTERMERE continued															
Rannerdale Croft, Rannerdale Farm.	Mrs. Elaine Beard, Rannerdale Farm, Buttermere, Nr. Cockermouth, Cumbria, CA13 9UY. Tel. (059 685) 232.	●	–	–	1	–	–	–	–	–	4–6	40.00 / *40.00*	85.00 / *85.00*	1–12	5 GE M LN
CALDBECK (Cumbria) B2															
Fellside Mansion Cottage, Fellside,	P. A. Chapman, 18 South Parade, York, Tel. York (0904) 35367.	●	–	–	1	–	–	–	–	–	6–7	50.00 / *60.00*	80.00 / *105.00*	1–12	GE M LN
† Whelpo House.	Diana Greenwood, Whelpo House, Caldbeck, Nr. Wigton, Cumbria, CA7 8HQ. Tel. (069 98) 270.	●	1	–	–	–	–	–	–	–	6	65.00 / *75.00*	115.00 / *140.00*	1–12	LF
CARLISLE (Cumbria) B1															
† The Garden Cottage, Corby Castle Estate,	Mrs. J. P. Howard, Corby Castle, Carlisle, Cumbria, CA4 8LR. Tel. Wetheral (0228) 60246.	●	–	–	1	–	–	–	–	–	5–6	80.50 / *80.50*	92.00 / *115.00*	1–12	GE LH
† Millstone Cottage, Blackhall Wood, by Carlisle.	Country Farm Holidays, The Place Ham La., Powick, Worcester, WR2 4RA. Tel. Worcester (0905) 830899. Telex 336957.	●	–	–	1	–	–	–	–	–	2–8	30.00 / *100.00*	65.00 / *145.00*	1–12	LH
† Newbiggin Hall.	David & June Bates, Newbiggin Hall, Carleton, Carlisle, Cumbria, CA4 0AJ. Tel. (0228) 27549.	●	–	–	1	–	2	–	–	–	2–8	40.00 / *90.00*	80.00 / *180.00*	1–12	GE M LH
† Orton Grange Caravan Park,	Lady Ley or Mr. Alan Dobson, Orton Grange Caravan Park, Wigton Rd., Carlisle, Cumbria, CA5 6LA. Tel. (0228) 710252.	●	–	–	–	5	–	–	–	2	2–6	28.75 / *69.00*	40.25 / *80.25*	1–12	GE M LH
CARTMEL (Cumbria) B3															
† Aynsome Manor Park.	Mrs. B. Smith, Aynsome Manor Pk., Cartmel, Cumbria, LA11 6HH. Tel. (044 854) 433.	●	–	–	1	–	4	–	–	–	4	25.00 / *35.00*	60.00 / *90.00*	1–12	12 GE M LH
† Church Town House, Market Sq.	Westbourne Hotel Ltd., 10 Lake Rd., Lytham St. Annes, Lancs., FY8 1BE. Tel. Lytham (0253) 734736.	●	–	–	–	–	1	–	–	–	4	100.00 / *100.00*	100.00 / *100.00*	1–12	12 GE M LF
Long Barn.	Mr. or Mrs. A. C. Gregory, The Farmhouse, Overridge, Cartmel, Grange-over-Sands, Cumbria, LA11 7SP. Tel. (044 854) 351.	●	1	–	–	–	–	–	–	–	4–8	50.00 / *60.00*	90.00 / *110.00*	3–11	GE M LN
Longlands Farm Cottage.	Mrs. J. A. Dixon, Longlands Farm, Cartmel, Grange-over-Sands, Cumbria, LA11 6HJ. Tel. (044 854) 406.	●	–	–	1	–	–	–	–	–	6	42.00 / *55.00*	75.00 / *120.00*	1–12	GE M LH
† Longlands.	Mr. & Mrs. J. R. S. Wilkie, Longlands, Cartmel, Grange-over-Sands, Cumbria, LA11 6HG. Tel. (044 854) 475.	●	–	–	3	–	3	–	–	–	2–8	45.00 / *–*	97.00 / *168.00*	1–12	GE M LH

 You are advised to read the introductory notes and to check prices and other details when booking accommodation

SELF-CATERING ACCOMMODATION

Name and Address: Town (County) / Establishment	Map Ref.	Contact for reservations: Name and address, Telephone number, Telex	Tourist Board Standards	Self-contained: House (or part)	Bungalows	Cottages	Chalets/caravans	Flats/flatlets	Houseboats	Not self-contained: Flats/flatlets	Chalets	Number of persons per unit	Prices per unit per week: Low season (£ Min. / *£ Max.*)	High season (£ Min. / *£ Max.*)	Months open (1–12)	Symbols (Key: see fold-out)
CASTLE CARROCK (Cumbria) (4m S. Brampton)	**C1**															
Greenwell.		Miss M. H. Bird, 1710 Greenwell, Castle Carrock, Carlisle, Cumbria, CA4 9NH. Tel. Hayton (022 870) 518.	●	–	–	1	–	–	–	–	–	4	40.00 / *40.00*	45.00 / *45.00*	5–10	4 ◉ GE M ▢ ⊙ LN ✻
CLEATOR (Cumbria)	**B2**															
Devonshire Bungalow,		Mrs. M. L. Martin, Ehenhall Gardens, Cleator, Cumbria, CA23 3BZ. Tel. Cleator Moor (0946) 810277.	●	–	1	–	–	–	–	–	–	2–9	66.00 / –	– / *120.00*	1–12	◉ GE M ▢ TV ⊙ LN
CLIBURN (Cumbria) (6m ESE. Penrith)	**C2**															
1–3 Rectory Dene, Cliburn, Penrith		A. J. & D. Chapelhow, Keystones, Rectory Dene, Cliburn, Penrith, Cumbria, CA10 3AL. Tel. Morland (093 14) 289.	●	–	3	–	–	–	–	–	–	4–6	50.00 / *94.00*	50.00 / *94.00*	1–12	◉ GE ▢ TV ⊙ LH
COCKERMOUTH (Cumbria)	**B2**															
Benson Court Cottage, 10 St. Helens St.,		Mrs. E. Pearson, 12 St. Helens St., Cockermouth, Cumbria, CA13 9HX. Tel. (0900) 824316.	●	–	–	1	–	–	–	–	–	6	40.00 / *50.00*	50.00 / *75.00*	1–12	◉ GE M ▢ R TV ⊙ LH S
Brow How, Pardshaw, Cockermouth.		Mrs. T. Dunstan, Greenacre Cottage, 42 North St., W. Butterwick, Scunthorpe, S. Humberside, DN17 3JW. Tel. Scunthorpe (0724) 782873.	●	–	–	1	–	–	–	–	–	6	50.00 / *75.00*	90.00 / *115.00*	1–12	◉ GE M ▢ R TV ⊙ LN ✻
Chestnut Cottage, 26 Kirkgate,		Mrs. J. M. Hurst, Fleetwith, 19 Harrot Hill, Cockermouth, Cumbria, CA13 0BL. Tel. (0900) 823984.	●	–	–	1	–	–	–	–	–	4–5	35.00 / *35.00*	50.00 / *80.00*	4–10	◉ GE M ▢ TV ⊙ LN
† Croft Cottages & Flats.		Grey Abbey Properties Ltd., P.O. Box 23, Coach Rd., Whitehaven, Cumbria, CA28 9DF. Tel. Whitehaven (0946) 3773.	●	–	–	1	–	9	–	–	–	4–6	37.00 / *88.00*	100.00 / *125.00*	1–12	◉ GE M ▢ TV ⊙ LH
Fieldside Cottage, Pardshaw Hall,		Mrs. D. E. Armstrong, 14 Dairylands Rd., Church Lawton, Stoke-on-Trent, Staffs., ST7 3EU. Tel. Alsager (093 63) 3186.	●	1	–	–	–	–	–	–	–	9	– / *85.00*	– / *150.00*	4–10	◉ GE M ▢ R TV LN ✻
33 Greyrigg Ave.,		Mrs. K. Konarek, 32 Platford Green, Nelmes Park, Hornchurch, Essex, RM11 2TA. Tel. Hornchurch (040 24) 56031.	●	–	1	–	–	–	–	–	–	6	– / *35.00*	– / *80.00*	1–12	▢ TV ⊙ LH
† Hillcrest & Hilltop.		Mrs. J. E. Mattinson, Marron House, Ullock, Workington, Cumbria, CA14 4TP. Tel. Lamplugh (094 686) 314.	●	2	–	–	–	–	–	–	–	2–9	45.00 / –	– / *110.00*	1–12	◉ GE M ▢ TV ⊙ LN ✻

SELF-CATERING ACCOMMODATION

Name and Address: Town (County), Map Ref., Establishment	Contact for reservations: Name and address, Telephone number, Telex	Accommodation: Tourist Board Standards	Self-contained: House (or part)	Bungalows	Cottages	Chalets/caravans	Flats/flatlets	Houseboats	Not self-contained: Flats/flatlets	Chalets	Number of persons per unit	Prices per unit per week: Low season £ Min. / £ Max.	High season £ Min. / £ Max.	Months open (1–12)	Symbols (Key: see fold-out)
COCKERMOUTH contd.															
Holiday Flats & Cottage.	Mr. & Mrs. W. Jackson, Woodhall, Cockermouth, Cumbria, CA13 0NX. Tel. (0900) 823585 & 822281.	●	-	-	1	-	7	-	-	-	7	- / -	- / *90.00*	4–10	GE M LH
† Hundith Hill Hotel.	Mrs. Hayton, Hundith Hill Hotel, Cockermouth, Cumbria, CA13 9TH. Tel. (0900) 822092.	●	1	-	-	-	1	-	2	-	2–7	40.00 / *70.00*	75.00 / *150.00*	1–12	GE LF
Jenkin Cottage.	Mrs. M. E. Teasdale, Jenkin Farm, Embleton, Cockermouth, Cumbria, CA13 9TN. Tel. Bassenthwaite Lake (059 681) 387.	●	-	-	1	-	-	-	-	-	6	45.00 / *60.00*	75.00 / *90.00*	1–12	LN
† The Old Corn Mill, Papcastle, Cockermouth.	Grey Abbey Properties Ltd., P.O. Box 23, Coach Rd., Whitehaven, Cumbria, CA28 9OE. Tel. Whitehaven (0946) 3773.	●	-	-	3	-	3	-	-	-	2–6	38.00 / *93.00*	110.00 / *128.00*	1–12	GE M LH
CONISTON (Cumbria) B3															
† Coniston Co-operative Soc. Ltd.	Mr. Stephenson, Yewdale Rd., Coniston. Cumbria, LA21 8DX. Tel. (096 64) 247.	●	-	-	-	-	2	-	-	-	6–8	45.00 / *60.00*	65.00 / *100.00*	1–12	GE M LN
Cruachan	Mrs L. Grant, 21 Collingwood Clo., Coniston Cumbria, LA21 8DZ. Tel. Langdale (096 67) 245.	●	1	-	-	-	-	-	-	-	6	70.00 / -	- / *130.00*	1–12	GE M LN
1 Devonshire Ter.,	Mrs Y. Williams, The Old Man, Antiques, Coniston Cumbria, LA21 8DU. Tel. (096 64) 389.	●	-	-	1	-	-	-	-	-	6	50.00 / *50.00*	60.00 / *100.00*	1–12	GE M LN
Flats 3 & 4 Richmond House, Tilberthwaite Ave.	Mrs. J. Johnson, Esk Villa, Tilberthwaite Ave., Coniston Cumbria, LA21 8ED. Tel. (096 64) 319.	●	-	-	-	-	2	-	-	-	2–8	50.00 / -	- / *130.00*	1–12	GE M LN
How Head Cottage,	Mrs. B. Thompson, How Head Cottage, Coniston, Cumbria, LA21 8AA. Tel. (096 64) 594.	●	-	-	-	-	1	-	-	-	2–4	55.00 / -	- / *100.00*	1–12	GE M LH
Lakeland House,	Mrs. M. Lee, Lakeland House, Tilberthwaite Ave., Coniston, Cumbria, LA21 8ED. Tel. (096 64) 303.	●	2	1	-	-	-	-	-	-	2–6	40.00 / *60.00*	85.00 / *135.00*	1–12	GE M LH
Low Bank Ground	Mrs. K. Smith, Low Bank Ground, Coniston, Cumbria, LA21 8AA. Tel. (096 64) 314.	●	-	-	-	-	5	-	-	-	4–8	74.75 / *149.50*	97.75 / *195.50*	1–12	GE M LN
† Spoon Hall	E Youdell, Spoon Hall, Coniston, Cumbria, LA21 8AW. Tel. (096 64) 391.	●	-	-	-	1	-	-	-	-	6	30.00 / *35.00*	35.00 / *40.00*	1–12	GE LH
Thurston House, Tilberthwaite Rd.,	Mr. D. W. Smith, Shepherds Villa, Tilberthwaite Rd., Coniston, Cumbria, LA21 8EE. Tel. (096 64) 337 or (0448) 31223.	●	-	-	-	-	5	-	2	-	2–6	20.00 / *40.00*	55.00 / *85.00*	1–12	GE M LH

You are advised to read the introductory notes and to check prices and other details when booking accommodation

SELF-CATERING ACCOMMODATION

Town (County) / Establishment	Map Ref.	Contact for reservations: Name and address, Telephone number, Telex	Tourist Board Standards	Self-contained: House (or part)	Bungalows	Cottages	Chalets/caravans	Flats/flatlets	Houseboats	Not self-contained: Flats/flatlets	Chalets	Number of persons per unit	Per unit per week: Low season £ Min. / £ Max.	High season £ Min. / £ Max.	Months open (1–12)	Symbols (Key: see fold-out)
CONISTON continued																
Townson Ground		Mrs. B. E. Nelson, Townson Ground, Coniston, Cumbria, LA21 8AA. Tel. (096 64) 272.	●	-	-	1	-	-	-	-	-	4	40.00 *55.00*	65.00 *80.00*	1–12	2 GE M LF
Wine Shop & Restaurant, Lake Rd.,		Mrs. E. A. Robinson, Under Brow, The Brow, Coniston, Cumbria, LA21 8EW. Tel. (096 64) 256.	●	-	-	-	-	2	-	-	-	5–6	40.00 -	75.00 *95.00*	1–12	GE M TV LH
Winton Shelt Gill, Haws Bank.		Rosalind Dean, 51 Winchester Cres., Sheffield, Yorks SI0 4ED.	●	-	-	1	-	-	-	-	-	5–6	55.00 -	- *120.00*	1–12	GE M LN
CROOK (Cumbria) (4m NW. Kendal)	C3															
† Birksey Brow Cottage, Birksey Brow.		Mrs. B. E. Bibby, 26, St.Mary's Park, Windermere, Cumbria, LA23 1AZ. Tel. Windermere (096 62) 2527.	●	-	-	1	-	-	-	-	-	5	55.00 *75.00*	85.00 *105.00*	1–12	GE TV LH
Brow Head Farm.		Mrs. Isabel Atkinson, Brow Head Farm, Crook, Kendal, Cumbria, LA8 8LR. Tel. Crosthwaite (044 88) 322.	●	1	-	-	-	-	-	-	-	6–8	- -	- *50.00*	4–10	TV LN
Holiday Cottages,		Mrs. B. Adams, Low Crag, Crook, Nr. Kendal, Cumbria, LA8 8LE. Tel. Crosthwaite (044 88) 268.	●	-	-	3	-	-	-	-	-	2–8	35.00 -	60.00 *140.00*	1–12	GE M TV LN
CROSTHWAITE (Cumbria) (5m WSW. Kendal)	C3															
Heath Cottage, Crosthwaite, Nr. Kendal,		Mrs. J. Schofield, The High Farm, Crosthwaite, Nr. Kendal, Cumbria. Tel. (044 88) 205.	●	-	-	1	-	-	-	-	-	6–7	50.00 *80.00*	90.00 *160.00*	1–12	GE TV LN
DENT (Cumbria) (5m SE. Sedbergh)	C3															
Low Chapel Farm, Dent, Nr. Sedbergh,		Mr. T. E. Capstick, Hall Bank Farm, Dent, Nr. Sedbergh, Cumbria, LA10 5TD. Tel. (058 75) 352.	●	1	-	-	-	-	-	-	-	6	40.00 *60.00*	60.00 *90.00*	1–12	GE M LN
Seeds Gill House, Main St.		R. I. Taylor, Netley Farmhouse, Gawthrop, Dent, Sedbergh, Cumbria, LA10 5TA. Tel. (058 75) 391.	●	-	-	-	-	2	-	-	-	2–4	35.00 *49.00*	60.00 *97.00*	1–12	5 GE M TV LF
EAMONT BRIDGE (Cumbria) (1m SE. Penrith)	C2															
Ash Lea, Southwaite Green La., Eamont Bridge, Pooley Bridge, Penrith,		Mrs. Dorothy Studholme, Newlands Grange, Hesket Newmarket, Caldbeck, Wigton, Cumbria, CA7 8HP. Tel. Calbeck (069 98) 676.	●	-	-	1	1	-	-	-	-	6	60.00 -	85.00 -	4–10	GE M TV LN

SELF-CATERING ACCOMMODATION

Name and Address: Town (County) / Establishment	Map Ref.	Contact for reservations: Name and address, Telephone number, Telex	Tourist Board Standards	Self-contained: House (or part)	Bungalows	Cottages	Chalets/caravans	Flats/flatlets	Houseboats	Not self-contained: Flats/flatlets	Chalets	Number of persons per unit	Prices per unit per week: Low season (£ Min. / £ Max.)	High season (£ Min. / £ Max.)	Months open (1–12)	Symbols (Key: see fold-out)
EGREMONT (Cumbria)	**B2**															
5 Cross Side.		Mrs. S. Marston, 34 Dane Ave., Barrow-in-Furness, Cumbria, LA14 4JS. Tel. (0229) 21891.	●	-	-	1	-	-	-	-	-	4	- *65.00*	- *100.00*	1–12	GE M LN
† Wodow Bank Farm Cottage.		Mrs. I Thomas, Wodow Bank Farm, Egremont, Cumbria, CA22 2UE. Tel. (0946) 820284.	●	-	-	1	-	-	-	-	-	10	100.00 -	150.00 -	1–12	GE LN
ELTERWATER (Cumbria)	**B2**															
Lane Ends Cottages. Elterwater, Nr. Ambleside,		Mrs. M. E. Rice, Fellside Lane Ends, Elterwater, Nr. Ambleside, Cumbria, LA22 9HS. Tel. Langdale (096 67) 678.	●	-	-	2	-	-	-	-	-	6	60.00 -	80.00 -	1–12	GE M LN
Oak Bank.		Mrs. F. Moseley, Oak Bank, Elterwater, Ambleside, Cumbria, LA22 9JA. Tel. Langdale (096 67) 683.	●	-	-	1	-	-	-	-	-	6	45.00 -	- *75.00*	3–11	GE M LN
Wheelwrights,		Ian & Anne Price, Wheelwrights, Elterwater, Ambleside, Cumbria, LA22 9HS. Tel. Langdale (096 67) 635.	●	-	-	1	-	1	-	-	-	4	65.00 *65.00*	180.00 *180.00*	1–12	10 GE M LF
ENNERDALE (Cumbria)	**B2**															
Bleach Green Cottages,		C. J. Mayson, 12 Finkle St., St. Bees, Cumbria, CA27 0BN. Tel. St. Bees (094 685) 641 & 616.	●	-	-	3	-	-	-	-	-	2–5	60.00 -	85.00 -	1–12	GE LN
The Byres, Ennerdale Bridge		D. Whitfield Bott., Shepherd's Arms Hotel, Ennerdale Bridge, Cumbria, CA23 3AR. Tel. Lamplugh (094 686) 249.	●	-	-	1	-	-	-	-	-	6	50.00 -	- *80.00*	1–12	GE M LN
Croftfoot Cottage, Ennerdale, Cleator		Croftfoot Trustees (Ref. Met), P.O. Box 1, 44 Duke St., Whitehaven, Cumbria, CA28 7NR. Tel. Whitehaven (0946) 2194.	●	-	-	1	-	-	-	-	-	7	65.00 -	100.00 -	4–10	GE LN
Merlewood.		Mrs. V Kenmare, Merlewood, High Wath, Cleator, Cumbria, CA23 3AE. Tel. Cleatormoor (0946) 811105.	●	-	-	-	-	1	-	-	-	5	35.00 -	- *100.00*	1–12	GE M LH
Mireside Farm.		Mrs. E. J. Vickers, Mireside Farm Ennerdale, Cleator, Cumbria, CA23 3AU. Tel. Lamplugh (094 686) 276.	●	1	-	-	-	-	-	-	-	6	50.00 -	- *70.00*	3–10	GE M LH
ESKDALE (Cumbria)	**B3**															
The Cottage, Boot, Eskdale,		Lois Howard, 1 Vale View, St. Bees, Cumbria, CA27 0BP. Tel. St Bees (094 685) 320.	●	-	-	1	-	-	-	-	-	6	35.00 *35.00*	50.00 *85.00*	1–12	GE M LN

You are advised to read the introductory notes and to check prices and other details when booking accommodation

SELF-CATERING ACCOMMODATION

Name and Address: Town (County) / Map Ref. / Establishment	Contact for reservations: Name and address, Telephone number, Telex	Accommodation: Tourist Board Standards	Self-contained: House (or part)	Bungalows	Cottages	Chalets/caravans	Flats/flatlets	Houseboats	Not self-contained: Flats/flatlets	Chalets	Number of persons per unit	Prices per unit per week: Low season (£ Min. / *£ Max.*)	High season (£ Min. / *£ Max.*)	Months open (1–12)	Symbols (Key: see fold-out)
ESKDALE continued															
† Fisherground Farm,	Mrs. J. Hall, Fisherground Farm, Eskdale, Cumbria, CA19 1TF. Tel. (094 03) 319.	●	-	-	1	3	-	-	-	-	6–8	50.00 / *55.00*	85.00 / *120.00*	1–12	GE LN
High Ground Farm Flats, High Ground, Birker Moor, Eskdale,	Mrs. J. M. Heywood, Birkerthwaite, Birker Moor, Eskdale, Cumbria, CA19 1TJ. Tel. (094 03) 266.	●	-	-	-	-	2	-	-	-	6–8	46.00 / -	- / *90.00*	3–10	GE LN
GARSDALE HEAD (Cumbria) C3 (7m E. Sedbergh)															
10 Railway Cottages, Garsdale Head, Garsdale,	Mrs. S. F. McTiernan, 29 New St., Pudsey, W. Yorkshire, LS28 8PE. Tel. Leeds (0532) 577565.	●	1	-	-	-	-	-	-	-	6	35.00 / *75.00*	75.00 / *95.00*	1–12	GE LN
GILSLAND (Cumbria) C1															
Hill Farm House.	A. B. & A. Slade, Hill Farm House, Gilsland, Carlisle, Cumbria, CA6 7DA. Tel. (069 72) 214.	●	-	-	-	-	3	-	-	-	6	40.00 / *70.00*	100.00 / *100.00*	1–12	GE LF
GOSFORTH (Cumbria) B2															
3 Hardingill Cottage, Gosforth, Seascale.	Mrs. P. Lawson, High Boonwood Farm, Gosforth, Seascale, Cumbria, CA20 1EA. Tel. (094 05) 423.	●	-	-	1	-	-	-	-	-	6	70.00 / -	- / -	4–10	GE LN
Haverigg Moorside.	Mr & Mrs P. Richardson, Haverigg Moorside, Gosforth Seascale, Cumbria, CA20 1HP. Tel. (094 05) 410.	●	-	-	1	-	-	-	-	-	6	50.00 / -	- / *100.00*	3–10	GE LF
GRANGE-OVER-SANDS (Cumbria) B3															
Avondale, Kents Bank Rd.,	Mrs H. E. Fletcher, Lynwood, Windermere Rd., Grange-over-Sands, Cumbria, LA11 6JX. Tel. (044 84) 2633.	●	1	-	-	-	-	-	-	-	8	30.00 / *70.00*	90.00 / *110.00*	1–12	GE LH
Claremont & Glengarth.	Mrs. M. Knowles, Bowett, Lindale, Grange-Over-Sands, Cumbria, LA11 6LC. Tel. (044 84) 2546.	●	-	-	2	-	-	-	-	-	8	40.00 / *90.00*	40.00 / *90.00*	1–12	GE LH
Cottages in Grange-Over-Sands	Mr B. B. Wesley, 14, Brook Rd., Flixton, Urmston, Lancs. M31 3RY. Tel. Urmston (061) 748 4583.	●	-	-	3	-	1	-	-	-	4–10	55.00 / *75.00*	85.00 / *150.00*	1–12	GE LN
Ground Floor Flat, 3 Thornfield Rd.,	Mrs. K. M. Watson, 3 Thornfield Rd., Grange-Over-Sands, Cumbria, LA11 7DR. Tel. (044 84) 2551.	●	-	-	-	-	1	-	-	-	2–3	40.00 / -	45.00 / -	4–10	GE LF
Kent Holme Flats, Kents Bank Rd.	Mr. or Mrs. H. Poole, The Coach House, Seawood, Kents Bank, Grange-over-Sands Cumbria, LA11 7AR. Tel. (044 84) 3235.	●	-	-	-	-	2	-	-	-	4–7	35.00 / *60.00*	45.00 / *85.00*	1–12	GE LN

SELF-CATERING ACCOMMODATION

Name and Address: Town (County), Map Ref., Establishment	Contact for reservations: Name and address, Telephone number, Telex	Accommodation: Tourist Board Standards	Self-contained: House (or part)	Self-contained: Bungalows	Self-contained: Cottages	Self-contained: Chalets/caravans	Self-contained: Flats/flatlets	Self-contained: Houseboats	Not self-contained: Flats/flatlets	Not self-contained: Chalets	Number of persons per unit	Prices per unit per week: Low season	Prices per unit per week: High season	Months open (1–12)	Symbols
												£ Min. *£ Max.*	£ Min. *£ Max.*		Key: see fold-out
GRANGE-OVER-SANDS continued															
† Lyndene.	Mrs. A. Burgess, Lyndene, Kentsford Rd., Kentsbank, Grange-over-Sands, Cumbria, LA11 7BB. Tel. (044 84) 3189.	C	-	-	-	-	-	-	5.	-	4	20.00 *30.00*	30.00 *40.00*	1–12	GE LF
† Newlands Holiday Flats,	Mr. & Mrs. A. M. Staunton, 1 Newlands, Crown Hill, Grange-Over-Sands, Cumbria, LA11 6BD. Tel. (044 84) 2659.	●	-	1	1	-	1	-	-	-	2–6	40.00 *70.00*	65.00 *110.00*	1–12	GE LF
† Wycombe Holiday Flats.	Mrs. W. G. Benson, Wycombe, The Esplanade, Grange-Over-Sands, Cumbria, LA11 7HH. Tel. (044 84) 2297.	●	-	-	-	-	3	-	-	-	2–5	40.00 *43.00*	60.00 *110.00*	1–12	GE LF
GRASMERE (Cumbria) B2															
† Beck Allans,	Mr. Beverley Yates, Beck Allans, College St., Grasmere, Cumbria, LA22 9SZ. Tel. (096 65) 329.	●	-	-	-	-	6	-	-	-	2–5	75.00 *140.00*	105.00 *195.00*	1–12	GE LF
3 College St.,	Mr. R. A. Fowler, Beck Steps Guest House, College St., Grasmere, Cumbria, LA22 9SY. Tel. (096 65) 348.	●	-	-	1	-	-	-	-	-	2–5	50.00 *75.00*	100.00 *120.00*	1–12	GE LH
Fell Cottage, Pye La.,	Mrs. C. M. Emmerton, Braefield, Ambleside, Cumbria, LA22 0EG. Tel. Ambleside (096 63) 3427.	●	-	-	1	-	-	-	-	-	7	69.00 *95.00*	98.00 *139.00*	1–12	GE LN
Grey Crag Barn, Hollens,	C. V. Dodgson, Butter Crags, Grasmere, Cumbria, LA22 9QZ. Tel. (096 65) 259.	●	1	-	-	-	-	-	-	-	2–8	80.00 *100.00*	120.00 *180.00*	1–12	GE LN
† Lake View	Mrs. Beth Mosey, Lake View, Lake View Dr., Grasmere, Cumbria, LA22 9TD. Tel. (096 65) 384.	●	-	-	-	-	3	-	-	-	2–5	77.00 *95.00*	84.00 *115.00*	3–10	GE LH
Meadow Brow.	Mr. & Mrs. A. D. Bateman, Meadow Brow, Grasmere, Ambleside, Cumbria, LA22 9RR. Tel. (096 65) 275.	●	1	-	1	-	-	-	-	-	2–5	60.00 *-*	- *165.00*	1–12	GE LF
North Lodge, Hollens,	Mrs. V. Hughes, Carr Howe, Belle Vue La., Ambleside, Cumbria, LA22 9EZ. Tel. Ambleside (096 63) 3695.	●	-	-	1	-	-	-	-	-	6	75.00 *110.00*	100.00 *150.00*	1–12	GE LN
Rowan Cottage & Rowan Studio Cottage,	Mrs. D. G. Armstrong, Rowan, Grasmere, Ambleside, Cumbria, LA22 9TA. Tel. (096 65) 424.	●	-	-	2	-	-	-	-	-	2–6	80.00 *95.00*	90.00 *120.00*	4–12	GE LH
† Silver Howe Lodge,	Douglas & Judy Worrall, Cottage Life, Lane Ends Barn, 11, Elterwater, Ambleside, Cumbria, LA22 9HN. Tel. Langdale (096 67) 292.	●	-	-	1	-	-	-	-	-	5	70.00 *-*	100.00 *-*	1–12	GE LN
† Wood Close, How Head La., Town End.	Mrs. E. A. Simmons, 10 Tower Rd., Branksome Park, Poole, Dorset Tel. Bournemouth (0202) 762222.	●	1	-	-	-	6	-	-	-	2–9	30.00 *50.00*	90.00 *215.00*	1–12	GE LN

You are advised to read the introductory notes and to check prices and other details when booking accommodation

SELF-CATERING ACCOMMODATION

Name and Address: Town (County) / Establishment	Map Ref.	Contact for reservations: Name and address, Telephone number, Telex	Accommodation: Tourist Board Standards	Self-contained: House (or part)	Bungalows	Cottages	Chalets/caravans	Flats/flatlets	Houseboats	Not self-contained: Flats/flatlets	Chalets	Number of persons per unit	Prices: Per unit per week: Low season £ Min. / *£ Max.*	High season £ Min. / *£ Max.*	Months open (1–12)	Symbols (Key: see fold-out)
GREAT SALKELD (Cumbria) (4m NE. Penrith)	**C2**															
Mattinson House, Great Salkeld, Penrith		Mrs. M. Robinson, Village Stores, Great Salkeld, Penrith, Cumbria, CA11 9LW. Tel. Lazonby (076 883) 215.	●	-	-	1	1	-	-	-	-	5–8	60.00 / *60.00*	90.00 / *90.00*	1–12	GE M LF
GREYSTOKE (Cumbria) (5m W. Penrith)	**C2**															
Jefferson House.		David or Barbara Smallwood, Jefferson House, Berrier Rd., Greystoke, Penrith, Cumbria, CA11 0UE. Tel. (085 33) 576.	●	-	2	-	-	1	-	-	-	2–6	55.00 / *80.00*	80.00 / *110.00*	1–12	GE M LH
HAVERIGG (Cumbria)	**B3**															
† 134, Main St., Haverigg, Millom		Mrs. I. R. Park, Byways, Hallthwaites, Millom, Cumbria, LA18 5HP. Tel. Millom (0657) 2544.	●	1	-	-	-	-	-	-	-	8	70.00 / *80.00*	90.00 / *110.00*	1–12	GE LF T
HAVERTHWAITE (Cumbria)	**B3**															
Woodcroft House.		Mrs B. L. Carey, Woodcroft House, Haverthwaite, Nr. Ulverston, Cumbria, LA12 8AE. Tel. Newby Bridge (0448) 31545.	●	1	-	-	-	-	-	-	-	6	45.00 / –	– / *100.00*	1–12	GE M LN
HAWKSHEAD (Cumbria)	**B3**															
Barn Syke, Main St.,		K. E. L. Garside, Jasmine Cottage, Vicarage La., Hawkshead, Nr. Ambleside, Cumbria, LA22 0PB. Tel. (096 66) 418.	●	-	-	1	-	-	-	-	-	8	55.00 / *75.00*	80.00 / *120.00*	1–12	GE M LN
† The Coppice, Rough Close		Mrs. E. J. Hewitson, Rough Close Hawkshead, Ambleside, Cumbria, LA22 0QF. Tel. (096 66) 370.	●	-	1	-	-	-	-	-	-	6	50.00 / –	– / *130.00*	1–12	GE M LN
† The Croft, North Lonsdale Rd.,		Holidays in Lakeland (C.H.) Stock Park Estates, Newby Bridge, Ulverston, Cumbria, LA12 8AY. Tel. Newby Bridge (0448) 31549.	●	-	-	-	-	6	-	-	-	3–5	61.00 / –	– / *131.00*	1–12	LF T
Estcote Rogerground,		Mrs. D. B. Marsh, Galloway Loun, Rogerground, Hawkshead, Ambleside, Cumbria, LA22 0QG. Tel. (096 66) 261.	●	-	-	-	-	2	-	-	-	4–5	80.00 / *85.00*	80.00 / *85.00*	1–12	GE M LN

SELF-CATERING ACCOMMODATION

Name and Address: Town (County) / Establishment	Map Ref.	Contact for reservations: Name and address, Telephone number, Telex	Tourist Board Standards	Accommodation: Self-contained: House (or part)	Bungalows	Cottages	Chalets/caravans	Flats/flatlets	Houseboats	Not self-contained: Flats/flatlets	Chalets	Number of persons per unit	Prices per unit per week: Low season (£ Min. / *£ Max.*)	High season (£ Min. / *£ Max.*)	Months open (1–12)	Symbols (Key: see fold-out)
HESKET NEWMARKET (Cumbria) (8m SE. Wigton)	**B2**															
Haltcliffe House, Hesket Newmarket, Wigton,		Mrs. M. A. Ridley, Lonning Head, Hesket Newmarket, Wigton, Cumbria, CA7 8JU. Tel. Caldbeck (069 98) 619.	●	1	–	–	–	–	–	–	–	10	70.00 –	90.00 –	1–12	GE M LN
Howbeck Farmhouse,		Andrew F. S. Chance, Howbeck Farmhouse, Hesket Newmarket, Wigton, Cumbria, CA7 8JN. Tel. Caldbeck (069 98) 306.	●	–	–	1	–	–	–	–	–	4	30.00 *40.00*	60.00 *75.00*	1–12	GE M LN
Hudscales Cottage. Hesket Newmarket, Wigton,		Mrs. V. Cowx, Hudscales, Hesket Newmarket, Wigton, Cumbria, CA7 8JZ. Tel. Caldbeck (069 98) 637.	●	–	–	1	–	–	–	–	–	8	– *60.00*	– *85.00*	1–12	GE M LN
IVEGILL (Cumbria) (8m S. Carlisle)	**B2**															
Cumbria, Ivegill, Carlisle.		Mrs. C. M. McCrone, Low Grange, Southwaite, Carlisle, Cumbria, CA4 0ND. Tel. Southwaite (069 93) 432.	●	–	1	–	–	–	–	–	–	2–7	60.00 *85.00*	100.00 *120.00*	1–12	GE M LH
KENDAL (Cumbria)	**C3**															
Byron For Hair, 6 New Rd.,		Linda Byron, Lowlands, The Shore, Hest Bank, Lancaster, Lancashire, LA2 6HW. Tel. Lancaster (0524) 824259 or Kendal (0539) 29319.	●	–	–	–	–	1	–	–	–	5	75.00 –	– –	4–10	GE M LF S
† 22 Castle Cres.,		Mrs. B. Stainton, Exchange Garage Old Shambles, Kendal, Cumbria, LA9 4TA. Tel. (0539) 20331.	●	1	–	–	–	–	–	–	–	5	65.00 *75.00*	75.00 *85.00*	4–10	GE M LF
Curlew Cottage, 5 High Tenterfell,		Mrs. A. Whitehouse, The Manse, Ravenstonedale, Nr. Kirkby Stephen, Cumbria, CA17 4NQ. Tel. Newbiggin-on-Lune (058 73) 323.	●	–	–	1	–	–	–	–	–	4	42.00 *63.00*	77.00 *77.00*	1–12	GE M LH
Dowsonfold, 2 Summerhow,		Mr. & Mrs. P. Crewdson, Summerhow, Kendal, Cumbria, LA9 6NY. Tel. (053 9) 20763. Telex 65125.	●	–	–	1	–	–	–	–	–	6	– –	– *197.00*	4–10	GE M LN
Force Cottage Holidays, Force Cottages, Sedgwick, Kendal.		A. Hoggarth & Son, 52 Kirkland, Kendal, Cumbria, LA9 5AP. Tel. (0539) 22592.	●	–	–	2	–	–	–	–	–	2–6	55.00 *65.00*	70.00 *95.00*	4–10	GE M LH
Garth Cottage, Castle Garth.		Mrs. Elizabeth Steele, Walkdene, 53 Burton Rd., Kendal, Cumbria, LA9 7JA. Tel. (0539) 23400.	●	–	–	1	–	–	–	–	–	2–5	35.00 *50.00*	– –	1–12	GE M LN
Great Eskrigg End,		Mrs. Megan Hill, Great Eskrigg End, Old Hutton, Kendal, Cumbria, LA8 0NU. Tel. (0539) 24833.	●	–	–	–	3	–	–	–	–	4–6	40.00 *60.00*	50.00 *80.00*	3–10	GE LN

 You are advised to read the introductory notes and to check prices and other details when booking accommodation

SELF-CATERING ACCOMMODATION

Name and Address: Town (County) / Establishment	Map Ref.	Contact for reservations: Name and address, Telephone number, Telex	Tourist Board Standards	Self-contained: House (or part)	Bungalows	Cottages	Chalets/caravans	Flats/flatlets	Houseboats	Not self-contained: Flats/flatlets	Chalets	Number of persons per unit	Per unit per week: Low season	High season	Months open (1–12)	Symbols
													£ Min. *£ Max.*	£ Min. *£ Max.*		Key: see fold-out
KENDAL continued																
Jasmin Cottage, Church View, Natland, Nr. Kendal,		Mrs. M. E. Moorhouse, High House, Helm La., Natland, Nr. Kendal, Cumbria, LA9 7QW. Tel. Sedgwick (0448) 60564.	●	–	–	1	–	–	–	–	–	6	– *50.00*	– *90.00*	1–12	GE LF
Lambrigg View. Grayrigg,		Mrs. Rhona Bentham, Mire Head Grayrigg, Nr. Kendal, Cumbria, LA8 9EU. Tel. Grayrigg (0539 84) 244.	●	–	–	1	–	–	–	–	–	6	30.00 *60.00*	– –	4–12	GE LH
Low Rigg Barn,		Mrs. V. J. Dixon, Morton Rigg, Garth Row, Skelsmergh, Kendal, Cumbria, LA8 9AT. Tel. Selside (053 983) 662.	●	–	–	1	–	–	–	–	–	5–6	60.00 *90.00*	100.00 *130.00*	4–10	LN
† Plumgarths Holiday Flats, Plumgarths, Crook Rd.,		Mr. & Mrs. Jonathan Somervell, Braithwaite, Crook, Kendal, Cumbria, LA8 8LE. Tel. Staveley (0539) 821325.	●	–	–	–	1	5	–	–	–	2–6	55.00 *80.00*	120.00 *185.00*	1–12	GE LN
Raw End Bungalow, Endmoor, Nr. Kendal,		Mrs. M. Maudsley, Raw End Farm, Endmoor, Nr. Kendal, Cumbria, LA8 0ED. Tel. Sedgwick (0448) 60295.	●	–	1	–	–	–	–	–	–	4	50.00 –	70.00 –	1–12	7 GE LN
Uplands, 167 Windermere Rd.,		Mrs. M. Kitchen, 50 Windermere Rd., Kendal, Kendal, Cumbria, LA9 5EP. Tel. (0539) 21309.	●	1	–	–	–	–	–	–	–	6–7	35.00 –	– *75.00*	1–12	GE LH
† Waterhouse Farm,		Mrs. C. Birchall, Waterhouse Farm, Burneside, Kendal, Cumbria, LA8 9AY. Tel. (0539) 24034.	●	–	–	–	1	–	–	–	–	6	45.00 –	– *70.00*	3–10	GE LF
KENTMERE (Cumbria) (9m NW. Kendal)	**C2**															
† Browfoot Farm, Kentmere Valley, Nr. Staveley, Kendal,		Tiffen King Nicholson, Lake Rd., Windermere, Cumbria, LA23 3BJ. Tel. Windermere (096 62) 2291.	●	2	–	1	–	–	–	–	–	6–8	65.00 *105.00*	95.00 *210.00*	1–12	GE LN
KESWICK (Cumbria)	**B2**															
Applethwaite,		Mrs. J. Ray, Applethwaite Farm, Keswick, Cumbria, CA12 4PN. Tel. (0596) 72608.	●	1	–	–	–	–	–	–	–	2–5	55.00 *70.00*	80.00 *95.00*	1–12	GE LN
Balestrand 21 Briar Rigg.		Mrs. M. Taylor, 19 Briar Rigg, Keswick, Cumbria, CA12 4NN. Tel. (0596) 73396.	●	1	–	–	–	–	–	–	–	8	75.00 *110.00*	110.00 *195.00*	1–12	LH
† Balmoral House, Lake Rd.,		Grey Abbey Properties Ltd., P.O. Box 23, Coach Rd., Whitehaven, Cumbria, CA28 9OF. Tel. Whitehaven (0946) 3773.	●	–	–	–	–	7	–	–	–	4–8	38.00 *93.00*	108.00 *154.00*	1–12	GE LH
The Barn,		Miss S. Brook, Barn Cottage, Stair, Newlands, Nr. Keswick, Cumbria, CA12 5UF. Tel. Braithwaite (059 682) 328.	●	–	–	–	–	2	–	–	–	5	40.00 *55.00*	55.00 *65.00*	1–12	GE LN

SELF-CATERING ACCOMMODATION

Name and Address: Town (County) / Map Ref. / Establishment	Contact for reservations: Name and address, Telephone number, Telex	Accommodation: Tourist Board Standards	Self-contained: House (or part)	Bungalows	Cottages	Chalets/caravans	Flats/flatlets	Houseboats	Not self-contained: Flats/flatlets	Chalets	Number of persons per unit	Prices per unit per week: Low season (£ Min. / £ Max.)	High season (£ Min. / £ Max.)	Months open (1–12)	Symbols (Key: see fold-out)
KESWICK continued															
Beechwood, High Hill,	Mr. J. V. Lancaster, Pillar House, 21 Main St., Keswick, Cumbria, CA12 5BL. Tel. (0596) 73037.	●	-	1	-	-	-	-	-	-	6	85.00 -	- *185.00*	1–12	GE M LN
† Bobbin Mill Cottages & Flats, Low Briery Holiday Village,	Grey Abbey Properties Ltd., P.O. Box 23, Coach Rd., Whitehaven, Cumbria, CA28 9DE. Tel. Whitehaven (0946) 3773.	●	-	-	2	-	6	-	-	-	6–8	52.00 *102.00*	133.00 *154.00*	1–12	GE M LH
† Brigham Farm Flats, Low Brigham, Keswick,	Olga Hunter, 12 Derwent St., Keswick, Cumbria, CA12 5AN. Tel. (0596) 74392.	●	-	-	-	-	6	-	-	-	2–4	30.00 *60.00*	50.00 *130.00*	1–12	GE M LF
43 Castlehead Clo.,	D. J. Marshall, School House, St. Bees, Cumbria, CA27 0DT. Tel. St. Bees (094 685) 374.	●	-	-	-	-	1	-	-	-	4	65.00 -	- *90.00*	4–10	4 GE LN
† Castlerigg Farmhouse.	Mrs. D. V. Tanner, 5 Spencer's Bellevue, Lansdown Rd., Bath, Avon. Tel. Bath (0225) 22788.	●	1	-	-	1	-	-	-	-	2–7	40.00 *100.00*	55.00 *150.00*	4–10 12	5 GE M LN
3 Catherine Cottages,	Mrs. D. Allison, 2 Raven La., Applethwaite, Keswick, Cumbria, CA12 4PW. Tel. (0596) 74153.	●	-	-	1	-	-	-	-	-	5	50.00 *67.00*	77.00 *82.00*	1–12	GE M LN
Chestnut Cottage, Millbeck.	Mrs Brownrigg, Spoutclose Cottage, Millbeck, Keswick, Cumbria, CA12 4PS. Tel. (0596) 73697.	●	-	-	3	-	-	-	-	-	4–8	62.00 *72.00*	62.00 *72.00*	4–10	GE M LN
† Derwentwater Hotel,	Derwentwater Hotel, Portinscale, Keswick, Cumbria, CA12 5RE. Tel. (0596) 72538. Telex 64418.	●	-	1	-	-	2	-	-	-	5	65.00 *70.00*	150.00 *180.00*	1–12	GE LF T
Fawe Park Lakeside Flats,	Mrs. M. C. Pigott, Fawe Park, Keswick, Cumbria, CA12 5TY. Tel. (0596) 72126 or 01-5841832.	●	-	-	-	-	2	-	-	-	2–6	70.00 *100.00*	80.00 *110.00*	1–12	GE LN
† Fieldside Grange	Sam Hicks, Fieldside Grange, Keswick, Cumbria, CA12 4RN. Tel. (0596) 74444.	●	-	-	-	-	7	-	-	-	2–7	35.00 *60.00*	60.00 *100.00*	1–12	GE M LF
† Fir Bank, 67 The Headlands, & Lyzzick Bungalow.	Mrs. M. Atkinson, Lyzzick Hall, Nr. Keswick, Cumbria, CA12 4PY. Tel. (0596) 72277.	●	1	2	-	-	-	-	-	-	6	65.00 -	100.00 -	1–12	GE M LH
† Greta Side Court, Otley Rd.,	Grey Abbey Properties Ltd., P.O. Box 23, Coach Rd., Whitehaven, Cumbria, CA28 9DF. Tel. Whitehaven (0946) 3773.	●	-	-	-	-	9	-	-	-	4–6	38.00 *93.00*	100.00 *125.00*	1–12	GE M LH
22 Greta St., 33 & 35 Blencathra St.	Mr. Abbott, Fayreholm, Blencathra St., Keswick, Cumbria, CA12 4HW. Tel. (0596) 72228.	●	-	-	-	-	4	-	-	-	2–6	40.00 -	- *85.00*	4–10 12	GE M LH
† 26 Heads Rd.	Mrs. B. A. Kirk, 25 Heads Rd., Keswick, Cumbria, CA12 5EX. Tel. (0596) 73408.	●	1	-	-	-	-	-	-	-	5	60.00 -	- *100.00*	1–12	M LH

 You are advised to read the introductory notes and to check prices and other details when booking accommodation

SELF-CATERING ACCOMMODATION

Town (County) / Establishment	Map Ref.	Contact for reservations: Name and address, Telephone number, Telex	Tourist Board Standards	House (or part)	Bungalows	Cottages	Chalets/caravans	Flats/flatlets	Houseboats	Flats/flatlets (Not self-contained)	Chalets (Not self-contained)	Number of persons per unit	Low season (£ Min. / *£ Max.*)	High season (£ Min. / *£ Max.*)	Months open (1–12)	Symbols (Key: see fold-out)
KESWICK continued																
45 High Portinscale, Nr. Keswick,		Mrs. E. J. Needham, Stonewell, Portinscale, Nr. Keswick, Cumbria, CA12 5RQ. Tel. (0596) 73043.	●	1	-	-	-	-	-	-	-	5	70.00 / –	80.00 / –	5–10	GE LN
Horse Shoe Crag, Fieldside Close,		Mrs. J. Swainson, Lime Grove, Fieldside Close, Keswick, Cumbria, CA12 4LN. Tel. (0596) 72150.	●	-	-	-	-	2	-	-	-	2–6	50.00 / *70.00*	100.00 / *110.00*	1–12	GE LF
Lakeland Self Catering Holidays.		Susan Graham, Maple Bank, Springs Rd., Keswick, Cumbria, CA12 4AN. Tel. (0596) 72911.	●	-	-	-	-	3	-	-	-	2–8	50.00 / *70.00*	70.00 / *150.00*	1–12	GE LF
Latrigg, 4 Park Holme.		Mrs. K. W. Johnson, 2 Holemire Cottages, High Lorton, Cockermouth, Cumbria, CA13 9TU. Tel. Lorton (090 085) 648 & Bolton (0204) 491293.	●	-	-	1	-	-	-	-	-	7	65.00 / *90.00*	100.00 / *140.00*	3–12	GE LN
Littlebeck.		Catherine Braithwaite, Littlebeck, Chestnut Hill, Keswick, Cumbria, CA12 4LT. Tel. (0596) 72972.	●	-	-	-	-	1	-	-	-	4	– / *70.00*	75.00 / *80.00*	2–11	GE LH
Lord's Seat, Terrace Rd., Applethwaite, Keswick.		R. V. Arnfield, Yew Tree Cottage, Westhorpe, Southwell, Notts. Tel. Southwell (0636) 813769.	●	-	-	-	-	2	-	-	-	2–6	60.00 / *75.00*	95.00 / *125.00*	1–12	GE LN
5 Lydias Cottages,		Mrs. C. Baker, Conservative Club, 14 Penrith Rd., Keswick, Cumbria, CA12 4HF. Tel. (0596) 72518.	●	-	-	1	-	-	-	-	-	2–6	60.00 / *75.00*	75.00 / *85.00*	1–12	GE LN
Manesty Farm, Manesty, Nr. Keswick,		Mr. J. R. Leyland, 24 The Meadows, Todwick, Nr. Sheffield, S31 0JG. Tel. Worksop (0909) 770508.	●	1	-	-	-	-	-	-	-	12	80.00 / –	– / *125.00*	4–10	GE LN
1–2 Markholme Cottages, Crosthwaite Rd.,		M. E. Hinde, Bray Hill, 9 Briar Rigg, Keswick, Cumbria, CA12 4NW. Tel. (0596) 72975.	●	-	-	-	-	2	-	-	-	4	52.00 / *55.00*	62.00 / *65.00*	4–11	GE LF
† Mountain View,		Mrs. R. Robertson, Mountain View, Penrith Rd., Keswick, Cumbria, CA12 4LJ. Tel. (0596) 72382.	●	-	-	-	-	1	-	-	-	6	55.00 / –	75.00 / –	1–12	GE LH
† The Old Vicarage, Littletown, Newlands, Keswick,		Mr. & Mrs. J. Grange, Yew Tree Cottage, Ullock, Portinscale, Keswick, Cumbria, CA12 5SP. Tel. Braithwaite (059 682) 493.	●	1	-	-	-	-	-	-	-	6	85.00 / –	– / *220.00*	1–12	GE LF
7 & 13 Otley Rd.,		D. U. Hodgson, Greta Lodge, Keswick, Cumbria, CA12 5ND. Tel. (0596) 72388.	●	-	-	2	-	-	-	-	-	4	– / *70.00*	– / *85.00*	4–10	GE LN
18 Poplar St.,		Mmes. D. & M. Allison, 1 Raven La., Applethwaite, Keswick, Cumbria, CA12 4PW. Tel. (0596) 73011.	●	-	-	1	-	-	-	-	-	4–6	55.00 / *55.00*	70.00 / *80.00*	1–12	GE LN

SELF-CATERING ACCOMMODATION

Name and Address: Town (County) / Map Ref. / Establishment	Contact for reservations: Name and address, Telephone number, Telex	Tourist Board Standards	House (or part)	Bungalows	Cottages	Chalets/caravans	Flats/flatlets	Houseboats	Flats/flatlets (not self-contained)	Chalets (not self-contained)	Number of persons per unit	Low season (per unit per week) £ Min. / £ Max.	High season £ Min. / £ Max.	Months open (1–12)	Symbols (Key: see fold-out)
KESWICK continued															
15 Ratcliffe Place,	Mr. & Mrs. J. Grange, Yew Tree Cottage, Ullock, Portinscale, Keswick, Cumbria, CA12 5SP. Tel. Braithwaite (059 682) 493.	●	1	–	–	–	–	–	–	–	6	65.00 / –	– / *125.00*	1–12	GE M LF
20 Ratcliffe Place,	Mrs. S. M. Eynon, Holme View, Deanscales, Cockermouth, Cumbria, CA13 0SL. Tel. Cockermouth (0900) 822436.	●	1	–	–	–	–	–	–	–	4–5	55.00 / *65.00*	65.00 / *75.00*	1–12	GE M LF
24 Ratcliffe Pl.,	Mrs. W. Plant, St. Bartholomew's Vicarage, Wesley Rd., Leeds, W. Yorks. LS12 1SR. Tel. Leeds (0532) 638620.	●	–	–	1	–	–	–	–	–	4	40.00 / *60.00*	60.00 / *70.00*	1–12	GE M LN
Refectory Keep, Pear Tree Cottage & Pamlet, Storms,	G. Spedding, Storms, Keswick, Cumbria, CA12 4RN. Tel. (0596) 72009.	●	1	–	2	–	–	–	–	–	2–8	45.00 / –	– / *125.00*	1–12	GE M LN
Riverside Holiday Flats,	Mr. & Mrs. Stephenson, Burleigh Mead, The Heads, Keswick Cumbria, CA12 5ER. Tel. (0596) 72750.	●	–	–	–	–	12	–	–	–	2–6	41.00 / *55.00*	80.00 / *117.00*	3–11	GE M LH
Rose Cottage, 24 Rose Ter., Penrith Rd.,	G. M. Hallatt, Twa Dogs Inn, Penrith Rd., Keswick, Cumbria, CA12 4JU. Tel. (0596) 72599.	●	–	–	1	–	–	–	–	–	2–5	50.00 / *70.00*	70.00 / *100.00*	1–12	GE M LN
4 St. Herbert St.,	Mrs. L. E. Houston, Little Dodd, Underskiddaw, Keswick, Cumbria, CA12 4PY. Tel. (0596) 73734.	●	1	–	–	–	–	–	–	–	6	– / *60.00*	75.00 / *100.00*	1–12	GE M LN
Smithy Flat, 54 Main St.,	Mr. R. Wilson, Roodlands, Portinscale, Keswick, Cumbria, CA12 5RF. Tel. (0596) 72986.	●	–	–	–	–	1	–	–	–	5	25.00 / –	– / *120.00*	1–12	4 GE M LF
Stoneycroft Hotel,	Mrs. R. Edmondson, Stoneycroft Hotel, Newlands, Keswick, Cumbria, CA12 5TS. Tel. Braithwaite (059 682) 240.	●	–	–	–	–	2	–	2	–	2–8	50.00 / *70.00*	100.00 / *130.00*	1–12	GE M LF
Sydenham House, Applethwaite, Keswick,	Mrs. M. Wilson, The Pheasant Inn, Bassenthwaite Lake, Nr. Cockermouth, Cumbria, CA13 9YE. Tel. Bassenthwaite Lake (059 681) 234.	●	1	–	–	–	–	–	–	–	6	60.00 / *75.00*	100.00 / *150.00*	1–12	5 GE M LN
† Tall Pines, Fieldside Clo.,	Mr. A. Hughes, Causey Pike, Fieldside Close, Keswick, Cumbria, CA12 4LN. Tel. (0596) 73353.	●	–	–	–	–	2	–	–	–	6	60.00 / *85.00*	95.00 / *130.00*	1–12	GE M LF
KIRKBY LONSDALE (Cumbria) **C3**															
Old Post Office, Hutton Roof, Kirkby Lonsdale,	Mrs. L. Andrews, Dents Barn, Hutton Roof, Kirkby Lonsdale, Carnforth, Lancs., LA6 2PG. Tel. (0468) 71134.	●	–	–	1	–	–	–	–	–	3	30.00 / *35.00*	40.00 / *50.00*	1–12	10 GE M LF

You are advised to read the introductory notes and to check prices and other details when booking accommodation

SELF-CATERING ACCOMMODATION

Name and Address: Town (County) / Establishment	Map Ref.	Contact for reservations: Name and address, Telephone number, Telex	Tourist Board Standards	Self-contained: House (or part)	Bungalows	Cottages	Chalets/caravans	Flats/flatlets	Houseboats	Not self-contained: Flats/flatlets	Chalets	Number of persons per unit	Prices per unit per week: Low season	High season	Months open (1–12)	Symbols
													£ Min. *£ Max.*	£ Min. *£ Max.*		Key: see fold-out
KIRKOSWALD (Cumbria)	**C2**															
† Staffield Hall, Nr. Kirkoswald, Penrith,		Grey Abbey Properties Ltd, PO Box 23, Coach Rd., Whitehaven, Cumbria, CA28 9OF. Tel. Whitehaven (0946) 3773.	●	–	–	1	–	9	–	–	–	2–9	37.00 *88.00*	108.00 *154.00*	1–12	GE LH
LAMPLUGH (Cumbria)	**B2**															
Ghyll Cottage, Lamplugh Green, Nr. Workington,		The Rev. & Mrs. F. C. Hambrey, Colton Vicarage, Nr. Ulverston, Cumbria, LA12 8NF. Tel. Greenodd (022 986) 361.		1	–	–	–	–	–	–	–	4	65.00 *65.00*	75.00 *90.00*	3–11	GE LN
Lamplugh Holiday Centre, Lowmillgillhead, Lamplugh Workington,		Lady Moon, 79 Woodstock Rd., Oxford, OX2 6HL. Tel. Oxford (0865) 57687.	●	2	–	–	–	1	–	–	–	2–9	35.00 *65.00*	45.00 *90.00*	1–12	GE LN
LANGDALE (Cumbria)	**B2**															
† Azalea Cottage, Skelwith Bridge, Langdale, Nr. Ambleside,		Douglas & Judy Worrall, Cottage Life, Lane Ends Barn, 11 Elterwater, Ambleside, Cumbria, LA22 9HN. Tel. (096 67) 292.	●	–	–	1	–	–	–	–	–	8	85.00 –	– *225.00*	1–12	GE LN
Fir Garth Holiday Cottages.		J. T. W. Sanderson, Fir Garth Holiday Cottages, Gt. Langdale, Nr. Ambleside, Cumbria, LA22 9JL. Tel. (096 67) 283.	●	–	4	9	2	–	–	–	–	4–5	45.00 –	95.00 –	1–12	GE LN
Thrang View & Oakdene Maisonette, Chapel Stile,		Mrs. P. Long, Oakdene, Chapel Stile, Gt. Langdale, Nr. Ambleside, Cumbria, LA22 9JE. Tel. (096 67) 629.	●	–	1	–	–	1	–	–	–	6	65.00 –	– *130.00*	1–12	GE LF
† 3 Weir Cottages, Chapel Stile, Gt. Langdale, Ambleside,		Mr. or Mrs. K. L. Farrar, Langdales Hotel, Gt. Langdale, Ambleside, Cumbria, LA22 9JF. Tel. (096 67) 253.	●	–	–	1	–	–	–	–	–	3–4	90.00 –	100.00 –	1–12	GE LF
LAZONBY (Cumbria) (7m NE. Penrith)	**C2**															
† Banktop Courtyard,		Mrs. M. Carlyle, Banktop House, Lazonby, Nr. Penrith, Cumbria, CA10 1AQ. Tel. (076 883) 268.	●	4	–	–	–	–	–	–	–	2–6	30.00 *70.00*	75.00 *115.00*	1–12	GE LH
† Edengrove Holiday Cottages,		Mrs. E. P. Bell, The Post Office, Lazonby, Penrith, Cumbria, CA10 1BG. Tel. (076 883) 242 & 437.	●	–	–	5	–	–	–	–	–	5–6	40.00 *60.00*	80.00 *110.00*	1–12	GE LN
LEVENS (Cumbria)	**C3**															
† Greengate Farm, Levens, Kendal,		Mrs. E. Edmondson, High Barns, Levens Bridge, Kendal, Cumbria, LA8 8EG. Tel. Sedgwick (0448) 60291.	●	1	–	1	–	–	–	–	–	4–8	45.00 –	– *80.00*	4–10	GE LH
Old Barn, Underhill,		R. Marshall, Underhill, Levens, Cumbria, LA8 8PH. Tel. Sedgwick (0448) 60298.	●	–	1	–	–	–	–	–	–	4	– *50.00*	– *50.00*	4–10	GE LN

SELF-CATERING ACCOMMODATION

Name and Address: Town (County), Map Ref., Establishment	Contact for reservations: Name and address, Telephone number, Telex	Tourist Board Standards	Self-contained: House (or part)	Bungalows	Cottages	Chalets/caravans	Flats/flatlets	Houseboats	Not self-contained: Flats/flatlets	Chalets	Number of persons per unit	Prices per unit per week: Low season (£ Min. / £ Max.)	High season (£ Min. / £ Max.)	Months open (1–12)	Symbols (Key: see fold-out)
LITTLE CLIFTON (Cumbria) **B2** (5m SW. Cockermouth)															
† Crossbarrow Motel & Self Catering Studio Apartments, Little Clifton, Nr. Workington,	Border (Crossbarrow), P.O. Box 23, Coach Rd., Whitehaven Cumbria, CA28 9DF. Tel. Whitehaven (0946) 3773.	●	-	-	-	-	10	-	-	-	2–6	38.00 *93.00*	100.00 *125.00*	1–12	GE M LH
LONGSLEDDALE (Cumbria) **C3**															
Low Swinklebank,	Mrs. P. M. Owens, Low Swinklebank, Longsleddale, Nr. Kendal, Cumbria, LA8 9BD. Tel. Selside (053 983) 251.	●	-	1	-	-	-	-	-	-	4	- *40.00*	- *50.00*	1–12	GE M LN
Tills Hole, Longsleddale, Kendal	Mrs. R. M. Fishwick, Middle Sadghyll, Longsleddale, Kendal, Cumbria, LA8 9BE. Tel. Selside (053 983) 283.	●	-	-	1	-	-	-	-	-	7–8	50.00 -	65.00 *80.00*	1–12	GE M LN
LORTON (Cumbria) **B2** (4m SE. Cockermouth)															
High Armaside Cottage,	Mrs. R. E. Thom-Postlethwaite, Armaside, Lorton, Cockermouth, Cumbria, CA13 9TL. Tel. (090 085) 212.	●	-	-	1	-	-	-	-	-	6	35.00 *75.00*	75.00 *90.00*	1–12	GE M LH
Midtown House, High Lorton, Nr. Cockermouth,	David Billington, Silver Birches, 27 St. Georges Rd., Formby, Merseyside, L37 3HH. Tel. Formby (070 48) 77962.	●	1	-	-	-	-	-	-	-	8	75.00 *100.00*	150.00 *200.00*	1–12	GE LF T
† Wayside Cottage, Lorton, Nr. Cockermouth,	M. E. Thompson, Scale Hill Hotel, Loweswater, Nr. Cockermouth, Cumbria, CA13 9UX. Tel. (090 085) 232.	●	-	-	1	-	-	-	-	-	6	80.00 *115.00*	115.00 *175.00*	1–12	GE LF
LOW HESKET (Cumbria) **C2** (7m SE. Carlisle)															
† The Manor	The Receptionist, Barrock Park, Low Hesket, Cumbria, CA4 0JS. Tel. Southwaite (069 93) 681.	●	-	-	14	-	-	-	-	-	2–7	80.50 *115.00*	103.50 *287.50*	1–12	LF S T
LOWESWATER (Cumbria) **B2**															
The Cottage,	Mrs. E. K. Bond, Jenkinson Pl., Loweswater, Cockermouth, CA13 0SU. Tel. Lamplugh (094 686) 748.	●	-	-	1	-	-	-	-	-	6	45.00 -	- *95.00*	3–12	GE M LN
Iredale Place, Loweswater, Nr. Cockermouth,	Mrs. A. Spencer, Gatra Farm, Lamplugh, Workington, Cumbria, CA14 4SA. Tel. Lamplugh (094 686) 279.	●	1	-	-	-	-	-	-	-	7	50.00 -	- *110.00*	1–12	GE M LN
† Lorton Park, High Lorton, Cockermouth,	Mr. & Mrs. B. I. Hill, Lorton Pk., High Lorton, Cockermouth, CA13 9DG. Tel. Lorton (090 085) 223.	●	-	-	-	-	1	-	-	-	4	50.00 -	- *120.00*	1–12	GE M LF

You are advised to read the introductory notes and to check prices and other details when booking accommodation

SELF-CATERING ACCOMMODATION

Name and Address: Town (County), Map Ref., Establishment	Contact for reservations: Name and address, Telephone number, Telex	Tourist Board Standards	Self-contained: House (or part)	Bungalows	Cottages	Chalets/caravans	Flats/flatlets	Houseboats	Not self-contained: Flats/flatlets	Chalets	Number of persons per unit	Per unit per week: Low season £ Min. / £ Max.	High season £ Min. / £ Max.	Months open (1–12)	Symbols (Key: see fold-out)
LOWESWATER continued															
Nether Close, Loweswater, Cockermouth,	Mrs. E. Vickers, Howside, Ennerdale, Cleator, Cumbria, CA23 3AU. Tel. Lamplugh (094 686) 334.	●	-	-	1	-	-	-	-	-	6	40.00 / -	- / *80.00*	1–12	GE M LH
Rose Cottage, Loweswater, Cockermouth.	Mrs. G. H. White, Jenkin, Loweswater, Cockermouth, Cumbria, CA13 0RU. Tel. Lorton (090 085) 234.	●	-	-	1	-	-	-	-	-	4	55.00 / *55.00*	65.00 / *65.00*	3–11	GE M LN
† Scale Hill Holiday Flats,	M. E. Thompson, Scale Hill Hotel, Loweswater, Nr. Cockermouth, Cumbria, CA13 9UX. Tel. Lorton (090 085) 232.	●	1	-	-	-	2	-	-	-	2–4	50.00 / *90.00*	100.00 / *125.00*	1–12	12 GE LF
LOWICK (Cumbria) B3 (5m N. Ulverston)															
† Romanile, Lowick Bridge, Nr. Ulverston,	H. Patton, To-in-Yan, Bouth, Nr. Ulverston, Cumbria, LA12 8JB. Tel. Greenodd (022 986) 419.	●	1	-	-	-	-	-	-	-	8	25.00 / *40.00*	65.00 / *90.00*	1–12	GE M LN
MALLERSTANG (Cumbria) C3 (5m S. Kirkby Stephen)															
Aisgill Moor Cottages, Mallerstang, Kirkby Stephen,	M. & N. Wiseman, 34 Edward St., Blackpool, Lancs. Tel. Blackpool (0253) 28936 (Day) 43471 (Evening).	●	-	2	1	-	-	-	-	-	4–5	40.00 / *70.00*	75.00 / *120.00*	1–12	GE M LN T
MILLOM (Cumbria) B3															
† Broadgate Furnished Lettings,	Miss K. M. Coulthard, Broadgate, Thwaites, Nr. Millom, Cumbria, LA18 5JZ. Tel. Broughton-in-Furness (065 76) 295.	●	3	1	2	-	2	-	-	-	1–7	25.00 / *70.00*	40.00 / *130.00*	4–10	6 GE M LN
† Yarfield Hall Flats, Festival Rd.,	D. Ross, 2 Lancashire Rd., Millom, Cumbria, LA18 4BX. Tel. (0657) 2934.	●	-	-	-	-	8	-	-	-	2–4	60.00 / -	80.00 / -	1–12	LN T
MORLAND (Cumbria) C2 (6m NW. Appleby-in-Westmorland)															
Bourn Edge, Morland, Penrith,	Mrs. Harwood, The College, Lowther Newtown, Penrith, Cumbria, CA10 2HH. Tel. Hackthorpe (093 12) 243.	●	-	-	1	-	-	-	-	-	6	50.00 / -	90.00 / -	4–9	GE M LN T
MUNGRISDALE (Cumbria) B2															
Thwaite Hall, Hutton Roof, Greystoke, Penrith,	Mrs. E. Taylor, Hill Top, Penruddock, Penrith, Cumbria, CA11 0RX. Tel. Greystoke (085 33) 340.	●	-	-	2	-	-	-	-	-	6	80.00 / -	100.00 / -	1–12	GE M LN

SELF-CATERING ACCOMMODATION

Name and Address: Town (County) / Map Ref. / Establishment	Contact for reservations: Name and address, Telephone number, Telex	Tourist Board Standards	Self-contained: House (or part)	Bungalows	Cottages	Chalets/caravans	Flats/flatlets	Houseboats	Not self-contained: Flats/flatlets	Chalets	Number of persons per unit	Prices per unit per week: Low season (£ Min. / £ Max.)	High season (£ Min. / £ Max.)	Months open (1–12)	Symbols (Key: see fold-out)
PENRITH (Cumbria) C2															
Dalkeith	Mr. K. G. Dudson, Bayshields Ltd., Dalkeith, Monks Clo., Penrith, Cumbria, CA11 9JG. Tel. (0768) 63574.	●	–	–	1	–	3	–	–	–	5–8	45.00 *65.00*	75.00 *100.00*	1–12	GE LN
Grayrigg, Plumpton Head,	Mrs. B. Ridley, Ravencroft, Plumpton, Penrith, Cumbria, CA11 9NP. Tel. Plumpton (076 884) 225.	●	1	–	–	–	–	–	–	–	2–8	60.00 *70.00*	75.00 *120.00*	1–12	GE LH
The Old Smithy, Catterlen,	Mr. T. S. Simpson, The Old Smithy, Catterlen, Penrith, Cumbria, CA11 0BQ. Tel. (0768) 64230.	●	–	–	–	–	1	–	–	–	3	50.00 *60.00*	60.00 *80.00*	4–10	LN
PENTON (Cumbria) C2 (7m NE. Longtown)															
† Bessiestown Farm,	Mrs. Margaret Sisson, Bessiestown Farm, Penton, Carlisle, Cumbria, CA6 5QP. Tel. Nicholforest (022 877) 219.	●	–	–	3	3	–	–	–	–	4–6	40.00 *–*	– *120.00*	4–10	GE LH
Craigburn Farm.	Mrs. Jane Lawson, Craigburn Farm, Penton, Longtown, Carlisle, Cumbria, CA6 5QP. Tel. Nicholforest (022 877) 214.	●	1	1	–	1	1	–	–	–	2–6	25.00 *40.00*	40.00 *70.00*	1–12	GE LH
Liddel Park	Mrs. J. E. Newton, Liddel Park, Penton, Nr. Carlisle, Cumbria, CA6 5QB. Tel. Nichol Forest (022 877) 317.	●	–	3	–	–	–	–	–	–	4–6	59.00 *–*	– *111.00*	1–12	GE LF
PRESTON PATRICK (Cumbria) C3 (3.5m NE. Milnthorpe)															
Beckside Cottage, Preston Patrick, Kendal,	P. H. Houghton, Gt. Croft, Yealand Redmayne, Carnforth, Lancashire, LA5 9TA Tel. Burton (0524) 781727.	●	–	–	1	–	–	–	–	–	2	– *60.00*	– *90.00*	4–10	GE LF
RAVENGLASS (Cumbria) B3															
Cropple How, Birkby, Ravenglass,	Mrs. D. Taylor, Cross House Farm, Bootle, Millom, Cumbria, LA19 5TJ. Tel. Bootle (065 78) 234.	●	1	–	–	–	–	–	1	–	2–8	30.00 *70.00*	45.00 *80.00*	4–10	GE LN
ROADHEAD (Cumbria) C1															
† Lynebank Holiday Cottages, Roadhead, Carlisle,	Mrs. Dorothy Downer, Bank End Farm, Roadhead, Carlisle, Cumbria, CA6 6NU. Tel. (069 78) 644.	●	–	–	2	–	–	–	–	–	2–6	50.00 *52.00*	90.00 *110.00*	1–12	GE LH
RYDAL (Cumbria) B2															
Rydal Estate, Rydal, Ambleside,	A. Hoggarth & Son, 52 Kirkland, Kendal, Cumbria, LA9 5AP. Tel. Kendal (0539) 22592.	●	1	1	–	–	–	–	–	–	2–6	50.00 *110.00*	110.00 *125.00*	1–12	GE LN

 You are advised to read the introductory notes and to check prices and other details when booking accommodation

SELF-CATERING ACCOMMODATION

Name and Address: Town (County) / Establishment	Map Ref.	Contact for reservations: Name and address, Telephone number, Telex	Accommodation: Tourist Board Standards	Self-contained: House (or part)	Bungalows	Cottages	Chalets/caravans	Flats/flatlets	Houseboats	Not self-contained: Flats/flatlets	Chalets	Number of persons per unit	Prices per unit per week: Low season (£ Min. / *£ Max.*)	High season (£ Min. / *£ Max.*)	Months open (1–12)	Symbols (Key: see fold-out)
ST. BEES (Cumbria)	**B2**															
Bide-a-While, Sea Mill La.,		Mrs. Dorothy H. Reid, Meadow House, St. Bees, Cumbria, CA27 0BZ Tel. (094 685) 217.	●	-	1	-	-	-	-	-	-	7	90.00 *110.00*	100.00 -	4–10	GE LN
Fairladies Holiday Homes,		George & Victoria Patterson, Fairladies Barn, St. Bees, Cumbria, CA27 0AD. Tel. (094 685) 718.	●	-	-	-	-	6	-	-	-	2–6	50.00 *65.00*	90.00 *120.00*	1–12	GE LH T
SATTERTHWAITE (Cumbria) (4m SSW. Hawkshead)	**B3**															
No. 2 Church Cottage,		Mrs. E. Walton, Townhead, Satterthwaite, Nr. Ulverston, Cumbria, LA12 8LS. Tel. (022 984) 203.	●	-	-	1	-	-	-	-	-	2–6	50.00 -	100.00 *130.00*	1–12	GE LN
Farra Grain,		Mrs. R. N. Buckley, The Old Vicarage, Satterthwaite, Ulverston, Cumbria, LA12 8LN. Tel. (022 984) 212.	●	-	-	1	-	-	-	-	-	6	70.00 -	100.00 *130.00*	1–12	GE LN
SAWREY (Cumbria)	**B3**															
Esthwaite Farm Holidays,		Mrs. T. W. Taylor, Esthwaite How Farm, Nr. Sawrey, Ambleside, Cumbria, LA22 0LB. Tel. Hawkshead (096 66) 331.	●	-	-	2	-	4	-	-	-	4–5	69.00 -	110.00 -	4–10	GE LN
SEASCALE (Cumbria)	**B3**															
Meadowside Cottage Whitriggs Farm,		Mrs. Margaret Taylor, Whitriggs Farm, Seascale, Cumbria, CA20 1NZ Tel. (0940) 28306.	●	-	-	1	-	-	-	-	-	7	45.00 -	- *90.00*	4–10	GE LN
SEBERGHAM (Cumbria) (10m SSW. Carlisle)	**B2**															
Beach Cottage, Sebergham, Carlisle,		M. A. Brough, How Gill, Hesket Newmarket, Wigton, Cumbria, CA7 8JB. Tel. Caldbeck (069 98) 213.	●	-	-	1	-	-	-	-	-	2–6	50.00 -	80.00 -	1–12	LF
† Monkhouse Hill Farm, Sebergham, Welton, Nr. Carlisle,		Mrs. D. Shaw, 23 Stonecross Rd., Kendal, Cumbria, LA9 5HR. Tel. Kendal (0539) 21897.	●	-	-	-	-	5	-	-	-	4–6	78.20 *90.85*	156.40 *198.95*	1–12	GE LH T
SILECROFT (Cumbria) (10m SE. Ravenglass)	**B3**															
Hartrees House & Cottages, Shore Rd.,		Mrs. S. Mansergh, Kellet Farm, Silecroft, Nr. Millom, Cumbria, LA18 4NU. Tel. Millom (0657) 2727.	●	2	-	2	-	-	-	-	-	2–10	35.00 *65.00*	55.00 *110.00*	4–10	GE LN
1 The Nook, Silecroft, Nr. Millom,		Mrs. P. Long, Oakdene, Chapel Stile, Ambleside, LA22 9JE. Tel. Langdale (096 67) 629.	●	-	-	1	-	-	-	-	-	4	60.00 -	- *85.00*	4–10	GE LN

SELF-CATERING ACCOMMODATION

Name and Address: Town (County) / Establishment	Map Ref.	Contact for reservations: Name and address, Telephone number, Telex	Tourist Board Standards	Self-contained: House (or part)	Bungalows	Cottages	Chalets/caravans	Flats/flatlets	Houseboats	Not self-contained: Flats/flatlets	Chalets	Number of persons per unit	Prices per unit per week: Low season (£ Min. / £ Max.)	High season (£ Min. / £ Max.)	Months open (1–12)	Symbols (Key: see fold-out)
SILECROFT continued																
Shore Meadow, Silecroft, Millom		Mrs. Susan Capstick, Whicham Hall, Silecroft, Millom, Cumbria, LA18 5LT. Tel. Millom (0657) 2637.	●	-	1	-	-	-	-	-	-	7	– *60.00*	75.00 *120.00*	1–12	GE M LN
SILLOTH (Cumbria)	**B1**															
5 Marine Ter.		T. Twentyman, Beach Holme, Allonby, Maryport, Cumbria, CA15 6QH. Tel. Allonby (090 084) 247.	●	-	-	-	-	2	-	-	-	6–7	25.00 *50.00*	75.00 *75.00*	5–10	GE M LN
32 Skinburness Dr.		Mrs. E. Shuttleworth, Hawkshead Hill, Ambleside, Cumbria, LA22 0PW. Tel. Hawkshead (096 66) 432.	●	1	-	-	-	-	-	-	-	6	40.00 *60.00*	65.00 *80.00*	2–11	GE LF
SPARK BRIDGE (Cumbria) (3m S. Coniston Water)	**B3**															
† Dicky Cragg Spark Bridge, Ulverston,		Mrs. B. Bailey, Down Court, Courts Hill Rd., Haslemere, Surrey, Tel. Haslemere (0428) 3993.	●	2	-	-	-	-	-	-	-	6–10	60.00 *70.00*	180.00 *240.00*	1–12	LF
STAVELEY (Cumbria)	**C3**															
7 The Banks, Staveley, Kendal,		Mrs. C. A. Black, Bridgestone, Kentmere, Kendal, Cumbria, LA8 9JP. Tel. (0539) 821550.	●	-	-	1	-	-	-	-	-	4	50.00 –	80.00 –	1–12	GE LN
Cottage Pie, 3 The Banks		Mrs. V. W. Wilson, 15 North Craig, Windermere, Cumbria, LA23 2ET. Tel. Windermere (096 62) 4888.	●	-	-	1	-	-	-	-	-	4	40.00 –	95.00 –	1–12	M LH
Fairfield & Nos. 2 & 6 Church View, Staveley, Kendal,		Mrs. D. E. Cannon, Eagle and Child Hotel, Staveley, Kendal, Cumbria, LA8 9LP. Tel. (0539) 821320.	●	1	-	2	-	-	-	-	-	5–8	40.00 –	60.00 –	1–12	GE M LF
† Gatefoot Mill, Windermere Rd.,		Mrs. B. E. Bibby, 26 St Mary's Park, Windermere, Cumbria, LA23 1AZ. Tel. Windermere (096 62) 2527.	●	-	-	-	-	4	-	-	-	4	40.00 *50.00*	65.00 *75.00*	1–12	GE M LH
TEBAY (Cumbria)	**C2**															
2 Chapel Cottages,		Mrs. Dora Carrington, 4 Shanny La., Natland, Kendal, LA9 7QX. Tel. Sedgwick (0448) 60170.	●	-	-	1	-	-	-	-	-	4–5	– *40.00*	– *60.00*	4–10	GE LN
THORNTHWAITE (Cumbria) (3m NW. Keswick)	**B2**															
Beckside Cottage,		Mrs. A. M. Lawson, Beckside, Thornthwaite, Keswick, CA12 5SA. Tel. Braithwaite (059 682) 395.	●	-	-	1	-	-	-	-	-	2–4	60.00 *120.00*	110.00 *140.00*	1–12	6 GE M LF
Seat Howe,		Mrs. D. Bell, Seat Howe, Thornthwaite, Keswick, Cumbria, CA12 5SQ. Tel. Braithwaite (059 682) 371.	●	-	-	1	-	-	-	-	-	4	80.00 *100.00*	100.00 *120.00*	1–12	7 GE LF

You are advised to read the introductory notes and to check prices and other details when booking accommodation

SELF-CATERING ACCOMMODATION

Name and Address: Town (County) / Establishment	Map Ref.	Contact for reservations: Name and address, Telephone number, Telex	Tourist Board Standards	Accommodation: Self-contained: House (or part)	Bungalows	Cottages	Chalets/caravans	Flats/flatlets	Houseboats	Not self-contained: Flats/flatlets	Chalets	Number of persons per unit	Prices per unit per week: Low season £ Min. *£ Max.*	High season £ Min. *£ Max.*	Months open (1–12)	Symbols (Key: see fold-out)
THORNTHWAITE contd.																
† Thornthwaite Holidays,		Mrs. R. E. Wakefield, Thornthwaite Galleries, Thornthwaite, Keswick, Cumbria, CA12 5SA. Tel. Windermere (096 62) 3856 or Braithwaite (059 682) 248.	●	2	–	–	–	–	–	–	–	6	100.00 *130.00*	160.00 *200.00*	3–11	GE M TV LF ✱
Thwaite Hill Barn,		Mrs. S. E. Walls, Thwaite Hill, Thornthwaite, Keswick, Cumbria, CA12 5SA. Tel. Braithwaite (059 682) 412.	●	–	–	1	–	–	–	–	–	4–6	55.00 –	– *110.00*	1–12	GE M TV LH ✱
THRELKELD (Cumbria)	**B2**															
† Blencathra Centre		The Manager, Blencathra Centre, Threlkeld, Keswick, Cumbria, CA12 4SG. Tel. (059 683) 601.	●	1	–	4	–	3	–	–	–	2–6	70.00 –	– *130.00*	1–12	☎ GE M TV LH ✱ ♿
1 Blencathra View, Threlkeld, Keswick		Mrs. P. M. C. Bish, 3 Squires Rd., Shepperton, Middlesex TW17 0LQ. Tel. Chertsey (093 28) 65857.	●	–	1	–	–	–	–	–	–	5	70.00 –	– *100.00*	1–12	☎ GE M TV LF
3 Blencathra View, Threlkeld, Keswick,		N. J. & S. M. Barlow, 19 Milton Clo., Marple, Stockport, Cheshire, SK6 7JT. Tel. 061–449 8453.	●	–	1	–	–	–	–	–	–	6	50.00 *70.00*	70.00 *100.00*	1–12	GE M R TV LN
The Bungalow		Mr. & Mrs. P. & V. J. Sunley, The Bungalow, Sunnyside, Threlkeld, Keswick, Cumbria CA12 4SD. Tel. (059 683) 679.	●	–	2	1	–	–	–	–	–	6–7	56.00 *65.00*	65.80 *100.00*	1–12	☎ GE TV LN ✱ ♿
Mire House Farm.		Mrs. I. Birkett, Birkett Mire, Threlkeld, Keswick, Cumbria, CA12 4TT. Tel. (059 683) 608.	●	1	–	–	–	–	–	–	–	8	60.00 –	– *130.00*	1–12	GE M R LH
† Setmabanning Farm,		G. L. & Mrs. M. E. Hutton, Setmabanning Farm, Threlkeld, Keswick, Cumbria, CA12 4TT. Tel. (059 683) 229.	●	–	–	2	–	–	–	–	–	5	60.00 *80.00*	80.00 *120.00*	1–12	GE M TV LN
Underknott, Blease Rd.		The Rev. & Mrs. F. C. Hambrey, Colton Vicarage, Nr. Ulverston, Cumbria, LA12 8HF. Tel. Greenodd (022 986) 361.		1	–	–	–	–	–	–	–	8	70.00 *80.00*	90.00 *115.00*	1–12	☎ GE M LN ✱
TROUTBECK, PENRITH (Cumbria)	**B2**															
Wallthwaite		Mrs. M. Harper, Wallthwaite, Troutbeck, Penrith, Cumbria, CA11 0SX. Tel. Threlkeld (059 683) 210.	●	–	–	2	–	–	–	–	–	6	40.00 –	50.00 –	1–12	GE M LN
TROUTBECK, WINDERMERE (Cumbria)	**B3**															
† Birkhead Guest House		Miss Dawson, Birkhead Guest House, Troutbeck, Windermere, Cumbria, LA23 1PQ. Tel. Ambleside (096 63) 2288.	●	–	–	3	–	–	–	–	–	4	50.00 *70.00*	80.00 *100.00*	1–12	GE M TV LH

SELF-CATERING ACCOMMODATION

Name and Address: Town (County), Map Ref., Establishment	Contact for reservations: Name and address, Telephone number, Telex	Tourist Board Standards	Self-contained: House (or part)	Bungalows	Cottages	Chalets/caravans	Flats/flatlets	Houseboats	Not self-contained: Flats/flatlets	Chalets	Number of persons per unit	Prices per unit per week: Low season £ Min. / £ Max.	High season £ Min. / £ Max.	Months open (1–12)	Symbols (Key: see fold-out)
TROUTBECK, WINDERMERE continued															
High Green House,	Mrs. J. Cochrane, Stoneyhills, Alnwick, Northumberland, NE66 2AB. Tel. Alnwick (0665) 602530.	●	–	–	1	–	–	–	–	–	8	60.00 / *60.00*	80.00 / *90.00*	4–12	GE M LN
Rose Cottage, Robin La.	Mrs. A. Kelly, 1 Robin La., Troutbeck, Windermere, Cumbria LA23 1PF. Tel. Ambleside (096 63) 2780.	●	–	–	1	–	–	–	–	–	8	70.00 / –	– / *160.00*	1–12	5 GE M LN
ULLSWATER (Cumbria) C2															
Amey's Cottage & Winn's Cottage, Pooley Bridge, Penrith	Mrs. W. H. P. Loftie, Bowerbank, Pooley Bridge, Penrith, Cumbria, CA10 2NG. Tel. Pooley Bridge (085 36) 304 or 01-730 2547.	●	–	–	2	–	–	–	–	–	2–7	55.00 / –	– / *110.00*	1–12	GE M LN
† Arcos	Raymond Cowperthwaite, Arcos, Hutton John, Penrith, Cumbria, CA11 0LZ. Tel. Greystoke (085 33) 300.	●	–	2	2	–	–	–	–	–	4–6	75.00 / –	– / *160.00*	1–12	LH
† Beckses Garage Caravan & Camping Site	J. Teasdale, Beckses Garage Caravan & Camping Site, Penruddock, Penrith, Cumbria, CA11 0RX. Tel. Greystoke (085 33) 224.	●	–	–	1	4	–	–	–	–	2–8	50.00 / *65.00*	60.00 / *95.00*	4–10	GE LN
Bonscale Farmhouse & Auterstone Cottage, Howtown, Penrith,	W. H. Parkin, Swarthbeck Farm, Howtown, Penrith, Cumbria, CA10 2ND. Tel. Pooley Bridge (085 36) 432.	●	1	–	1	–	–	–	–	–	6–10	65.00 / –	– / *120.00*	1–12	GE M LN T
Cross Cottage, Askham, Penrith,	Mrs. C. Charlton, Howfoot, Pooley Bridge, Penrith, Cumbria, CA11 0NQ. Tel. Pooley Bridge (085 36) 234.	●	–	–	1	–	–	–	–	–	6	– / *100.00*	– / *150.00*	1–12	GE M LN T
Cuthbert House	Mrs. M. Kelso, Cuthbert House, Glenridding, Penrith, Cumbria, CA11 0GG. Tel. Glenridding (085 32) 285.	●	–	1	–	–	–	–	–	–	5	70.00 / *75.00*	85.00 / *95.00*	2–10	GE M LN
† Dalemain Estates.	The Agent, Estate Office, Dalemain, Penrith, Cumbria, CA11 0HB. Tel. Pooley Bridge (085 36) 450.	●	–	1	3	–	–	–	–	–	4–10	60.00 / *80.00*	80.00 / *110.00*	4–10	GE M LN
Fell View Holiday Flats.	Mrs. M. E. Burnett, Fell View, Grisedale Bridge, Glenridding, Nr. Penrith, Cumbria, CA11 0PJ. Tel. Glenridding (085 32) 342.	●	–	–	–	–	2	–	–	–	4	– / *70.00*	– / *80.00*	1–12	GE M LN
† Glenridding House, Glenridding, Penrith	Border Holiday Homes, Bute House, Rosehill, Carlisle, Cumbria, CA1 2SA. Tel. Carlisle (0228) 34371.	●	–	–	–	–	2	–	2	–	5–6	45.00 / –	– / *140.00*	1–12	GE M LH
2 Low Glenridding, Glenridding, Penrith,	Mrs. A. M. McCreadie, Patterdale Hall, Glenridding, Penrith, Cumbria, CA11 0PN. Tel. Glenridding (085 32) 436.	●	–	–	1	–	–	–	–	–	5	60.00 / *65.00*	65.00 / *75.00*	4–10	M LN

 You are advised to read the introductory notes and to check prices and other details when booking accommodation

SELF-CATERING ACCOMMODATION

Name and Address: Town (County), Map Ref., Establishment	Contact for reservations: Name and address, Telephone number, Telex	Tourist Board Standards	Accommodation: Self-contained: House (or part)	Bungalows	Cottages	Chalets/caravans	Flats/flatlets	Houseboats	Not self-contained: Flats/flatlets	Chalets	Number of persons per unit	Prices per unit per week: Low season (£ Min. / *£ Max.*)	High season (£ Min. / *£ Max.*)	Months open (1–12)	Symbols (Key: see fold-out)
ULLSWATER continued															
Mains House, Pooley Bridge & Yew Cottage, Dacre,	Lt. Col. & Mrs. T. J. C. Washington, Dacre Lodge, Penrith Cumbria, CA11 0HH. Tel. Pooley Bridge (085 36) 221.	●	1	–	1	–	–	–	–	–	4–10	69.00 *103.50*	92.00 *138.00*	1–12	GE M LN
Parcey House.	Mrs. B. Thomson, Parcey House, Hartsop, Penrith, Cumbria, CA11 0NZ. Tel. Glenridding (085 32) 413.	●	1	–	–	–	–	–	–	–	2	35.00 –	– *60.00*	1–12	GE M LH
Park Foot.	Mrs. Allen, Park Foot, Howtown Rd., Pooley Bridge, Penrith, CA10 2NA. Tel. Pooley Bridge (085 36) 309.	●	–	5	2	6	–	–	–	–	2–6	50.00 –	– *150.00*	1–12	GE LN
Rose Bank Cottage,	Colonel or Mrs. R. P. Baily, Rose Bank, Dacre, Nr. Penrith, Cumbria, CA11 0HL. Tel. Pooley Bridge (085 36) 258.	●	1	–	–	–	–	–	–	–	4	70.00 *90.00*	100.00 *120.00*	4–9	GE M LN
† Thackthwaite Holiday Cottages,	Mr. & Mrs. V. F. Cash, High House, Thackthwaite, Dacre, Penrith, Cumbria, CA11 0ND. Tel. Pooley Bridge (085 36) 385.	●	1	–	2	–	–	–	–	–	3–6	37.00 –	62.00 –	1–12	GE M LH
Ullswater Caravan Camping & Marine Park,	Mr. D. Dobinson, Ullswater Caravan Camping & Marine Park, Watermillock, Penrith, Cumbria, CA11 0LR. Tel. Pooley Bridge (085 36) 666.	●	–	2	5	–	–	–	–	–	5–6	46.00 *70.00*	70.00 *150.00*	1–12	GE M LH
Ullswater House, Glenridding, Ullswater, Penrith.	Mr. T. J. Fynn, Daweswood Patterdale, Penrith, Cumbria, CA11 0NW. Tel. Glenridding (085 32) 221.	●	1	–	–	–	–	–	–	–	11	150.00 *150.00*	200.00 *200.00*	1–12	GE M LF
† Ullswater Sailing School.	A. Longworth, Ullswater Sailing School, Landends, Watermillock, Nr. Penrith, Cumbria, CA11 0NB. Tel. Pooley Bridge (085 36) 438.	●	–	–	–	4	–	–	–	–	3–6	25.00 *47.50*	70.00 *157.50*	1–12	GE M LN
Walton Holiday Homes.	Mrs. D. Hetherington, Waltons Pl., Stainton, Penrith, Cumbria, CA11 0EP. Tel. Penrith (0768) 62714.	●	4	–	–	1	–	–	–	–	6–8	60.00 *70.00*	80.00 *100.00*	3–10	GE M LF
ULVERSTON (Cumbria) **B3**															
Brookwood. Newland,	H. Stevenson, Newland, Ulverston, Cumbria, LA12 7QG. Tel. (0229) 53825.	●	–	1	–	–	–	–	–	–	2	35.00 *35.00*	35.00 *35.00*	1–12	GE LF
The Bungalow, Greenmoor, Nr. Pennington, Ulverston,	Crayrock Ltd., 39 Rampside, Barrow-in-Furness, Cumbria, LA13 0PY. Tel. Barrow-in-Furness (0229) 25772.	●	–	1	–	–	–	–	–	–	2–8	60.00 *60.00*	150.00 *150.00*	1–12	GE M LN
† The Falls,	Geoff Dellow, The Falls, Mansriggs, Ulverston, Cumbria, LA12 7PX. Tel. (0229) 53781.	●	1	–	2	–	2	–	–	–	2–10	55.00 *90.00*	135.00 *285.00*	1–12	GE LF S T

SELF-CATERING ACCOMMODATION

Town (County) / Establishment	Map Ref.	Contact for reservations: Name and address, Telephone number, Telex	Tourist Board Standards	House (or part)	Bungalows	Cottages	Chalets/caravans	Flats/flatlets	Houseboats	Flats/flatlets (not self-contained)	Chalets (not self-contained)	Number of persons per unit	Low season £ Min. / *£ Max.*	High season £ Min. / *£ Max.*	Months open (1–12)	Symbols (Key: see fold-out)
UNDERBARROW (Cumbria)	**C3**															
Parks Farm, Underbarrow, Kendal,		Mr. B. Slater, 13 Hillgarth Underbarrow, Kendal, Cumbria, LA8 8HN. Tel. Crosthwaite (044 88) 458.	●	-	-	1	-	-	-	-	-	6	60.00 *60.00*	60.00 *60.00*	1–12	GE M TV LN
WASDALE (Cumbria)	**B2**															
† Church How Cottage		Mrs. S. M. Friend, The Old Vicarage, Netherwasdale, via Seascale, Cumbria, CA20 1ET. Tel. Wasdale (094 06) 232.	●	-	-	1	-	-	-	-	-	7	82.50 *104.50*	104.50 *165.00*	1–12	M R TV LF
† Greendale.		Mr. & Mrs. M. D. Burnett, Greendale, Wasdale, Nr. Seascale, Cumbria, CA20 1EV. Tel. (094 06) 243.	●	-	-	-	-	11	-	-	-	4–6	80.00 *100.00*	100.00 *140.00*	1–12	TV LH
† Row Foot Cottage,		Reception Wasdale Head Inn, Wasdale Head, Nr. Gosforth, Cumbria CA20 1EX. Tel. (094 06) 229.	●	1	-	1	-	1	-	-	1	2–8	70.00 *190.00*	100.00 *210.00*	1–12	LF
WELTON (Cumbria) (8m SW. Carlisle)	**B2**															
Smithy Cottage, Nether Welton, Dalston, Carlisle,		Mr. John I. Fawkes, Blackwell House, Blackwell, Carlisle, Cumbria, CA2 4TS. Tel. Carlisle (0228) 22504.	●	-	-	1	-	-	-	-	-	4	125.00 *150.00*	160.00 *200.00*	1–12	GE R TV LF T
Well Cottage, Welton, Nr. Dalston, Carlisle		Mrs. A. E. Ivinson, Green View, Welton, Nr. Dalston, Carlisle, Cumbria, CA5 7ES. Tel. Raughton Head (069 96) 230.	●	-	-	1	1	-	-	-	-	2–6	45.00 -	60.00 -	1–12	GE M TV LH T
† Welton Plains Holiday Cottages,		Capt. H. V. Hubbard, Welton Plains, Welton, Cumbria, CA5 7ET. Tel. Raughtonhead (069 96) 459.	●	-	-	6	-	-	-	-	-	2–8	60.00 *118.00*	80.00 *195.00*	1–12	GE TV LF T
WHITEHAVEN (Cumbria)	**B2**															
Bleabank, Low Moresby, Whitehaven,		Mr. & Mrs. D. A. C. Smith, Whin Garth, Low Moresby, Whitehaven, Cumbria, CA28 6RT. Tel. (0946) 3033.	●	-	1	-	-	-	-	-	-	6	67.00 *74.00*	115.00 *159.00*	1–12	R TV LN
The Maisonette, 47 Lowther St.,		Miss M. R. Gray, Moordyke, Unthank, Dalston, Carlisle, Cumbria, CA5 7BA. Tel. Dalston (0228) 710381.	●	-	-	-	-	1	-	-	-	6	35.00 *55.00*	65.00 *75.00*	1–12	TV LN
WIGTON (Cumbria)	**B2**															
The Craggs, Rosley, Wigton,		Mrs. D. E. Shaw, Causa Grange, Rosley, Wigton, Cumbria, CA7 8DD. Tel. (096 54) 2450.	●	-	-	1	-	-	-	-	-	5	45.00 *65.00*	75.00 *100.00*	1–12	GE M TV LN
2 Railway Ter.,		Mr. R. C. Beaty, 45 Broadlands, Netherfield, Milton Keynes, Buckinghamshire, MK6 4HJ. Tel. Milton Keynes (0908) 679359.	●	-	-	1	-	-	-	-	-	4	- *50.00*	- *65.00*	1–12	GE M TV LN

 You are advised to read the introductory notes and to check prices and other details when booking accommodation

SELF-CATERING ACCOMMODATION

Name and Address: Town (County) / Establishment	Map Ref.	Contact for reservations: Name and address, Telephone number, Telex	Tourist Board Standards	Self-contained: House (or part)	Bungalows	Cottages	Chalets/caravans	Flats/flatlets	Houseboats	Not self-contained: Flats/flatlets	Chalets	Number of persons per unit	Per unit per week: Low season £ Min. / *£ Max.*	High season £ Min. / *£ Max.*	Months open (1–12)	Symbols (Key: see fold-out)
WIGTON continued																
The Stables, Rosley, Wigton		Dr. & Mrs. F. M. Elderkin, Rosley House, Rosley, Wigton, Cumbria, CA7 8BZ. Tel. (096 54) 2665.	●	–	–	1	–	–	–	–	–	6	30.00 –	100.00 –	3–10	GE LF
Tarrangower,		Mr. & Mrs. K Batey, Tarrangower Filling Station, West Woodside, Wigton, Cumbria, CA7 0LP. Tel. (096 54) 2263.	●	–	1	–	–	–	–	–	–	4–7	65.00 *65.00*	100.00 *100.00*	4–10	GE M LH
Wheyrigg Farm,		Mrs. D. Wilson, Wheyrigg Farm, Wigton, Cumbria, CA7 0DH. Tel. Abbeytown (096 56) 200.	●	1	–	–	–	–	–	–	–	6	69.00 *69.00*	69.00 *69.00*	4–10	GE LN
WINDERMERE (Cumbria)	**B3**															
† Abbotsgarth, Beaumont, Thornbarrow Rd.,		Mr. P. Chance, Beaumont, Thornbarrow Rd., Windermere, Cumbria, LA23 2DG. Tel. (096 62) 5144.	●	–	3	–	–	–	–	–	–	2–3	50.00 –	– *130.00*	1–12	10 GE M LF
† Applethwaite Luxury Holiday Flats		F. & E. Coates, Applethwaite Luxury Holiday Flats, The Heaning, Heaning La, Windermere, LA23 1JW. Tel. (096 62) 3453.	●	–	–	–	–	6	–	–	–	2–6	35.00 *65.00*	73.00 *150.00*	1–12	5 GE M LH
The Barn Old Heathwaite,		Mrs. J. E. Law, Old Heathwaite, Windermere, LA23 2DH. Tel. (096 62) 2410.	●	–	–	–	–	1	–	–	–	4	55.00 –	– *120.00*	1–12	GE M LH
† Beaumont Luxury Holiday Flats.		Mrs. S. Chance, Beaumont Luxury Holiday Flats, Thornbarrow Rd., Windermere, Cumbria, LA23 2DG. Tel. (096 62) 5144.	●	–	3	–	–	5	–	–	–	2–5	50.00 –	– *140.00*	1–12	10 GE M LF
Biskey Howe Flats.		Mrs. Marjorie Mullen, 1a Biskey Howe Rd., Windermere, Cumbria, LA23 3AP. Tel. (096 62) 2323.	●	–	–	–	–	3	–	–	–	2–5	45.00 *85.00*	65.00 *108.00*	1–12	GE M LF
Bowering Holiday Flats, 6 Park Rd.		Mrs. Taylor, Belle Mere, Newby Bridge, Cumbria, LA12 8NL. Tel. Newby Bridge (0448) 31202.	●	–	–	–	–	5	–	–	–	2–6	50.00 *65.00*	55.00 *100.00*	1–12	GE M LH
† Briscoe Lodge.		Mrs. J. W. N. Cook, Briscoe Lodge, Ellerthwaite Rd., Windermere, Cumbria, LA23 2AH. Tel. (096 62) 2928.	●	–	–	–	–	2	–	–	–	3–4	60.00 *65.00*	60.00 *65.00*	1–12	GE M LF
Buntings, 28 Meadowcroft Cottages, Storrs Park,		Mr. F. P. Aubrey, Otters Pool, Blackbeck Wood, Windermere, Cumbria, LA23 3LS. Tel. (096 62) 4488.	●	–	–	1	–	–	–	–	–	6	40.00 *80.00*	100.00 *135.00*	1–12	5 M LN
† Canterbury Flats, Quarry Rigg, Lake Rd., Bowness-on-Windermere,		Mr. H. E. Betham, Flat 41A Quarry Rigg, Lake Rd., Windermere, Cumbria, LA23 3DT. Tel. (096 62) 5216 or Canterbury (0227) 69803.	●	–	–	–	–	22	–	–	–	2–9	78.20 *120.75*	138.00 *230.00*	1–12	M LF

SELF-CATERING ACCOMMODATION

Name and Address: Town (County) / Map Ref. / Establishment	Contact for reservations: Name and address, Telephone number, Telex	Accommodation: Tourist Board Standards	Self-contained: House (or part)	Bungalows	Cottages	Chalets/caravans	Flats/flatlets	Houseboats	Not self-contained: Flats/flatlets	Chalets	Number of persons per unit	Prices per unit per week: Low season (£ Min. / £ Max.)	High season (£ Min. / £ Max.)	Months open (1–12)	Symbols (Key: see fold-out)
WINDERMERE continued															
Chestnut Cottage.	Mrs. V. J. Greenwood, The Chestnuts, Prince's Rd., Windermere, Cumbria, LA23 2EF. Tel. (096 62) 5295.	●	–	–	–	–	1	–	–	–	2	50.00 –	– *60.00*	1–12	GE M LF
† The Coach House, Bank Rd.,	Windermere Holidays, Homewood, Storrs Pk., Windermere, Cumbria, LA23 3IT. Tel. (096 62) 4175.	●	1	–	–	–	–	–	–	–	5	90.00 *120.00*	120.00 *150.00*	3–11	GE M LH
15 Cross St.,	Mrs. M. L. Moss, 5 Oak St., Windermere, Cumbria, LA23 1BH. Tel. (096 62) 4610.	●	–	–	1	–	–	–	–	–	5	60.00 *60.00*	60.00 *90.00*	1–12	GE M LH
1, The Crosses.	Mrs. G. Thompson, 2 The Crosses, Windermere, Cumbria, LA23 1JU. Tel. (096 62) 3599.	C	1	–	–	1	–	–	–	–	6	25.00 *80.00*	40.00 *125.00*	3–11	GE M LN
† Deloraine,	Mrs. P. M. Fanstone, Deloraine, Helm Rd., Windermere, Cumbria, LA23 2HS. Tel. (096 62) 5557.	●	–	–	–	–	4	–	–	–	2–9	50.00 –	95.00 –	1–12	GE M LH
Derby Cottage Flat, Off Crescent Rd.,	Mr. P. Laidler, Rose Cottage, Spooner Vale, Windermere, Cumbria, LA23 1BE. Tel. (096 62) 3339.	●	–	–	–	–	1	–	–	–	5	30.00 *55.00*	65.00 –	1–12	GE M LF
† Dove Nest Estate & Farm.	Mrs. Susan H. Jones, Dove Nest, Windermere, Cumbria, LA23 1LR. Tel. Ambleside (096 63) 2286.	●	1	–	2	1	5	–	–	–	2–6	50.00 *150.00*	75.00 *200.00*	1–12	GE M LF
Ecclerigg Close,	H. Clifford Holt, The Squirrels, 2, Beechwood Ave., Earlsdon, Coventry, W. Midlands, CV5 6DF. Tel. Coventry (0203) 74991.	●	–	–	–	–	1	–	–	–	2–9	40.00 *75.00*	75.00 *135.00*	1–12	GE LN
3 Elim Ct., Craig Walk & Old Mill Cottage, Brigsteer,	Mrs. I. J. Hackett, The Grange, Windermere, Cumbria, LA23 1AX. Tel. (096 62) 2604.	●	–	–	1	–	1	–	–	–	4–7	45.00 *45.00*	80.00 *150.00*	1–12	GE M LF
Ellerdene Chalet.	Mr. or Mrs. Bowness, Ellerdene, 12 Ellerthwaite Rd., Windermere, Cumbria, LA23 2AH. Tel. (096 62) 2752.	●	–	–	–	1	–	–	–	1	2	– –	– *28.00*	1–12	GE M LF
Fair Rigg Luxury Flats.	Mrs. N. J. Riley, Fair Rigg, Ferry View, Windermere, Cumbria, LA23 3JB. Tel. (096 62) 3555.	●	–	–	–	–	3	–	–	–	2–4	50.00 *75.00*	70.00 *90.00*	3–10	10 GE M LF
Fellside, 33 Craig Walk,	Mrs. J. Hunt, 104 Cecil Rd., Hale, Cheshire, WA15 9NU. Tel. 061-928 8116.	●	–	–	1	–	–	–	–	–	6	60.00 *80.00*	80.00 *120.00*	1–12	GE M LN
Grey Roofs.	Mrs. P. Kirk, Grey Roofs, Beech Hill, Windermere, Cumbria, LA23 3PR. Tel. (096 62) 3791.	●	–	–	–	1	1	–	–	–	4	45.00 –	60.00 *85.00*	4–10	GE M LN
2 & 3 Hazelhurst Flats, Hazel St.,	Mr. A. Booth, Hazelhurst Cottage, Hazel St., Windermere, Cumbria, LA23 1EL. Tel. (096 62) 4626.	●	–	–	–	–	2	–	–	–	2–6	60.00 –	90.00 –	4–10	GE M LN

 You are advised to read the introductory notes and to check prices and other details when booking accommodation

SELF-CATERING ACCOMMODATION

Name and Address: Town (County) / Establishment	Map Ref.	Contact for reservations: Name and address, Telephone number, Telex	Tourist Board Standards	Self-contained: House (or part)	Bungalows	Cottages	Chalets/caravans	Flats/flatlets	Houseboats	Not self-contained: Flats/flatlets	Chalets	Number of persons per unit	Prices per unit per week: Low season (£ Min. / £ Max.)	High season (£ Min. / £ Max.)	Months open (1–12)	Symbols (Key: see fold-out)
WINDERMERE continued																
Heathwaite Howe, Heathwaite,		Mrs. J. Law, Old Heathwaite, Heathwaite, Windermere, Cumbria, LA23 2DH. Tel. (096 62) 2410.	●	1	–	–	–	–	–	–	–	7	75.00 *150.00*	150.00 *250.00*	1–12	LH
High Riding,		Mr. D. Latham Warde, High Riding, Windermere, Cumbria, LA23 3LS. Tel. (096 62) 4313.	●	1	–	–	–	–	–	–	–	4–5	80.00 *100.00*	120.00 *160.00*	4–10	10 GE LF
Holbeck Ghyll Cottage, Holbeck Ghyll, Windermere		Derek & Catherine Wallace, 75 New Hall La., Bolton, Lancs., BL1 5LF. Tel. Bolton (0204) 46769.	●	–	–	1	–	–	–	–	–	6	50.00 –	– *115.00*	1–12	GE LN
Holehird Farm,		Mrs. S. Bragg, Holehird Farm, Windermere, Cumbria, LA23 1NP. Tel. (096 62) 2678.	●	–	–	–	–	1	–	–	–	2–3	30.00 –	– *40.00*	1–12	GE LF
Howe Foot Holiday Flats,		Mrs. M. E. Thexton, Hillside, Oakthwaite Rd., Windermere, Cumbria, LA23 2BD. Tel. (096 62) 2792.	●	–	–	–	–	12	–	12	–	2–8	52.90 *90.85*	75.90 *136.85*	1–12	GE LF
Ivythwaite Cottage,		Mrs. M. Park, Ivythwaite, Prince's Rd., Windermere, Cumbria, LA23 2DD. Tel. (096 62) 4023.	●	–	–	1	–	–	–	–	–	4	40.00 –	80.00 –	1–12	GE LN
22 Lake Rd.,		Mrs. C. W. Tyson, 14 Lickbarrow Clo., Windermere, Cumbria, LA23 2NF. Tel. (096 62) 2064.	●	–	–	–	–	1	–	–	–	2–6	60.00 –	– *95.00*	4–10	GE LH
† Lilac Cottage, Old College La.,		Mr. & Mrs. C. Heighton, Lipwood, Old College La., Windermere, Cumbria, LA23 1BY. Tel. (096 62) 3494.	●	–	1	–	–	–	–	–	–	4–7	61.00 –	125.00 –	1–12	GE LN
† Lipwood,		Mr. & Mrs. C. Heighton, Lipwood, Old College La., Windermere, Cumbria, LA23 1BY. Tel. (096 62) 3494.	●	–	–	–	–	3	–	–	–	4–8	53.00 –	86.00 –	1–12	GE LN
† Low Wood Self Catering Apartments,		Reception, Low Wood Hotel, Windermere, Cumbria, LA23 1LP. Tel. Ambleside (096 63) 3338. Telex 65273.	●	–	–	–	–	8	–	–	–	6	40.00 *150.00*	105.00 *215.00*	1–12	GE LF
† Ottersholme & Granton Lodge, Storrs Pk.,		Mrs. L. C. Sinfield, Granton Investments Ltd, 40 Greenways Dr., Low Pk., Endmoor, Nr. Kendal, Cumbria, LA8 0EL. Tel. Sedgwick (0448) 60394.	●	–	–	2	–	–	–	–	–	4	83.00 *255.00*	137.00 *300.00*	1–12	LN
Pinethwaite,		Mrs. S. Legge, Pinethwaite, Lickbarrow Rd., Windermere, Cumbria, LA23 2NQ. Tel. (096 62) 4558.	●	–	–	2	–	4	–	–	–	2–6	25.00 *72.00*	48.00 *120.00*	1–12	GE LH
† The Priory Hotel,		Reception, Priory Hotel, Rayrigg Rd., Windermere, Cumbria, LA23 1EX. Tel. (096 62) 4377.	●	–	–	14	–	–	–	–	–	4	– *140.00*	– *192.00*	1–12	GE LF
34 Quarry Rigg,		Mrs. M. Nettleton, 99 Craig Walk, Windermere, Cumbria, LA23 2JS. Tel. (096 62) 4482.	●	–	–	–	–	1	–	–	–	4	45.00 *60.00*	60.00 *85.00*	3–10	5 LN

SELF-CATERING ACCOMMODATION

Name and Address: Town (County) / Map Ref. / Establishment	Contact for reservations: Name and address, Telephone number, Telex	Tourist Board Standards	Self-contained: House (or part)	Self-contained: Bungalows	Self-contained: Cottages	Self-contained: Chalets/caravans	Self-contained: Flats/flatlets	Self-contained: Houseboats	Not self-contained: Flats/flatlets	Not self-contained: Chalets	Number of persons per unit	Prices per unit per week: Low season (£ Min. / *£ Max.*)	Prices per unit per week: High season (£ Min. / *£ Max.*)	Months open (1–12)	Symbols (Key: see fold-out)
WINDERMERE continued															
Sandylands, Thorthwaite Rd.,	Mrs. R. M. Holliday, Lonsdale Hotel, Lake Rd., Bowness-on-Windermere, Cumbria, LA23 2JJ. Tel. (096 62) 3348.	●	1	–	–	–	–	–	–	–	5	– *70.00*	– *100.00*	1–12	3 GE R TV LF T
10 South Ter.,	David & Judith Hargreaves, Bowerswood House, Bowers La., Nateby, Preston, Lancashire, PR3 0JD. Tel. Garstang (099 52) 3322.	●	–	–	1	–	–	–	–	–	2–6	60.00 *80.00*	80.00 *142.00*	1–12	GE M TV LN
† Spinnery Cottage Holiday Flats.	Mr. & Mrs. R. Allman-Smith, Spinnery Cottage, Brantfell Rd., Bowness-on-Windermere, Cumbria, LA23 3AE. Tel. (096 62) 4884.	●	–	–	–	–	3	–	–	–	2–6	40.00 *–*	– *167.00*	1–12	GE TV LN
† Winander Luxury Holiday Flats,	Mr. & Mrs. J. R. Greenhalf, Winander Luxury Holiday Flats, Ferry View, Bowness-on-Windermere, Cumbria, LA23 3JB. Tel. (096 62) 3835.	●	–	–	–	–	7	–	–	–	2–4	80.00 *100.00*	90.00 *130.00*	3–10	10 GE TV LF T
1 Woodland Clo.	Mrs. M. Evans, 14A Old School House, Old Main St., Bingley, W. Yorks., BD16 2RH. Tel. Bradford (0274) 567312.	●	1	–	–	–	–	–	–	–	6	65.00 *–*	– *105.00*	3–10	R TV LN
† Wordsworth Court Holiday Cottages, Brantfell Rd.,	Mr. W. Stanton, Fell Cottage, Winster, Windermere, Cumbria, Tel. (096 62) 3302.	●	7	–	–	–	–	–	–	–	2–8	60.00 *60.00*	75.00 *195.00*	1–12	TV LF
WINSTER (Cumbria) **B3** (2m S. Windermere)															
Woodlea, Winster, Windermere	Mrs. C. E. Brockbank, Common Head, Staveley, Kendal, Cumbria, LA8 9NG. Tel. Staveley (0539) 821237.	●	1	–	–	–	–	–	–	–	8	86.25 *96.25*	100.00 *150.00*	1–12	GE M TV LN
WITHERSLACK (Cumbria) **C3**															
† Old Mill Cottage, Mill Side, Witherslack, Grange-over-Sands,	Mrs. Dorothy A. Scott, Overleigh House, East Cliff, Preston, Lancashire, PR1 3JF. Tel. Preston (0772) 53545.	●	–	–	1	–	–	–	–	–	6	55.00 *–*	– *130.00*	1–12	GE M R TV LN T
WREAY (Cumbria) **C2** (5m SE. Carlisle)															
Holly Flat,	Mrs. F. Sherrard, Holly Cottage, Wreay, Carlisle, CA4 0RL. Tel. Southwaite (069 93) 425.	●	–	–	–	–	1	–	–	–	2–6	60.00 *75.00*	85.00 *115.00*	1–12	GE M R TV LF S

 You are advised to read the introductory notes and to check prices and other details when booking accommodation

CAMPING AND CARAVAN SITES

TOURIST BOARD STANDARDS FOR CARAVAN SITES AND STATIC HIRE CARAVANS/CHALETS

The Tourist Board Standards for caravan sites and static hire caravans and chalets are given below. Sites which conform to these standards are indicated by a ●. We have also printed our recommendations on the kind of information which site owners should provide to people enquiring about a reservation. This will serve as a useful check list of questions which you may want to ask.

CARAVAN AND CHALET SITES

1. The site must have planning permission and site licence readily available.
2. Facilities must be clean and in wholesome condition.
3. The site must be well managed and maintained and kept in a clean and presentable manner and attention paid to the road-side sign and entrance.
4. The site must have reception arrangements at appropriate times from which visitors can be directed to their caravan/chalet/pitch and where advice and assistance can be obtained if necessary.
5. The site operator must be capable of arranging or carrying out repairs to caravans and equipment.
6. Supplies of gas and replacement bottles together with essential spares must be made available by the site operator at all reasonable times.
7. A minimum of 10% of toilets to be lit internally and externally during the hours of darkness, whilst the site is open.
8. An adequate first-aid kit must be readily available, and emergency notices displayed.
9. It is the site operator's responsibility to ensure that all caravans offered for hire on his site have insurance cover for public liability as letting caravans.
10. The site must have fire fighting equipment and notices which conform with the conditions of the site licence.

STATIC HIRE CARAVANS AND CHALETS

1. All caravans must be of proprietary make.
2. All caravans/chalets must be in a good state of internal and external repair and decoration with no internal dampness.
3. The caravans/chalets must not be occupied by more than the number of persons for which they are designed by the manufacturer i.e. four persons in a 4 berth.
4. Equipment must be provided as listed below. An inventory of this equipment must be available for each caravan/chalet.
5. All caravans/chalets must have adequate storage space for luggage and food for the maximum of occupants.
6. All doors, windows, skylights and all ventilation in the caravan/chalet must function correctly. All windows must be properly fitted with opaque curtains or blinds.
7. All caravans/chalets must have adequate internal lighting.
8. All caravans/chalets must be thoroughly cleaned and checked before every letting and equipment maintained and replaced as necessary.
9. Where linen is provided it must be changed on each change of occupier and as appropriate during lets of 2 weeks or more; all mattresses must be in a sound condition.
10. The sink and its waste pipe must be in a sound condition with a draining board. A fixed impervious work top for food preparation must be provided.
11. All caravans/chalets must have a cooker with at least two boiling rings. The cooker must be in a sound and clean condition and functioning properly.
12. All caravans/chalets must have adequate heating according to season.

INFORMATION FOR HIRERS

The booking form should be accompanied by details of the site and caravan(s)/chalet(s) stating clearly:–
1. The number of berths as designed by the manufacturer and, where possible, the make and other relevant details, such as length, width and whether berths are single or double.
2. Whether caravans are connected to:
Mains water.
Mains drainage.
Mains sewerage.
Electricity (stating voltage).
3. Type of lighting.
Electricity.
Gas.
4. The type of cooking equipment.
Electricity.
Gas.

5. A description of site and amenities:
Whether cars park by caravan or in a car park.
Whether pets allowed.
Details of shower and bathrooms.
Whether grocery shop on site or distance to nearest shop.
Licensed bar.
Laundry facilities.
Dancing, entertainments.
TV Room.
Sports facilities.
Public transport.
Distance from sea and nature of accessibility to beach (coastal sites only).
Whether advance booking is necessary during the peak season.

6. The charges for the accommodation/pitch for the period booked and details of any further additional charges e.g. electricity, gas, showers, etc. as well as any optional charges e.g. holiday insurance.

Note: If VAT is payable but not included this must be clearly stated.

7. Any special conditions for payment of deposits or balance.

8. Wherever possible a map showing the location of the site and its proximity to main centres and attractions should be provided.

INVENTORY OF EQUIPMENT FOR STATIC HIRE CARAVANS AND CHALETS

The accommodation should contain the following: -

3 Blankets or 1 continental quilt and cover per bed (for winter, late or early season lettings, the scale of bedding should be increased and adequate heating provided).

1 per person
Pillow.
Knife (table & dessert).
Fork (table & dessert).
Spoon (dessert & tea).
Plate (large & small).
Tea cup and saucer.
Cereal/soup plate.
Tumbler.
Egg cup.

2 per person
Coathangers.

1 per caravan/chalet
Kettle.
Teapot.
Tea caddy.
Saucepan & lid (large, medium and small).
Frying pan.
Colander.
Oven roasting tray.
Casserole dish.
Carving knife and fork.
Bread knife.
Bread/cake container.
Bread and cake plate.
Bread/chopping board.
Fish slice.
Small vegetable knife.
Tin opener.
Corkscrew/bottle opener.
Potato peeler.
Large fruit dish.
Butter dish.
Sugar basin.
Tray.
Milk jug.
Condiment set (2 piece).
Washing-up bowl.
Water carrier (not required where mains water is connected to caravan).
Dustpan and brush.
Broom.
Floor cloth.
Pot scourer/dish mop.
Bucket (an extra bucket is required if sink waste is not connected to a 'soak away' or main drainage).
Mirror.
Doormat.
Covered kitchen refuse container.
Fire extinguisher.

2 per caravan/chalet
Table spoons.
Mixing bowls or basins.
Dusters.
Ash trays.

CAMPING AND CARAVAN SITES

Name and Address: Town (County) / Establishment / Address / Telephone number, Telex	Map Ref.	Tourist Board Standards	Site capacity: Acreage of site	Pitches: Caravans	Pitches: Tents	Pitches: Total	Units for hire: Static holiday caravans	Units for hire: Chalets and similar units	Caravans and chalets not for hire	Prices: Car, caravan and two people overnight	Prices: Motor caravan and two people overnight	Prices: Car, tent and two people overnight	Static caravans and chalets per unit per week: Low season	Static caravans and chalets per unit per week: High season	Months open (1–12)	Symbols
										£ Min. / £ Max.	£ Min. / £ Max.	£ Min. / £ Max.	£ Min. / £ Max.	£ Min. / £ Max.		Key: see fold-out
ALLONBY (Cumbria)	**B2**															
† Manor House Caravan Park, Edderside Rd., Allonby, Maryport, CA15 6RA. Tel. (090 084) 238.		●	14	60	10	70	3	–	100	– / *2.50*	– / *2.50*	– / *2.50*	35.00 / *40.00*	– / *50.00*	3–10	
AMBLESIDE (Cumbria)	**B2**															
† Neaum Crag, Loughrigg, LA22 9HG. Tel. (096 63) 3221.		●	13	37	45	82	–	6	33	3.00 / *6.00*	2.50 / *5.00*	2.50 / *2.50*	84.84 / *84.84*	110.60 / *110.60*	3–11	
Skelwith Fold Caravan Park Ltd., Skelwith Fold, LA22 0HX. Tel. (096 63) 2277.		●	125	125	–	125	–	–	300	– / *2.50*	– / *2.50*	– / –	– / –	– / –	3–11	
APPLEBY-IN-WESTMORLAND (Cumbria)	**C2**															
† Wild Rose Caravan & Camping Park, Ormside, Appleby-in-Westmorland, CA16 6EJ. Tel. Appleby (0930) 51077.		●	27	160	60	220	–	–	180	3.30 / *4.00*	3.30 / *4.00*	3.30 / *4.00*	– / –	– / –	4–10	
ARNSIDE (Cumbria)	**C3**															
† Holgates Caravan Park Ltd., Cove Rd., Silverdale, Nr. Arnside, Carnforth, Lancs. LA5 0SH. Tel. Silverdale (0524) 701508.		●	106	50	20	70	12	–	338	3.00 / *5.50*	3.00 / *5.50*	3.00 / *5.50*	48.00 / *88.00*	95.00 / *170.00*	3–11	
BASSENTHWAITE (Cumbria)	**B2**															
Robin Hood Caravan Pk., Robin Hood Farm, Bassenthwaite, Nr. Keswick, CA12 4RJ. Contact Mrs. A. E. Ivinson, Green View, Welton, Nr. Dalston, Carlisle, Cumbria CA5 7ES. Tel. Raughton Head (069 96) 230.		●	3	–	–	–	1	–	–	– / –	– / –	– / –	25.00 / *70.00*	35.00 / –	4–10	
† Scarness Bay Caravan Site, Bassenthwaite, Keswick, CA12 4QZ. Tel. Bassenthwaite Lake (059 681) 367.		●	9	5	–	5	25	–	30	4.00 / *5.00*	4.00 / *5.00*	– / –	50.00 / *80.00*	90.00 / *140.00*	4–10	
BRAITHWAITE (Cumbria)	**B2**															
Scotgate Caravan Site, Braithwaite, Keswick, CA12 5TJ. Tel. (059 682) 343.		●	10	15	120	135	35	–	15	3.00 / *5.00*	1.80 / *2.50*	2.10 / *2.80*	55.20 / *87.40*	57.50 / *92.00*	4–10	
CARLISLE (Cumbria)	**B1**															
† Dandy Dinmont Caravan & Camping Site, Blackford, Carlisle, CA6 4EA. Tel. Rockcliffe (022 874) 611.		●	4	27	20	47	–	–	15	2.50 / –	2.50 / –	1.80 / *2.00*	– / –	– / –	3–10	
† Orton Grange Caravan & Camping Site, Wigton Rd., CA5 6LA. Tel. (0228) 710252.		●	5	30	20	50	5	2	16	2.70 / *3.60*	2.70 / *3.60*	2.70 / *3.60*	28.75 / *69.00*	40.25 / *80.25*	1–12	

 You are advised to read the introductory notes and to check prices and other details when booking accommodation

CAMPING AND CARAVAN SITES

Name and Address: Town (County) / Establishment, Address, Telephone number, Telex	Map Ref.	Tourist Board Standards	Site capacity: Acreage of site	Pitches: Caravans	Pitches: Tents	Pitches: Total	Units for hire: Static holiday caravans	Units for hire: Chalets and similar units	Caravans and chalets not for hire	Prices: Car, caravan and two people overnight (£ Min. / £ Max.)	Motor caravan and two people overnight (£ Min. / £ Max.)	Car, tent and two people overnight (£ Min. / £ Max.)	Static caravans and chalets per unit per week: Low season (£ Min. / £ Max.)	High season (£ Min. / £ Max.)	Months open (1–12)	Symbols (Key: see fold-out)
CASTERTON (Cumbria) (1m N. Kirkby Lonsdale)	C3															
† Woodclose Caravan Park, Laitha La., Casterton, Kirkby Lonsdale. LA6. Mrs. P. A. Wilman, Crossway, Bentinck Dr., Kirkby Lonsdale, Carnforth, Lancs., LA6 2DQ. Tel. Kirkby Lonsdale (0468) 71403.		●	6	30	–	30	–	–	30	3.00 *3.50*	3.00 *3.50*	– –	– –	– –	3–10	
COCKERMOUTH (Cumbria)	B2															
Skiddaw View Caravan Park, Bothel, Nr. Sunderland, Cockermouth, CA5 2ET. Tel. Aspatria (0965) 20919. Contact Mrs. Pattinson, Orchard House, Plumbland, Aspatria, Carlisle, Cumbria, CA5 2ET. Tel. Aspatria (0965) 20404.		●	7	40	30	70	7	–	63	2.00 *2.50*	2.00 *2.50*	1.50 *2.00*	45.00 *55.00*	50.00 *65.00*	4–11	
† Violet Bank Caravan Site, Off Lorton Rd., CA13 9TG. Tel. (0900) 822169.		●	5	37	37	37	7	–	33	3.50 *4.50*	3.00 *4.50*	3.00 *4.50*	50.00 *50.00*	65.00 *99.00*	4–10	
CONISTON (Cumbria)	B3															
† Coniston Hall Camp Site, LA21 8AS. Contact John Barlow, Rentacamp Leisure Hire, Station Buildings, Windermere, Cumbria, LA23 1AH. Tel. Windermere (096 62) 4786. Frame tents. Fully equipped, ready erected on site.		●	22	–	5	–	–	–	–	– –	– –	2.00 *3.70*	– –	– –	5–8	
DENT (Cumbria)	C3															
High Laning Farm, LA10 5QJ. Tel. (058 75) 239.		●	2	10	20	30	3	–	–	– *2.50*	– *2.00*	– *2.00*	40.00 –	– *80.00*	3–10	
ESKDALE (Cumbria)	B3															
† Fisherground Farm, CA19 1TF. Tel. (094 03) 319.		●	3	5	25	30	3	–	–	– –	1.30 *1.30*	1.30 *1.30*	50.00 *55.00*	85.00 *110.00*	4–10	
FLOOKBURGH (Cumbria) (2m SW. Cartmel)	B3															
Lakeland Caravan Park, Moor La., LA11 7LS. Tel. (044 853) 235. Contact Bourne Leisure Group Ltd., 51-55 Bridge St., Hemel Hempstead, Herts, HP1 1EQ. Tel. Hemel Hempstead (0442) 48661. Telex 826362.		●	41	95	30	125	75	10	315	3.00 *4.00*	3.00 *4.00*	3.00 *4.00*	44.00 *70.00*	70.00 *135.00*	4–10	
GRANGE-OVER-SANDS (Cumbria)	B3															
Greaves Farm Caravan Site, Field Broughton, Grange-over-Sands, LA11 6HR. Contact Mrs. E Hutchinson, Cornerways Field Broughton, Grange-over-Sands, Cumbria LA11 6HR. Tel. Cartmel (044 854) 282.		●	1	–	–	–	2	–	18	– –	– –	– –	50.00 *55.00*	55.00 *60.00*	4–10	

CAMPING AND CARAVAN SITES

Name and Address Town (County) — Map Ref. Establishment Address Telephone number, Telex	Site capacity: Tourist Board Standards	Acreage of site	Pitches: Caravans	Pitches: Tents	Pitches: Total	Units for hire: Static holiday caravans	Units for hire: Chalets and similar units	Caravans and chalets not for hire	Prices: Car, caravan and two people overnight	Prices: Motor caravan and two people overnight	Prices: Car, tent and two people overnight	Static caravans and chalets per unit per week: Low season	Static caravans and chalets per unit per week: High season	Months open (1–12)	Symbols
									£ Min. *£ Max.*	£ Min. *£ Max.*	£ Min. *£ Max.*	£ Min. *£ Max.*	£ Min. *£ Max.*		Key: see fold-out
GRANGE-OVER-SANDS continued															
† Whitestone Caravan Site, Ayside, Grange-over-Sands, LA11 6JD. Tel. Newby Bridge (0448) 31770.	●	10	5	–	5	1	–	79	2.50 *2.50*	2.50 *2.50*	– –	45.00 *45.00*	50.00 *50.00*	3–10	
HAWKSHEAD (Cumbria) B3															
† The Croft Caravan & Camp Site, North Lonsdale Rd., Hawkshead, Nr. Ambleside, LA22 0NX. Contact Mr. Smith or Mrs. Barr, The Croft, North Lonsdale Rd., Hawkshead, Nr. Ambleside, Cumbria, LA22 0NX. Tel. (096 66) 374.	●	4	3	72	75	15	–	–	3.00 –	2.55 –	2.60 –	53.00 –	– *126.00*	3–10	
KENDAL (Cumbria) C3															
† Millcrest Caravan Park, Skelsmergh, Kendal, LA9 6NY. Tel. (0539) 21075.	●	2	36	–	36	–	–	–	2.00 *2.50*	2.00 *2.50*	– –	– –	– –	4–10	
Pound Farm Caravan Site, Crook, Nr. Kendal, LA8 8JZ. Tel. Staveley (0539) 821220.	●	1	–	–	–	11	–	–	– –	– –	– –	35.00 –	– *60.00*	4–10	
KESWICK (Cumbria) B2															
Burnside Caravan Park, Underskiddaw, Keswick, CA12 4PF. Tel. (0596) 72950.	●	3	24	–	24	6	–	19	2.50 *3.50*	2.00 *2.50*	– –	35.00 *45.00*	45.00 *60.00*	3–10	
† Low Briery Holiday Village, Penrith Rd., CA12 4RN. Tel. (0596) 72044. Contact Grey Abbey Properties Ltd., PO Box 23, Coach Rd., Whitehaven, Cumbria, CA28 9DF. Tel. Whitehaven (0946) 3773.	●	5	–	–	–	29	1	14	– –	– –	– –	54.00 *82.00*	91.00 *133.00*	4–10	
† Morte Point Caravans, Threlkeld, Keswick, CA12 4TT. Contact D. A. Conroy (EL), 17 South Rd., Stourbridge, W. Midlands, DY8 3YA. Tel. Stourbridge (038 43) 5960.	●	5	–	–	–	16	–	–	– –	– –	– –	30.00 *40.00*	45.00 *70.00*	3–10	
† North Lakes Caravan & Camping Park, Bewaldeth, Bassenthwaite Lake, Nr. Keswick, CA13 9SY. Tel. Bassenthwaite Lake (059 681) 510.	●	30	145	50	195	–	–	–	3.50 –	3.50 –	2.00 –	– –	– –	3–11	
KIRKBY THORE (Cumbria) C2															
Low Moor Caravan Site, Kirkby Thore, Penrith, CA10 1XG. Tel. (093 06) 231.	●	2	12	12	12	8	–	17	1.40 *1.40*	1.40 *1.40*	1.40 *1.40*	20.00 *40.00*	20.00 *40.00*	4–10	
LAMPLUGH (Cumbria) B2															
† Inglenook Caravan Park, Fitz Bridge, Lamplugh, CA14 4SH. Tel. (094 686) 240.	●	4	36	6	40	4	–	8	2.50 *2.50*	2.50 *2.50*	2.30 *2.30*	50.00 *90.00*	50.00 *90.00*	3–11	
LANGDALE (Cumbria) B2															
† Greenhowe Caravan Park, Great Langdale, Ambleside, LA22 9JU. Tel. (096 67) 231.	●	3	–	–	–	40	–	3	– –	– –	– –	35.00 *55.00*	70.00 *120.00*	1–11	

 You are advised to read the introductory notes and to check prices and other details when booking accommodation

CAMPING AND CARAVAN SITES

Name and Address: Town (County), Establishment, Address, Telephone number, Telex	Map Ref.	Tourist Board Standards	Site capacity: Acreage of site	Pitches: Caravans	Pitches: Tents	Pitches: Total	Units for hire: Static holiday caravans	Units for hire: Chalets and similar units	Caravans and chalets not for hire	Prices: Car, caravan and two people overnight	Prices: Motor caravan and two people overnight	Prices: Car, tent and two people overnight	Static caravans and chalets per unit per week: Low season	Static caravans and chalets per unit per week: High season	Months open (1–12)	Symbols
										£ Min. *£ Max.*	£ Min. *£ Max.*	£ Min. *£ Max.*	£ Min. *£ Max.*	£ Min. *£ Max.*		Key: see fold-out
LEVENS (Cumbria)	**C3**															
† Gilpin Bridge Caravan Pk., Bridge End, Levens, Nr. Kendal, LA8 8EP. Tel. Witherslack (044 852) 430.		●	2	-	-	-	4	-	-	- -	- -	- -	50.00 *65.00*	75.00 *100.00*	4–10	
LORTON (Cumbria) (4m SE. Cockermouth)	**B2**															
Wheatsheaf Inn & Caravan Pk., Low Lorton, Cockermouth, CA13 9UW. Tel. (090 085) 268.		●	1	15	-	15	1	-	-	3.25 *3.50*	2.50 *3.00*	- -	40.00 *50.00*	50.00 *60.00*	3–11	
Whinfell Hall Caravan Pk., Whinfell Hall Farm, Lorton, Cockermouth, CA13 0RQ. Tel. (090 085) 260.		●	2	5	30	35	4	-	13	3.25 *3.50*	2.50 *2.50*	- *2.25*	40.00 *40.00*	- *60.00*	4–10	
MEALSGATE (Cumbria) (6m SW. Wigton)	**B2**															
† The Larches Caravan Park, Mealsgate, Carlisle, CA5 1LQ. Tel. Low Ireby (096 57) 379.		●	18	73	73	73	-	-	177	3.00 *5.00*	3.00 *5.00*	3.00 *5.00*	- -	- -	3–10	
MILNTHORPE (Cumbria)	**C3**															
Fell End Caravan Park, Slackhead Rd., Hale, Milnthorpe, LA7 7BS. Tel. (044 82) 2122.		●	28	50	18	68	-	-	215	2.60 *3.20*	2.00 *2.20*	2.00 *3.20*	- -	- -	3–10	
MUNGRISDALE (Cumbria)	**B2**															
Morte Point Caravans, Hutton Roof, Mungrisdale, C A11. Contact A. F. Conroy, (EL) 17 South Rd., Stourbridge, W. Midlands, Tel. Stourbridge (038 43) 5960.		●	5	-	-	-	35	-	-	- -	- -	- -	30.00 *40.00*	45.00 *70.00*	3–10	
Thanet Well Caravan Park, Hutton Roof, Mungrisdale, CA11 0XX. Contact Mrs. A. E. Ivinson, Green View, Welton, Nr. Dalston, Carlisle, Cumbria, CA5 7ES. Tel. Raughton Head (069 96) 230.		●	5	-	-	-	3	-	-	- -	- -	- -	25.00 -	45.00 -	3–10	
PENRITH (Cumbria)	**C2**															
Greenacres Caravan Park, Plumpton, Penrith, CA11 9PF. Tel. Plumpton (076 884) 206.		●	3	16	-	16	2	-	22	3.00 *3.50*	3.00 *3.50*	- -	80.00 *80.00*	80.00 *80.00*	4–10	
† Lowther Caravan Park, Eamont Bridge, Penrith, CA10 2JB. Tel. (0768) 63631.		●	50	146	50	196	8	-	375	3.50 *4.50*	3.50 *3.50*	3.50 *4.50*	70.00 -	120.00 -	3–10	
† White Horse Caravan Site, Kings Meaburn, Penrith, CA10 3BU. Contact Mrs. R. J. S. Addison, Greystone House, Kings Meaburn, Penrith, Cumbria, CA10 3BU. Tel. Morland (093 14) 226.		●	3	5	-	5	6	-	24	2.50 *3.00*	2.50 *3.00*	- -	45.00 *55.00*	45.00 *55.00*	3–10	
PRESTON PATRICK (Cumbria) (3m NE. Milnthorpe)	**C3**															
Millness Hill Caravan & Camping Site, LA7 7NU. Tel. Crooklands (044 87) 306.		●	2	14	12	26	1	-	14	2.00 -	2.00 -	1.65 -	35.00 -	- *40.00*	3–10	

You are advised to read the introductory notes and to check prices and other details when booking accommodation

CAMPING AND CARAVAN SITES

Name and Address: Town (County), Establishment, Address, Telephone number, Telex	Map Ref.	Tourist Board Standards	Site capacity: Acreage of site	Pitches: Caravans	Pitches: Tents	Pitches: Total	Units for hire: Static holiday caravans	Units for hire: Chalets and similar units	Caravans and chalets not for hire	Prices: Car, caravan and two people overnight (£ Min. / £ *Max.*)	Prices: Motor caravan and two people overnight (£ Min. / £ *Max.*)	Prices: Car, tent and two people overnight (£ Min. / £ *Max.*)	Static caravans and chalets per unit per week: Low season (£ Min. / £ *Max.*)	Static caravans and chalets per unit per week: High season (£ Min. / £ *Max.*)	Months open (1–12)	Symbols (Key: see fold-out)
ST. BEES (Cumbria)	**B2**															
Beachcomber Caravan Site, CA27 0ES. Tel. (094 685) 540.		●	3	18	–	18	25	–	–	2.50 *3.00*	2.50 *3.00*	– –	40.25 *80.50*	57.50 *115.00*	4–10	
St. Bees Chalet & Trailer Park, CA27 0ET. Tel. (094 685) 335.		●	20	175	100	240	20	–	84	2.00 *3.00*	2.00 *3.00*	2.00 *3.00*	65.00 *80.00*	75.00 *100.00*	1–12	
SEDBERGH (Cumbria)	**C3**															
Pinfold Caravan Site, LA10 5JL. Tel. (0587) 20576.		●	6	28	24	52	6	–	56	– *2.50*	– *2.50*	– *2.50*	60.00 –	– *85.00*	3–10	
SILECROFT (Cumbria) (10m SE Ravenglass)	**B3**															
† Silecroft Caravan & Camping Site, Silecroft, Millom LA18 4NX. Tel. Millom (0657) 2659.			25	54	8	62	–	–	118	3.00 *3.50*	3.00 *3.50*	1.50 *1.50*	– –	– –	3–10	
SILLOTH (Cumbria)	**B1**															
Abbey Holme, Beckfoot, Silloth, CA5 4LA. Contact Mr. & Mrs. J. A. Biglands, Alanco, Beckfoot, Silloth, Silloth, Cumbria CA5 4LA. Tel. (0965) 31653.		●	4	20	5	25	1	–	24	2.25 –	2.25 –	2.25 –	30.00 –	– *60.00*	4–9	
Silloth Caravan Pk., CA5 4AY. Tel. (0965) 31707. Contact Stanwix Pk. Holiday Centre, West Silloth, CA5 4HH. Tel. (0965) 31671.		●	18	93	93	93	50	–	215	2.50 *3.50*	2.50 *3.50*	2.50 *3.50*	50.00 *80.00*	60.00 *100.00*	3–10	
† Solway Lido Holiday Centre, CA5 4QQ. Tel. (0965) 31236.		●	135	600	600	600	90	85	340	2.90 *4.50*	2.90 *4.50*	2.90 *4.50*	42.00 *52.00*	105.00 *150.00*	5–9	
Stanwix Park Holiday Centre, West Silloth, CA5 4HH. Tel. (0965) 31671.		●	15	50	50	100	100	28	186	3.20 *4.10*	3.20 *4.10*	3.20 *4.10*	50.00 *100.00*	70.00 *140.00*	3–10	
Tanglewood Caravan Park, Causewayhead, CA5 4PE. Tel. (0965) 31253.		●	6	21	10	31	6	–	38	2.00 *2.00*	2.00 *2.00*	2.00 *2.00*	35.00 *88.00*	35.00 *88.00*	4–10	
STAVELEY (Cumbria)	**C3**															
† Ashes La. Caravan & Camping Pk., Ashes La., Staveley, Nr. Kendal, LA8. Tel. (0539) 821119. Contact Address above or Mr & Mrs. Taylor, Belle Mere, Newby Bridge, Ulverston, Cumbria, LA12 8NL. Tel. Newby Bridge (0448) 31202.		●	25	100	200	300	–	–	–	2.75 *3.50*	2.25 *3.25*	2.60 *3.00*	– –	– –	3–10	
THIRLMERE (Cumbria)	**B2**															
Thirlspot Farm, Thirlmere, Keswick, CA12 4TW. Contact Mrs. E. Gaskell, 4 Fisher Pl., Thirlmere, Keswick, Cumbria, CA12 4TW. Tel. Keswick (0596) 72224.		●	13	3	24	27	4	–	2	2.00 –	2.00 –	1.60 –	45.00 *60.00*	55.00 *75.00*	1–12	

 You are advised to read the introductory notes and to check prices and other details when booking accommodation

CAMPING AND CARAVAN SITES

Name and Address: Town (County) / Establishment, Address, Telephone number, Telex	Map Ref.	Tourist Board Standards	Site capacity: Acreage of site	Pitches: Caravans	Pitches: Tents	Pitches: Total	Units for hire: Static holiday caravans	Units for hire: Chalets and similar units	Caravans and chalets not for hire	Prices: Car, caravan and two people overnight (£ Min. / £ Max.)	Prices: Motor caravan and two people overnight (£ Min. / £ Max.)	Prices: Car, tent and two people overnight (£ Min. / £ Max.)	Static caravans and chalets per unit per week: Low season (£ Min. / £ Max.)	Static caravans and chalets per unit per week: High season (£ Min. / £ Max.)	Months open (1–12)	Symbols (Key: see fold-out)
THRELKELD (Cumbria) (4m NE. Keswick)	B2															
† Setmabanning Farm, Threlkeld, Keswick, CA12 4TT. Tel. Threlkeld (059 683) 229.		●	5	22	–	22	28	–	–	2.00 / *3.00*	2.00 / *2.50*	– / –	35.00 / *55.00*	40.00 / *70.00*	3–10	
TROUTBECK, PENRITH (Cumbria)	B2															
† Hutton Moor End Caravan & Camping Site, CA11 0SX. Tel. Threlkeld (059 683) 615.		●	4	20	15	35	–	–	15	1.00 / *1.50*	1.00 / *1.50*	1.00 / *1.50*	– / –	– / –	4–10	
ULLSWATER (Cumbria)	C2															
† Beckses Garage Caravan & Camping Site, Penruddock, Penrith, CA11 0RX. Tel. Greystoke (085 33) 224.		●	5	16	5	21	5	–	13	3.50 / –	3.50 / –	2.00 / –	50.00 / *65.00*	60.00 / *95.00*	4–10	
Knotts Hill Caravan Chalet Site, Watermillock, Ullswater, Penrith, CA11 0JR. Tel. Pooley Bridge (085 36) 328.		●	42	21	–	21	6	6	18	2.50 / *3.00*	2.50 / *2.50*	– / –	16.00 / *55.00*	25.00 / *80.00*	3–11	
Park Foot Caravan & Camping Site, Howtown Rd., Pooley Bridge, Penrith, CA10 2NA. Tel. Pooley Bridge (085 36) 309.		●	15	10	95	105	2	4	90	3.00 / –	3.00 / –	3.00 / –	57.50 / –	– / *115.00*	3–10	
The Quiet Caravan & Camping Site, Watermillock, Penrith, CA11 0LS. Tel. Pooley Bridge (085 36) 337.		●	10	10	50	60	5	–	16	2.75 / *4.00*	2.75 / *4.00*	2.50 / *3.00*	75.00 / –	– / *115.00*	3–11	
Seat Farm Caravan Site, Howtown, Penrith, CA10 2NA. Tel. Pooley Bridge (085 36) 208.		●	1	–	–	–	1	–	9	– / –	– / –	– / –	45.00 / –	65.00 / –	3–10	
Sykeside Camping Site, Brotherswater, Patterdale, Nr. Penrith, CA11 0NZ. Tel. Glenridding (085 32) 239.		●	5	–	80	80	–	–	–	– / –	– / –	2.50 / *3.40*	– / –	– / –	3–11	
Ullswater Caravan, Camping & Marine Pk., Watermillock, Penrith, CA11 0LR. Tel. Pooley Bridge (085 36) 666.		●	13	40	75	115	20	7	35	2.50 / *5.00*	2.50 / *4.00*	2.50 / *4.00*	31.00 / *57.00*	70.00 / *115.00*	3–11	
† Waterfoot Caravan Estate, Pooley Bridge, Nr. Penrith, CA11 0JF. Tel. Pooley Bridge (085 36) 302.		●	22	65	–	65	–	–	115	4.00 / *4.00*	4.00 / *4.00*	– / –	– / –	– / –	3–10	
ULVERSTON (Cumbria)	B3															
† Blackbeck Caravan Park, Bouth Nr. Ulverston, LA12 8JJ. Contact Mr. & Mrs. A. Mingay, Byways, Blackbeck Caravan Pk., Bouth, Nr. Ulverston, Cumbria, LA12 8JN. Tel. Greenodd (022 986) 274.		●	39	45	12	57	–	–	220	3.00 / –	2.50 / –	2.00 / –	– / –	– / –	3–10	
WASDALE (Cumbria)	B2															
Church Stile Farm, Church Stile, Wasdale, Seascale, CA20 1ET. Tel. (094 06) 252.		●	4	15	50	65	–	–	15	2.00 / *2.50*	2.00 / *2.00*	2.00 / *2.50*	– / –	– / –	3–11	

CAMPING AND CARAVAN SITES

Name and Address — Town (County), Map Ref. — Establishment, Address, Telephone number, Telex	Tourist Board Standards	Site capacity: Acreage of site	Pitches: Caravans	Pitches: Tents	Pitches: Total	Units for hire: Static holiday caravans	Units for hire: Chalets and similar units	Caravans and chalets not for hire	Prices: Car, caravan and two people overnight (£ Min. / £ Max.)	Prices: Motor caravan and two people overnight (£ Min. / £ Max.)	Prices: Car, tent and two people overnight (£ Min. / £ Max.)	Static caravans and chalets per unit per week: Low season (£ Min. / £ Max.)	Static caravans and chalets per unit per week: High season (£ Min. / £ Max.)	Months open (1–12)	Symbols (Key: see fold-out)
WINDERMERE (Cumbria) **B3**															
† Blakeholme & Hill of Oaks Caravan Estate, Tower Wood, Windermere, LA23 3PJ. Tel. Newby Bridge (044 83) 417.	●	84	43	-	43	-	-	219	5.00 / *5.00*	5.00 / *5.00*	- / -	- / -	- / -	3–10	
† Braithwaite Fold Touring Caravan Park, Glebe Rd. LA23 3HB. Tel. (096 62) 2177. Contact (Summer) Address above, (Winter & Advance bookings), South Lakeland District Council, A.R.T. Dept., Ashleigh, Windermere, LA23 2AG. Tel. (096 62) 2244.	●	17	65	-	65	-	-	-	3.00 / *5.00*	3.00 / *5.00*	- / -	- / -	- / -	4–10	
† Fallbarrow Park, Rayrigg Rd., LA23 3DL. Tel. (096 62) 4427 (hire) & 4428 (Tour).	●	32	80	-	80	90	-	177	3.50 / *8.50*	3.50 / *8.50*	- / -	63.00 / *82.00*	137.00 / *190.00*	3–11	
† Limefitt Park, LA23 1PA. Tel. Ambleside (096 63) 2300.	●	113	355	355	355	10	-	-	2.70 / *5.40*	2.00 / *4.00*	2.70 / *5.40*	73.00 / *73.00*	158.00 / *158.00*	4–10	
Park Cliffe Caravan & Camping Site, Birks Rd., LA23 3PG. Tel. Newby Bridge (0448) 31344.	●	12	50	200	250	-	-	50	2.40 / -	1.80 / *2.70*	2.40 / *3.60*	- / -	- / -	3–10	
† White Cross Bay Caravan Park, Troutbeck Bridge, Windermere, LA23 1LF. Tel. (096 62) 3937.	●	60	125	-	125	-	-	353	3.32 / *3.90*	3.32 / *3.90*	- / -	- / -	- / -	3–10	

KEEP BRITAIN TIDY

BOOKING ENQUIRY COUPONS

When enquiring about accommodation you may find it helpful to use the enquiry coupons on this page which can be cut out and mailed to the establishment(s) of your choice.

Before completing the coupon read the advice about making a booking in the introductory notes.

When enquiring about self-catering accommodation remember to send your coupon to the contact address and indicate which property you are interested in.

Remember to include your name and address and please enclose a stamped addressed envelope for each reply or an international reply coupon if writing from outside Britain.

Where to Stay '82

Published by the English Tourist Board

ENQUIRY COUPON

Name and address of establishment where you wish to stay:

Please send me information about your accommodation and other facilities, including a brochure if available and details of prices charged. — Tick box required. ☐

On the reverse of this coupon I have given details of the accommodation in which I am interested. Would you please advise, as soon as possible, if you have accommodation available on the dates given. ☐

Name (block letters):

Address (block letters):

Telephone number: P.T.O.

Where to Stay '82

Published by the English Tourist Board

ENQUIRY COUPON

Name and address of establishment where you wish to stay:

Please send me information about your accommodation and other facilities, including a brochure if available and details of prices charged. — Tick box required. ☐

On the reverse of this coupon I have given details of the accommodation in which I am interested. Would you please advise, as soon as possible, if you have accommodation available on the dates given. ☐

Name (block letters):

Address (block letters):

Telephone number: P.T.O.

BOOKING ENQUIRY COUPONS

I am interested in accommodation for adults and children (ages:)
(Give number of persons and the ages of the children if applicable)
From (date of arrival): To (date of departure):

or alternatively from: to:

Accommodation required would be:

Meals required would be:

Other/special requirements:

I enclose a stamped addressed envelope (or international reply coupon) for your reply to this enquiry.

Signed: Date:

I am interested in accommodation for adults and children (ages:)
(Give number of persons and the ages of the children if applicable)
From (date of arrival): To (date of departure):

or alternatively from: to:

Accommodation required would be:

Meals required would be:

Other/special requirements:

I enclose a stamped addressed envelope (or international reply coupon) for your reply to this enquiry.

Signed: Date:

BOOKING ENQUIRY COUPONS

When enquiring about accommodation you may find it helpful to use the enquiry coupons on this page which can be cut out and mailed to the establishment(s) of your choice.

Before completing the coupon read the advice about making a booking in the introductory notes.

When enquiring about self-catering accommodation remember to send your coupon to the contact address and indicate which property you are interested in.

Remember to include your name and address and please enclose a stamped addressed envelope for each reply or an international reply coupon if writing from outside Britain.

Where to Stay '82

Published by the English Tourist Board

ENQUIRY COUPON

Name and address of establishment where you wish to stay:

____

____

____

____

____

____

Tick box required.

Please send me information about your accommodation and other facilities, including a brochure if available and details of prices charged. ☐

On the reverse of this coupon I have given details of the accommodation in which I am interested. Would you please advise, as soon as possible, if you have accommodation available on the dates given. ☐

Name (block letters): ____________________

____

Address (block letters): ____________________

____

____

Telephone number: ____________________ P.T.O.

Where to Stay '82

Published by the English Tourist Board

ENQUIRY COUPON

Name and address of establishment where you wish to stay:

____

____

____

____

____

____

Tick box required.

Please send me information about your accommodation and other facilities, including a brochure if available and details of prices charged. ☐

On the reverse of this coupon I have given details of the accommodation in which I am interested. Would you please advise, as soon as possible, if you have accommodation available on the dates given. ☐

Name (block letters): ____________________

____

Address (block letters): ____________________

____

____

Telephone number: ____________________ P.T.O.

BOOKING ENQUIRY COUPONS

I am interested in accommodation for adults and children (ages:)
(Give number of persons and the ages of the children if applicable)
From (date of arrival): To (date of departure):

or alternatively from: to:

Accommodation required would be:

Meals required would be:

Other/special requirements:

I enclose a stamped addressed envelope (or international reply coupon) for your reply to this enquiry.

Signed: Date:

I am interested in accommodation for adults and children (ages:)
(Give number of persons and the ages of the children if applicable)
From (date of arrival): To (date of departure):

or alternatively from: to:

Accommodation required would be:

Meals required would be:

Other/special requirements:

I enclose a stamped addressed envelope (or international reply coupon) for your reply to this enquiry.

Signed: Date:

ENGLISH LAKELAND
CUMBRIA

ENGLISH LAKELAND
CUMBRIA

PUBLICATIONS ORDER FORM

The following useful publications can be obtained by sending this order form to:

Cumbria Tourist Board,
Ellerthwaite,
Windermere,
Cumbria LA23 2AQ.

Please supply the publication(s) which I have ticked below:

The Most Beautiful Corner of England.
Price 50p. ☐

Where Shall We Go in Cumbria.
Price 40p. ☐

Britain's Border Country.
Price 50p. ☐

Lakes and Seas around Cumbria.
Price 50p. ☐

English Lakeland Leisure and Holiday Planning Map.
Price £1.20p. ☐

Freedom of Cumbria.
A guide including accommodation for disabled people. Price 30p. ☐

Public Transport Map.
Price 25p. ☐

Sites for Caravans and Tents.
Price 30p. ☐

Postage and packing on the above publications:
One publication 35p.
Two publications 50p.
Three or more publications 65p.

Information Leaflets.

Houses, Castles and Gardens.* 10p ☐
Art Galleries, Museums & Visitor Centres.* 10p. ☐
Fairs, Festivals and Traditional Events.* 10p. ☐
Nature, Forest and Town Trails. 10p. ☐
Hound Trailing and Sheep Dog Trials.* 5p. ☐
Launching Sites for Small Boats.* 10p. ☐
Cycling and Cumbria Cycle Way. 10p. ☐
Swimming. 10p. ☐
A Taste of Cumbria. 10p. ☐
Riding and Pony Trekking.* 10p. ☐
Golf Courses. 10p. ☐
Craft Workshops.* 10p. ☐
Fishing (National Park Publication). 10p. ☐

*Published jointly with the Lake District Special Planning Board.

Postage and packing on the information leaflets: 15p for any number of leaflets.

Insert your name and address here (in **BLOCK CAPITALS** please).

Name ______________________________

____

Address ______________________________

____

____

____

____

WTS'82

I enclose a cheque/postal order for the total amount of..................made payable to the **Cumbria Tourist Board.**

TOURIST INFORMATION CENTRES

Throughout England over 470 tourist information centres are ready to help you enjoy your holiday. Look out for the above sign.

Use these centres to get the most out of your holiday. They provide information on what to see and do; entertainments; sporting facilities; how to get there; when it's open; and where to stay.

All tourist information centres have information on local accommodation and for a small charge many provide a booking service for personal callers. Centres offering the Book-a-Bed-Ahead scheme can make a provisional reservation for you at any other town which has a centre also operating the scheme.

Tourist information centres in this region are listed below. The symbol 🛏 means that an accommodation booking service is provided. Please note that some centres are only open during the summer months - these are indicated by a * against the town name.

Alston, 🛏
Railway Station,
☎ (049 83) 696

Ambleside, 🛏 *
The Old Courthouse,
Church Street,
☎ (096 63) 2582

Appleby, 🛏 *
Moot Hall, Boroughgate,
☎ (0930) 51177

Barrow-in-Furness, 🛏
Civic Halls,
Duke Street,
☎ (0229) 25795

Bowness-on-Windermere, 🛏
Bowness Bay,
☎ Windermere
(096 62) 2244 Extn. 43

Brampton, *
Moot Hall,
Market Square,
☎ (06977) 3433

Brough, 🛏
The 'One Stop Shop',
☎ (093 04) 260

Carlisle, 🛏
Old Town Hall,
Green Market,
☎ (0228) 25517/25396

Cockermouth, 🛏 *
Riverside Car Park,
Market Street,
☎ (0900) 822634

Coniston, 🛏 *
Village Car Park,
☎ (096 64) 533

Egremont, 🛏 *
Lowes Court Gallery,
12/13 Main Street,
☎ (0946) 820693

Glenridding, 🛏 *
Car Park,
☎ (085 32) 414

Grange-over-Sands, 🛏 *
Victoria Hall,
Main Street,
☎ (044 84) 4026

Grasmere, 🛏
Broadgate Newsagency,
☎ (096 65) 245

Hawkshead, 🛏 *
Main Street,
☎ (096 66) 525

Kendal, 🛏
Town Hall,
Highgate,
☎ (0539) 25758

Keswick, 🛏
Summer –
The Moot Hall,
Market Square,
Winter –
Council Offices,
50 Main Street,
☎ (0596) 72645

Kirkby Lonsdale, 🛏
The Art Store,
18 Main Street,
☎ (0468) 71603

Kirkby Stephen, 🛏
The Bookshop,
22 Market Street,
☎ (0930) 71804

Longtown, 🛏
21 Swan Street,
☎ (0228) 79201

Maryport, 🛏
Maritime Museum,
1 Senhouse Street,
☎ (090 081) 3738

Millom, *
Millom Folk Museum,
St. George's Road,
☎ (0657) 2555

Penrith, 🛏 *
Robinson's School,
Middlegate.
☎ (0768) 64671 Extn. 33

Pooley Bridge, 🛏 *
Car Park,
☎ (085 36) 530

Ravenglass, 🛏 *
The Car Park,
Ravenglass & Eskdale
Railway Station,
☎ (065 77) 278

Sedbergh, 🛏 *
Main Street,
☎ (0587) 20125

Silloth,
Mobile Unit,
The Green,
☎ (0965) 31944

Southwaite, 🛏
M6 Service Area,
Southwaite,
Nr. Carlisle,
☎ (069 93) 445

Ulverston,
17 Fountain Street,
☎ (0229) 52299

Whitehaven, 🛏
Whitehaven Museum,
Market Place,
☎ (0946) 5678

Windermere, 🛏 *
Victoria Street,
☎ (096 62) 4561

PLEASE MENTION 'WHERE TO STAY '82' WHEN MAKING A BOOKING

THERE'S SO MUCH TO SEE & DO (But where do you start?)

There are Tourist Information Centres in over 470 locations throughout England to see that you get the most out of your holiday.

You'll find friendly staff to suggest new ideas on what to see and do and help with your accommodation and journey. There are always plenty of brochures & pamphlets for you to take away and often maps & guides for you to buy.

A list of Tourist Information Centres is available from centres or by writing to the English Tourist Board, 4 Grosvenor Gardens, London SW1W 0DU.

You can easily spot a Tourist Information Centre – they all display this sign.

MAP AND INDEX

Based upon the Ordnance Survey map with the permission of the Controller of Her Majesty's Stationery Office, Crown Copyright reserved.

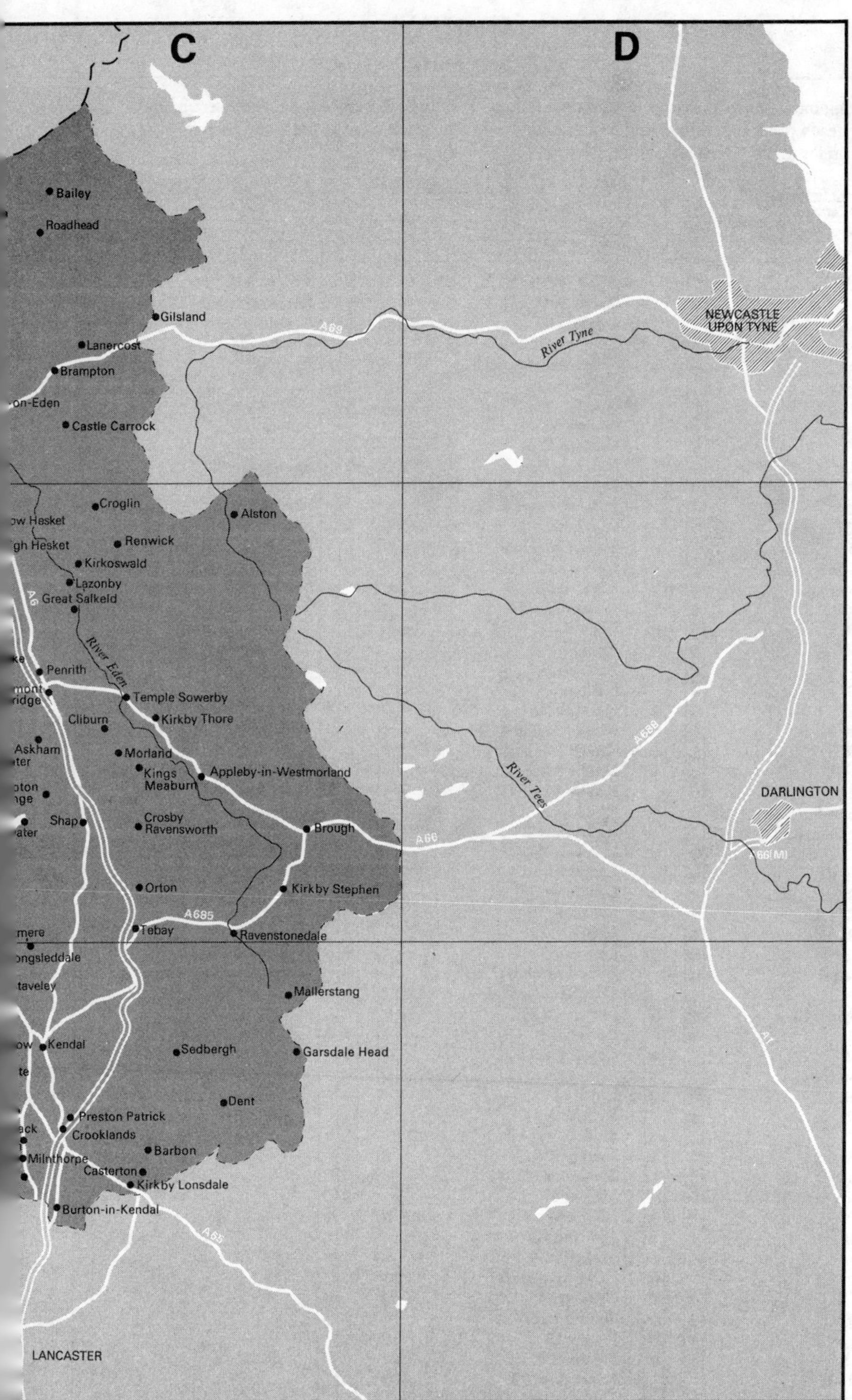

Produced by Engineering Surveys Reproduction Limited

The following index shows the types of accommodation listed under each place name appearing in this guide. For details, refer to the place name in the relevant section. A number of entries were included just before the guide went to press and therefore may not appear in the index.

Town Map ref.	Hotels, Motels etc.	Group and Youth	Self-Catering	Caravan and Camping
Ainstable B1	*			
Allonby B2	*		*	*
Alston C2	*	*	*	
Ambleside B2	*	*	*	*
Appleby-in-Westmorland C2	*		*	*
Arnside C3	*		*	*
Askham C2	*			
Aspatria B2			*	
Backbarrow B3			*	
Bailey C1			*	
Bampton Grange C2	*			
Barbon C3	*			
Barrow-in-Furness B3	*			
Bassenthwaite B2	*	*		*
Beckermet B2	*			
Beckfoot B2			*	
Beetham C3	*		*	
Berrier B2	*			
Blawith B3	*			
Bootle B3	*		*	
Borrowdale B2	*		*	
Braithwaite B2	*		*	*
Brampton C1	*		*	
Brough C2			*	
Broughton-in-Furness B3	*		*	
Burgh-by-Sands B1			*	
Burton-in-Kendal C3	*		*	
Buttermere B2	*		*	
Caldbeck B2	*		*	
Calderbridge B2	*			
Carlisle B1	*		*	*
Cartmel B3	*		*	
Cartmel Fell B3	*			
Casterton C3	*			*
Castle Carrock C1	*		*	
Cleator B2			*	
Cliburn C2			*	
Cockermouth B2	*		*	*
Coniston B3	*		*	*
Croglin C2	*			
Crook C3			*	
Crooklands C3	*			
Crosby-on-Eden C1	*			
Crosby Ravensworth C2	*			
Crosthwaite C3			*	
Dalston B1	*			
Dent C3	*	*	*	*
Eamont Bridge C2			*	
Egremont B2	*		*	
Elterwater B2	*		*	
Ennerdale B2	*		*	
Eskdale B3	*		*	*
Flookburgh B3				*
Garsdale Head C3			*	
Gilsland C1	*		*	
Gosforth B2	*		*	
Grange-over-Sands B3	*		*	*
Grasmere B2	*		*	
Great Salkeld C2	*		*	
Gretna B1	*			
Greystoke C2		*	*	
Haverigg B3	*		*	
Haverthwaite B3			*	
Haweswater C2	*			
Hawkshead B3	*		*	*
Hesket Newmarket B2	*		*	
Heversham C3	*			
High Hesket C2	*			
Holmrook B3	*			
Ireby B2	*			
Ivegill B2			*	
Kendal C3	*		*	*
Kentmere C2	*		*	
Keswick B2	*	*	*	*
Kings Meaburn C2	*			
Kirkby Lonsdale C3	*		*	
Kirkby Stephen C2	*			
Kirkby Thore C2				*
Kirkoswald C2	*		*	
Kirksanton B3	*			
Lakeside B3	*			
Lamplugh B2			*	*
Lanercost C1	*			
Langdale B2	*		*	*
Lazonby C2			*	
Levens C3			*	*
Little Clifton B2	*		*	
Longsleddale C3			*	
Longtown B1	*			
Lorton B2	*		*	*
Low Hesket C2	*		*	
Loweswater B2	*		*	
Lowick B3			*	
Lyth Valley C3	*			
Mallerstang C3			*	
Maryport B2	*			
Mealsgate B2				*
Millom B3			*	
Milnthorpe C3	*			*
Morland C2			*	
Mungrisdale B2	*		*	*
Newby Bridge B3	*			
Orton C2	*			
Penrith C2	*		*	*
Penton C1	*		*	
Preston Patrick C3				*
Ravenglass B3	*		*	
Ravenstonedale C2	*			
Renwick C2	*			
Roadhead C1			*	
Rydal B2	*		*	
St. Bees B2	*		*	*
Satterthwaite B3	*		*	
Sawrey B3	*		*	
Seascale B3	*		*	
Sebergham B2	*		*	
Sedbergh C3	*			*
Shap C2	*			
Silecroft B3	*		*	*
Silloth B1	*		*	*
Spark Bridge B3	*		*	
Staveley C3	*		*	*
Tebay C2	*		*	
Temple Sowerby C2	*			
Thirlmere B2	*			*
Thornthwaite B2	*		*	
Threlkeld B2	*	*	*	*
Troutbeck, Penrith B2	*		*	*
Troutbeck, Windermere B3	*		*	
Ullswater C2	*		*	*
Ulverston B3	*	*	*	*
Underbarrow C3	*		*	
Wasdale B2	*		*	*
Welton B2	*		*	
Whitehaven B2	*		*	
Wigton B2	*		*	
Windermere B3	*		*	*
Winster B3			*	
Witherslack B3	*		*	
Workington B2	*			
Wreay C2			*	